THE
ARMS
CRISIS
OF
1970

THE
ARMS
CRISIS
OF
1970

MICHAEL HENEY

HEAD
of ZEUS

First published in the UK in 2020 by Apollo, an imprint of Head of Zeus Ltd

9 8

A catalogue record for this book is available from
the British Library.

ISBN (FTP): 9781789545593
ISBN (E): 9781789545616

Typeset by Divaddict Publishing Solutions Ltd

Printed and bound in Great Britain by
CPI Group (UK) Ltd, Croydon CR0 4YY

Head of Zeus Ltd
First Floor East
5–8 Hardwick Street
London EC1R 4RG

WWW.HEADOFZEUS.COM

This book is dedicated to the late Jim and Sheila Kelly

Contents

Arms crisis: Key dates and events

13 August 1969 Northern Ireland erupts after Apprentice
Boys march, with shootings, killings and
Catholic families burned from their homes;
Jack Lynch delivers his 'we cannot stand
by' speech on television; after a government
meeting, the Irish army is deployed to the
border.

14–16 August Refugees begin to stream across the border;
the Irish government hold a further series
of crisis meetings to determine the response
to the Northern unrest; as fears remain of
further sectarian assaults, the government
makes contingency plans and decides that a
sum of money will be provided for Northern
relief.

20 September Lynch delivers a policy speech on Northern
Ireland in Tralee, Co. Kerry, setting out a
peaceful approach to ending partition.

3–4 October Meeting of Northern Defence Committees
in Bailieboro, Co. Cavan, convened by
Captain James Kelly – the beginning of the
plan to import arms.

6 February 1970   Minister for Defence, James Gibbons,
                       delivers a government directive to the Chief
                       of Staff of the Defence Forces; he orders him
                       to prepare for possible military intervention
                       by the Irish army across the border in
                       Northern Ireland.

February–March   Captain James Kelly visits the Continent
                       several times in an effort to acquire arms for
                       the Northern Defence Committees.

2 April   Army lorries loaded with weapons and
                       ammunition are sent as far north as
                       Dundalk Army Barracks, as rioting and
                       disturbances in Ballymurphy in Belfast
                       threaten to get out of hand.

18 April   With an arms consignment expected at
                       Dublin Airport over the weekend, the
                       Garda Special Branch mount a blockade
                       around the airport; when Charles Haughey
                       telephones Department of Justice Secretary
                       Peter Berry and asks for the incoming
                       consignment to be allowed through
                       unhindered, Berry refuses.

20 April   Taoiseach Jack Lynch receives a Garda
                       report from Peter Berry, setting out details
                       of the unsuccessful attempt to import arms
                       covertly into Dublin Airport on the previous
                       weekend.

5 May   Leader of Fine Gael, Liam Cosgrave,
                       confronts Lynch with an anonymous leaked
                       document on Garda-headed notepaper; this

alleges that cabinet ministers were involved in an illegal effort to bring in guns for Northerners.

6 May

Lynch sacks ministers Charles Haughey and Neil Blaney at 2 a.m. for their involvement in the attempted gun-running; other ministers resign in protest.

8–9 May

A marathon confidence debate takes place in Dáil Éireann after Jack Lynch re-forms his government; Lynch wins the vote.

27–28 May

Criminal charges are issued by the Attorney General against Charles Haughey, Neil Blaney, Captain James Kelly, John Kelly and Albert Luykx.

2 July

Charges are withdrawn against Neil Blaney at a preliminary hearing in the Dublin District Court.

22–29 September

First arms trial takes place at the Central Criminal Court in Dublin, under Judge Aindrias Ó Caoimh; it collapses when Ó Caoimh suddenly withdraws.

6–23 October

Second arms trial takes place under Judge Seamus Henchy; all four accused are acquitted by the jury.

**January–
November 1971**

Evidence is taken at inquiry hearings conducted by the Dáil Committee of Public Accounts into the expenditure of money voted for Northern Ireland relief.

July 1972   The Committee of Public Accounts releases
                         its inquiry report; it finds almost £35,000
                         had been misappropriated, spent on
                         purposes other than what it termed 'the
                         relief of distress'.

Introduction

Although the 1970 Arms Crisis was a key event in the history of twentieth-century Ireland, half a century later conflicting views of it abound. In the generally dominant view, the crisis arose when Taoiseach Jack Lynch uncovered a dangerous conspiracy within his own government, one that has been seen as threatening democratic rule in the Irish Republic. The perceived plot was aimed at rearming the IRA, and as such risked generating an all-Ireland, thirty-two-county sectarian conflagration; Lynch, after vacillating for a time; was seen as having foiled the plot by sacking the supposed culprits, his two most powerful ministers, Charles Haughey and Neil Blaney, for their involvement in a failed gun-running attempt. This display of a new-found steel by Lynch reasserted his control over the government south of the border, and has been seen as narrowly averting tragedy on the island of Ireland.

This is a view of the Arms Crisis that, although not unchallenged, has retained sway both in the popular mind and in academia. This is despite the emergence into the public realm since 2001 of substantial documentation that, on closer analysis, should point to a very different narrative. This book relies heavily on the Irish and British State papers for 1969–70, but also on a range of new and hitherto unprocessed material presented here for the first time; it offers a rebalancing of the 1970 Arms Crisis, with a very different take on Lynch and on most of the other principals in the affair.

At the time, Lynch's sudden sacking of Haughey and Blaney caused a political convulsion. It generated widespread fears that the Irish Republic, after almost fifty years of partition, would be drawn into civil conflict inside Northern Ireland. The spark for the upheaval was the discovery of a failed attempt to import arms for republicans in Northern Ireland, involving not just some of Lynch's cabinet but also an Irish army intelligence officer, Captain James Kelly. When the Leader of the Dáil Opposition, Fine Gael's Liam Cosgrave, confronted Lynch with this information on 5 May 1970, Lynch's response, the immediate dismissal from cabinet of his two most senior ministers, created shock waves in the country. It became clear shortly afterwards that Lynch had known of allegations against Haughey and Blaney for several weeks, but had failed to act against them.

At the time, Northern Ireland was in a volatile state, following serious disturbances six months earlier in August 1969; Catholic families had been burned out of their homes in Belfast and thousands of refugees had streamed south across the border into the Irish Republic. There were widespread concerns in Dublin that further pogroms against Northern Catholic nationalists might be imminent.

The ministerial sackings were followed by a criminal prosecution, played out in dramatic fashion in two arms trials in Dublin's Central Criminal Court. Charged alongside Haughey & Blaney were the junior army officer who organized the arms importation, Captain Kelly; an expatriate Belgian businessman, Albert Luykx, who had acted as interpreter on arms-buying trips to the Continent; and a Northern republican, John Kelly (no relation to Captain James Kelly). The proceedings unfolded against a backdrop of open political warfare in the governing Fianna Fáil party. Blaney had the charges against him thrown out for lack of evidence at District Court level. The trials later in 1970 brought further reverses for the State when a Dublin jury acquitted Haughey, the two Kellys and Luykx of conspiracy to import arms illegally.

While the crisis passed, its impact on the political careers of Lynch and his main rival, Haughey, was long-standing; it also marked a watershed in the Republic's involvement with its northern neighbour. Having been forced, as one historian has put it, 'for the first time since 1925 to take a real look over the border', the Republic under Lynch stepped firmly away from any role in the military defence of Northern nationalists vulnerable to sectarian assault.[1]

But at issue is whether Lynch's hands were as clean as he maintained, and whether the arms importation, which he re-nounced, had really been a betrayal of his trust and of government policy. The alternative view was that it had been substan-tially authorized, whether officially or unofficially, and that the treachery in the matter lay rather with Lynch's disavowal of responsibility. Central to the historical debate on these issues, and to Lynch's defence of his role, has always been the embattled Minister for Defence, Jim Gibbons, and it is on Gibbons that the research contained in this book ultimately focuses.

Gibbons's suspected role has remained for almost half a century a key aspect of the research challenge facing historians of the Arms Crisis. The full disclosure of his frailties as a witness is in many ways central to this book. The hapless former Minister for Defence, by turns assertive and error-prone, dominates the narrative of the Arms Crisis from start to finish with his own extraordinarily self-destructive approach. He was the key figure in the trials, and he remains a key figure for historians in coming to terms with Lynch's subterfuges, deceptions and a terminal reluctance to discuss in detail the events of the period.

Gibbons opens an important window on the hidden Taoiseach. Even a well-disposed biographer writing in 1991 could find that Lynch, in retirement, was on the subject of the Arms Crisis 'resistive to investigation, hostile to exploration... mysterious... elusive and remarkably reticent'.[2] Lynch in truth had much to hide, and in his vulnerability, it was Gibbons who constituted his Achilles heel. It was Gibbons who took the heat in the witness box for the inconsistencies and contradictions in the government's stance, despite the full weight of the Taoiseach's office being deployed then and throughout the 1970s to shield him from his loss of reputation.

The moment that sparked the Arms Crisis came at 8 p.m. on 5 May 1970, when the Leader of the Opposition, Liam Cosgrave, arrived at the office of Taoiseach Jack Lynch in Government Buildings in Dublin. He carried with him a note typed on Garda-headed notepaper, containing disturbing information. 'A plot to bring in arms has been discovered,' it warned. Signed simply 'Garda', it informed Cosgrave that three members of Lynch's cabinet – Minister for Finance Charles Haughey, Minister for Agriculture Neil Blaney and Minister for Defence James Gibbons – plus several others, including an Irish army officer, Captain James Kelly, were involved in a secret, and seemingly criminal, attempt to import guns for the use of Northern Ireland republicans.[3] The involvement of the Minister for Defence, alongside a senior army officer, suggested that the gun-running might have official State backing.

Cosgrave's arrival at Lynch's door caused several remarkable things to happen. The most obvious of these was the sacking from the cabinet of Haughey and Blaney within hours. But less conspicuous was the way Lynch, demonstrating a political agility that would serve him well over the coming months, somehow persuaded Cosgrave on the spot that, while parts of his information were valid, other parts were not. The valid elements concerned Haughey and Blaney; their involvement Lynch appeared not to contest. The inclusion of Gibbons among the supposed conspirators was a different matter.

Cosgrave's note said that Gibbons was involved in the gun-running, but, as with the rest of the note's contents, the Fine Gael leader had no additional information to back up its contents, and Lynch persuaded him that the note was mistaken about Gibbons. Their conversation was private, so how Lynch persuaded Cosgrave to exclude the Minister for Defence is not known. But that was the outcome: first came the sacking, within hours, of Haughey

and Blaney, but when Cosgrave explained to the Dáil next day
what had happened, he dropped Gibbons's name from the list he
had given to Lynch. In a strangely misleading account, he told the
Dáil that he had presented to the Taoiseach the names of just two
ministers, Haughey and Blaney.

Nor was this failure to mention Gibbons Cosgrave's only
omission. There was another significant name, apparently, on the
list he showed Lynch, which the Dáil was not told about: this was
that of Captain Kelly's boss, Colonel Michael Hefferon, the army's
Director of Military Intelligence.[4] The note had said that Hefferon
too was part of the plot. Cosgrave never mentioned Hefferon to the
Dáil; effectively, both the Army Intelligence chief and his minister,
Gibbons, were written out of the story.[5] Neither Cosgrave nor
Lynch ever divulged any details of what they had talked about on
5 May and Cosgrave, despite his role as Leader of the Opposition,
for the duration of his life declined all invitations to clarify the
matter. This was despite the gradual emergence at the 1970 arms
trials of clear evidence that both Gibbons and Hefferon had known
of and tolerated the gun-running attempt. Hefferon never made the
slightest attempt to deny that he was personally involved. Gibbons
attempted to deny it, but was never convincing in his denials.

The involvement of these two men is central to the narrative of
the Arms Crisis contained in this book; beyond that, the handling
of the private Lynch–Cosgrave encounter on 5 May 1970, and
the way they featured in it, is deeply illustrative of the difficulties
presented to historians by the entire subsequent saga of the
Arms Crisis. The outcome of that meeting directly precipitated
the Arms Crisis, yet the refusal by both Cosgrave and Lynch to
reveal details of their discussion caused obfuscation to set in
almost immediately. Cosgrave made a Dáil statement that was
essentially false, while Lynch simply maintained silence on the
matter. The result was a fog of uncertainty over a pivotal moment.
The importance of the issue cannot have escaped Cosgrave. It was
whether or not the Minister for Defence, James Gibbons, had a
hand in the attempted gun-running. The Garda note said that he

had, but Cosgrave, after talking to Lynch, appears to have decided otherwise. What assurances did Lynch give him, and why were they so readily accepted?

The confusion around Cosgrave's meeting with Lynch on 5 May quickly extended over the full Arms Crisis narrative, which came to be characterized on all sides by a persistent strain of false testimony, silence, evasion and various forms of subterfuge. The general effect of the large number of deceptions – outlined in this book for the first time in detail – has been to leave both contemporary writers and future historians struggling to reach agreement on the basic facts of 1969–70, and on the rights and wrongs of the case. Given the extent of Lynch, Gibbons and Haughey's provable evasions, and against a background of concealed facts on a variety of fronts, it is hardly surprising that the result has been conflicted analysis and fractious discussion.

It is one of the claims of this book, on the basis of the State files, plus much hitherto unexplored documentary evidence, that the Arms Crisis has produced an exceptional set of historical myths. These extend far beyond the Lynch–Cosgrave meeting, and they are long in need of redressing. Chief among the myths of 1970 is that of Lynch as hero, the gentle, honest leader who asserted himself at the last moment to surprise those who, in the mythology, were plotting his downfall. The dominant, though far from universal, perception has been that the plot in 1970 involved plans that would have undermined the State's democratic institutions and brought the island close to a bloody civil war. At least partly on the back of defeating such evil intentions, Lynch acquired an immense status in later years as a strong and charismatic leader.

The other myth is of Charles Haughey and Neil Blaney as conspirators and fellow travellers with the IRA: the perception that, at the time, they believed in using force to break partition and were prepared to subvert the democratic institutions of the State in order to seize power from a Taoiseach they held in contempt. This second myth is essential to the first, as Lynch could avoid responsibility for the uncovered gun-running plan only if others could be identified and blamed. Without Haughey and Blaney as culprits, the government would have been left naked before some uncomfortable facts. Chief among these, as the Garda note that Cosgrave brought to Lynch implied, was the apparent entanglement in the gun-running scheme of Gibbons and Hefferon, as Minister for Defence and top-ranking Army Director of Military Intelligence respectively. This book explores the reality behind the two linked myths of 1970: Lynch as hero, and Haughey and Blaney as sinister plotters.

It has never been satisfactorily established whether the gun-running was the result of a plot by Lynch's two sacked cabinet colleagues, or whether it was an authorized project, at least unofficially. This book challenges the dominant view that Lynch was the aggrieved party. Using the most comprehensive array of source material yet assembled, it claims that Lynch scapegoated his two ministers, after having done much to create a crisis that historians and journalists, perversely, have given him credit for resolving. Question marks will be placed here against theories that Haughey and Blaney were operating a disloyal 'government within a government', or were plotting to unseat Lynch as Taoiseach.

The evidence is that Lynch had an effectively hidden policy on Northern Ireland, which in part involved the provision of guns – in emergencies – to Northern nationalists. Lynch never admitted this. It is one of the claims here that while he was Taoiseach, and thereafter, Jack Lynch engaged in a long-term cover-up of the contents of a directive given to the Defence Forces on 6 February 1970. The directive largely, although not totally, encapsulated the hidden policy. This book also contains the first serious examination of the criminal prosecution that led to the arms trials; it raises fresh doubts over whether charges should ever have been preferred, and offers new and unique insights into how the jury decided to acquit Haughey, Captain James Kelly and the other accused.

Overall, the book argues for a reassessment of the historical significance of the Arms Crisis. It calls for a recasting of the roles played by the two dominant figures of the period, Lynch and Haughey, as well as other central players such as Blaney. It suggests the two army officers involved, Kelly and Hefferon, were essentially collateral damage in a larger conflict being played out substantially within Fianna Fáil. Their treatment, it is argued, has been unjust.

The uncovering of the myths about 1970 has not been helped by the existence of a different conspiracy identifiable from the time, one based on silence and deception. The untruths that litter the evidence are so persistent that it is not possible to develop a clear Arms Crisis narrative without first distinguishing between those witnesses whose evidence appears broadly credible, and those whose evidence, generally speaking, is questionable. This exercise quickly establishes the value of testimony from public servants such as Anthony Fagan of the Department of Finance and senior army officer Michael Hefferon; their broadly trustworthy testimony proved a sharp contrast to the frequently unreliable claims from almost all the senior politicians. The evidence of Peter Berry, Secretary of the Department of Justice, and an important player in the events considered below, exists in a category of its own and will be considered accordingly.

But even with an enhanced approach to witness credibility, all attempts to pierce through the contradictions and dead ends of the dominant narrative have to contend with a further suffocating reality: the Arms Crisis, in significant part, was internal Fianna Fáil business, and the sectional interest of the party has never been in full disclosure. This is illustrated in the elaborate subterfuges of James Gibbons, Jack Lynch and Charles Haughey. Silence and reticence alone were never going to be enough to protect Fianna Fáil's hold on office, and complete truth-telling, it seems, was never an option.

While Haughey's capacity for twisting the record is one of the worst-kept secrets of the Arms Crisis, less conspicuous is the fact that throughout 1970 and beyond, extending even to November 1980, Lynch and Gibbons were responsible for a large number of false statements to the Dáil and, in Gibbons's case, for false and misleading statements to Garda investigators. Gibbons's struggles with veracity caused him to suffer humiliation at the hands of senior counsel in the arms trials, but the extent to which Lynch's public statements, to the Dáil and otherwise, fail to stand up, may surprise many. As the British ambassador remarked in the aftermath of the trials, the entire episode reflected poorly on nearly everyone involved, with Fianna Fáil, in his view, 'putting party and power above principles'.[6] It was a view with which Peter Berry, the formidable Secretary of the Department of Justice, from a very different vantage–point, completely concurred. In his *Diaries*, written retrospectively and published posthumously in 1980, Berry reached an acid conclusion: 'The necessity to keep the Fianna Fáil government in power at all costs was the over-riding consideration.'[7]

This book has been prompted in part by the unsatisfactory nature of the literature on the Arms Crisis. Apart from Captain Kelly, only two of the authors who have ventured into the field, Justin O'Brien in *The Arms Trial* (2000)[8] and Angela Clifford in *The Arms Conspiracy Trial, Ireland 1970: The Prosecution of Charles Haughey, Captain Kelly and Others* (2009),[9] devote their books exclusively to the events surrounding the Arms Crisis. The rest – among them Stephen Collins with *The Power Game* (2000), Bruce Arnold with *Lynch: Hero in Crisis* (2001) and Dermot Keogh with *Jack Lynch: A Biography* (2008) – address the subject only as part of biographical or other wider studies.[10] In fact, the most perceptive work on the period has come from non-academics Clifford and journalist Vincent Browne.

Another reality is that among writers and historians who have considered the tangled nature of the 1970 Arms Crisis, very little agreement exists after nearly fifty years. What is not disputed is the importance of the events: for Arnold, the crisis represented 'the most momentous political event in the State's history',[11] while Keogh saw it as 'the worst crisis since the Civil War'.[12] Collins believed it caused 'the near-collapse of the Government of the

Irish Republic, and led directly to the creation of the Provisional IRA'.[13] Even Clifford, whose view of events was radically different from many other commentators in the field, conceded that 'the arms crisis was crucial in shaping Irish political life in succeeding decades'.[14]

But beneath this umbrella of apparent agreement on the importance of 1970, there are conflicting interpretations of key events, and differing, often ambiguous, views on the roles played by some key participants, such as Minister for Defence Jim Gibbons. The extensive documentation made public since 2001 in the National and Military Archives in Dublin and in the British Archives in Kew should have helped dispose of many of the fanciful theories that have abounded, but few other than Clifford appear to have rigorously interrogated all the available primary sources.

Perhaps partly as a result, Hefferon is one of the great neglected figures in the literature on the Arms Crisis. A central player who knew of Kelly's plans and even gave critical advice on how his junior officer should get the arms into the country without disturbance, he fits uneasily into narratives of subversion and plotting led by ministers Haughey and Blaney. Hefferon has been disparaged by some writers as a result of a series of critical memoranda written by his successor as Director of Military Intelligence, Colonel P. J. Delaney, but the research for this book, as detailed below, offers a different perspective on Delaney and how he may have been used and abused by his minister, Jim Gibbons.

The early chapters of this book chart how plans to bring in guns for the Northern Defence Committees developed in tandem with the Lynch government's more general contingency planning, in the aftermath of the events of August 1969. In Chapter 1, military files from the time suggest that Lynch's 'cannot stand by' television address on 13 August may not have been, as many have suggested, an idle threat, and that cross-border intervention was a real possibility. Dublin feared a repeat of August 1969, and made contingency plans so that it would be better prepared. A 'cold shoulder' policy adopted by the British government, which refused any role or consultative rights to the Irish government over Northern Ireland, left Lynch with few diplomatic options in the event of any recurrence of such disturbances. In these circumstances, it appears questionable whether the Lynch cabinet was as divided over Northern Ireland policy after August 1969 as many writers have asserted.

In Chapter 2, Captain Kelly's alleged status as a maverick officer is queried. His project to bring in guns for the Northern Defence Committees is charted, focusing in part on a key meeting with republicans in Bailieboro, Co. Cavan in early October 1969. In the background to the Bailieboro meeting, military papers show that senior officers in the Chief of Staff's office at Army GHQ were proposing at the time a remarkable, almost unimaginable, working relationship with republicans. This was viewed as a necessary part of plans to protect nationalists over the border. The evidence raises major doubts over whether the Bailieboro meeting was the subversive event claimed for it. Kelly's role in seeking to split the IRA is considered in the context of a cabinet memorandum that urged such a policy.

Chapter 3 queries claims that Blaney and Haughey were engaged in a conspiracy to unseat Lynch as Taoiseach, with plans to use a rearmed IRA as a tool in this process. A critical assessment is made of the frequently voiced assertions in the literature that both ministers favoured the use of force as a means of gaining Irish unity. Their main concern, it is suggested, was the defence of nationalists under threat, and there appears to be no evidence that they favoured the use of force to end partition.

New evidence on Haughey is discussed in Chapter 4, querying claims that he was disloyal and running 'a government within a government' in the autumn of 1969. Haughey was seen as an unlikely plotter, and his involvement with gun-running surprised close observers. Also subject to critical scrutiny in this chapter is Haughey's management of the £100,000 voted for Northern relief.

The Dáil Committee of Public Accounts, in its report published in July 1972, assumed the money had been misappropriated to buy arms, but significant reasons are considered for the belief that the committee was mistaken in this view.

The covert aspect of Lynch's two-sided Northern Ireland policy before May 1970 is documented in Chapter 5. Hidden from public view was the training of Northern nationalists in arms–handling, contingency planning for arming them, and possible Irish army humanitarian incursions over the border. While Lynch publicly stressed his peaceful intentions on the border, he said nothing of the more interventionist and militarized plans being made to assist nationalists if there was a more serious recurrence of the events of August 1969. The two dimensions to Northern Ireland policy, public and private, are shown to have progressed hand-in-hand from autumn 1969 to spring 1970. The 6 February directive, embodying the hidden policy, led to the emergency transfer of 500 rifles north to Dundalk on 2 April 1970, while riots raged in Ballymurphy in Belfast. Evidence is identified in military files suggesting that the plan to provide arms for the defence of Northern nationalists had been abandoned by early June 1970; this was an apparent change of policy, coinciding with Lynch's repudiation of the gun-running. This appears to support Captain James Kelly's persistent claims that it was a government change of policy that ended the gun-running attempt.

Chapter 6 produces evidence that before January 2001 there was an official cover-up by Lynch and his ministers of the full contents of the 6 February directive. A 1971 personal memorandum from the Taoiseach, not previously considered in the literature, describes in questionable terms assurances he had given to the chairman of the Public Accounts Committee, Patrick Hogan TD (Fine Gael). According to former Labour deputy Justin Keating, who resigned from the committee in protest at the government's attitude, the language he saw in the directive, thirty years later, indicated that decades of modern Irish history needed to be reassessed. Keating concluded that the arms trials were unjustified and that too many official lies had been told for the historical record to stand.

In Chapter 7, it is suggested that Lynch and Gibbons colluded in making a false denial that Peter Berry warned Lynch at a meeting in Mount Carmel Hospital in Dublin, on 17 October 1969, of how Captain Kelly, at a meeting in Bailieboro, Co. Cavan, had offered money to republicans to buy guns. The claims made by Berry corroborated evidence given by Colonel Hefferon and Captain Kelly nine years earlier in 1971, at the Committee of Public Accounts. The evidence, it is argued, has exposed Gibbons and Lynch as being deceitful over the matter. Their apparent collusion has fundamental implications for their credibility six months later in April 1970, when Kelly's role in the gun-running attempt became evident.

A detailed forensic analysis of Gibbons's various public statements on the Arms Crisis in 1970–71, including his earliest statements of evidence to gardaí, forms a central part of Chapter 8; it reveals a pattern of evasion on Gibbons's part, plus further seeming collusion with Lynch in deception. Conspicuously, Gibbons's memory became greatly improved in 1971, after the crisis was over. In his evidence at the Committee of Public Accounts inquiry that year, he contradicted extensively the witness statements and sworn evidence he had provided throughout 1970. The extent of Gibbons's knowledge of the gun-running, it is argued, suggests that if the failed attempt was part of a conspiracy against Lynch, any such conspiracy had to include Gibbons.

Fresh perspectives on Neil Blaney are explored in Chapter 9, including the extent to which there was a split inside the Lynch cabinet before May 1970. This includes a revealing comparison between the language used by Blaney in his controversial Letterkenny speech of December 1969, and the language used privately by his colleague Gibbons just two months later in the 6 February directive. Files from the British State papers at Kew are used to show how Lynch used Blaney's public unruliness over Northern policy to his advantage in dealing with the British government. Blaney's true allies in Northern Ireland, evidence suggests, were not the IRA, but the Nationalist Party, led by Eddie McAteer. A prospective future leader of that party, Derry community leader Paddy 'Bogside' Doherty, is shown to have played a key role in events leading to the 6 February directive.

The events of the climactic weekend in the gun-running project – 17–20 April 1970 – are the subject of analysis in Chapter 10, raising further questions over Gibbons's claimed failure to notify Taoiseach Jack Lynch earlier of what he knew. Haughey's pivotal phone conversation with Peter Berry on Saturday evening, 18 April 1970 is analysed; while it was used against him at the arms trials, claims that Haughey was attempting to suborn Berry into acts of treason against the State are described as highly problematic. The chapter also includes fresh evidence, unearthed in the State files, that casts new light on Gibbons's conversation with Haughey on Monday afternoon, 20 April; this suggests that a second, undisclosed meeting took place between Haughey and Gibbons on that day, and that Judge Seamus Henchy lacked the full facts when he famously declared at the second arms trial that one or the other of the two ministers had been guilty of perjury over their meeting.

The following fifteen days, from 20 April to 5 May 1970, characterized by Lynch's sluggish response to the dramatic information Berry had brought to him, are considered in Chapter 11. Until the unexpected intervention of Liam Cosgrave, the evidence suggests that the situation was very fluid. Lynch was keeping his options open over how to deal with Captain Kelly and with ministers involved in the gun-running; meanwhile, the frustration of the Garda Special Branch and of their effective civil service controller, Peter Berry, kept mounting.

The important role played by Colonel Michael Hefferon during the Arms Crisis is the focus of Chapter 12. While his evidence was a vital part of the two arms trials, it is argued that his general significance in the events of the time has been under-appreciated. As with Gibbons, Hefferon's participation in the planning of the gun-running suggests difficulty in excluding him from any supposed conspiracy against Lynch. In a compare-and-contrast assessment of the two documented schemes to provide arms to nationalists, both of them covert, the chapter concludes that Hefferon was justified in regarding the schemes as connected by means of government policy.

In Chapter 13, evidence is assembled that Jack Lynch failed to tell the truth not just in several statements to Dáil Éireann in 1970, but also in other public and private instances. In a context of apparent collusion between Lynch and Gibbons in denying receipt of Peter Berry's warning, the chapter also assesses other seeming contradictions in the evidence regarding the two men. Through the eyes of several different observers – two British ambassadors to Dublin, Lynch's cabinet colleague Kevin Boland and civil servant Peter Berry – a devious side to the Taoiseach's personality is identified.

The first forensic examination of the arms trial prosecution and the accompanying Garda Special Branch investigation is contained in Chapters 14 and 15. Department of Justice files, including witness statements, are used to create for the first time a prosecution timeline; this throws new light on the decision to bring criminal charges. The Attorney General, it is argued, was in possession of evidence casting suspicion on Minister Jim Gibbons, but showed little interest. A hitherto unpublished document discovered in the National Archives, the final Garda investigation report from Detective Chief Superintendent John Fleming, is assessed. This reveals further problematic behaviour concerning Gibbons. The controversial editing of Hefferon's witness statement for the Book of Evidence, removing his references to Gibbons's advance knowledge of the gun-running, is shown to have been part of a questionable pattern in the Attorney General's prosecution. A critical assessment is made of an official 2001 report by former Attorney General Michael McDowell SC, which viewed the editing as *bona fide*.

The conduct of the second arms trial under Judge Seamus Henchy, and the background and reasoning behind the acquittals, are critically examined in Chapter 16, again employing original source material and offering fresh lines of analysis. Unique extended interviews with two arms trial jurors explain the basis for the verdicts; these describe specific problems the jury encountered over Charles Haughey, and why Haughey was the last of the accused to be acquitted. The analysis identifies how an apparently strong legal case for a guilty verdict remained at the end of the trial, and how the jury reconciled the conflicting issues before them, in deciding to acquit.

Chapter 17 assesses the historical significance of the book's findings. It argues that there is now a case for a root-and-branch historical revision of what happened in the 1970 Arms Crisis. This includes Lynch's role and his apparent scapegoating of Haughey and Blaney, along with the treatment of Captain James Kelly and the other accused in the arms trials. The criminal prosecution, it is argued, was probably unwarranted, and the historical significance of the Arms Crisis in twentieth-century Irish history may have been overstated.

The book concludes that the activities of Haughey and Blaney did not assist significantly in the emergence of the Provisional IRA; it suggests that a different, little considered opinion may have more credibility, that the actions of Jack Lynch helped the Provisional IRA more, by leaving a vacuum they could exploit, and allowing them to claim to be the sole defenders of the minority community.

1

Aftermath of August 1969

The search for the roots of the 1970 Arms Crisis inevitably begins by focusing on the events of August 1969. The convulsion that month within Northern Ireland, with whole streets in Belfast being burned out, followed by mass movements of population, left a spectre hanging heavily over the Irish government in Dublin; the fear was of a repeat event, perhaps with even fiercer consequences and with much higher fatalities. The deep underlying issue of the Arms Crisis was how, or whether, an administration in Dublin could provide protection and physical help to Catholic/nationalist people across the border, if there were further sectarian assaults. This was the issue that crystallized in August 1969.

Different choices appeared to be open to Jack Lynch and his cabinet at that time, and the tensions generated by these choices reverberated over the following months. On the one hand, there appeared a prospect to some in the cabinet that perhaps the end of partition was in sight, and that a historic reunification of the island of Ireland could be realized; other more practically minded ministers could see a clear need to ensure that the Irish authorities were not found wanting a second time. Should a similar upheaval occur, they could see the Irish Republic had to be able to offer endangered nationalists some semblance of assistance, *in extremis*. If a third group existed, those who felt the Republic could sit on its hands in the event of another Northern emergency and offer no physical comfort to Northern Catholics under assault, they never found their voice in late 1969.

Trauma across the border raised challenging questions for Fianna Fáil in government and, at whatever level it presented, was certain to generate stress and internal disagreement. That the events of August 1969 caused tensions in Lynch's cabinet is undeniable; what may need to be treated with more caution are assertions that those tensions led inevitably to the splits perceived within the Lynch government in May 1970. The core question raised here is the extent to which the Lynch government was divided internally in the months from August 1969 to May 1970. It seems possible that the divisions that did exist may have been over emphasized by being seen through a prism of hindsight, and a hindsight that, additionally, arose from a questionable perception of the events of May 1970.

The common view in the literature has been that the Lynch cabinet was so riven after the events of August 1969 in Northern Ireland that a governmental crisis, such as emerged, was an almost inevitable consequence. Historian Ronan Fanning was not untypical when he stated that it was the fissures inside Lynch's government that 'triggered the cataclysm of the Arms Crisis' in May 1970.[1] According to general perception, after the events of 13 August in Belfast and Derry, the cabinet divided into hawks and doves; the perceived point of division between the factions was the relative willingness of some ministers to support the use of military force to secure the end of partition.[2] Other factors, too, appeared to be aggravating cabinet divisions: these included an ill-concealed sense of frustrated ambition among some of Lynch's colleagues, who, it is claimed, could see in Northern Ireland's instability an opportunity to unseat Lynch as Taoiseach.

These underlying assumptions about Jack Lynch's cabinet, post-August 1969, merit closer scrutiny. To what extent was the government actually split into so-called hawks and doves? While the Northern Ireland situation was uncertain and fear-ridden, it is hard to discern precisely the policy divide between Lynch and his supposed rivals in August 1969. Real differences of temperament and personality were certainly in play; Lynch and his government colleagues on the night of 13 August contemplated facing some impossible choices, of a kind not encountered by any Irish government since the Provisional Government headed by Michael Collins in 1922. Already the choice seemed stark: to send the Irish army over the border, or not? But it is open to query whether the shorthand terminology of hawks and doves adequately describes the complexity of responses around Lynch's cabinet table in August 1969 and over the following months. Particular difficulty is created by the proposition that the supposed hawks within the government believed, contrary to the evolution of Fianna Fáil thinking under Eamon de Valera and Seán Lemass, that the use of force could end partition.

Lynch, listed among the doves, was certainly no warmonger, but his immediate response to the events of August 1969 was at best ambiguous. He warned in a televised address that the Irish government could no longer afford to 'stand by and see innocent people injured and perhaps worse'.[3] In a move seemingly designed to reassure Northern Catholics, but which from a unionist or British viewpoint had to appear threatening, he announced that the Irish army would be installing itself along the border with Northern Ireland, ostensibly to set up a number of field hospitals. The somewhat bellicose tone of his statement left many expecting some form of imminent cross-border intervention. The British government, watching closely, was concerned that Lynch was signalling an invasion of some kind.[4]

Historians, however, have tended to represent Lynch's actions on 13 August 1969 as mere posturing, a thin concealment for the impotence of the Republic in the face of threats to the Northern Catholic minority.[5] J. J. Lee believed that Lynch was trying to prod the British into action; of course, the following day, 14 August, the British army was sent onto the streets of Derry's Bogside. However, the State files released in 2000 and 2001 contain no evidence that the Irish government at any point ruled out intervention across the border.

Lynch and his colleagues faced an extremely fluid situation. A rolling government meeting began at 2.15 p.m. and throughout the afternoon was receiving information from officials and making periodic decisions. Eventually, it was announced 'in the early evening' that Lynch would be making a television address to the nation at 9 p.m.[6] Ministers did not know that the British army would be sent in the following day; nor indeed was there any expectation that such an action would help calm the situation. On the contrary, the government statement made clear that the involvement of the British army was not welcomed, nor did ministers believe it *would* in fact restore peace.[7] Their fears and uncertainties were on full view.

The evidence is that after a fractious debate, during which Blaney proposed that the Irish army cross the border – it seems immediately – and go straight into the Bogside, the cabinet decided firmly against such a course at that point. Lynch later said that the 'most cogent' reason for the government's rejection in August of what he called an 'armed invasion' of the North was the very practical consideration 'that the use of force would not advance our long-term aim of a united Ireland'.[8] Blaney, some two decades later, said that his intention had been to create an international incident, leading to the involvement of the United Nations.[9] The naivety of this approach was apparent to most of his colleagues, who realized that any such move would expose Catholics in Belfast – who were greatly outnumbered generally in the city and surrounded by Protestants in areas such as the Short Strand – to an extreme sectarian backlash.

This emerges from the account of Kevin Boland, who has provided the earliest, most complete and most convincing of the internal cabinet versions of the discussions that day. He resigned from cabinet at the height of the crisis, in a principled stand supporting Haughey and Blaney. In a little-referenced book published just two years later, Boland acknowledged that some ministers had seen the situation as an opportunity to advance the party's goal of a united Ireland; but none of them, he claimed, believed the opportunity should be taken by the use of force. This was the general understanding 'even if adequate force was available, which it was well known was not the case'.[10] Boland said the substantial argument advanced on 13 August 1969 was 'that the situation was getting worse hourly, and that if it became really catastrophic – and it was recognized that it had not by any means reached that stage as yet – then it would be our duty to give whatever protection we could'.

Boland said cabinet members recognized the particular difficulties posed by the situation in Belfast. 'We all appreciated the fact that, while effective protection against the attackers could be given in Derry, Newry and other border towns, the people in Belfast and other isolated areas could be wiped out if any action of ours gave the signal.' In the end, he felt that a temporary consensus was reached: 'There was then completely unanimous realization that there could be no suggestion of any crossing of the border, unless the situation was already so bad that no action of ours could make it worse.'

But, as noted above, the situation in the North was not static on 13 August, and the decision on that day to deploy the Irish army to the border was clearly made in the knowledge that circumstances north of the border could well sharply deteriorate. The public atmosphere neared hysteria. Newspaper reports referred to a 'massive mobilization' and suggested that 'very large forces and convoys are moving near border areas'. Rumours were reported to be sweeping the Bogside that help from Dublin was at hand.[11] The ostensible purpose of the deployment, as announced publicly at the time, was the creation and defence of field hospitals to cater for refugees and others injured in the disturbances. A bulletin from the Government Information Bureau in Dublin sought to calm speculation about the extent of the troop movements, stating somewhat questionably that 'the only troops involved are those engaged either in a direct medical or supporting capacity in setting up the military hospitals'.[12]

The official line has always been that, even if the circumstances had worsened, there was no contemplation in August 1969 of the Irish army crossing the border into Northern Ireland.[13] That, however, is unlikely to represent the full truth. It is noteworthy that the State papers released in 2000 do not reveal the official instructions from the Minister for Defence to the Chief of Staff on 13 August 1969, and also fail conspicuously to identify the precise mission given to the army. The Chief of Staff's instructions to his troops left all options open by stating that the deployment to Donegal was 'with a view to rendering such assistance as may be desirable'. The actual mission being given to the army was unstated; it would be 'as explained verbally by CF [Chief of Staff] to officer commanding Donegal area'.[14] The Operation Order (OO) included only what it termed 'a gen[eral] outline' of instructions for the 'execution' of the mission, an outline that did include 'the establishment of field hospitals' as part of the task.

It may be significant that, whereas this Operation Order deployed only a small force of three infantry companies (about 420 troops) to establish field hospitals, other documents in the State papers reveal that in fact a far larger force of 1,500 troops was actually mobilized, and also that the army had immediately sought extra military equipment of a kind normally associated with artillery units. Information on the numbers deployed and the equipment they required was contained in a 19 August 1969 memo from Army Quartermaster General Colonel MacDonnachadha to the Secretary of the Department of Defence, Seán Ó Cearnaigh, entitled 'Supply Requirements'.[15] MacDonnachadha referred to 'the possibility of our forces being engaged in sustained operations'. He sought the urgent resupply of heavy weaponry and anti-tank missiles. In a later follow-up letter on this question of supplies from Ó Cearnaigh to his minister, James Gibbons, there is reference to 'conditions where the Defence Forces would be involved in hostilities'.

In the light of these references to heavy weaponry, it seems highly unlikely that when Gibbons ordered the army to the border, he made no reference to the possibility – however unsought, however undesired, and even however unlikely – that in the course of its mission, the army might be required in the coming days to cross into Northern Ireland. It may also be significant that the deployment of troops to the border area was not speedily reversed when the British army established control after August 1969; a memorandum from a senior official in the Department of External Affairs show that the troops were still there in mid-November.[16] Even at the end of January 1970, British Ambassador Andrew Gilchrist noted that the Irish army was 'still fairly thick on the ground along the border'.[17]

Although some of the military documents referred to here have been public since January 2000, only two writers have given them serious attention. Angela Clifford, the first to identify their importance, may have exaggerated when she wrote that 'preparations were being made for war',[18] yet she argued convincingly that the instructions to the army went beyond the simple defence of hospitals and refugee camps within the state. The military weapons requested by the Quartermaster General, she wrote, were 'both defensive and offensive. High-explosive anti-tank mortar and machine gun ammunition and Energa grenades were not going to be needed to defend field hospitals and refugee camps from low level assaults, but would be required for the intervention of the Defence Forces in Northern Ireland in order to secure the safety of the minority population'.[19] It was a conclusion with which political scientist Donnacha Ó Beacháin broadly agreed. He felt the items sought showed that the mission the government envisaged 'went far beyond providing humanitarian assistance on the Republic's side of the border'. He noted particularly the request for 'large quantities of 25-pounder and 100 mm ammunition… for artillery… and for large mortars, both offensive weapons'.[20] Neither of these writers has argued that Jack Lynch ever contemplated a crossing of the border for the purpose of breaking partition, should that have been proposed by any faction in his cabinet. The only pretext for an incursion to which Lynch would conceivably have assented was a humanitarian one, for the protection of Catholic lives.

Blaney's view of the army's mission in 1969, as he insisted twenty years later, was that it was open-ended, with some intervention possible if circumstances deteriorated. He noted that after the cabinet had rejected his argument for the creation of an international incident by sending the troops into Derry or Newry, it was then

> ...agreed by the Government to send the Army to the border, under the cover of field hospitals.... The field hospitals idea we went along with. I didn't give a goddamn how they went up as long as the Army went up and were there to go in. And that was what was in the minds of, I'd say, the majority of our cabinet that day.[21]

Lynch himself years later sought to dismiss the military deployment after 13 August as merely a smokescreen to lift the pressure he was under from some of his cabinet colleagues.[22] Historian Michael Kennedy, however, appeared to find Blaney's 'open-ended' view of the August 1969 mobilization more convincing than Lynch's, despite the Irish army being out-gunned and unprepared for any confrontation with the British army. According to Kennedy, 'The cabinet agreed, off the record, the contingency of a doomsday scenario in which Southern troops would invade Northern Ireland to create an international incident and thereby bring in the United Nations.'[23] Although he cited no authority for this view, Kennedy's suggestion is that, as early as mid-August 1969, there was within the cabinet a generally shared support for cross-border intervention to protect Northern nationalists from sectarian assault, *in extremis*.[24] If this is correct, the cabinet was prepared to act, but not immediately. For the time being, a sensible majority view had prevailed. There was an understandable reluctance to cross the border, to make what could be considered to be an act of war against a friendly neighbour and also to risk inciting an anti-Catholic pogrom. But for an Irish government staring at a combustible, unstable situation over the border on 13 August 1969, this could only be a holding position.

So, if there were fissures over Northern Ireland between Lynch and his colleagues, as claimed by Fanning and others, where did they lie? A problem here, as historian Mary Daly observed, is the difficulty of knowing precisely 'what were Lynch's views?' in the autumn of 1969.[25] Daly's uncertainty here is indicative of a general perception that Lynch, in his TV address on 13 August 1969, was under some duress from his colleagues and effectively was coerced into a statement that was not fully his. British Ambassador Gilchrist gave early expression to this in his annual report to London: 'The Taoiseach, in order to maintain party unity, was forced to go a considerable way to meet the strongly interventionist views of the Fianna Fáil right wing, led by such men as Mr Neil Blaney.'[26] And Blaney in later years contributed to this impression of Lynch when he insisted that the televised address had been drafted communally: 'That speech was composed word for word, every comma, every iota, as a collective cabinet speech. It was not Jack Lynch's speech, made on behalf of his government. It was a cabinet speech, made by Jack Lynch.'[27]

What is undeniable is that it was Lynch who delivered the somewhat hawkish address, Lynch who appeared to threaten Irish army intervention, Lynch who dismissed the capacity of the British army or the RUC to bring peace, and Lynch who declared at that point that Irish unity was the only permanent solution. Nor did the Taoiseach make any attempt to resile from this position two months later when he insisted in the Dáil that he stood over everything that he had said and done on 13 August.[28]

It is also significant that Lynch's implied threat on 13 August – that the Irish government could not 'stand by' while innocent people were slaughtered – cannot be dismissed as an isolated one-off remark. The files show that it was repeated by his cabinet ally,

External Affairs Minister Patrick Hillery, in an entirely private meeting in London almost six months later. In February 1970, in discussions with the Chancellor of the Duchy of Lancaster, George Thomson, and top Foreign Office and Northern Ireland officials, Hillery was at pains to point out the fears still being expressed at that stage by Northern nationalists to the Irish government. Their concern, he said, centred on the number of private guns in the hands of Protestant extremists. The Irish official minutes of the meeting show that Hillery stressed the need to avoid violence, but then asked the British delegation what the Irish government should say to 'these frightened [nationalist] people when they inquired as to their fate if they were attacked'. When a British senior official responded by saying the British army was there, Hillery insisted that there was a danger of a false alarm, or false start,

> ...in the sense that the frightened people of the minority... might possibly react against a threat which might not be actual, but which they believed to be a real threat, and a situation might then arise where *we could not stand by* and leave these unfortunate people defenceless in such a situation [emphasis added].[29]

Hillery's private use of the incendiary phrase 'not stand by', six months after it was issued by Lynch on 13 August 1969, was hardly accidental. It speaks volumes about the continuing apprehensions in Dublin through the winter and spring of 1969–70, concerned that some military cross-border intervention could be forced on them. It also underlines that Lynch's implicit threat to intervene on 13 August should not be dismissed as mere posturing.

The many writers, such as Stephen Collins, who have argued that as the autumn of 1969 drew in, battle lines on Northern Ireland were already firmly drawn within the cabinet, find little support for their theory in the way Lynch deployed his ministers to deal with the new Northern Ireland situation. He took a series of decisions that greatly enhanced the power and responsibility of Haughey, Blaney and Gibbons in this regard. Lynch had already, after the June general election, re-established Haughey in the powerful position of Minister for Finance, ahead of George Colley in the pecking order, and restored Blaney to his senior portfolio as Minister for Agriculture and Fisheries. Both Blaney and Haughey had shown their electoral worth in securing for Lynch an impressive overall majority in the June 1969 general election. On Northern Ireland, clearly a pressing issue after the 12 August disturbances, and of considerable significance for any Fianna Fáil administration, Blaney's credentials were unrivalled. For all his dour, dogmatic public persona, he was the minister most closely connected to Northern nationalists, and was the cabinet's point man for information on affairs north of the border.

By mid-August, Lynch was fully aware of where his two senior ministers stood on Northern Ireland; if his government was split into so-called hawks and doves, as claimed, then Haughey and Blaney were clearly identifiable on the militant side. They had argued initially for cross-border army intervention into Derry, and then, however reluctantly, had accepted the more practical majority view, which was that such a move could be disastrous for Catholic nationalists in Belfast. Gibbons, significantly, was also among the supposed hawks; he had apparently aligned himself with Blaney and Haughey in the discussions around 13 August and the following days.[30]

It is a challenge for those writers and historians who have depicted a cabinet already split into factions, that Lynch, who at that point had the measure of his various colleagues' views on Northern Ireland, decided to assign responsibilities as he did. He delegated responsibility for ensuring that the Defence Forces were prepared for all contingencies that might arise in Northern Ireland jointly to Gibbons as Minister for Defence and Haughey as Minister for Finance.[31] On 16 August 1969, at cabinet, he delegated to Haughey unique control over a fund of money intended for the aid of victims of the August troubles in the

North. Haughey alone would decide on the amount to be paid, and on the channel of disbursement. Thirdly, Lynch appointed a cabinet sub-committee to liaise with Northern Ireland opinion, on which two of the four members were Blaney and Haughey.[32]

These important decisions, taken in August 1969 by a cabinet chaired by Jack Lynch, have often been represented, on the basis of hindsight after May 1970, as mistakes by the Taoiseach. They have been seen as evidence of Lynch's weak leadership pre-May 1970, and a key moment in his supposed loss of control over his cabinet. The premise is that he was negligent and foolhardy to delegate power to a strong faction who had shown that they opposed his views on Northern Ireland.[33] Lynch apologists would later represent the Taoiseach as a politician somehow transformed by the critical events of May 1970; the uncertain, error-prone figure they identified from the autumn of 1969 became, actually overnight, the decisive and steely leader who dispensed with his treacherous rivals Haughey and Blaney with aplomb, and emerged, in Arnold's memorable description, as a 'Hercules' within his party and government.[34]

What is not at all clear is that the evidence can support such a stirring analysis, or that it backs up the Lynch theory of miraculous transformation. What it fails to explain is why Lynch, fresh from his electoral triumph only six weeks earlier, assigned this level of responsibility to such men in August 1969 if he knew them to hold views on Northern Ireland with which he fundamentally disagreed. A different and perhaps more likely explanation is that Lynch did not see himself as being in fundamental disagreement with these colleagues. Is this possible? Here one comes back to the question posed by Mary Daly, asking – what *were* Lynch's views? Was it the case that he and Neil Blaney differed fundamentally on the use of force and military intervention in Northern Ireland? Or might their views have to a degree overlapped, at least more than has been generally acknowledged?

The question this raises is central to the whole Arms Crisis – it concerns the meaning of the phrase 'use of force in Northern

Ireland'. Force, classically, can be used for purposes that are defensive or aggressive – and conceivably for both. In the context of Northern Ireland in 1969–70, it could be used for defensive purposes and with the humanitarian goal of saving lives, or it could be employed for aggressive purposes, with the intention of smashing partition. Weapons used for defence could also be used for attack, and drawing a clear line between the two functions may perhaps be impossible. However, this inherent difficulty cannot negate the fact that the use of force may not, necessarily, have aggressive intent or purpose, but could be for the protection of lives and property. Martin Mansergh, who later served as Haughey's adviser when he became Taoiseach, has argued that there was no division in Lynch's cabinet after August 1969 – whether with Blaney or any other minister – over a willingness to take necessary cross-border action in the event of a so-called 'doomsday situation' in the North.[35] This important issue will be discussed further below.[36]

What seems certain is that Blaney's influence over Northern Ireland policy was strong in this period from August 1969 to May 1970. It had perhaps been enhanced, as Michael Kennedy has argued, by the departure from the cabinet of veteran republican Frank Aiken after the June election. Aiken had been 'the main advocate of common sense and moderation' in the government's previous Northern Ireland policy, and with his departure Kennedy believed 'the aggressive Northern Ireland policy advocated by Neil Blaney had no opponent' within the cabinet.[37] What is in question is the extent to which Blaney's influence extended over Lynch himself, going beyond any kind of duress, or reluctant tolerance, to an actual level of agreement.

Lynch and Blaney had clear differences of temperament, personality and background, and they came from very different constituencies; on Northern Ireland, Blaney, the Donegal man, was driven and impulsive, while the Cork-based Lynch was less personally involved, more cautious and tentative. Lynch, in public, seemed far from Blaney over the autumn and winter of

1969–70, as he appeared to be inching towards accepting the right of Northern unionists to withhold their consent from a united Ireland. In private, however, the story was different. Outside the public view, Lynch appears at this time to have been much closer to his outspoken colleague. He appears to have accepted that a Fianna Fáil administration, at a time of crisis in Northern Ireland, had some ultimate thirty-two-county responsibilities that could not be shrugged off. Post-August 1969, Lynch and his cabinet appear to have been united in seeing an opportunity, at least through the route of the United Nations and otherwise petitioning the British government, to make the ending of partition a real possibility.

A significant factor for Lynch in these matters was the response by the British government in the aftermath of August 1969, leaving him with severely restricted policy options on Northern Ireland. The British State papers for the period show how the Irish government was very publicly informed by the UK government on 15 August 1969 that Northern Ireland was seen as an internal concern of the British government, and that the Irish Republic had no role there. This stern line was spelled out in the clearest terms by junior Minister Lord Chalfont to Patrick Hillery in London on 15 August 1969. Hillery had travelled hot-foot to London to demand either a joint Anglo-Irish force to police troubled areas, or United Nations intervention. Chalfont dismissed both. He told Hillery that the Irish government proposal for a UN force to be despatched to Northern Ireland was unnecessary and irrelevant, and that the British government had no intention of taking such a course. 'Northern Ireland', Chalfont asserted, 'is part of the United Kingdom and we are confident we can deal with the situation.' Nor, he stated, would Dublin be consulted on future plans. 'We will consider as useful normal diplomatic consultations, but we could not undertake to consult the Irish government on how to solve a problem which is essentially a problem of the United Kingdom.'[38] Hillery was sent packing in no uncertain terms, and returned to

Dublin, it can be safely assumed, burning with indignation.

This unbending British attitude meant that Lynch's oppor-
tunities for any effective or discernible diplomatic response to
unpredictable events across the border were severely curtailed. It
threatened to leave the Irish government with tied hands if there
were further disturbances and unrest in the North.[39] And the
British attitude that Hillery had experienced was no passing fancy.
UK files are replete with indicators from British officials over the
following year holding to the line that the North was simply no
business of the Irish government. No concessions – even to the
point of discussions on more routine matters – could be made
to Dublin on the constitutional position of Northern Ireland; the
border was not, and could not be, an issue.[40] The British priority
was the protection of the unionist regime of Major Chichester
Clark in Stormont; they were aware that any involvement by them
with the Irish government, even on the level of consultation,
would tend to bring immediate adverse repercussions north of
the border.[41] It was a refusal to engage jointly on Northern Ireland
policy that would have consequences beyond anything the British
may have calculated.

At the same time, the British government was not oblivious
to the difficulties they were posing for Lynch by restricting Irish
diplomatic options. The State papers in Kew in London show that
alongside the hard line rejecting any consultation, there was a
matching anxiety to assist Lynch, at least in short-term matters,
and to seek to do nothing that might weaken him in facing down
the more aggressive instincts of the Blaney camp. There would be
encouragement and support for Lynch, but on the border he could
be offered nothing more than what Gilchrist termed 'a distant and
slow-moving gleam of light at the end of the tunnel'.[42]

A perceptive early analysis of these issues, entitled 'Lynch's
Dilemma', was sent by Ambassador Gilchrist to London in
October 1969. He pointed out that cooperating with the British
government's internal reform plans for Northern Ireland would
do nothing for Fianna Fáil's goal of a united Ireland. The better

the Stormont plans worked, the further off Irish unity would be. This meant, Gilchrist reasoned, that Britain could expect from Lynch only 'a policy of fits and starts, so that we must jolly him along and get what cooperation we can with the aid of vague confidential carrots, but without giving him any visible or quotable commitment in the sense he wants'. Gilchrist opined, somewhat smugly, 'So far we have not done badly.'[43] The British clearly recognized the dilemma facing Lynch and his party after August 1969, but they were over-complacent over the possible consequences of their strict hands-off attitude.

The reality was that the British refusal to allow any kind of advisory or consultative role over Northern Ireland was bound to create pressures on Lynch and his government to develop its own contingency planning for Northern Ireland. Such plans would never be anything but top secret. Lynch had a genuine commitment to the peaceful ending of partition, something the British, on the evidence of the official papers, did not doubt, but that was not his only responsibility. The Fianna Fáil government had responsibilities to Northern nationalists, and also was obliged to protect itself from a republican backlash in the event of a repetition of the events of August 1969.

Lynch could see the dangers to the Irish state if his government appeared again to do nothing to help defend Northern nationalists; he could see how an Irish government could be vulnerable to the IRA presenting itself in time of crisis as the only true defender of the threatened cross-border minority. Here it is significant that the Taoiseach spoke to the British ambassador privately in the autumn of 1969 of the danger that, as Gilchrist put it, the IRA might 'by some traditionally violent intervention, recapture the moral leadership of Ireland'.[44] In another private meeting in September 1969, Lynch warned Gilchrist that his Foreign Minister, Hillery, during the previous month had 'twice come back from London with hurt feelings'. Lynch also informed Gilchrist on that occasion that the cold shoulder from the British government on 15 August had forced his government to ask the United Nations directly to intervene. And he said that what he needed was a concession on consultation.[45] Gilchrist was unmoved.

What Lynch omitted to state was that the British policy of shutting out the Irish government would have consequences beyond a predictably ineffectual resort to the United Nations. The Irish government, its capacity to influence British policy through diplomatic channels having been reduced to almost nothing, was being forced into covert planning for a possible disaster in the North. The secret contingency plans already being formulated would be a fundamental factor in the Arms Crisis of 1970, and arose, at least partly, because of the hardline refusal of London to concede to the Irish government any public or attributable role over Northern Ireland. The challenge to historians is to see this situation and these events, in the aftermath of August 1969, as they were, and to avoid being influenced by the argument-laden and highly contrived versions of events that emerged after the Arms Crisis of the following May.

2

Captain Kelly: Maverick Officer?

One historian, not short on cynicism, has described James Kelly scathingly as 'a would-be Lawrence of Arabia'.[1] This description, laced with sarcasm, has the virtue of at least capturing the notoriety Kelly achieved in many quarters in 1970 and thereafter. To his critics, he has appeared a maverick – a republican-minded Irish army officer perceived as desiring to lead Northern Catholics to the promised land of Irish unification. It is a perception that has seen Kelly as out of sync with the government's peaceful approach to Northern Ireland, a soldier led astray by his personal zeal for a united Ireland. Kelly always vigorously contested this image of himself as a pro-IRA maverick, and ultimately succeeded in satisfying the jury in the Central Criminal Court that his role throughout the saga had been known of and approved by his military superiors.

Despite coming under intense fire, politically and legally, the junior officer turned out to be a much tougher opponent than anyone could have anticipated. The Attorney General and his lawyers discovered this the hard way when it became evident that, as a *sine qua non* for the State's case to triumph in the arms trials, it was necessary for Kelly's credibility as a witness to be destroyed. He was accordingly subjected to what one observer called 'savage infighting' in his cross-examination by State counsel Seamus McKenna SC.[2] There was little in his experience up to that point to prepare the army officer for such high-profile, life-or-death legal grappling.

James Kelly was 41 years old in 1970. He had been born into a strongly nationalist family, the eldest of ten children of a Co. Cavan farmer from outside the town of Bailieboro. He joined the Irish army in 1949 and went on to serve with the United Nations in Palestine. He won glowing testimonials from his Chief of Staff there, who described him as 'a clear, logical thinker, cool and unruffled in emergencies', while also possessing 'a sharp wit and astute intelligence', which caused him to be liked and respected by his associates.[3]

Back in Ireland, Kelly became editor of the Defence Forces journal, *An Cosantoir*, while also working in the sensitive position of staff officer to the Director of Military Intelligence, Colonel Michael Hefferon. In the arms trials, although he was always centre stage, he presented himself not as a controlling force over the attempted gun-running, but as more of a functionary. At the trial, Tom MacIntyre described him as 'a neat, erect figure, open-faced, humour in him, and a sensibility – quintessentially native – alive to the slither-and-twist of thought, a native vehemence in him also... doesn't look in the least like an Intelligence Officer, except in one important respect – his alertness'.[4]

Kelly's essential story was that he acted as a link between government ministers and the Northern Defence Committees; he said he worked with the committees, and, where the Northern Relief Fund was concerned, under the direction of the Northern account-holders. Although before March 1970 he had little or no direct involvement with Gibbons, his evidence was that throughout March and early April he received the Minister for Defence's personal approval for his actions. It was a claim that appeared to help sway the jury in the second arms trial towards his acquittal.[5] Kelly's version of events was set out not just at the second arms trial and at the proceedings of the Committee of Public Accounts in 1971, but also in his two books, *Orders for the Captain?* (1971) and *The Thimble Riggers* (1999). His description has been supplemented to some degree by the accounts of his co-accused, John Kelly, and through the evidence of his immediate boss, Colonel Hefferon, at both the arms trials and at the Committee of Public Accounts inquiry. His account of how the gun-running project originated is the earliest on record, and remained substantially unchallenged.

One key perspective that has been missing from Kelly's story, however, is that of Neil Blaney, then Minister for Agriculture, with whom Kelly was meeting on a weekly basis in the autumn of 1969. Charges brought initially against Neil Blaney were dropped at District Court level early on, and – somewhat surprisingly – Blaney was never called as a witness for Kelly and the other accused in the arms trials. A partial consequence was that Blaney's detailed insights into the origins and development of the arms plan have never been properly set down. Captain Kelly's various extensive accounts did not fill this gap, since they conspicuously do not include any detail on Blaney's role. His reticence over Blaney may have been the result simply of deference, an acknowledgement that the minister was entitled to make his own statement as he saw fit, but it left unaddressed a giant, Blaney-sized hole in the detailed historical narrative of the Arms Crisis. And while Kelly emerges from the record as a generally truthful and important chronicler of events, not everything in his story is completely convincing, in particular when it comes to the likely fate of any weapons that might have been imported in mid-April 1970.

The most important of the many issues in the Arms Crisis which involve James Kelly is the extent to which his actions were authorized by his minister, James Gibbons. Other questions arise over how much he revealed to his immediate military boss, Colonel Hefferon, a senior officer who cynics have noted was on the verge of retirement. An indignant Hefferon had to bat away suggestions at the Committee of Public Accounts inquiry in 1971 that he might have been 'hoodwinked' by his subordinate over his arms dealing.[6] Kelly also had to explain his particularly close dealings with Blaney and Haughey, two ministers without obvious authority to issue orders to an army officer. Concern has centred on whether these two ministers inserted themselves improperly into the military chain of command over Kelly. The blunt question has been asked: did Hefferon, Kelly's commanding officer, effectively lose control of him in the events leading up to May 1970? Some of these questions will surface throughout this book and are dealt with as they arise.

The main concern in this chapter is the origin of the gun-running attempt, and Kelly's dealings regarding money and guns with republicans who were effectively members of the IRA. Here his controversial meeting in Bailieboro on 4–5 October 1969 with members of the Northern Defence Committees is of central importance. Kelly never hid the fact that money was on offer at this meeting for the purchase of guns, and it has been a persistent question since whether the guns were intended for defensive or aggressive purposes, and what grouping was to receive them. Much helpful new data has become available in the State papers for 1969 and 1970, and from the memoirs of various key participants.

Kelly's initial involvement in the events leading to the Arms Crisis was entirely accidental. He was on holiday in the North when the disturbances of August 1969 broke out, visiting his brother, a priest in Belfast. Personal and professional curiosity caused the two brothers to travel to Derry, where they witnessed the Apprentice Boys parade on 12 August degenerate into widespread communal violence, leading to the so-called Battle of the Bogside. Kelly then saw the disturbances spread to Belfast, from where he made his return to Dublin on 14 August. Although still technically on holiday, he immediately reported what he had seen and heard to Colonel Hefferon in Military Intelligence. This resulted in Hefferon ordering him to continue to develop the contacts he had made in Belfast and Derry, and to focus his intelligence work for the foreseeable future exclusively on Northern Ireland. Over the following days, Kelly noted later, several unnamed Northerners visited him in Dublin, 'looking for arms for defence, if violence should ever break out again'.[7]

In further visits to Belfast in early September, locals further impressed on him their need for arms for defence. During this time he met John Kelly (no relation), a Belfast republican who was organizer 'on a six-county basis' for the Northern Defence Committees. These were the voluntary groupings that had sprung up after 13 August 1969 to provide defence and organization to nationalists in barricaded areas of Belfast and elsewhere in the North.[8] Contact between Kelly and two government ministers, Neil Blaney and Charles Haughey, followed shortly afterwards.

At some point in September 1969, having returned from a later visit to Belfast, Captain Kelly became aware that a cabinet sub-committee had been appointed on 16 August 1969, charged with 'maintaining permanent liaison with opinion in the Six Counties', and that one of its members was Neil Blaney.[9] A meeting with Blaney was followed by a further impromptu meeting arranged by Blaney on the same evening with Charles Haughey, Blaney's government colleague on the sub-committee. The stage was then set for an ensuing collaboration between the army officer and these cabinet members. Kelly never met the other two members of the largely dormant sub-committee, Minister for Social Welfare Joe Brennan and Minister for Education Padraig Faulkner, but he insisted always that he kept Hefferon informed of his contacts with Haughey and Blaney,[10] a claim that Hefferon endorsed.

Whether Kelly was ever formally appointed to act as liaison between the government and the Defence Committees has never been fully determined. This is at least partly because Judge Henchy, in the second arms trial, ruled out evidence on cabinet discussions that might have clarified it. Gibbons, the Minister for Defence, denied afterwards knowing anything of Captain Kelly at this time, but Kevin Boland, Minister for Local Government, challenged this, insisting that Kelly's name came up more than once at cabinet.[11] Whatever the truth, Kelly became the individual who connected Haughey and Blaney with the Northern Defence Committees, a matter Haughey confirmed to the second arms trial.[12]

When Haughey, as Minister for Finance, had to determine to whom the funds for Northern Relief allocated by the government on 16 August 1969 should be disbursed, it was to Captain Kelly he turned for information and assistance. Kelly's job, essentially, was to vet the various Northern applicants. And when efforts began in the autumn of 1969 to acquire arms for the Defence Committees, Kelly's perceived military expertise and familiarity with weapons left him perfectly placed to assist, if required. In fact, his direct assistance appears to have been sought only from January 1970 onwards. Before that he appears to have been essentially an onlooker as the Northern Defence Committees looked to the United States for arms, seeking out groups there with a long history of supporting Irish republicanism.

The earliest mention of a plan to import arms in the autumn of 1969 occurs in Captain Kelly's report to his boss, dated 6 October 1969, on his controversial meeting the previous week-end with representatives of the Defence Committees in Bailieboro. At this meeting, Kelly made it known that money would be available from Dublin, and that the Irish authorities were prepared to provide it for arms. He wrote later that the purpose of the meeting was to get the views of those 'who would be responsible for the use and control of arms that might be issued by the Dublin government'.[13] Almost all the Defence Committees across Northern Ireland were represented at the Bailieboro meeting. Kelly wrote that many of them 'were aware of the promise of money by Dublin, which they understood could be used to fund the purchase of arms'. In these talks with republicans about guns and money, Kelly was acting with the knowledge and authority of his commanding officer, Hefferon, and, it appears, also with the approval of ministers Haughey and Blaney.[14]

Bruce Arnold has described the Bailieboro meeting as the 'first major focus' of what he termed an 'elaborate and complicated

plot orchestrated by Haughey and Blaney'.[15] Kelly never accepted
the idea that there was such a plot, but agreed that the meeting
was 'the genesis' of the later attempted arms importation.[16] His
6 October report to Colonel Hefferon is revealing about the nature
of that genesis. It states that the 'N.I. Republican Movement's first
priority is the acquisition of arms for defensive purposes'. Already,
he told Hefferon, it 'has the finance to accomplish this', and 'it is
the intention to import arms through the South'.

This almost contemporaneous account by Kelly of the outcome
of the Bailieboro meeting is important, as it identifies the origins of
the gun-running plan that eventually sparked the Arms Crisis. It
appears to show that the decision to import arms did not originate
with either Haughey or Blaney, but with the Defence Committees
north of the border. Kelly reported that the committees already
had funds in hand – although not enough, it seems, to make a
project practicable – and had the intention of purchasing and
importing arms. Later, Kelly would assist in setting up an account
at the Bank of Ireland in Clones, Co. Monaghan, for channelling
monies allocated by the Irish government in August 1969 for
Northern Relief, but in early October that account did not exist,
and it would be months before any money from the Relief Fund
would be provided to the Defence Committees.

What happened at Bailieboro gave impetus to an arms
acquisition plan that had already been conceived, but the promise
of money from Dublin, while boosting such plans, also had the
effect of significantly complicating the ownership of the project
now in train. Whose plan was it? Kelly was offering funds, which
meant there would be a new paymaster in Dublin, and this
paymaster might be expected to have a view on who should receive
the money/arms, and by what means. But that did not mean, if
problems were to arise, that senior government figures in Dublin
would be willing to take public responsibility for seeing that the
arms were delivered efficiently. This of course was not an issue at
the time, but it would become so. Captain James Kelly stood at the
centre of the operation, but to whom did the operation actually

belong? It seems it never fully belonged to the Irish government, at any level. It may be that its ultimate undoing, and what proved to be its largely ramshackle organization, can be traced back to this initial confusion over ownership, funding and origin.

Official Department of Defence papers released in 2001 show that Kelly's activities in Bailieboro were not just known to his boss Hefferon, but were also broadly in harmony with the thinking of other senior Defence Forces officers in the Planning and Operations Section of the Chief of Staff's office at Army GHQ. Two documents in particular indicate this: the Interim Report of the Planning Board on Northern Ireland Operations, 27 Mean Fómhair, 1969, and a second paper entitled Recommendations of Planning Board, 13 Deire Fómhair, 1969. These records, prepared just in advance of Bailieboro by senior officers in Army GHQ, cast a new if indirect light on the Bailieboro encounter, and also on the directive to the Defence Forces that would be issued by Minister Gibbons on 6 February 1970.

The first document, the Interim Report, was produced by a panel of officers comprising two commandants and a lieutenant colonel, while the second, the Recommendations, was an unsigned assessment of that report, probably prepared by a more senior officer within the Planning and Operations Section of GHQ. What these records reveal is that, distant from Captain Kelly, in September–October 1969 senior army personnel in the Planning and Ops nerve centre were already thinking hitherto unthinkable thoughts about how the Northern Ireland situation might require it to work with illegal republican groups such as the IRA.[17]

The importance of the Interim Report is that it advised how, despite significant stated doubts, cross-border military operations by the Irish army could to a degree be made feasible. It was prefaced with the view that the Irish army was unprepared for cross-border operations in Northern Ireland, and that *any* kind of military action, conventional or unconventional, including invasion, would be militarily unsound. Despite this, it recommended considering 'supporting the minority in the North by training and the supply of arms and equipment'; such a course, it frankly acknowledged, would entail cooperation with 'republican groups in the North' and also 'with illegal groups in the Republic'. The report found that 'conventional operations' could be conducted by the army inside Northern Ireland, but only if restricted to 'company level', and only in areas where there was a Catholic/nationalist majority. The feasible areas were those adjoining the border, including Derry and Newry, but ruled out were areas such as Belfast, where there was a strong Protestant/ unionist majority; for these areas, 'only unconventional oper- ations' were deemed suitable.

The view of the army planners was that 'the support and assistance of a substantial part of the minority would be essential for success in Defence Force [sic] operations in Northern Ireland'.[18] Since only unconventional army operations could be conducted in areas like Belfast, where Catholics/nationalists were in the minority, it was felt – significantly – that 'it is to these latter areas that supplies of arms and equipment should be chiefly directed'.[19] The report stressed the extreme dangers to the State of following a course of intervention. It finally stressed the importance of an intensified intelligence effort in the North before and during any such operations.

This extraordinary – and given its source, somewhat startling – advice was further assessed in the Recommendations of the Planning Board document. Dealing with the proposal that the minority could be given training and arms and equipment, this noted pointedly that the number of people in the nationalist community 'who would be prepared to take an active part against the security forces in Northern Ireland' could be assumed to be 'NOT great' (emphasis as given). Nonetheless, it felt that training could be provided through the Fórsa Cosanta Áitiúil (FCA), the army's territorial reserve, on a full-time, one-month basis. It agreed that an intensified intelligence effort should be mounted.

The document then sounded another warning: training could not be given, nor weapons supplied, 'to members of organizations whose motives would not be in the best interests of the State'. To arm and train 'an element which may not have the best interests of the State as their motive' could, it warned, seriously prejudice political aims.[20] This appeared to be a coded reference to the IRA of the time, led by Cathal Goulding, and edging as it was towards socialism.

The relevance of these important documents to the activities associated with Captain Kelly is four-fold. Firstly, the importance they placed on finding reliable allies for the Defence Forces within Northern Ireland, allies capable of defending nationalist areas without threatening the interests of the State; secondly, their positive recommendation that consideration be given to supplying training, arms and equipment to Northern nationalists; thirdly, the central role given to Army Intelligence in implementing these actions; and fourthly, the implicit message in the documents that the one group to whom guns should *not* be provided was Goulding's IRA.

If any conventional operations were to be attempted by the Irish army – such as rescue incursions to border towns like Derry, Strabane, Enniskillen and Newry – in the Planning Board's view these would depend on unconventional military assistance being in place in areas where Catholics were outnumbered. In other words, army incursions could not succeed on their own, but would depend on the provision of arms and training in areas where a unionist backlash could be anticipated.

These high-level army reports, disclosed only in January 2001, provide an important broader context for the meeting in Bailieboro. They offer a yardstick for measuring whether Captain James Kelly was operating within recognizable Defence Forces norms, as opposed to harbouring subversive intentions. What they reveal is a remarkable consistency between Kelly's activities and the GHQ planners' cautious advice. What is extremely telling is the shared perception of a need to engage with republicans – i.e., members of the IRA – which in normal times would be a mark of sedition, but in these documents is revealed as the (somewhat nervous) calculation of senior army officers.

The armed assistance of Northern nationalists/republicans was viewed as essential to any cross-border operation geared to the defence of the Northern minority. Angela Clifford, the Belfast writer who has been almost unique in her detailed analysis of the Planning Board reports, has described them as representing 'direct evidence that Captain Kelly was not acting independently or subversively in 1969/70'.[21] She might also have observed that a similar argument could be made on behalf of Blaney and Haughey.

Yet the reports were advisory only; they cannot be taken as confirmed Defence Forces policy, and to that extent they cannot fully vindicate Kelly, Blaney or Haughey's activities. This advisory status may partly explain the limited attention given to these documents since they were released to the National Archives in 2001. Furthermore, and perhaps unsurprisingly, they appear to have generated controversy at the time in the army's upper echelons. According to the Hefferon Papers, a cold reception was given to the reports at least by some of the top brass. Hefferon wrote that they were initially 'buried' by some senior officer in GHQ,[22] to the great displeasure of the three-man board that produced the Interim Report. One of the three board members was an officer reporting to Hefferon.[23]

The reports were intended to prepare general staff for a meeting of a rarely convened body, the Council of Defence, but the minutes of that meeting make no reference to them.[24] Gibbons, who chaired the meeting in his office on 13 October 1969, is recorded as stating at one point that 'there should be military plans for extreme contingencies arising from the situation in the North'; this had been precisely the purpose of the Planning Board's reports. Hefferon, in his papers, also noted that the Chief of Staff, MacEoin, appeared surprised to learn in early February 1970 that the reports had not been sent directly to the minister in early October.

In all this confusion, there are glimpses of the simmering tensions the Northern situation was creating within the Defence Forces in the autumn and winter of 1969–70. The persistent message from the military to the government in this period was to stress how under-resourced and ill-equipped it was for any Northern intervention[25] – yet, despite this, the army found itself being directed towards exactly such an intervention. Cross-border adventures, however necessary their contemplation might appear to be to the civil power, could easily spell both immediate and long-term military disaster. The Planning Board recommendations, in anticipating such a cross-border venture and discussing uncharted alliances between the State's security forces and subversive groups, were offering just another strong stick for the army's already creaking back. Hefferon's own view, as shown in his papers, was that the Planning Board reports were 'worthy to receive deep consideration'. He felt they could have been used as a starting point for more detailed studies. But the upshot was that it took four months for the reports finally to reach the minister's desk, at some point shortly after 6 February 1970, and nothing in the files indicates what happened to their proposals thereafter.

Regarding Captain Kelly, one of the main issues at this time, partly arising from the Bailieboro meeting, is whether – as has often been alleged – the arms being sought were for the emergent Provisional IRA. Since the Provisional IRA did not exist in early October 1969, to some extent the question is disingenuous. The arms could not have been, at that stage, for them. A more relevant question is whether the arms were to be used to break partition, or rather were intended for purely defensive purposes. Kelly, who convened the Bailieboro meeting, always insisted that the arms to be brought in were for the Defence Committees, and were intended for purposes of defence.

In his 1971 book *Orders for the Captain?*, Kelly insisted that he was not dealing with the IRA;[26] his entire focus was on the defence of Northern nationalists, not on attacking partition. In *The Thimble Riggers*, published in 1999, he noted that the attendance at the Bailieboro meeting 'was unanimous and very adamant that they [*the arms*] would only be used for defensive purposes'. His contemporaneous record of the meeting's outcome appears at least consistent with this.[27] On the other hand, British journalist and historian Peter Taylor took the view that 'it was axiomatic that the Defence Committees were dominated by the IRA',[28] while John Kelly, Captain Kelly's close associate in the gun-running project, observed that 'they [*meaning the Defence Committees and the IRA*] were, by and large, the same'.[29]

However, the 'by and large' in that comment cannot be regarded as insignificant. Although the Defence Committees relied on IRA muscle for their security, and to that limited extent could be termed a front organization, they drew on a bigger, more representative pool of citizens which included priests, businessmen and lawyers, and their focus was unquestionably on defending their communities from potential attack. The allegiances of the Defence Committees varied according to locale: eight months after the IRA split in December–January of 1969–70, some of them were working with the Provisionals, some were working with the Officials, and some were independent of both.[30]

What seems critical from Kelly's perspective is that between August 1969 and January 1970, when the plan to import arms was set in motion, the IRA was fracturing. Its Chief of Staff, Cathal Goulding, was trying to 'modernize', taking it towards socialism and away from a total fixation on removing the British presence from the island. The process was ongoing throughout the late 1960s and had generated fatal internal tensions which were further aggravated by the events of August 1969.

How the splintering of republicanism would work out was far from clear. Some break-up certainly appeared imminent, because a Northern faction had staged an internal *coup d'état* on 22 September, and had severed links with the Goulding leadership in Dublin.[31] At the time of the Bailieboro meeting, Goulding's writ within the IRA no longer ran fully north of the border. But while this represented a split of sorts, the *real* split, when it came, would be different in scale, in personnel and even in causation from that which seemingly emerged in the early autumn. The national grouping that became known as the Provisional IRA, led and commanded as it was by republicans from the South, was as yet nowhere in evidence.[32]

Accordingly, the use of the terms 'IRA' and 'Defence Committee' can be problematic in describing the origins and focus of Captain Kelly's arms importation scheme. The republicans on the Northern Defence Committees with whom Kelly was dealing were chafing under IRA control from Dublin. Kelly viewed them less as IRA than as malcontented Northern republicans, unhappy with the direction in which Goulding was leading the IRA, and most of all unhappy about the body's failure to defend Catholic areas of Belfast in August 1969. Many of these dissidents appeared intent on going their own way, whether inside or – as seemed at that stage more likely – outside the IRA.

Seán MacStiofáin, the Provisional IRA's first Chief of Staff and a member of its Army Council, cast cold water in his 1975 memoir on the idea that the arms being imported in April 1970 were for the Provisionals. He said they were not intended for the IRA. He wrote that he had been told early in 1970 that a consignment of weapons, paid for out of Dublin government funds and meant for the Belfast Defence Committees, would be arriving – he did not state where – within weeks. 'I had no other information, except that the consignment would consist of various types of weapons suitable for defensive action.... All the arrangements had been made the previous autumn, prior to the formation of the Provisional Army Council.'[33]

This view supports Captain Kelly's claims, and confirms that the focus was on defence. It seems likely, nonetheless, given how events had developed and the key role played by John Kelly, who operated at Captain Kelly's shoulder and later became an important figure in the Provisional IRA, that whatever Captain

Kelly, Hefferon or indeed Blaney expected or intended, at least some of the arms were likely to have gone eventually into the hands of that organization. This of course is very different from saying that the importation was *for* the Provisional IRA. MacStiofáin, in his interview with Justin O'Brien, provided some other clues as to the likely outcome of a successful arms importation:

> John [Kelly] came to me a few days before Christmas, a few days after the new Convention for the Army Council, and told me about the arrangements made to bring in arms, and he told me that 'once they come in I will give them to you'. I said, 'John, I do not want any details. Give me a report now and again through your brother [Billy Kelly]. Just give me a list of the weapons you ordered.'[34]

This is a significant account, and it offers a rare glimpse of possibly different agendas between army officer Captain James Kelly – and therefore probably Blaney – and Kelly's namesake John, who was representing the Northern Defence Committees but later joined the Provisionals. MacStiofáin's comments about what John Kelly told him run counter to everything Captain Kelly told the second arms trial regarding his intentions for the imported arms. In this respect, some writers have accused the army officer of naivety, in thinking the emerging Provisionals would not have immediately seized the weapons on their arrival in Dublin.[35]

That Captain Kelly genuinely intended the arms to go into storage in a Cavan monastery under his lock and key appears convincing, not least because that was what he told his commanding officer at the time. Both Hefferon and he testified to this in court, and Hefferon made the further telling revelation that he went on to inform Gibbons of the intended location in Co. Cavan.[36] While this evidence of an intention to store the arms, pending a future decision to release them, appears compelling, some scepticism may be warranted about the plan's practicality, and also over whether it covered *all* the weapons being imported.

Captain Kelly told the Committee of Public Accounts that the arms were 'owned' not by the Defence Forces but by the Northerners, who he said had provided money of their own and to whom funds for their purchase had been gifted by the Irish authorities.[37] It might be thought unlikely, if the arms were 'owned' by this group in the face of defence needs perceived as immediate and pressing, that they would easily accept a plan to put them into storage across the border under James Kelly's sole control, awaiting an Irish government decision to release them that might never come. Belfast was the centre of anxiety for Northern nationalists and was seen as the hardest area to protect.[38] Republicans such as Billy Kelly – a senior IRA figure in Belfast whose activism preceded the IRA split and continued under the banner of the Provisionals – clearly wanted guns on-site and readily available for defensive use, not locked in a monastery across the border.[39] This provides a further reason to question the likely fate of the arms consignment, if imported. It may be speculated that *some* of the arms consignment was intended to go to Belfast, with the rest being stored under Captain Kelly's control, as was indicated to the minister.

Apart from his liaising with the Northern Defence Committees, in the autumn of 1969 Captain Kelly was also part of a broader military intelligence strategy led by Hefferon, directed at splitting the IRA. Its ultimate aim, in line with the Planning Board reports considered above, appears to have been to find reliable republican partners who could help provide defensive measures in the event of a repeat of the attacks of August 1969. In effect, it was an effort to separate the Northern wing of the IRA from its socialist-oriented Cathal Goulding leadership in Dublin. It became a recurring feature in Special Branch reports at the time that money was on offer from the Dublin government if a separate IRA Northern Command was created, one free from the control of Goulding's leadership and geared to exclusively Northern Irish-based activities.[40] Such accounts have been broadly confirmed in the years since 1969 by various writers, such as the English journalist Peter Taylor, who conducted personal interviews with participants.

However short-sighted or dangerous these Army Intelligence dealings with republicans may with hindsight appear to have been, the efforts of Captain Kelly, his boss Hefferon and the others involved appears to have had the secondary intention of protecting the Irish State from the possibility of future assault by any group using arms the State had given them. To that extent it was a prudent approach. In subsequent interviews, Blaney admitted his own role; it was part of his close liaison with Captain Kelly through this period.[41] But what is significant in regard to Kelly is that he was not the only officer in Army Intelligence who participated in these efforts to divide republicans. The evidence for this comes partly from the Official IRA, but also from Garda intelligence reports reaching Assistant Commissioner Pat Malone at the time.

An IRA pamphlet entitled *Fianna Fáil and the IRA*, published in the early 1970s, identified 'Free State Army Intelligence officers Kelly, Drohan and Duggan' as part of this effort.[42] Duggan and Drohan were also named on television by Seamus Ó Túathail, according to the writer Justin O'Brien, who claimed that MacStiofáin, the first Chief of Staff of the Provisional IRA, named Drohan to him personally as one of those involved.[43] From their side, Special Branch gardaí similarly believed that Colonel Hefferon was directing a team of intelligence officers – one being James Kelly – in what they felt was an official 'army intelligence operation'.[44] Again, this is information that belies the much-touted image of Kelly as a maverick officer, under the external influence of Neil Blaney. Hefferon himself, as noted earlier, had no direct contact with Blaney,[45] so it is hard to see how he could have come under Blaney's spell. Hefferon was never asked at the arms trials, or at the Committee of Public Accounts inquiry, about his orchestration of this seeming attempt to split the IRA. Had it arisen, he would probably have declined to discuss it, on the grounds that he was excluded from so doing under the Official Secrets Act.

A further challenge to the theory that Kelly was a maverick army officer lies in the State papers released in 2000–01, where it is shown that the tactic of seeking to split the IRA was a policy option strongly advanced in a cabinet memorandum in the first months of 1969 by no less than the Secretary of the Department of Justice, Peter Berry. The memorandum was circulated to all cabinet members in March 1969, and even submitted again, slightly updated, to the new cabinet four months later, after the June general election.[46] Ministers were advised in the memo that a rift had developed within Goulding's organization because of his attempts to modernize the IRA; its new-found socialist leanings were alienating more traditional-minded republicans. The situation was depicted as ready for exploitation by the Irish government. Berry wrote: 'It is thought in the Department of Justice that if the facts of the new [IRA] policy were publicised sufficiently by State and Church authorities, a result would be a split in the IRA organisation, and the communist element would become discredited.' The fact of this advice was first revealed in Berry's *Diaries*, posthumously published in 1980,[47] and later confirmed and elaborated on in the State papers released in 2000.[48] Berry's advice preceded the events of August 1969, at which point the IRA, perceived as having failed to protect nationalists in Belfast, became even more vulnerable to a split.[49]

While Berry's 1969 memorandum for government cannot be seen as an official endorsement for the sort of tactics used in the autumn of 1969 to facilitate an IRA split, it does make it difficult to view the efforts in this direction by Captain Kelly, Blaney and others as any kind of sedition or covert initiative behind Lynch's back. It remains the case – hardly surprising in itself – that no record is to be found in the files of an actual government decision to seek the splintering of the IRA.

3
Haughey–Blaney: Where's the Plot?

It has been a staple part of the literature on the Arms Crisis that Neil Blaney and Charles Haughey were conspiring behind Jack Lynch's back in May 1970, and were caught out; their plan, as generally represented, was to rearm and regenerate the IRA, use the force of arms to break partition, and in the process remove Lynch as Taoiseach. The proposition gained credibility from the fact that neither minister had ever made a secret of their ambition to lead the party.[1] Yet while events linked their fortunes closely for a period in 1970 and thereafter, before the Arms Crisis erupted Haughey and Blaney had very different public profiles.

Blaney, who held the position of Minister for Agriculture and Fisheries, had a unique reputation within the government as a hardline republican. From his political base in Donegal, flanking the border, he had issued a series of uncompromising speeches on Northern Ireland throughout 1968 and 1969 which were widely seen as a challenge to Lynch's cautious style of leadership. A machine politician with an intimate knowledge of the party's grass-roots, like Haughey, he was one of the party's most powerful figures.[2]

Haughey, the other Fianna Fáil 'strong man', was Minister for Finance and a more obvious leader-in-waiting than Blaney. But he had travelled under the radar so far as any public criticism of Lynch was concerned, and rarely if ever had made public reference to Northern Ireland. Accordingly, Haughey's dismissal by Lynch for alleged seditious behaviour on 6 May 1970 was a cause for astonishment in many well-informed quarters. Immediately after the sackings, the British ambassador, Sir John Peck, noted that while Blaney's differences with Lynch had seemed apparent for some time, 'The position of Haughey has been much more discreet.... He has refrained from public comment and his differences with the Taoiseach have received no publicity.'[3] An article by the Dublin correspondent of the *Financial Times* reported, the day after the sackings, that Charles Haughey 'remains the great enigma. Why was he sacked? No one would count him in the ranks of the hardliners'.[4] Even writing many years later, Desmond O'Malley, a staunch Lynch loyalist, confessed that he had been 'flabbergasted' and 'mystified' by Haughey's involvement.[5]

To many, ambition seemed the key to Haughey's involvement. In August 1969, his status in the Fianna Fáil party, as well as that of Blaney, had been underscored by the way they had jointly masterminded Lynch's emphatic general election victory just two months earlier. But in helping to consolidate Lynch's position in this way, they had created obstacles in the way of their own ambition to succeed him. Historian J. J. Lee felt that the election outcome had left them restless and frustrated. Lynch had been transformed from a leader with only caretaker, provisional status to one with authority and strong electoral support. In Lee's view, after the election Blaney and Haughey 'could now anticipate long years of frustrated ambition'.[6] Against this background, the theory that they could be conspiring against Lynch took early form in the months after August 1969. It surfaced in the Sinn Féin newspaper *United Irishman* as early as November 1969, where it was claimed that Haughey and Blaney were plotting to take over and subvert the Northern Ireland civil rights movement.[7]

So when Lynch sacked Blaney and Haughey in May 1970 for allegedly conspiring behind his back to import arms illegally for use in Northern Ireland, the news, while it surprised and shocked, also fed into a perception that here were two ambitious and unscrupulous senior ministers, each having become a *bête noire* to members of the opposition parties, Fine Gael and Labour. Though he helped initiate the idea of a plot, Lynch never fully detailed how it might have operated. As a theory, it has endured through the decades since, despite the absence of any evidence of an actual Haughey–Blaney pact, or any specifics on their supposed conspiracy. Nor has it ever been established precisely how they envisaged that the Northern Ireland situation might topple Lynch.

While increasing numbers have accepted that Captain Kelly (and by association, John Kelly and Albert Luykx) may have *believed* that they were involved in a government-sanctioned operation,[8] Blaney and Haughey have been accorded no such excuse. Most writers have taken the view that the two ministers were working covertly to unseat Lynch, and the arms importation was part of their 'plot'. As a result, they are assumed to have deserved their dismissal by Lynch in May 1970 for disloyal and treacherous behaviour. Their actions were seen as contrary to Lynch's peace-minded approach to the issue of Northern Ireland. 'The entire tenor of government policy was in the opposite direction [to the gun-running attempt],' Garret FitzGerald TD (FG) told Colonel Hefferon at the Committee of Public Accounts inquiry in 1971.[9] Dick Walsh, in his analysis of Fianna Fáil, *The Party* (1986), wrote that 'the autumn of 1969 provided fertile ground... for conspiratorial politics, whether designed to hijack the party or to subvert the State, or to achieve both ambitions at once'.[10] Writing in 2008, historian Eunan O'Halpin noted that 'the arms importation scheme went against the entire thrust of government policy'.[11]

A popular assessment has been that whether or not the attempted arms importation was illegal, it was engineered by the two sacked ministers and was unknown to the bulk of the cabinet, including probably Lynch; its intention was to build up the IRA, destabilize the North, and somehow, within this process, topple Lynch. It was a picture of two scheming and disloyal colleagues who operated 'a government within a government'.[12] In this scenario, Lynch in the end simply out-manoeuvred his treacherous opponents in the Arms Crisis, besting them with his surprisingly tough and calculated actions when the crunch point arrived.

This theory of a Blaney-Haughey plot was forcefully outlined in three books published between 2000 and 2001, from writers with a background in journalism: Justin O'Brien's *The Arms Trial* (2000), Stephen Collins's *The Power Game: Ireland under Fianna Fáil* (2001) and Bruce Arnold's *Jack Lynch: Hero in Crisis* (2001). Their arguments appeared to draw on the State papers for 1969 and 1970, released after thirty years to the National Archives. This chorus of three became a quartet in 2008 when the voice of Lynch's biographer, Dermot Keogh, was added, in his sympathetic *Jack Lynch: A Biography*.[13] These writers drew broad conclusions about Blaney and Haughey's manoeuvrings during the Arms Crisis which have become embedded in popular understanding.

Justin O'Brien's central theory has been that the Arms Crisis derived from a power play for the soul of Fianna Fáil; it came from a conspiracy within Lynch's government, led by Blaney and Haughey, who were effectively running a shadow administration. Each planned to take over from Lynch, using Military Intelligence and one of its officers, Captain Kelly, in a plan to bring about Irish unity. While plotting to split the IRA and unseat Lynch, they helped to finance the emergence of the Provisional IRA.

Stephen Collins, in broad agreement with this analysis, assigned to Blaney and Haughey political and moral responsibility for the arms 'plot', arguing that they were the only ones who should have been charged. Echoing O'Brien, Collins has seen the two ministers as running an alternative government. In his view, they opposed Lynch on the use of force in Northern Ireland, and while Lynch tried to hold the line in defence of the rule of law and democratic principles, they planned for a final solution on partition, regardless of the consequences. They plotted to use taxpayers' money to bring in arms for the IRA; their secret strategy helped to give rise to the Provisionals, and thereby fuelled the thirty-year Troubles.

In Bruce Arnold's view, the two ministers, though not particularly close, had a Northern policy that was covert and conspiratorial, and opposed to that of Lynch. They took over Military Intelligence, intruding on Captain Kelly's normal chain of command in an elaborate and dangerous plot, one that to Arnold resembled treason. Drawing on the evidence of Peter Berry, Secretary of the Department of Justice, Arnold has insisted that there was a plot from within the government to subvert the State. The arms being imported were intended for the IRA, and the law had clearly been broken.

Keogh, for his part, believed that Blaney and Haughey did not accept Lynch's peaceful policy on Northern Ireland; Blaney was the leader of a shadow government that rejected Lynch's non-violent approach. The two ministers privately wished to arm Northern nationalists and finish the job of restoring national unity. When Lynch eventually confronted this subversion within his government, he saw off the sinister elements that Keogh argued would have put the country at mortal risk. The Blaney-Haughey alternative involved the removal of Lynch as Taoiseach, with bloody consequences for Northern Ireland.

The effect of these writings was to confirm and amplify a perception of Blaney and Haughey that had been present from the start, i.e., as the 'bad guys' in 1970, treacherous towards their Taoiseach and in receipt ultimately of their just deserts by being dismissed. Nonetheless, some apparent frustration at the lack of confirming evidence for the plotting was evident in Arnold's lament about the State papers released in 2001. 'The extent of the damage inflicted on Ireland by Neil Blaney and C. J. Haughey will never be fully explained,' Arnold wrote, before noting: 'The more the archives deliver up supposedly revelatory material, the less it seems to tell us of the nature or extent of the conspiracy in which they had both been involved.'[14]

In a heavily contested landscape, some aspects of the Blaney-Haughey plot theory appear non-contentious: both men were restless and ambitious ministers, and both appear to have held Lynch in low esteem. While Lynch's declared policy on Northern Ireland was for unity by peaceful means and by agreement, Blaney in particular repeatedly took a more aggressive public tone towards partition. As a matter of fact, taxpayers' money, voted for Northern aid, was used secretly to buy guns, and the guns were clearly intended for Northern republicans. Haughey, as Minister for Finance, was responsible for the disbursement of this money, and Blaney, despite being minister for an unrelated portfolio – Agriculture and Fisheries – was very active in efforts to bring in guns bought with the money in question. James Kelly, the army officer centrally involved, freely acknowledged he had been working closely with Blaney and Haughey, and thus appeared to be taking direction from outside his normal military chain of command.

Faced with this degree of broadly proven data, it may seem relatively unsurprising if the writers listed above, supported to a greater or lesser degree by biographers such as T. Ryle Dwyer, John Walsh and Patrick Maume[15] have been harsh in their judgements of both Blaney and Haughey. Even writers such as Vincent Browne and Diarmaid Ferriter, sceptical of Lynch's and Gibbons's claims to be ignorant of the arms importation in advance, have used the word 'plot', implying – whatever the verdict in the arms trial – that a conspiracy of some sort was afoot. That could refer only to Haughey and Blaney.[16]

Meanwhile, just a handful of writers – Angela Clifford, Conor Lenihan and Donnacha Ó Beacháin in particular – have to different degrees favoured a reverse conspiracy theory: they have seen the arms importation attempt as the result of a loose government *sub rosa* operation, one that was at least unofficially authorized, although probably always deniable. These writers have avoided using the pejorative terms 'plot' or 'conspiracy', preferring the more neutral 'attempted arms importation'. Clifford, writing in 2009, felt that the Arms Crisis arose when Lynch 'abruptly and unilaterally changed the policy his cabinet had been conducting since August 1969'.[17] Despite the evidence that Lynch requested the resignations of Haughey and Blaney in the days after 20 April 1970, she argued that it was only when the Taoiseach came under pressure from Leader of the Opposition Liam Cosgrave that he moved decisively against the two ministers; they were made scapegoats for an undercover operation that had gone wrong, but which in Clifford's view had full government authority.

Conor Lenihan, younger son of Lynch's Minister for Transport and Power in 1970, Brian Lenihan, in a deceptively slight biography of Haughey in 2015, drew partly on privately expressed opinions by his late father to claim that Lynch knew of the arms importation, that it was covert and deniable, and that eventually Lynch had backed off and 'thrown to the wolves' his two ministers and Captain Kelly, while remaining unscathed himself by what had happened.[18] Lenihan was emphatic that the involvement of Hefferon in the arms importation 'destroys any argument that somehow rogue elements had taken over government policy'.[19] Ó Beacháin, whose focus was on Fianna Fáil's relationship with republicans rather than on the Arms Crisis itself, felt that the State papers released in 2001 showed that the arms importation plan was not inconsistent with Lynch's policy on Northern Ireland at the time. It was, he concluded, official policy to provide arms for distribution in the North in certain circumstances; at the same time, Ó Beacháin did not query that Blaney and Haughey, although vindicated in the arms trial, had been seeking to further their leadership ambitions.[20]

The major question with Haughey and Blaney, however, is the policy issue of whether they opposed Lynch's peaceful approach to the ending of partition, and whether, as so often claimed, they favoured the use of force to that end. There is little in the record to suggest that Haughey, before the Arms Crisis, had been nurturing a hidden republicanism that came to light only after August 1969. There had been no doubt about his firm stance against the IRA while Minister for Justice in the early 1960s; in fact, Haughey won plaudits from Peter Berry, his Secretary in that department at the time, for having effectively crushed the 1950s IRA border campaign against partition, through the introduction of military courts and internment in the Republic.[21]

Regarding the events of August 1969, Haughey expressed no views publicly, then or later, on the use of force to end partition. Despite this, he – along with Blaney – is widely identified in the literature as favouring such an approach. Precise evidence to support this proposition remains hard to find. Nonetheless, historian Stephen Kelly was not untypical of writers on the period when he asserted that 'in a blatant act of defiance of an essential constitutional obligation on any Irish minister, that of collective responsibility of the government, Haughey played an integral role in a subversive scheme to arm Northern Ireland nationalists with guns and ammunitions'.[22] The proposition that any such arming or use of force might have been intended for defensive purposes, rather than for subversion, appeared not to be considered.

Some valuable insight into Haughey's private views on the use of force over Northern Ireland can be gleaned from the personal papers of T. K. Whitaker, deposited in the University College Dublin Archive (UCDA) in successive stages between 1994 and 1999. These contain a record of a fascinating private exchange in early January 1968 between Haughey, as Minister for Finance, and Whitaker, who had recently retired from the position of Secretary in Haughey's department to become Governor of the Central Bank. The discussion arose from a memo Whitaker had sent to Haughey, supporting a recommendation from the Dáil Committee on the Constitution which urged the removal of Article 3 of the Constitution. This Article claimed on behalf of the Irish State the right to exercise jurisdiction over the Six Counties of Northern Ireland, and Whitaker was strongly in favour of removing the Article. 'I am', he told Haughey, 'in entire agreement with the principle underlying the Committee's recommendations... It is quite obvious that having eschewed the use of force to bring about the reunification of the national territory, we must be content to wait for the agreement of Northern Ireland to reunification proposals.'

In his response, dated 5 January 1968, handwritten at the foot of Whitaker's memo, Haughey disagreed. He said their different views on Article 3's retention came from 'issues of principle'. His position was: 'We could never abandon the moral right to use force. We have the right to use force to defend the national territory. The national territory is all Ireland and we would be quite justified in using force to throw out the British army if that were feasible. We recognize that to try to compel the people of the North by force to do something is out of the question, but that is an entirely different matter.'

In this response to Whitaker in 1968, Haughey distinguished between the legitimacy of using force to end partition, and its impracticality. It was a position that appears manifestly consistent with Éamon de Valera's 1937 Constitution, with Haughey not prepared to abandon the constitutional claim to jurisdiction over the North. This was a classic Fianna Fáil position from which neither de Valera nor his party had ever resiled. But more provocatively, Haughey was also setting down a corollary to such a position: this was that a state that claimed a right to jurisdiction over a piece of territory implicitly claimed the right to enforce that jurisdiction – even if, for reasons of practicality, it chose not to do so. It was a statement, in unusually direct terms, of twin aspects of Fianna Fáil orthodoxy: just as partition had been created by force, so nationalists retained at least a moral right to use force to end it. No public statement by de Valera ever asserted the contrary.[23] It was also, however, fundamental to Fianna Fáil's position as it evolved, that such use of force, if not morally objectionable, was certainly impractical; in consequence it was, as Haughey described it, 'out of the question'.

Whitaker responded to Haughey some weeks later by saying that, while the moral issue was open to dispute, in practical terms the government had defined its position: 'We have eschewed the use of force as a means of ending the partition of Ireland, and we see the reunification of the Irish people as a matter for Irishmen in Ireland [*underlined in original*], to be achieved by agreement between them, the British being expected to display goodwill, or at least indifference.'[24] No response from Haughey is recorded. He may have felt Britain had a greater responsibility to help resolve the situation than Whitaker had suggested. In any regard, his comments in this exchange provide no support for claims that he favoured the use of force to end partition.[25]

Another possible insight into Haughey's supposedly hidden republicanism before May 1970 was unearthed by Stephen Kelly in 2013, when he discovered a 1955 memorandum on partition in the Fianna Fáil Papers in the UCDA. The document was produced by the Tomás Ó Cléirigh cumann in the Dublin North-East constituency, and was submitted to the party executive by its honorary Secretary at the time, a young C. J. Haughey. The document, according to Kelly, 'offered an aggressive case as to why Fianna Fáil should use physical force to secure Irish unity'. Cumann membership at the time included party notables such as George Colley, Harry Boland and Oscar Traynor,[26] and the document was written in the first person plural, using phrases such as 'we believe' and 'it seems to us'; it was presented therefore as the product of a collective effort.

The memorandum's argument, born of frustration at the lack of progress in the mid-1950s towards ending partition, was for a campaign of civil disobedience in selected border areas, supported covertly by military backup from the Irish government. Its authors felt that the public disavowal by the party leadership 'of any intention of using force… is a strategic error of the first magnitude'. While Haughey clearly had contributed to the memorandum, and possibly in a major way, the absence of any signature makes it impossible to assign individual responsibility for its contents. In the event, the proposals in the memorandum received short shrift from Lemass at the time.

The one other notable remark from Haughey on the use of force in Northern Ireland occurs in *Paddy Bogside*, the 2001 memoir of Derry community leader Paddy Doherty. Describing an important meeting he attended with Blaney, Haughey and Jim Gibbons in Government Buildings in Dublin in February 1970, Doherty wrote that he had told the three ministers of the intense existing fears of an impending Protestant assault on their area of Northern Ireland. His book went on: 'Another pogrom against the Catholic population of Northern Ireland was on the cards. Charles Haughey, who had not spoken often during the meeting, addressed his two colleagues: "Let's take the North. We should not apologise for what is our right."[27] Doherty's book – reporting here just a brief interjection in a conversation being recalled after thirty-one years – contains no elaboration from Haughey on how he felt the North might be 'taken'. Such a record, with its startlingly bullish views, clearly has to be received with caution.

What seems clear generally is that evidence on the nature and extent of Haughey's militant republicanism before 1970 is scant or non-existent. In fact, Haughey seems to have placed his best hopes for resolving the North's problems at this time on the possibility of a United Nations intervention. At some early stage he appears to have written off the British army's prospects of ever being seen as an impartial peacekeeping force. Only a UN presence offered an honourable way out, he argued at the time; his suggestion was that it could lead to a major international 'Marshall Plan' for the redevelopment of Northern Ireland.[28] This position appears in principle consistent with his reported support at the cabinet meeting on 13 August 1969 for Blaney's proposed cross-border army thrust into Derry. Blaney's intention, at least as he later described it, was to create an international incident by drawing in the UN.[29]

★

Blaney, like Haughey, has been widely seen in the literature on the Arms Crisis as a supporter of the use of force to end partition, and this has been represented as his chief disagreement with Lynch. At the cabinet meeting on 13 August 1969, with Blaney leading, the two ministers are generally reported to have argued, in the course of fractious discussions, that the Irish army should cross the border into Derry's Bogside. No formal record exists of these discussions, and historians, as shown earlier, have had to rely on those few ministers who over time chose to set down their recollections in writing. Blaney's demand for a strong approach, it seems, was supported by Minister for Local Government Kevin Boland, Justice Minister Mícheál Ó Móráin and, interestingly, Defence Minister James Gibbons, in company with Brian Lenihan (Transport and Power) and Seán Flanagan (Health).[30] In the end, a compromise approach resulted in an announced decision to move the army to the border, with the stated purpose of setting up field hospitals to deal with casualties of the conflict. This was outlined in a television address to the nation from the Taoiseach that night, in which he issued his ambivalent warning that 'the Irish government could no longer stand by and see innocent people persecuted and perhaps worse'.[31]

From newspaper reports of the cabinet arguments on 13 August, from the later published recollections of some of the participants and from various bellicose speeches made around this time by Blaney in particular, many writers concluded that Blaney and Haughey favoured the use of force to end partition. John Walsh, in his 2008 biography of Patrick Hillery, concluded: 'It soon became apparent that an influential section of the government did not share the views of the Taoiseach or his Foreign Minister on the use of force to resolve the long-standing grievance of partition.'[32] Ryle Dwyer said of Blaney that he 'seemed intent on going to war over the North'.[33] James Downey believed Blaney sought to provoke a civil war, maintaining that 'it would not be disastrous, that it would end quickly, and that the unionists would see that they could have a satisfactory future in a united Ireland'.[34] More recently, historian Stephen Kelly, drawing on the same mixture of contemporary newspaper leaks and published memoirs, noted that on 13 August, 'led by an aggressive Blaney, both Boland and Haughey maintained that physical force had always represented official Fianna Fáil policy'.[35]

Although Blaney denied on several occasions after his sacking by Lynch that he supported the use of force as a means of ending partition, his protests in this regard have been given little serious attention. This is problematic, for his denials arguably raise real and significant issues over the meaning of the term 'use of force in Northern Ireland'. Almost universally in the historiography, as indicated above, it has been taken to mean force for the removal of partition, and for the creation of a united Ireland. However, in the unique circumstances created by the upheaval of August 1969, when nationalist areas had come under serious sectarian assault, it was also a term with more limited connotations. Force for the purpose of defending people's lives in the face of a pending feared assault should – at least in principle – be entirely distinguishable from force to remove the border and end partition. Making such a differentiation is not without its difficulties, but no informed assessment of Blaney or Haughey's role in the Arms Crisis can avoid facing the issue.

Lynch himself set out the dilemma on using force when, in the aftermath of the crisis, he argued that one reason his government had – as he claimed – decided against issuing guns to Northerners was the difficulty of preventing arms that were intended for defensive purposes from being used in a more aggressive mode.[36] Clearly, this was a genuine issue. Nonetheless, in the unique circumstances in Northern Ireland in late 1969 and early 1970, for a Catholic community perceived by itself and its southern neighbours to be at imminent risk of calamitous assault, the question of distinguishing means of defence from means of attack was largely academic.

The sense of vulnerability at the time was palpable, especially among Catholic nationalists in Belfast and areas distant from the border with the Irish Republic. Even Conor Cruise O'Brien, who opposed all efforts to provide military assistance to the minority in 1970, acknowledged the problem faced by people who considered themselves to be defenceless. He described in *States of Ireland* (1972) how he attempted to persuade Northern Catholics after August 1969 that having guns might make them more prone to danger, not less, but also noted wryly: 'I was asked: what would you do if your own house was attacked? A good question.'[37]

Writers like Arnold and O'Halpin have suggested that the arrival of the British army on Northern streets from mid-August 1969 significantly reduced the vulnerability to attack of the nationalist population.[38] Even if that assessment proved ultimately to be broadly correct, there is ample evidence that this was far from universally perceived to be so at the time, whether by Northern nationalists or in Government Buildings in Dublin. Having been partially overrun in August 1969 and burned out of places like Bombay Street in Belfast, in the early months of 1970 nationalists could not be certain that the British authorities would have either the will or the capacity to protect them. These concerns were not just shared by Blaney from his constituency in Donegal just across the border, but also by his Irish government colleagues and their advisers, as the State files illustrate.

In early February 1970 a memorandum from the Department of External Affairs for the Taoiseach referred to 'the possibility that the North will fall apart'.[39] On 20 February 1970, External Affairs Minister Patrick Hillery expressed personally to British minister Lord Thomson his anxiety that frightened members of the Northern minority might overreact against a perceived threat to their safety in a way that could force the Irish government to intervene.[40] In early March, Derry MP Ivan Cooper was advising officials in Dublin that he did not believe the British army could control rural areas and 'the problem was how many lives would be lost before troops arrived'.[41]

In London, the Irish ambassador, Dr D. O'Sullivan, was himself unimpressed with assurances he received on 23 March 1970 that the British forces were confident of being able to get to any trouble spot within thirty minutes. He commented in reply: 'There could be a lot of bloodshed even in that short space of time.'[42] Eamonn Gallagher, the senior official from the Department of External Affairs on the ground in the North, noted that the ambassador's meeting of 23 March showed 'clear indications... that the British assessment of the situation in the Six Counties is erroneous'.[43] Further warnings on security came from Liberal Party leader Jeremy Thorpe on 20 April 1970, when he advised Ambassador O'Sullivan that the situation in Northern Ireland was 'completely getting out of hand' and that General Sir Ian Freeland, the officer commanding British forces, was 'becoming strongly of the view that the military strength in the North may not be at all adequate to cope with the situation which could arise'.[44]

A meeting in London between Ambassador O'Sullivan and British officials in late April 1970 showed the extent of the continuing anxiety present in Irish government circles, and continuing tension over British attitudes:

The Ambassador insisted... that the situation had become very grave – graver, in fact, than it had been at any time since last August.

Mr Burroughs [Foreign and Commonwealth Office] interjected: 'Potentially grave.'

The Ambassador replied, 'No, actually grave.'... The Ambassador said he must be brutally frank. The fact was that he and they saw things quite differently – perhaps because their information was coming from different sources. His people thought the situation was much more explosive than their people seemed to think.[45]

These despatches leave no doubt that anxiety remained high within Irish diplomatic and government circles through the winter and spring of 1969–70. The presence of the British army had only partially allayed fears over the vulnerability of the Northern minority. Given these concerns, remarkably little attention has been paid in the historical literature to the distinction between initiatives that involved force to assist and defend a beleaguered population, and more aggressive efforts using force with the intention of breaking partition. It is a distinction that, while far from clear-cut, is important in understanding the situation within Fianna Fáil leading up to the Arms Crisis, and particularly in considering whether the principal so-called hawks in the cabinet – Blaney, Haughey and Boland – were advocating that force be used to end partition.

A perfect illustration of the confusion surrounding the phrase 'use of force in Northern Ireland' is provided in historian Ronan Fanning's *Independent Ireland* (1983), in which he compared the challenge facing the Dublin government in 1969–70 with that faced almost fifty years earlier by Michael Collins's Provisional Government. At that point in the spring of 1922, in the interval between the signing of the Anglo-Irish Treaty and the start of the Civil War, serious sectarian assaults against Catholics took place in Belfast, with many deaths. Partition was already a reality at this stage, but Collins was under pressure to assist Northern nationalists. Fanning wrote:

What was at issue was what, if any, extra-constitutional steps a Dublin government might take in their efforts to assist the

Catholic minority in the North. The outcome was the same in 1970 as in 1922. The Dublin government pledged itself to peaceful means and foreswore the use of force in their endeavours to resolve the Northern problem.[46]

Fanning here judged the response of Lynch's government to be similar to that of Collins, in the sense that Collins did not choose to use force to undermine the recently established border. But Fanning himself, earlier in the same book, acknowledged that the response of Collins and his Minister for Defence to attacks on Catholics in 1922 also had a covert and military dimension, thereby contradicting the historian's claim that [Michael Collins] had been fully 'pledged... to peaceful means'.

Fanning wrote: 'Their anguish and fury at the plight of Northern Catholics led Collins and Mulcahy [Collins's Minister for Defence] to continue supplying them with arms (albeit secretly and indirectly through the IRA).'[47] It is not immediately evident from the text whether Fanning, a declared admirer of Lynch's record in 1970, realized that he appeared to have concluded that Lynch's government, it seems in his view officially, had agreed, as Collins had, to provide weapons to Northern nationalists. Fanning's view of 1922 was that Collins had pledged himself to peaceful means and forsworn the use of force vis-à-vis partition, but this, as he himself observed, had actually gone hand-in-glove with the secret provision of guns. Fanning appears (perhaps unconsciously) to have accepted that this too was Lynch's policy for a time in 1970, with the same hidden military dimension as Collins.

Neil Blaney's stance on the use of force to end partition has been defined not just by his call that the Irish army should have entered Derry in August 1969, but also by his controversial speech in Letterkenny, Co. Donegal, in December 1969. The speech was actually part of a series of militant statements from the Donegal deputy in the period 1968 to 1970, leading to widespread calls for Lynch to sack him from the cabinet. Lynch effectively ignored the clamour. The Letterkenny episode is highly revealing, though not necessarily for the conventionally understood reasons. The speech Blaney made there requires – and repays – careful reading. Its tone was bellicose and threatening, probably intentionally so, but the threat was not from any firm statement of purpose, but from the calculated ambiguity of his words.[48]

Blaney made it clear that, in the mainstream tradition of de Valera and the Fianna Fáil party, he did not accept the moral right of the majority in the Six Counties to decide on partition. To accede to such a claim would be to accept that partition had been justified in the first place, whereas Blaney saw Northern Ireland as an artificial creation, set up against the majority wishes of the Irish people. He went on:

We have heard much in recent times concerning the use of force. We should be clear about where we stand here. In the discussion on October 22/23rd last in Dáil Éireann on the Six County situation, the Taoiseach, in opening the debate, said: 'The Government in this part of Ireland has no intention of mounting any armed invasion of the Six Counties'. Mr. Cosgrave, the leader of the Fine Gael party, speaking in his turn, went further by stating that his party's consistent attitude was that 'the only way to achieve ultimate unity was by peaceful means and cooperation'. Mr. Corish, the leader of the Irish Labour Party, when he came to speak, went still further and stated that, as far as he is concerned, 'force is out'. I believe, as do the vast majority, that the ideal way of ending partition is by peaceful means. But no one has the right to assert that force is irrevocably out. No political party or group at any time is entitled to predetermine the right of the Irish people to decide what course of action on this question may be justified in given circumstances. The Fianna Fáil party has never taken a decision to rule out the use of force if the circumstances in the Six Counties so demand. The situation last August in Belfast and Derry was such that, had the violence continued, the question of the use of force in defence of our own people under attack would have had to be urgently considered. If a situation were to arise in the Six Counties in which the people who do not subscribe to the Unionist regime were under sustained and murderous assault, then, as the Taoiseach said on August 13th, we 'cannot stand idly by'.[49]

This speech was clearly carefully written and prepared,[50] but at the time, and frequently since, it has been mistakenly seen as an argument for the use of force to end partition. Stephen Collins was not unrepresentative among writers in describing it as 'a straightforward defiance of Lynch's policy'.[51] While his speech may well have been intended as a kind of defiance, Blaney at Letterkenny did not actually advocate force to end partition. He stressed the *right* to use force, including for the ending of partition, and omitted to explain why this right had never been invoked – which was because his party had long viewed it as unrealistic and impractical. But by referring to the existence of such a right, he was stating publicly what Lynch had opted to leave unsaid. Blaney was being careful not to transgress against actual Fianna Fáil policy. What he explicitly favoured in Letterkenny was the use of force to protect and defend nationalists if, as he described it, they should find themselves subjected to murderous assault.

At the time of the Letterkenny speech, it was taken as a sign of weakness that Jack Lynch did not discipline or even sack Blaney. The following day, the Taoiseach, having restated the commitment he gave at Tralee three months earlier to pursue reunification of the country by peaceful means, said only that Blaney 'knows and endorses government policy on this issue, as he did in his speech at Letterkenny last night'.[52] Blaney himself, after being sacked in May 1970, sought in the Dáil to put the record straight on Letterkenny:

> I have been misrepresented, grossly misrepresented, by the architects of partition both in this House and in Stormont on the question of force. I have never advocated the use of force as a means of bringing about the unity of this land – never. Those who say otherwise are liars.[53]

In an interview with *This Week* magazine in August 1970, Blaney again complained of being misquoted and that his words had been taken out of context. He stressed that the use of force he had referred to was in a defensive context:

> I believe that the nationalists of the Six Counties have the right to defend themselves from murderous aggression in every way they can. I believe it is our duty to help them so to defend themselves.... If we claim a right to all Ireland then it is the duty of the Irish Army to defend the Unionists in the Shankill just as much as to protect Catholics in Cork.[54]

Blaney restated this position later that year in the Dáil in November 1970:

> I have been misrepresented when I referred to the use of force in another context. What I have said, and now repeat, is that if the minority in the Six Counties were to come under the threat of annihilation by armed murderous assault – as they did in certain parts of the Six Counties in August 1969 – then we in the 26 Counties could not, cannot, and should not stand idly by.[55]

This position was backed by Blaney's party colleague Kevin Boland, writing in 1977. According to Boland, in Letterkenny Blaney 'had said nothing contrary to well-established party

policy'.[56] Blaney in later interviews noted how he had argued on
13 August for the Irish army to enter the Bogside, but insisted that
he had seen this in a 'protective' mode, not as an invasion.[57] It seems
correct to say his call for the Irish army to cross the border into Derry,
while undeniably provocative, dangerous and even potentially
suicidal, was presented less as a military intervention than as a
device to internationalize the Northern crisis. This was the view
taken by historian and political scientist Donnacha Ó Beacháin,
following the expression of similar views by veteran journalist
James Downey.[58]

Even Bruce Arnold, a writer convinced that Blaney and
Haughey were plotting sedition, agreed that 'neither Boland nor
Blaney favoured force in order to achieve reunification'.[59] In his
biography of Lynch, Arnold went further, stating that 'Blaney
never had'.[60] Historian Thomas Hennessey saw no division
over Northern Ireland policy between Lynch and Blaney at this
time: 'Blaney,' he wrote, 'far from dissenting from established
government policy, was at the heart of it. And so was Jack Lynch.'[61]
Ó Beacháin, while struggling somewhat to identify the precise
difference between the Blaney camp and Lynch, agreed it was not
over the use of force:

> Neither side advocated force as a solution to partition; indeed
> Boland argued that no one adhered to such a view. Neither
> side denied that partition was undemocratic, nor did they fail
> to stress their desire to promote re-unification. The essential
> divergence was between those who pinned the responsibility
> for the situation in the North on Britain, and those who
> advocated a *rapprochement* with the Northern Government.[62]

Stephen Kelly agreed with Ó Beacháin that Blaney in these
speeches was not opposing Fianna Fáil policy. 'In fact, it was
the reverse,' he said, because by restating old policy when Lynch
was seeking to update it, Blaney was creating 'an ideological
straitjacket on Lynch'.[63] It seems clear from all this, as argued

above, that attempts to identify policy differences on Northern Ireland as a basis for Haughey and Blaney's mythical conspiracy against the Taoiseach encounter the same difficulties as those that beset the whole conspiracy proposition.

4

Haughey: Treacherous Schemer?

Charles Haughey's powerful position as Minister for Finance in Jack Lynch's government in 1969–70 reflected his exceptional ability and influence within Fianna Fáil. The son-in-law of Seán Lemass, Haughey was already a controversial politician as a result of the wealth he had amassed in the course of a ten-year career in public life, and his swaggering, ostentatious lifestyle. He lived like a country squire in a Gandon-designed mansion on the north side of Dublin, wore expensive shirts, dined in the city's finest restaurants and was known among the chattering classes to keep a mistress. But Haughey was also recognized as a clever and resourceful politician, one of the brightest of his generation. His role in the 1970 Arms Crisis is interlinked with that of Neil Blaney, particularly in the context of their supposed joint conspiracy against Jack Lynch. Yet in May 1970 Haughey's situation was markedly different from Blaney's. This was partly because of their cabinet responsibilities, but also because of their very different public profiles over Northern Ireland.

Many of those who believe Haughey was plotting against Lynch in 1970, in seeking to explain his motivation, have seen in the Arms Crisis the exposure of an unchecked ambition for leadership. Bruce Arnold regarded ambition as Haughey's driving force, causing him to be 'frightened' of Blaney as a future rival for the party leadership. His envy of Blaney's strength on the North 'was the over-riding motivation for his direct involvement in Northern Ireland affairs'.[1] Michael Kennedy has argued that

Blaney's influence over the government's Northern Ireland policy increased with the departure from the cabinet (after the June 1969 general election) of party veteran Frank Aiken, who had taken a more cautious approach to the North.[2] Justin O'Brien argued that 'Haughey used the uncertainty surrounding the Irish government's response to the Northern conflict as his opportunity to challenge the leadership'.[3] On the other hand, historian Stephen Kelly has challenged what he called 'a widely held myth' that Haughey's involvement in the Arms Crisis arose from 'little more than shrewd political opportunism on his behalf in a bid to topple and replace Jack Lynch as Fianna Fáil leader'. In his view, Haughey's actions 'were also motivated by a genuine and hitherto unrecognized deep-rooted commitment to a united Ireland'.[4]

One of the several claims against Haughey, arising from the State papers released in 2001, is that he was a disloyal and treacherous force within Lynch's cabinet. The argument is that in the period August 1969 to May 1970 he displayed a regular disregard for the Taoiseach's authority, at times with seditious intent. Three specific instances have been used in the literature to back up this proposition. These have been important in bolstering the image of Haughey as a renegade within the cabinet, additional to any part he may have played in the gun-running that led to his dismissal by Lynch.

The first of these three examples of Haughey's supposed errant behaviour involves his private meeting in his home in Kinsealy in Dublin with the British ambassador, Andrew Gilchrist, on 4 October 1969. At this meeting, Haughey presented to the British his view of the terms that could lead towards a united Ireland. This has been characterized as Haughey acting without authority, as if he was leading a government of his own. The second example of apparent disregard for Lynch's authority concerns Haughey's flouting of a clearly stated demand from Lynch in the autumn of 1969 that public money cease to be used to fund the propaganda newspaper *Voice of the North*. Lynch was upset at the paper's contents, which were critical of the government, and he wanted state support withdrawn. The funding continued, however. The picture is one of Haughey, as Minister for Finance and therefore controller of the funding mechanisms, giving Lynch a two-fingered sign of defiance. The third example of supposed disrespect for Lynch's authority is the claim that Haughey made a private deal with IRA Chief of Staff Cathal Goulding in the autumn of 1969. The supposed deal was that the IRA could move arms freely across the border in return for halting its attacks on foreign-owned property in the Irish Republic. This suggestion gained extra authority because it emanated from Peter Berry, Permanent Secretary in the Department of Justice, and was based on Special Branch intelligence reports. These three instances have been variously cited since 2001 to show Haughey as an out-of-control, disloyal member of Lynch's government, even before the gun-running attempt in April–May 1970. However, the full evidence, in each of these three instances, does not support the conclusions about Haughey that some have chosen to draw.

Firstly, the meeting with the British ambassador, Gilchrist. Here there has been confusion over the precise circumstances in which Haughey invited Gilchrist to visit him. The confusion apparently has arisen from a failure to consult the primary sources, held in the British National Archives in Kew in London, and a reliance on incomplete newspaper reports of the original documents. What the original files show is that the day before Haughey met Gilchrist, he had briefed a British writer, Constantine Fitzgibbon, on the Irish government's stance on the North. He had gathered that Fitzgibbon intended to report back on what was said to the British Embassy. He also learned that Gilchrist was about to travel to London to brief the Foreign Secretary personally on Irish government attitudes. Haughey, not unreasonably, was concerned that London was going to get a third-hand version of his opinions. He rang Gilchrist after talking to Fitzgibbon and explained his concerns, suggesting that the ambassador might wish to hear his views first-hand. Gilchrist agreed, and went to see Haughey at his home. There, Haughey expressed to him some bold thoughts on a possible eventual Irish settlement. He suggested that in return for British support for a united Ireland, the United Kingdom – and/or NATO – could be given access to the old treaty ports at Cobh and Berehaven in Co. Cork and Lough Swilly in Donegal, which had all been handed over to Irish control in the 1930s, following independence.

Haughey told the ambassador, according to Gilchrist's report to London, that to achieve a united Ireland there 'was nothing he would not sacrifice, including the position of the Catholic Church'. Haughey said he would also support a united Ireland rejoining the British Commonwealth. And he suggested that, in response, London could give a secret commitment that the border would be the subject of an inter-governmental review. In reporting this to London, Gilchrist explained how their meeting had come about, how Haughey had rung him after meeting Constantine Fitzgibbon the day before, and how he thought the ambassador should not have to rely on Fitzgibbon's version of what the Irish government thought.[5] Gilchrist appeared to find this plausible and reasonable. This important context for their meeting has not featured to date in the literature.

Other records in the British State papers show that Haughey's message to the British ambassador was far from being the solo run it has been represented as. The files show that five weeks before Haughey met Gilchrist, on 29 August 1969, the Taoiseach himself had provided a confidential off-the-record briefing for Patrick O'Donovan of the *Observer* newspaper, the contents of which – with Lynch's apparent agreement – had been relayed afterwards to the British Embassy and to Gilchrist.[6] Lynch's briefing of the journalist was broadly similar to that given four weeks later by Haughey to Gilchrist. He had told him that if partition was ended, there could be 'deletion of Section 2 and 3 of Article 44 of the Constitution', involving the 'special position of the Catholic Church'. O'Donovan was confused on the details of the Irish Constitution, but the sense is clear. Lynch had also said that he anticipated that unification would bring about a federal Ireland, with Stormont being retained but with Westminster's powers transferred to Dublin. Ireland would 'most certainly' consider rejoining the Commonwealth if the border was removed. A future relationship similar to that between Britain and India was envisaged. What this record shows is that when Haughey met Gilchrist, he was following a broadly similar strategy to that employed by his Taoiseach. On the basis of all this, there appears to be little ground for citing this meeting as evidence of supposedly disloyal and unwarranted behaviour by Haughey, as some writers have held.[7]

The second instance of Haughey's supposed insubordination was his failure to halt funding for the *Voice of the North* propaganda newspaper, after Lynch indicated that he wished the aid to stop. Even historian T. Ryle Dwyer, generally a detached and balanced commentator, saw this as showing a blatant disregard for the Taoiseach's instructions. It appeared to represent further defiance by Haughey, the Minister for Finance.[8] Yet this was not the burden of the evidence considered by the Dáil Committee of Public Accounts inquiry in 1971. Uncontested evidence before that inquiry from journalist Seamus Brady – who edited *Voice of the North* for a time – and from Captain James Kelly, who was liaising with the Northern account holders who were receiving money from Dublin, presented the matter very differently.

Brady explained to the Committee of Public Accounts that his minister, Haughey, had told him of the Taoiseach's wishes that the funding for *Voice of the North* should cease. He in turn had passed this on to Captain Kelly, who was acting as agent for the Northern account holders. Brady told Captain Kelly that *Voice of the North* might have to be closed down. Kelly, he said, initially agreed with him, but later came back to say that the Northern account holders wanted the paper kept going. They thought *Voice of the North* was 'doing a very good job, and were prepared to subsidize it'.[9] At the Committee of Public Accounts inquiry, Captain Kelly was asked from where he had received instructions to continue funding the newspaper. He said the instructions came from the people controlling the accounts in Northern Ireland, who wanted the paper to continue.[10] He stated that he was just their agent, acting on their instructions.

Although the committee, in its final report, did not accept this view of Kelly's role, his claims – that the Northern trustees of the account, who had been given money with no strings attached, were entitled to decide how it should be used – nonetheless appear convincing. Neither the government nor the Dáil had specified any limit on the use of the money. The evidence thus suggests that, in the end, it was not Haughey's call that the funding should continue, but that of the Northern recipients. The Taoiseach's wishes were not ignored; they were passed down, but the account holders took a different view, and this view prevailed.[11] While there were admittedly some contentious issues involved here about the control of the money that had been disbursed – issues going to the heart of the *modus operandi* of the Committee of Public Accounts, a matter considered later in this chapter – on balance there seems little ground for seeing this *Voice of the North* episode as evidence of Haughey defying the Taoiseach.

The final example of Haughey's supposed independence during this period is the alleged 'deal' he is reported to have made with IRA Chief of Staff Cathal Goulding in the early autumn of 1969. This was a story circulated by Peter Berry in 1970, and one that emerged, as with much of Berry's information, from Special Branch intelligence. Berry claimed that Haughey had met Goulding secretly in the week before 19 August 1969, and did a deal to permit the free movement of IRA arms to the North, in return for a halt to the IRA's campaign of attacks on foreigners' property in the Republic. The charge is similar to that attaching to Haughey's meeting with Gilchrist in early October; it implied that he saw himself as operating a government of his own, separate from the cabinet, only on this occasion dealing directly with subversives. Berry noted, pointedly, that the attacks on foreigners' property stopped around the time Haughey was supposed to have made this deal.[12] Even presuming that to be true, Berry must have known it did not establish cause and effect, only a coincidence of timing; it could simply be evidence that, in the immediate aftermath of the convulsions of August 1969 in Belfast, the IRA, in new and drastically changed circumstances, had changed its priorities.

The question that arises is: how reliable was Berry's Special Branch information? A detailed examination of the Department of Justice files for 1969, along with Berry's *Diaries*, published posthumously in 1980, does not engender confidence in the accuracy of his claims. The files released in 2001 raise significant doubts over any such meeting or pact by Haughey – over whether it happened, when it happened, or with whom it happened. The earliest written reference to any such encounter with Haughey occurs in a memorandum from Berry to Jack Lynch, penned on 8 June 1970. In this, Berry wrote that nine months earlier, in September 1969 – not August – it had come to light that Haughey met, not Goulding, but Mick Ryan, described as the O/C of the Dublin Brigade of the IRA (and shortly afterwards Quartermaster General). A deal was made that the IRA would be facilitated in the movement of arms to Northern Ireland. In return, the IRA would call off its campaign of burning and destroying the property of foreign wealthy residents.[13] Another undated note from Berry, written around the same time on a copy of the statement he himself made to the gardaí in late May 1970, agreed that Haughey's consultations had been with the Quartermaster General of the IRA. However, also in Berry's handwriting, the words 'Quartermaster General' had been later crossed out and replaced by 'CS', an abbreviation for Chief of Staff.[14]

In his advisory memo to the Attorney General and to state counsel involved in the arms trial prosecution, probably written in late June 1970, Berry put the date of the encounter as before 20 August 1969, and changed the name of the person Haughey met from Ryan to Chief of Staff Goulding. He described a broadly similar purported deal, but this time in inverted commas, as in 'the deal', suggesting some uncertainty over the status of the information.[15] In this document Berry cited, as evidence that such a deal had been made, the fact that 'the burning and destruction of the property of aliens by the IRA ceased after that meeting – whether by design (as the gardaí reported) or by sheer coincidence'.[16]

Further insights into this matter came from journalist Seamus Brady, a close associate of Blaney and related to him by marriage. Brady's 1971 memoir, *Arms and the Men*, stated that following 'an important cabinet decision', a directive was sent by Minister for Justice Mícheál Ó Móráin to the gardaí around August 1969. This was that 'the movement of arms for the defence of the minority in the Six Counties across the border should not be inhibited by prosecution or harassment by the authorities in the South'.[17] Brady's close connections with Blaney mean that his account cannot be lightly dismissed, although no supporting evidence exists to back up his statement. What appears certain is that if there was such a directive as he stated, emanating from the cabinet and specifically from the Minister for Justice, it would totally alter any sense of a covert Haughey 'deal'; equally, such a directive – if it existed – should have been known to Berry, as Secretary of the Department of Justice.

It may also be significant that the Goulding IRA never claimed to have made a deal, as described by Berry, with Haughey or the Fianna Fáil government, not even in their combative *Fianna Fáil and the IRA* pamphlet published in the early 1970s. This did refer to an undated approach from Haughey to the IRA 'with an offer of money to buy arms, on certain conditions',[18] and a suggestion that this meant leaving politics alone in the Republic and concentrating on military activity in the North. The IRA pamphlet also contained a reference – which could be significant in view of Berry's confusion – to a meeting that Goulding had in mid-August 1969, not with Charles Haughey, but rather with Haughey's brother Padraig, known as Jock.[19] The pamphlet did not claim that any agreement had been made.

In his *Diaries*, written in the mid-1970s, Berry stated that in August 1969 he had informed his minister, Ó Móráin, of the intelligence on the supposed deal, and of reports that Goulding had met with an unnamed minister. Ó Móráin offered no comment on the question of a deal, but had an inconclusive discussion with his department Secretary, speculating about which minister might have been involved. He then went to cabinet, where he raised informally Berry's written report on the matter. After the meeting, he told Berry flatly that no minister had met Goulding. Haughey, it seems, had acknowledged to Ó Móráin that he had a casual meeting 'with some member of the IRA organization' who wanted to meet him, but said he had paid little attention and claimed it was of no consequence.[20] In his *Diaries*, Berry dropped the inverted commas around the word 'deal'; he wrote that the information came from top Branch officers Fleming and McMahon, and that the information was to the effect that 'a deal had been made' between IRA Chief of Staff Goulding and this unnamed minister, in the week before 19 August 1969.[21]

As a postscript to this jumble of unsubstantiated, incoherent and unverifiable claims from Berry and his garda informants in the Special Branch, the following year, 1971, Chief Superintendent John Fleming insisted in evidence to the Committee of Public Accounts inquiry that Haughey had met, not with Goulding, but with an unspecified 'leading member of the IRA' towards the end of the period August–September 1969, and had promised him £50,000. He made no mention of a deal on IRA arms crossing the border.[22]

The extent of the uncertainty over the claim that Haughey did a private deal with Goulding has been identifiable from the State papers since 2001. Although there are clear question marks over its provenance and reliability, perhaps as a result of being embraced and propagated by Berry it appears to have been accepted without adequate query. The more likely proposition is that Goulding met Haughey's brother Jock, as the IRA believed;[23] alternatively, Haughey himself may have met IRA officer Mick Ryan, but on a different date to his supposed meeting with Goulding.[24] It remains a mystery how any arrangement or 'deal' could have operated without the Minister for Justice, Ó Móráin, being across it at the time, or without Berry himself being informed, or the top echelons of the Garda Síochána. While the claim for it has little or no evidential value, it has been presented otherwise in the literature.

These three problematic instances where Haughey is supposed to have behaved as though he was running 'a government within a government' in the period after August 1969 are examples of a literature that has too often failed to interrogate the primary sources that became available after January 2001. They also seem to offer examples of the tendency to view this period immediately leading up to the Arms Crisis through a hindsight prism, governed by a particular view of what transpired in May 1970. An ill-founded conviction that Haughey and Blaney were later exposed as conspiring against Lynch inevitably generated a tendency to seek instances of conspiracy, or at least disloyalty, in these ministers' behaviour in earlier times. This, it is suggested, may at least partly explain why these three apparent misrepresentations of Haughey have gained currency.

But the case against Haughey does not rest there. Close to the heart of that case – and, to a degree, the case against Blaney also – is the argument that public funds intended for humanitarian purposes were secretly misappropriated for the purchase of arms, with the connivance of the two ministers. This is a theory that rests on several assumptions, none of which are entirely secure. One is that the Dáil and/or the government intended to tie the hands of those to whom the money was being given, despite the fact that the clear demand of Northerners had been for means of defence. It also appears to assume that the gun-running project was the brainchild of either Haughey or Blaney, rather than coming to them, already part-formed, from north of the border. It also assumes that Haughey – as the responsible minister – was the person who dictated that public money from the Northern Relief Fund should go to arms purchases. The evidence on these issues, as earlier indicated, is far from conclusive, and tends in a different direction. It appears that the intention to purchase arms abroad came first from the Northern Defence Committees, and there has been no evidence produced of a decision by Haughey and/or Blaney that the money the Irish government was providing should, or must, be spent on arms. There is no evidence that the purchase of arms was required of the account holders – nor indeed, given the total absence of accounting required from those recipients (see below), is it clear how it could have been.

What is indisputable is that Haughey, as Minister for Finance, was effectively in sole control of the disbursement of this money under a formal cabinet delegation of authority,[25] and that Blaney somehow became involved in its distribution. These undoubted facts left both men open to retrospective accusations that they engaged in illegal, disloyal, perhaps even treacherous behaviour. The issue historically therefore is less whether or not the two men were complicit in this use of the money to buy arms – which Haughey always sought, unconvincingly, to deny – but rather a series of other questions: was it ever specified by either the government or the Oireachtas that the money was to be used only for humanitarian purposes? Did the decision to buy arms come from Haughey or from Blaney? Did using the money in that way amount to a deliberate deception of Lynch and the rest of his government? And finally, was the buying of arms in this way part of a subversive plot to boost a resurgent IRA?

The 1971–72 Committee of Public Accounts inquiry into the disbursement of the Northern Relief Fund is central to these issues. Its inquiry was set up after the arms trials had conspicuously failed to convict Haughey and his three co-defendants. The acquittals left Lynch in no mood to resist the insistent demands from both Fine Gael and Labour that the matter be pursued further. Observers could see that the inquiry by the Dáil committee, launched with the enthusiastic participation of Fine

Gael and Labour, was likely to be effectively another prosecution – only this time seeking a different verdict.[26] The mission given by the Dáil, 'to examine specially the expenditure' of the monies voted,[27] was a straightforward fact-finding task, but such was the questioning of witnesses during the committee's proceedings throughout 1971 that at separate points Captain Kelly and Colonel Hefferon were driven to protest that it had became a 'third arms trial'.[28] If it was a prosecution, its target, to many observers, was always Haughey.

The inquiry had the weakness from the start that it was unable to compel the attendance of witnesses from outside the jurisdiction, resident in Northern Ireland. It was then further weakened by a Supreme Court judgement denying it the power to compel witnesses from *within* the jurisdiction.[29] While writers such as Dermot Keogh, despite these drawbacks, have nonetheless applauded the committee's work,[30] it is contended here that its findings were fatally undermined by some additional basic errors of the members' own choosing.

An underlying premise in the inquiry's proceedings, one that held an implicit criticism of how Haughey had discharged his guardianship responsibilities, was that any use of the disbursed money to buy arms was contrary to the intentions of the Dáil, and so amounted to misappropriation. It is striking that the committee had no discussions on this premise, nor did it ever reach a finding of fact on it. Misappropriation was simply taken for granted in the proceedings, and, in the years since, has been accepted as such without query by many writers in the literature.[31] In their questioning of witnesses, deputies made many references to 'the intentions of the Dáil' regarding use for the monies, as though those intentions were self-evident and required no further discussion.[32] In the same vein, the committee did not discuss, but simply assumed it to be the case, that the provision of solely humanitarian aid had been the Dáil's intention. This assumption guaranteed that any use of the Northern Relief Fund to purchase arms automatically represented 'misappropriation'.[33]

Had the committee probed further into the Dáil's intentions, as opposed to simply taking them as read, it would have encountered some difficulty, since there was almost no stated evidence on what either the Dáil or the government intended. The Dáil had no discussion whatever on the Supplementary Estimate for the Grant-in-Aid vote on 18 March 1970, and Haughey, as minister, made no reference to the Northern Relief Fund when presenting the Estimate.[34] Nor was there any official reference at the time to a term that became commonplace later, 'the relief of distress'.[35] When the Committee of Public Accounts inquiry was being set up after the arms trials, on 1 December 1970, there was still no discussion as to whether the money had been intended for exclusively humanitarian aid and, if it was, why this was left totally unsaid. In fact, there appears to be no evidence on the public record that identifies the intentions of the Dáil when the aid was voted.

Nor was the earlier government announcement of the aid allocation, on 16 August 1969, much more helpful by way of indicating what the cabinet's intentions were. It referred simply to 'aid for the victims of the current unrest'. The provision being made was far from normal: the announcement stated explicitly that Haughey, as Minister for Finance, would have total control of 'the amount and the channel of disbursement'.[36] Charles Murray, Secretary of the Department of Finance, underlined the uniqueness of the latitude given to Haughey over the fund's disbursement when he stated: 'In my experience, I have never seen a government decision that was drafted in such wide terms.'[37] He was noting the absence of constraints on the Minister for Finance's judgement on disbursement, plus the absence of any limit on the amount of money involved.

This silence at the time on the intended use of the money, and the failure to specify an intention of humanitarian usage only, appears telling, and it would be difficult to argue it was either accidental or due to simple negligence. The demands of the Northerners, as described memorably by defendant John Kelly at the second arms trial, could hardly have been clearer: 'We did not ask for blankets or feeding bottles, we asked for guns.'[38] What they got was money, and the recipients, focused as they were on urgent defensive measures, had already, as has been shown, determined how the money would be used.

An interesting insight into the intended use of the voted monies is provided by the conduct of two Northern Ireland MPs who shortly afterwards became trustees of the Northern Relief Fund bank accounts.[39] Paddy Devlin and Paddy Kennedy arrived in the Department of Foreign Affairs offices in Dublin on the evening of 16 August 1969, angrily demanding guns from the government. When Assistant Department Secretary Seán Ronan failed to give them an immediate positive response that evening, they reacted 'vehemently', with Devlin 'more angry and emotional than the others'.[40] Their remonstrations that day were fully documented by Ronan, and passed on to the Office of the Taoiseach. Earlier in the evening, Devlin had made a more public demand for guns at a gathering outside the GPO in Dublin.[41] Whether or not the Taoiseach knew that Devlin and Kennedy later became trustees of the Relief Fund is unclear, but it was information clearly available to him had he sought it. There seems no reason to suppose these men had altered their views on what kind of assistance was being sought.

In later years, Devlin was coy about his actions in August 1969. He had been involved in the IRA as a younger man, but by 1969 he was firmly on a constitutional path, representing the Northern Ireland Labour Party in Stormont. His public demand for guns outside the GPO proved a subsequent embarrassment to him, and in his memoir *Straight Left*, published in 1993, he sought to distance himself from it:

> Those words were to haunt me and be used against me for years to come, but I have to say again they were used in the heat of an emotional moment. I had long ago rejected the use of violence and severed my connections with the IRA.... My remarks at the

GPO did not accurately represent the thrust of my approach to the ongoing problem, and I did not of course get any guns or take any steps to do so.[42]

The State papers released in 2001 removed all room for misunderstanding concerning Devlin's stance in August 1969. As a future trustee of the Relief Fund, his example is significant but not unique. Whatever the actual reality, few elected representatives were later prepared to admit an association with acquiring arms at this time.[43] In this vein, Gerry Fitt MP subsequently complained that money from the Irish government had gone to republican groups in the North, yet Fitt is recorded in *The Thimble Riggers* as asking for guns himself in mid-September 1969,[44] and Vincent Browne has written that three separate interviewees – John Kelly, republican Billy Kelly and MP Paddy Kennedy – all told him that Fitt was asking for arms.[45]

If there was a logic to the way money voted as aid for Northern nationalists in 1969 was spent, only a handful of writers have acknowledged it. One of these, T. Ryle Dwyer, concluded that because unarmed nationalists in the Six Counties were living under mental stress and in dread of being attacked, the purchase of arms could be seen as consistent with the government's stated intention to provide aid and relief. Vincent Browne observed, simply: 'The primary relief for which most people were asking then was arms, and in the circumstances it was not unreasonable to accede to that request.'[46]

It is reasonable to conclude, on the balance of the evidence, that there was an unstated intention in autumn 1969 to allow the Northern Defence Committees the freedom to spend the funds they were being given as they wished, and clearly to spend the money without public scrutiny.[47] At the same time, it is also evident that the money did not come fully *carte blanche*: Blaney and officers from Military Intelligence sought to ensure that groups who might get money or guns would not be disposed to use them against the forces of the Irish state.

Haughey's evidence on the issue of supposed mis-appropriation complicates any analysis, since he appears to have been entirely disingenuous and less than honest in his claims at the time. He chose not to support claims that Captain Kelly's behaviour over arms was authorized or proper, but argued simply that he did not know the details. It was, he told the Committee of Public Accounts, 'astonishing' and 'a shock to me' to learn that money had gone to anything other than for the relief of distress.[48] While this appears untrue – judging by the evidence of his assistant, Department of Finance official Anthony Fagan, and also his co-accused, Captain Kelly – realistically Haughey probably had little choice in 1971 but to take a similar line to the sworn evidence he had given in the arms trial in 1970. There he had denied on oath knowing that Captain Kelly was importing arms when he ordered Revenue to clear the consignment in question through customs without examination. His position was that he had not been told of the contents of the consignment, and knew only that it was required by Army Intelligence. This contradicted his co-defendant Kelly, who gave evidence that Haughey knew exactly what he was authorizing from the moment Kelly approached him on 19 March 1970.[49] Kelly's position was spelled out clearly in *The Thimble Riggers*: it was that when the Northern Relief Fund was established, 'It was clearly understood by all, including Mr Haughey, that at the discretion of the Defence Committees, a major portion of the money was intended for the purchase of arms.'[50]

Haughey was clearly determined that he would not go to jail; also, by denying awareness that guns were involved, he was creating for himself an extra chance of being acquitted. His plea meant that even if his three co-defendants were convicted, he might himself avoid such a fate. They did not dispute that they were engaged in importing arms, but argued that it was an authorized importation; Haughey said he simply did not know that the consignment was of arms.

With this evidence, the former Minister for Finance appears to have been taking a cynical each-way bet on the outcome. Arguably, it was a kind of betrayal, and it certainly did his co-defendants few favours. They needed Haughey to state that the arms importation was known within the cabinet and to that extent sanctioned, at least unofficially. This Haughey would not do. When questioned in detail the following year, he was never likely to tell the Committee of Public Accounts that the Northern Relief Fund, over which he had sole control, could have been properly used for arms purchases, as Captain Kelly asserted. Haughey's legal defence at the arms trials, resting totally on his claimed ignorance, in turn led him to agree with members of the committee that the use of the Northern Relief Fund for the purchase of arms and ammunition, or indeed for propaganda, through the *Voice of the North* newspaper, was not proper, nor did he authorize it:

> Chairman: Do you accept that the intention behind the Vote was for the purpose of relief to the North and for no other purpose?
>
> Haughey: Absolutely.
>
> Chairman: You accept, therefore, that expenditure from that fund for propaganda purposes and for arms would be irregular?
>
> Haughey: Yes....
>
> Chairman: So payment from the Fund was made without your knowledge or permission?
>
> Haughey: Yes. [51]

Haughey was asked by Justin Keating TD (Labour) about the terms 'aid' and 'relief', which were part of the official government announcement in August 1969. What activity did he consider proper in that context?

Haughey: The provision of every type of facility and amenity which they would require... we envisaged providing financial assistance, providing food, clothing – a very wide basis of assistance....

Keating: Can I take it, in your thinking as the Minister at that time charged with the disbursement, that the use of these moneys for the provision of arms, even if that were for defensive purposes, was totally excluded from the terms of that decision?

Haughey: Absolutely.[52]

This position of Haughey, like that of the government in general, would have been more credible if this had ever been specified, or if anything had been done not just to exclude, but even to monitor, any such use of the money. It was a feature of the Northern Relief Fund as implemented by the Department of Finance, that it left the Northern recipients of the money almost untrammelled freedom over how they chose to use it. Its designation was as a 'grant-in-aid'; this meant that it would normally not be subject to audit by the Controller and Auditor General. It was hardly a secret that no real accounting for the funds, once delivered to the bank account of the designated recipients, was ever going to be required.

Haughey received support of a kind at the Committee of Public Accounts from his former Department Secretary, Charles Murray. Murray frustrated committee members by his insistence that the department had fulfilled its oversight responsibilities once the money had been passed on. He, of course, was not entirely a disinterested party, since his own reputation and that of his department were involved. But throughout the committee hearings, he stubbornly declined to be critical of his former minister. As the designated accounting officer, he insisted that there had been nothing improper or irregular in the way the Relief Fund was disbursed. He declined to use the word 'misappropriated' in relation to the money, but agreed that the title 'Northern Ireland Relief Fund' suggested that use of the money to buy arms was precluded. At the same time, Murray appeared to feel there was no real redress in that situation, because the money had gone to its correct destination, and there the department's responsibility had ended. The recipients had decided what they used the money for. He said that as accounting officer, in general he was satisfied 'both in regard to the appropriateness, and propriety, of these payments'.[53]

A significant matter not considered by the Committee of Public Accounts, and so not addressed in that forum by Haughey, was the practical difficulty that would have arisen *had* there been an attempt to insist on a purely humanitarian use of the money, ruling out more military or defence-oriented uses. The Committee's Final Report shows that while £30,000 was spent on arms purchases, a further £31,000 went to the Belfast Committee for the Relief of Distress, substantially as payments of wages to full-time volunteers in the Defence Committee areas. The committee could not establish that this money had been used 'for the relief of distress'. Murray was told in Belfast that the money was largely used for payments to men unable to reach their workplace because of the security situation. Other evidence, however, suggests that much of the money spent like this went to members of republican groups, those providing the defence 'muscle' in barricaded nationalist areas.[54] John Kelly, one of the arms trial defendants, told Peter Taylor years later how he had distributed money to republicans on the barricades:

Taylor: What sum of money did you receive to distribute?

Kelly: You'd be talking in terms of £1000–£1500.

Taylor: How often?

Kelly: Every week.

Taylor: And you'd take that money to Belfast?

Kelly: That's correct, yeah.

Taylor: And to whom would you give it?

Kelly: Well, Billy McMillen [Official IRA commander in Belfast] was alive at the time. Billy dispensed money to the Lower Falls people. And other monies were dispensed to people in New Lodge area who were manning the barricades. Anyone in fact who was manning the barricades got paid for their work.

Taylor: Billy McMillen was the Belfast O/C [of the Goulding-led IRA]?

Kelly: He was.

Taylor: In effect then, was the money from Dublin going into the hands of the IRA?

Kelly: Well, you could say it was, yeah.[55]

It is evident that, in the disturbed circumstances of the time, the line between humanitarian aid and defensive/military aid was impossibly blurred. But there is no evidence of any attempt to make such a distinction at the time, publicly or privately. It became an issue only in the aftermath of the arms trials, when the British army had reimposed some order on Northern Ireland and virtually everyone, North and South, wished to disassociate themselves from funding delivered in more fraught times to republican activists.

★

A further possible criticism of Haughey concerns his failure
to inform the Taoiseach, or his cabinet colleagues generally,
that public money was being spent on arms. This was regarded
by Bruce Arnold as a deception.[56] It is a view, however, that
disregards the unusual status of the project, with the Northern
Defence Committees in at least partial ownership, and it also
may overestimate the extent to which Lynch would have wished
to receive such information. Vincent Browne wrote, somewhat
disingenuously, that he could not understand why Haughey did
not simply acknowledge that the money had gone to buy guns,
when 'it was a perfectly legitimate thing to have done at the time,
in the light of the perceived danger in which large numbers of
nationalists found themselves in Northern Ireland'.[57]

The probable truth is that Haughey, although in the witness
box he denied knowledge of arms and thus committed himself to
that unconvincing line of argument, had in reality found himself
supervising the financing of a covert activity that ultimately
neither he nor almost any other public representative, North or
South, would be prepared to stand over publicly. By 1971, denial
was everywhere.

5

Lynch's Hidden Policy

Although the evidence for it emerged as early as the arms trials in autumn 1970, the process of acknowledging that Jack Lynch had a hidden policy on Northern Ireland has met with strong resistance. At the trials it was disclosed that from mid-August 1969, the government had become engaged in making top-secret militarized contingency plans to cater for future emergencies across the border. The embarrassing revelations came largely through the evidence of Colonel Hefferon. The State had little incentive to flesh them out in court. Accordingly, the full extent of the government's covert planning had to wait a further thirty years to be disclosed; this came with the public release in January 2001 of military records held by the Department of Defence. Yet even since then the process of coming to terms with the previously hidden aspects of Lynch's policy on Northern Ireland in 1969–70 has been slow, it seems largely because of confusion and disagreement over the significance of some of the disclosed documentation.

Scepticism over the covert aspects of Lynch's Northern Ireland policy prior to May 1970 has been most pronounced regarding one of the central revelations at the trials: the directive issued to the Defence Forces on 6 February 1970 by Jim Gibbons, Minister for Defence. This ordered the army to prepare, in certain circumstances, for incursions across the border, and to make surplus arms available which could be provided to Northern nationalists to defend themselves.[1] Gibbons agreed in the witness box that he had ordered rifles, ammunition and gas masks – significantly, *without* accompanying soldiers – to be transported urgently by the Defence Forces to Dundalk on 2 April 1970, as rioting in Ballymurphy in Belfast appeared on the verge of spiralling out of control. The direct connection between the February directive and the Dundalk rifles episode two months later was not evident at the arms trials, despite evidence to this effect from Hefferon; these two events appeared to be separate until, thirty years later, the State papers revealed that there was a direct connection.

Other evidence at the arms trials, again largely emanating from Hefferon, showed that in September 1969, Gibbons, as Minister for Defence, had ordered training facilities to be provided to Northern republicans by the Defence Forces at Fort Dunree in Co. Donegal. There was more detail on these events and on Gibbons's involvement in them in the State papers released in 2000 and 2001. But at the time, throughout 1969 and until the first arms trial in September 1970, these aspects of policy were completely hidden. The disclosures shone a bright light on the covert Northern Ireland policy of Jack Lynch's government in the period immediately before the Arms Crisis, and specifically from February to May 1970. Elements missing from Lynch's public policy pronouncements were strikingly set out in Department of Defence files, indicating a reality very different to the official picture at the time.

An example of how the complexity of Jack Lynch's Northern policy was hidden from view is provided by his important speech on Northern Ireland in Tralee, Co. Kerry, on 20 September 1969. This has often been seen as defining the Taoiseach's peaceful approach to the ending of partition. It was a speech drafted by T. K. Whitaker, former Secretary of the Department of Finance, and it has been generally seen as the moment Lynch set down, after the ambivalence of his 13 August television broadcast, a clear declaration that the Irish government had no intention of using force to undermine partition, and sought unity only by consent. Lynch stated:

> The unity we seek is not something forced but a free and genuine union of those living in Ireland based on mutual respect and tolerance.... It will remain our most earnest aim and hope to win the consent of a majority in the Six Counties to means by which the North and South can come together....[2]

But even as the Taoiseach was delivering this clarion call rejecting violence, arrangements were secretly being put in place, under the auspices of his Minister for Defence, to train nationalist citizens of Derry in the use of weaponry. The venue was Fort Dunree Irish army camp, near the border in Co. Donegal.[3] A group of twelve men, led by community leader Paddy 'Bogside' Doherty, were assembled at the camp just one week after the Tralee speech. They were inducted into the army's territorial reserve, the Fórsa Cosanta Áitúil (FCA), and received training in the use of firearms. More groups were expected to follow, but word of the training leaked out, and newspaper queries from the UK caused an abrupt cancellation of the scheme after just one week. The decision to abort the training was made by Colonel Hefferon; apart from being Director of Military Intelligence, he was also responsible for the army's press office at the time, and in consequence had received the first query from the British press about Fort Dunree. When he was unable to contact his minister late on a Friday afternoon, Hefferon took responsibility for calling off the next phase of the training, and reported his actions to his Chief of Staff, Lieutenant General MacEoin, the following Monday morning.[4]

When this question of Irish army training in firearms for Northern Ireland citizens was raised in the Dáil seven months later, in May 1970, Jim Gibbons initially refused to admit there had been any training.[5] But when confronted at the second arms trial with Hefferon's evidence to the contrary, Gibbons accepted that it had happened, and that he personally had instituted it. He ascribed no role to Hefferon, but said that when the press were alerted, Lynch had decided to end the training. Gibbons was subsequently pressed by Captain Kelly's counsel, Tom Finlay SC, on the basis that a decision to train Northerners in the use of firearms for their defence would have been pointless if they were not going to be given guns. Gibbons denied this, and argued unconvincingly that the training had been merely a gesture of sympathy with the fears and concerns of Northern nationalists. Although he agreed that he had authorized the training, he represented the Taoiseach as disapproving of it, and as the reason for its cancellation.[6] The image he conjured up was a familiar one to researchers of the Arms Crisis: a moderate Lynch continually reining in over-enthusiastic ministers – such as Gibbons himself– who were misguidedly attempting to assist beleaguered Northerners. The evidence for these interventions by Lynch, however, is somewhat elusive.

Regarding the training at Fort Dunree, the question is whether or not Lynch disapproved of it, and then ensured it did not continue in any form. He was not involved in the initial instruction to Donegal officers to call off the training; this came from Hefferon, who provided a detailed and convincing account of his actions in that regard.[7] This was backed up by Captain Kelly, who said he was present in Hefferon's office on the Friday evening in question, and had assisted in the cancellation.[8] While Gibbons's evidence was that he told Lynch of the problem after the weekend, the Taoiseach appears at that point to have simply endorsed the holding decision that Hefferon had already taken.

Although the impression given by Gibbons at the arms trials was that thereafter Lynch put a permanent stop to the training, there is some evidence that the halt was only temporary. The evidence for this lies partly in the minutes of a meeting of the Council of Defence on 13 October 1969. The Council was a body that met occasionally, when required, to advise the Minister for Defence on policy issues. It comprised mainly top army officers, including the

Chief of Staff, as well as the minister. The Council met a week after Captain Kelly's encounter with the Northern Defence Committees in Bailieboro – where delegates had expressed unhappiness at the sudden cancellation days earlier of the Fort Dunree training. A strong appeal for further training was made by those present at Bailieboro, a request submitted upwards through a written report from Captain Kelly to Colonel Hefferon.[9]

What appears significant is that, at the Council of Defence meeting on 13 October 1969, Gibbons instructed the army Chief of Staff to submit a programme of 'special courses of continuous training for elements of the FCA'.[10] Donnacha Ó Beacháin has argued, probably correctly, that these 'special courses' were intended for the further training of Northerners, as had happened at Fort Dunree and as had been proposed by the Army Planning Board on Northern Ireland Operations.[11] There is support for this view in the minutes of the Council of Defence meeting, where Gibbons warned those present that officers needed to be aware that the special training he proposed 'might give rise of public speculation'[sic]; this was an apparent acknowledgement from the minister of the press speculation that caused the Fort Dunree project to be aborted.

There are additional indications that the Irish Defence Forces training of Northerners in firearms use in the autumn of 1969 did not in fact end at Fort Dunree. These have come from Billy Kelly, one of the veteran Belfast republicans most closely involved in petitioning Dublin for firearms assistance in 1969–70. Kelly, who met the Taoiseach for this purpose in early February 1970,[12] stated in a 2001 interview with the author that, to his knowledge, forty to fifty republicans were trained by the Irish army in different army camps at this time. He believed they were trained under the auspices of the FCA in the period August–December 1969.[13]

Although Captain Kelly wrote that the Fort Dunree training was not resumed,[14] it seems likely, from all the evidence, that the Defence Forces did make further provision, and on the different basis that the minister had set out to the Council of Defence.

Since Gibbons claimed to have brought the Fort Dunree training directly to Lynch's attention, it must be judged unlikely that he would have subsequently authorized any resumption of such training without the explicit approval of the Taoiseach.

The discrepancy between the much-lauded sentiments Lynch expressed at Tralee in September 1969 and the training of Northerners in the use of firearms around the same time would have been seriously embarrassing had the training not been entirely secret, and hidden from public view. It was not judged to be feasible to acknowledge its existence, for obvious reasons. The danger – that it would be misunderstood both north of the Irish border and in Whitehall – needs no underlining. The subterfuge, not for the first time in the story of the Arms Crisis, was effectively mandatory.

It was left to Captain Kelly himself, writing in 1999, to seek to reconcile the contradiction between Lynch's Tralee speech and the training in firearms his government had authorized for nationalists from Derry:

> In common with the vast majority of the Irish people, Jack Lynch's most earnest wish was that the Six-County problem be solved by peaceful means, but governments have to be prepared for contingencies, the pertinently obvious one in the Irish case at this time being a complete breakdown of law and order in Northern Ireland, with a renewal of violence, again sparking off murderous attacks on the Nationalist minority... To me... this was the only way in which the apparent advocation of a policy of peace and the preparation for armed intervention, however low-key, could be reconciled.[15]

Kelly's entirely reasonable argument here was that the limited, but undoubtedly militarized, contingency planning being undertaken by the government did not mean that Lynch was repudiating a peaceful approach to ending partition. It was an explanation Jack Lynch himself might have offered, had it been at all practicable in the worrisome times of autumn 1969 for him to be open and transparent about Northern Ireland policy.

The Tralee speech has governed perceptions of Lynch's pre-May 1970 Northern policy, and the hidden elements, even since they have come to light, have tended to be understated. This is illustrated in historian Michael Kennedy's analysis of how the Irish government responded to the Northern trauma in August 1969.[16] Kennedy stated correctly of the Tralee speech that it moved the emphasis away from a military solution to partition to a peaceful one, but then added – perhaps less reliably – that in the speech 'he [Lynch] was telling Northern Ireland republicans that they would get no assistance from the Irish army'. When the hidden activities of Lynch's government are factored in, as in the Fort Dunree training, it seems clear the government had a more ambiguous message for republicans: it would not support violence directed against partition, but, for defensive purposes, it would make available some training in the use of firearms.

What was already operating in September 1969 was a Janus-faced policy on Northern Ireland, pursued in particular by Jim Gibbons as Minister for Defence from August 1969 to May 1970, and under Lynch's supervision. It was two-sided and it was two-faced, but it was focused on defence and was entirely within the framework of a peaceful approach to ending partition. The Minister for Defence had a central role in implementing this policy. It was not unauthorized and it was not rogue, nor was it a subversive plot engineered by scheming ministers contrary to the wishes of the Taoiseach. Recognition of this extra covert dimension to policy on Northern Ireland is critical to any analysis of the Arms Crisis. It is also critical to an understanding of the important event that occurred on 6 February 1970, the government directive to the Defence Forces, when Jack Lynch showed how far he was prepared to go – albeit in top secrecy – in providing defensive support for Northern nationalists.

★

News of the directive was a near-sensation when it emerged at the first arms trial in September 1970. The revelation came from Colonel Hefferon, who was actually present in the office when Minister Gibbons delivered the directive orally, without a note-taker present, to the army Chief of Staff, Lieutenant General Seán MacEoin. This was immediately after a Friday cabinet meeting in which the government had discussed a lengthy memorandum from the Minister for External Affairs on government policy in relation to Northern Ireland.[17] It was partly accidental that Hefferon was present in Gibbons's office at the time, because he had come, it seems, in relation to other business. However, when he rose in order to leave the Chief of Staff and the minister alone, he was waved back into his seat by Gibbons and told that this concerned him also.[18]

Hefferon's account of what Gibbons said, offered several months later at the arms trials, was largely drawn from memory and inevitably imprecise; it would be a further thirty years before the definitive version became public.[19] One top officer in GHQ remarked at the time to Hefferon: 'This is the most important directive that has ever been given to the Defence Forces.'[20] The import of the minister's instructions was sufficiently evident for MacEoin to set about, over the following days, a meticulous process of clarifying, with Gibbons's full cooperation, precisely what the instructions were and what they meant. One result is that the files relevant to the directive comprise a series of documents, not just one; another is that they are a historical source exhibiting an unusual and valuable precision.

The records were kept in the Planning and Operations Section of the Chief of Staff's office in Army GHQ. The first version of the directive was set down following a somewhat incoherent debriefing thirty minutes after the event.[21] Over the following days, MacEoin documented a much more precise record of the instructions. Here the key document is the addendum to the directive, dated 11 February 1970. This set down in quotation marks the direct speech Gibbons had used five days earlier:

'At a meeting of the Government held this morning (Friday 6 February, 1970), I was instructed to direct you to prepare the Army for incursions into Northern Ireland.

'The Taoiseach and other Ministers have met delegations from the North, At these meetings urgent demands were made for respirators, weapons and ammunition, the provision of which the Government agreed. Accordingly truck loads of these items will be put at readiness so that they may be available in a matter of hours.'[22]

This record established that there were two distinct elements to the directive: one involving preparation for cross-border incursions, the other making specific provision for guns for Northerners. The major revelation in the addendum, which went beyond anything revealed at the arms trials or at any time prior to 2001, was in Gibbons's phrase 'the Government agreed'. What was agreed was a decision to make respirators, weapons and ammunition available, for possible provision to the delegations who had asked for them. It was not a decision actually to hand over such items, only to have them available in case circumstances deteriorated sufficiently. It was also new that the arms, ammunition and respirators were to be loaded onto lorries, ready for despatch northwards 'in a matter of hours'.

Another significant military document relating to the directive also made public in 2001 was a briefing paper prepared for the Chief of Staff, MacEoin, in advance of a meeting with the Taoiseach on 9 June 1970. This was entitled Brief for the Ceann Fóirne [Chief of Staff]. The brief described discussions between Gibbons and MacEoin in the days after 6 February, undertaken with the purpose of clarifying exactly what the directive entailed. Direct questions were put by MacEoin to the minister on 13 February 1970; in his responses, Gibbons confirmed that the 'sole object' of the cross-border incursions referred to would be 'the protection of the lives and property of the [Catholic] minority'. They would only occur in the context of 'a complete breakdown of law and order in N. Ireland, where the security forces were unable or unwilling to protect the minority'. MacEoin questioned the minister specifically about the arms, ammunition and gas masks that were to be provided: how many were to be made available, to whom, and in what circumstances were they to be handed over? The reply was that 'the minister had no idea'; Gibbons stipulated nonetheless that stockpiles should be held in Dublin and Athlone. In reply to further direct questions from the Chief of Staff, Gibbons stated that the Northern delegations had not been told of these plans, and that there would be no diplomatic representations to the British before any incursions took place.[23]

Later the same document, Brief for the Ceann Fóirne, recorded that on 18 February 1970, both in Dublin and in Athlone barracks, there were assembled 500 rifles, 200 machine guns, 3,000 respirators, 80,000 rounds of .303 ammunition and 99,000 rounds of 9 mm ammunition. In a clear following reference to these stockpiled items, the briefing document noted how six weeks later, on 2 April, the Minister for Defence had decided 'material stored in Dublin should be moved forward'. This had been after he was warned by his cabinet colleague, Neil Blaney, that attacks were planned on the minority in the North and that British security forces would be withdrawn, leaving the nationalist minority unprotected. Accordingly, on the night of 2 April 1970, there were stored in Dundalk Barracks '500 rifles, 80,000 rounds of ammunition and 3,000 respirators'. This material – minus the 200 machine guns – was exactly half of that set aside on army lorries under the directive. The other half, waiting in Athlone Barracks, was undisturbed. The arms sent to Dundalk were never used, and were eventually all returned to Dublin.

It is notable that this series of actions and events on 2 April, as described in the Brief for the Ceann Fóirne, generated possibly the most dangerous moment of the entire Arms Crisis. Unlike Captain Kelly's unsuccessful project, in which the guns never arrived, these surplus army rifles were both available and sent urgently to the border that evening, with the clear purpose of potential distribution to persons unknown. Far from being a rogue action, these were Irish army weapons, sent on Irish army lorries by order of the Minister for Defence, Jim Gibbons. Moreover, they had been set aside two months earlier for just such an emergency purpose, on foot of the government's 6 February directive.[24] It was an operation that was formally authorized, at a time when the *sub rosa* plans for an arms importation by Captain James Kelly were still in gestation. If there was a high point of risk in the Arms Crisis, this may have been it.

Jack Lynch has been credited in the historiography in recent years with countermanding the sending of the rifles to Dundalk.[25] But the official military papers, while they describe the event in some detail, make no mention of Lynch being involved in any way. Nor, during his prolonged questioning by Tom Finlay SC (for Captain Kelly) at the first arms trial, did Gibbons make any mention of an intervention by Lynch; he stated more than once that he sent the rifles specifically 'to Dundalk', with no suggestion they were heading somewhere else only to be diverted there.[26] A different impression was given in *Hurler on the Ditch*, the 2005 memoir of former political correspondent Michael Mills, which contained an elaborate account of Lynch's supposed involvement in the Dundalk episode. Mills stated that Lynch, en route to his holiday home in west Cork, was told of the arms being sent northwards, and immediately contacted Gibbons; he instructed him, according to Mills, to countermand the order. Accordingly, the arms were taken into Dundalk Barracks. The suggestion is that this involved a diversion of the consignment from a different intended destination; Mills said the rifles were then 'kept there for the duration'.[27] No source for this information was given.

It appears that one of the main reasons the rifles sent to Dundalk stayed in Irish army hands was that – fortunately – by 2 April the riots in Ballymurphy were winding down, having persisted for several days. As the Irish army lorries rolled north that evening, by coincidence the panic that underlay the whole episode was already dissipating. According to the official record, 350 of the 500 rifles were returned to Dublin two days later 'because of storage problems in Dundalk'; perhaps significantly, the balance of 150 rifles, and *all* of the ammunition, were left in Dundalk through the whole month of April. They were returned to army stores in Dublin only on 1 May. The fact that these rifles and ammunition were kept in Dundalk Barracks for so long casts some doubt on Mills's assertion that Lynch had ordered an end to the operation; and subsequently Lynch himself, in a personal memo of a conversation with journalist Vincent Browne on 6 May 1980 dealing with the Dundalk rifles episode, made no reference to having countermanded the rifles' transfer north. The former Taoiseach (he had retired earlier in 1980) noted that the transfer 'was done without any recourse to me, although I believe there was an attempt to contact me in the middle of the night, but it was not successful'.[28] This document effectively disposes of the theory that Lynch intervened to halt or divert the movement of the army rifles. It raises the further question as to who provided Michael Mills with his mistaken account of Lynch's role.

The significance of the military documents relating to the 6 February directive has been acknowledged only sporadically in the literature since 2001. Many writers have simply ignored the directive entirely, while others have minimized its importance.[29] Yet the documents in which it is described are a valuable, confirmed record of a key statement of government policy from the time. They are arguably among the most important to have emerged in relation to the Arms Crisis. It is obvious from the actual terms of the directive that secrecy, and where necessary denial, was essential to its operation. This was not because it contradicted the essentially peaceful nature of Lynch's approach on Northern Ireland, which it indisputably did not, but because of its implications for Anglo-Irish relations.[30]

Lynch never discussed in public the directive and the reasoning behind it. While it appears to have arisen from a genuine concern to act to protect Northern nationalists in a time of perceived peril, and not from any covert or warlike intentions, it is understandable that no amount of humanitarian motives could persuade Lynch to admit publicly his government's intention to send the Irish army over the border, if the worst came to the worst. Even less publicly admissible was any idea that his government was making preparations to enable it to provide arms to nationalists for their self-defence. Lynch's inability to acknowledge the reality of the contingency planning, however understandable in terms of the interests of the State, left him obliged to dissimulate and to disguise the truth. As Donnacha Ó Beacháin, one of the few writers to recognize the directive's importance, points out, it 'demonstrates beyond doubt that the provision of arms for distribution in Northern Ireland when the government felt the situation warranted it was official policy'.[31] Planning for army incursions over the border was also official policy.

The implications of these hidden provisions for any considered historical assessment of the Arms Crisis are arguably immense. The value of the Brief for the Ceann Fóirne is that it sets out the military understanding in early June 1970 of the 6 February directive, and its consequences. Much at that stage had happened since the Dundalk rifles episode in early April – most notably, there had been the cabinet upheavals of 6 May, the sacking of Haughey and Blaney, and the start of a criminal prosecution. None of these are referred to in the briefing paper for MacEoin; nor is there any suggestion that the government's instructions of 6 February 1970 had been in any way misrepresented by Gibbons, or alternatively that the army had misunderstood the minister. It is evident that, contrary to some later accounts of the directive which suggested that no actions ensued from it,[32] the instructions had led to very specific actions, with guns, ammunition and gas masks first stockpiled on lorries, then later sent northwards to Dundalk in a perceived emergency in early April.

Further significant evidence confirming that the directive had Jack Lynch's personal authority, and also confirming Lynch's direct involvement in the contingency planning over Northern Ireland, is provided in the official minutes of Lynch's actual meeting with Lieutenant General MacEoin on 9 June 1970. These minutes also appear to reveal that an important unannounced change in government policy took place at some point between 2 April and 9 June 1970.[33] Two different sets of minutes of the meeting survive: a one-page memo from the Secretary of the department of Defence, Seán Ó Cearnaigh,[34] and a fuller, seven-page set from Army General Staff, dated 16 June and in the handwriting of Colonel Joe Adams.[35] Only four people were present: Lynch; his new Defence Minister, Jerry Cronin; the Secretary of Cronin's department, Seán Ó Cearnaigh; and MacEoin himself. A later memo from Cronin to Lynch revealed that the meeting was held in Lynch's own office.[36] There is no evidence of a set agenda, other than defence policy and planning in regard to Northern Ireland.

The army minutes show that MacEoin raised the question of the 6 February directive. He had continuing worries over the plan for Irish army incursions across the border. Could Lynch confirm that the army was correct in assuming that the word 'incursion' did not mean an invasion, but rather 'a short temporary stay to carry out a mercy mission'? Lynch, in reply, 'confirmed that the circumstances envisaged by the government were those assumed by the Chief of Staff'. The minute on 9 June also noted: 'The Taoiseach reaffirmed that it was the policy of the government that force would NOT [emphasis as per minute] be used to re-integrate the national territory.' Lynch had confirmed that cross-border army incursions would take place only 'in circumstances where there had been a complete breakdown in law and order, in which the lives of the minority would be in grave danger, and in which the security forces in Northern Ireland would be unable or unwilling to protect the lives of the minority'.

The later memo from Ó Cearnaigh was even more direct: 'The Taoiseach visualized the possibility of an extreme situation arising in which the government might feel impelled to employ the Defence Forces on rescue missions across the border.'[37] But this was something Lynch had specifically repudiated a month earlier. On 9 May, he told Dáil Éireann that neither cross-border troop incursions, nor the provision of guns, were contemplated:

> People have been coming down frequently from all parts of the Six Counties ever since and even before 12th August last year. They have come down for many purposes. Some of them have come down asking for guns and ammunition.... I told successive groups that we could not and would not send troops across the border... I told successive groups too – and they came I am sure in genuine fear and in the conviction that they needed guns – that we could not supply any guns either because I felt possession of arms on any side would be dangerous.[38]

Despite these assertions to the Dáil on 9 May, one month later, behind closed doors, the Taoiseach still contemplated sending troops over the border. His difficulties with frankness and transparency could hardly be clearer.

However, by 9 June it was a different story regarding the second element of the February directive – the provision of guns to Northern nationalists. Neither set of minutes makes any reference to this. As an issue, it had vanished from the agenda. The difference with mid-February 1970 is stark: at that point, MacEoin had unsuccessfully sought to get answers from Gibbons to questions that troubled him: Who would get the guns that were to be handed over across the border? How many guns? In what circumstances would they be handed over? Gibbons's unhelpful response on that earlier occasion had been that he 'had no idea'.[39] Now, after the Arms Crisis had blown up over the sacking of Haughey and Blaney, the matter was no longer an issue. No one brought it up, neither Taoiseach nor Chief of Staff, nor was there any indication as to *why* it had vanished from the military's concerns.

It is hard to avoid the conclusion that the provision of guns for nationalists in a doomsday situation, which had been government policy from at least 6 February 1970 through to 2 April, was no longer policy by 9 June. When was it dropped? Why was it dropped? After the political earthquake of a month earlier, when the cabinet had been convulsed over related issues, it could be fairly described as the elephant in the room between Lynch and MacEoin.

The historical value of this official record of the 9 June meeting is that it establishes, on a key issue, what Jack Lynch knew and when he knew it. Such precision regarding Lynch is rare in researching the Arms Crisis. The minutes position Lynch squarely within the process of contingency planning for Northern Ireland which he had broadly entrusted to Gibbons and Haughey, as Ministers for Defence and Finance respectively, at cabinet the previous August. Specifically, on 9 June the Taoiseach is seen to accept ownership of the directive issued on his behalf to the Defence Forces on 6 February 1970. It speaks volumes that Lynch made no mention of the provision of arms to Northerners at this particular moment, his point of acknowledgement that Gibbons had spoken with his and his government's authority. The minutes provide a definite date – 9 June – by which time it can be said that a key part of the policy that was laid out on 6 February had become no longer operational.

The documents do not reveal when the plan to provide arms for Northern nationalists was dropped, or why it was dropped, but the reasons appear obvious. It had become a political hot potato. It represented a covert policy that had never been publicly acknowledged, indeed one that the Taoiseach had repudiated to the Dáil – it seems falsely – on 9 May. If such a policy was revealed to have been officially communicated to the Defence Forces on 6 February 1970, it would not just suggest that Lynch had deceived the Dáil, but would also raise awkward questions over how he discriminated between that official policy and the arms provision project for which Haughey and Blaney had been sacked. There were obvious differences, but there were more obvious similarities, in particular through a stated government willingness to consider arming nationalists in the North.

These documents thus appear to provide a degree of corroboration for Captain Kelly's frequently advanced claim that it was a change of policy by Lynch and Gibbons in April 1970 which precipitated the Arms Crisis, rather than the discovery of the arms importation itself.[40] The coincidence of timing suggests that the events were directly linked. Almost every serious writer on this period – with a handful of notable exceptions – has seen Lynch in the Arms Crisis as the victim of underhand and conspiratorial activity by his close cabinet colleagues, up to the point on 6 May 1970 when he sacked them. Doubts about the existence of any such conspiracy have already been outlined above. A conclusion that Captain Kelly's arms importation was consistent with a government policy operational at least until the first week of April, and probably for a further four weeks after that, would fly in the face of most historical analysis of the Arms Crisis.[41] The idea that it was Lynch's simultaneous withdrawal from a clearly stated policy which brought about the sackings of Haughey and Blaney, and precipitated the 1970 arms trials, is subversive of much of what has been written since. The available evidence does however support such claims, and in so far as it does, it vindicates the activities of Captain Kelly, and casts doubt over Lynch's sacking of Haughey and Blaney.[42]

6

Directive Cover-up

The contents of the 6 February directive were so sensitive, almost shockingly so, that had Colonel Hefferon not given first-hand evidence of the directive's existence, and how the Minister for Defence issued it in his presence, it seems unlikely that anything of its nature would have been publicly confirmed, certainly before the State papers were released in 2001 – and perhaps not even then. As things were, it became the cause of much subterfuge and double-talk after Hefferon disclosed its existence, because Jack Lynch refused, either in public or private, to concede its real nature.

The importance of the directive in the Arms Crisis is indirectly shown by the extraordinary way Lynch handled it. Even within his government, it appears to have been treated with extreme secrecy, as the Taoiseach showed his capacity to keep his cards close to his chest when he wished to. For example, Desmond O'Malley, parliamentary Secretary to Gibbons at the time and shortly afterwards Minister for Justice, asserted in 2014: 'I knew nothing about any directive being issued to the army in January [sic] 1970,' adding that 'there was never a government proposal or any intention to buy arms or to supply arms to people in the North'.[1] It is also striking that neither Padraig Faulkner, in his memoir As I Saw It, nor Patrick Hillery, in Walsh's official biography, reveal any awareness of the 6 February directive. Hillery, in fact, told the author personally in 2001 that he did not know anything of the directive; he did not know that such instructions had been issued to the Defence Forces or that truckloads of arms had been loaded up and later sent to Dundalk. 'All that is new to me,' he said.[2] Padraig Faulkner, then Minister for Education, clearly believed the government had ruled out the cross-border army actions which Gibbons specified on 6 February.[3] If the remaining ministers – Mícheál Ó Móráin, Joe Brennan, George Colley, Brian Lenihan, Patrick Lalor and Seán Flanagan – were aware of the directive, they never gave any indication to that effect in the years after the Arms Crisis.

Even Kevin Boland, who produced a number of books on the period, makes no reference to it. Boland did, however, write that the movement of the rifles to Dundalk on 2 April – an action which, as shown above, stemmed directly from Gibbons's directive to MacEoin on 6 February 1970 – represented the government's 'contingency plan put into effect, in the belief that the hour of catastrophe had arrived'.[4] Whatever Boland's level of knowledge at the time, those clearly in the loop over the directive were just Gibbons, Blaney, perhaps Haughey, and Lynch himself.[5] It seems unlikely that Attorney General Colm Condon SC, when he initiated the prosecutions leading to the arms trials in late May 1970, had any idea of the secret instructions that had been given to the Defence Forces. The evidence is that only a handful of ministers were briefed on the government's covert policy on Northern Ireland. This could be seen as prudent, given the sensitivity of the issues involved, but it also shows Lynch in a particular controlling light.[6] It also means that, in choosing not to share with many of his cabinet colleagues the full nature of the instructions given to the Defence Forces, the Taoiseach took on even greater personal responsibility for those instructions, and for the policy they embodied.

The first public mention of the directive came in questioning from Captain Kelly's counsel, Tom Finlay SC, when he cross-examined Jim Gibbons at the first arms trial in September 1970; subsequently, after Hefferon had given first-hand evidence on its nature and extent, its existence in broad terms was confirmed at that trial by the man who issued it, the Minister for Defence, Gibbons. He initially sought to avoid answering questions by claiming privilege. Hefferon then explained how he was present when the directive was issued, and how he saw it as relevant to Kelly and his plans to help import arms for the Northern Defence Committees.

Hefferon elaborated on this at the Committee of Public Accounts inquiry in 1971.[7] He said his judgement was that Gibbons was stating government policy in the directive, and, hearing it thus stated, his view of what Kelly was engaged in was altered. The directive meant that arms were to be made available for possible future provision to Northern nationalists, and Kelly's work appeared to Hefferon to be consistent with that. He had previously felt strongly that Kelly needed to resign from the army if he was to continue his arms acquisition activities, and he told Gibbons so; but now the minister, in the aftermath of issuing the directive, told him not to proceed with Kelly's retirement, but to put it on hold. He also appeared to approve of Captain Kelly's arms-buying trips to the continent. Hefferon drew what might be considered some obvious conclusions about the approved status of Kelly's work.

When the directive was mentioned in evidence at the first arms trial, strange things happened. State counsel Seamus McKenna undertook to make immediate efforts to locate it within the State files, but then reported the following day to Judge Aindrias O'Caoimh that these efforts had failed, and the directive could not be found within GHQ records.[8] This was unusual, not to say suspicious, because just days earlier a senior army officer in GHQ, Colonel John O'Donovan, on a request from his retired colleague Hefferon, had successfully consulted the records, and had been able to confirm to Hefferon the accuracy of his recall of the directive's contents.[9] Nonetheless, the directive could not be found during the first trial – only for it to reappear, as if by magic, three days later. Between the two arms trials, the directive was made available to Gibbons to consult on 2 October 1970, after he requested access to it.[10]

In a further questionable episode, allegations surfaced in 1977 that the State had attempted to produce a forged version of the directive before the second arms trial got under way. This charge was first made in Kevin Boland's *Up Dev*, the former minister's account of why he resigned from Lynch's front bench in 1970.[11] Boland, himself a former Minister for Defence, wrote that he had been contacted towards the end of the first trial by a friend who was a serving senior official in the Department of Defence;[12] he was told that the directive had been rewritten, in the official's presence, in the office of Gibbons's successor as Minister for Defence, Jerry Cronin, with the assistance of phone calls to the Taoiseach, Jack Lynch. Boland wrote that he told defence counsel in the arms trials about this tip-off, with the result that the defence, having earlier at the first trial sought the official documents, conspicuously avoided calling for them to be produced at the second arms trial.[13] Whether or not Boland's informant was correct in his reports of evidence-tampering, no such 'forged' account – meaning a rewritten version, one which might have fudged the precision of the actual directions given – surfaced publicly either in the arms trials or in the State papers in 2001. Nonetheless, writers Angela Clifford and Vincent Browne, along with Boland and Captain Kelly himself, remained convinced that a forgery was attempted, before somehow being abandoned.[14]

Gibbons, having initially claimed privilege over the directive, was later required by the judge to answer questions about its precise contents; his replies were equivocal. But as shown in the previous chapter, in May 1970 Lynch had been far from equivocal when he denied to the Dáil that he would ever send the Irish army across the border, or that he would ever provide arms to the various groups of Northerners who had come seeking them. Why Lynch might have delivered a double assertion so far removed from the truth, as shown in the State papers in 2001, may be best explained by the blunt terms

used by Hefferon's successor as Director of Military Intelligence, Colonel P. J. Delaney, who advised privately during the trials on the need for absolute discretion over the directive. Delaney wrote:

> The Addendum [*the core document outlining the terms of the directive*] can NOT be released because NO Government can afford to publish openly what could be called its normal secret military plans, especially if these plans are directed against a friendly State. Such a revelation in open court would cause a diplomatic furore of the first order. This is just NOT done by any State regarded as friendly [*emphasis as in the original*].[15]

A further false statement about the directive was elicited from Lynch's government in April 1971, after Blaney had gone on the public record at a Fianna Fáil dinner in Arklow to state – correctly, as it transpired – that after 6 February 1970 arms had been loaded on trucks ready to move northwards. Blaney claimed the trucks had been sent to Dundalk in early April 1970, at the time of the Ballymurphy riots.[16] But Lynch's Minister for Defence, Jerry Cronin, specifically denied this two weeks later in the Dáil. Cronin stated bluntly, 'It is not true to say that the arms were loaded onto trucks and left ready to roll in a barracks in Dublin.'[17] The State papers, in particular the Brief for the Ceann Fóirne released in January 2001, showed Cronin's statement to be false.

Lynch's dissimulations do not appear to have stopped at his misstatements to the Dáil in May 1970, according to documents in the British State papers held in Kew, also released in 2001. On 19 May 1970, with the political crisis in Dublin dominating the news and public speculation continuing about the nature of the gun-running over which Blaney and Haughey had been dismissed, Lynch met with English journalist Owen Hickey, chief leader writer for *The Times*. Hickey relayed an account of this briefing immediately afterwards to the British Embassy in Dublin, which account was reported that same day to the Foreign and Commonwealth Office in London. Officials understood that Lynch knew, and accepted, that his words would be relayed back in this way. The report said that Lynch reaffirmed to Hickey what he had told the Dáil, that there would be no cross-border military involvement by the Irish Defence Forces. But responding to a specific question, he went further:

> He told Hickey that even if the predicted outbreak of serious disorders in the North this year were to develop into open insurrection which was beyond the resources of the British Army to contain, he would not permit the Irish Army to cross the border, or allow the passage of arms to the Catholics there.[18]

The least critical observation that can be made about this reported statement from Lynch about cross-border incursions is that it ran totally counter to what he would tell his Defence Forces Chief of Staff three weeks later. There are clearly serious issues over the veracity of what Lynch told the visiting journalist, and equally over the position he presented to the Dáil.

Further evidence that truthfulness over the directive was not on Lynch's agenda emerged when in 1971 he became involved in behind-the-scenes discussions on the Committee of Public Accounts inquiry into the disbursement of the Northern Relief Fund. The committee was seeking access to the terms of the directive, but early in its proceedings this was refused by Jerry Cronin, Gibbons's successor as Minister for Defence, on grounds of privilege. The Chief of Staff, Lieutenant General MacEoin, gave a letter to the committee containing what appeared to be a definitive statement:

> The directive gave no authority whatever, direct or indirect, to the Department of Defence or to any other body, officer or person, to purchase, procure or acquire arms or equipment. None of the matters covered by the directive is in any way relevant to the expenditure of the Grant-in-Aid, or any funds the subject matter of the inquiry.[19]

This view from MacEoin was of considerable consequence. It appeared to undercut totally the position taken by Hefferon at the arms trials[20] – where MacEoin, conspicuously, had not been called by the State as a witness. Hefferon, again in February 1970 in his evidence before the Committee of Public Accounts, said he viewed the directive as relevant to Kelly, and that it had altered his approach to Kelly's arms importation plans.[21] His belief, on intelligence grounds, was that if there was a possibility that arms were to be provided to Northerners, they should ideally be untraceable to the Irish army; he said he had stated this to Gibbons. After hearing the 6 February directive being delivered, it appeared to him that Kelly's efforts to bring in arms were in line with government policy. He was questioned about this at the Committee of Public Accounts inquiry:

> Dep. Eddie Collins (Fine Gael): You felt that he was working under Ministerial direction, did you?
>
> Hefferon: I felt, certainly after the 6th of February, that the possibility might arise, that this directive was a very plain and very responsible statement of policy by the Government... and I certainly did not feel I should do anything to stop him, to stop Capt. Kelly from—
>
> Collins: In other words it could have been part of Government policy to allow this activity?
>
> Hefferon: It could have been Government policy to prepare for the contingency, which indeed, in the climate of the time, seemed to be going that way.[22]

MacEoin's 1971 letter to the committee directly implied that Hefferon was mistaken in taking such a view. However, it then emerged, in a closed-door session of the committee which became public thirty years later, that the views contained in the Chief of

Staff's letter, although signed by him, were not in fact his. He revealed in private that he had been *ordered* by the minister to state in the letter that the directive had no relevance to their inquiry.[23] The words were dictated to him by Jerry Cronin. The committee did not reveal this significant information at the time.[24] MacEoin was barred from giving evidence in person to the committee, but it is unlikely he could ever have voluntarily written the letter he had signed. He was obviously familiar with Gibbons's precise language, as revealed in the addendum, and this showed that the directive could be at least *indirectly* relevant to acquiring arms that would be suitable for possible distribution, apparently the view Hefferon had taken.

Another official document, released to the National Archives in 2002 and which appears to have gone hitherto unnoticed by researchers, establishes that the views that Minister for Defence Cronin imposed on his Chief of Staff in 1971 were actually the views of the Taoiseach, Jack Lynch. A personal *aide-mémoire* written and signed by Lynch in February 1971 set out the contents of a conversation he had had just hours previously with Patrick Hogan TD (FG), chairman of the Committee of Public Accounts inquiry into the Northern Relief Fund.[25] Hogan met Lynch to request access to the actual directive on behalf of his committee. He showed the Taoiseach the letter the committee had received from the Chief of Staff, which stated the directive had neither direct nor indirect relevance to any matters before the committee. In his private note of their meeting, Lynch stood fully behind the letter Cronin had dictated:

> I told Deputy Hogan that the directive was a verbal one and as interpreted by the Chief of Staff he wrote it out; that the directive was given in order to ensure a degree of preparedness of the Defence Forces in the event of the 'Forces of Law and Order' in the North being unable or unwilling to protect the community if they were attacked by hostile groups such as the UVF, who were, as far as we knew, well armed. The purpose

would be mercy missions but no action would be taken without a Government decision. As the Chief of Staff indicated, there was no authorization or even suggestion that arms would be purchased by anyone... it [the directive] would establish that no authorization was given in it to Captain Kelly to purchase arms or to do anything else, as he had claimed....

This is an important document. It is firstly significant that Lynch, in describing the directive in this way to Hogan, made no mention of the two important elements in it which had made it appear relevant to Hefferon, i.e., the statement that the government had 'agreed' to provide arms to Northern nationalists for their own defence, and the related order that surplus arms, ammunition and gas masks should be loaded on army lorries in Dublin and Athlone, ready for instant delivery to the North. Lynch's exclusion of these matters, as if they had never been stated, appears further to confirm the dropping of these elements from official policy. But it also means he was misrepresenting the directive to the Committee of Public Accounts inquiry chairman, at the same time that he was refusing the request that the committee inspect the directive for itself. Lynch gave the excuse that it would set a precedent for security-screened material. He endorsed the letter dictated by his Minister for Defence, with its seemingly false message that nothing in the directive was relevant to the inquiry. Hogan had been given the extra assurance of the Taoiseach that it contained no authorization for Captain Kelly to purchase arms or 'to do anything', whereas in fact the directive had instructed the Defence Forces to make arms available for distribution to civilians in Northern Ireland.

If nothing else, Hefferon's evidence that the directive altered his attitude to his subordinate officer's activities meant that, regardless of what way he had read it, its precise terms were indisputably relevant to the inquiry. It was relevant if it contradicted what Hefferon had stated – on that same day, 2 February 1971 – to the committee, and even more relevant if it supported him. As can be seen in the transcript of his exchanges with Garret FitzGerald,

Hefferon never claimed the directive *directly* authorized the importation of arms.[26] To him, its relevance seemed indirect: it provided possible authorization for the *acquisition* – rather than the purchase or importation – of untraceable arms which might be, and certainly in his view would be, more suitable than the regular army-issue surplus rifles otherwise to be used. The directive had set out that the Defence Forces were to make arms available and, with his intelligence remit, Hefferon felt a direct responsibility to ensure that the arms made available were fit for purpose.

Support for the view Hefferon took at the time, and for the proposition that the committee was misled over the directive, can be found in the later experience of one of its Labour Party members, Justin Keating TD. He resigned from the Committee of Public Accounts inquiry in 1971 in protest at the Fianna Fáil government's failure to provide access to the directive, and what he felt was the government's general failure to assist the inquiry. Keating's views have particular force, coming from a lifelong political opponent of both Haughey and Blaney. He was shown by the author, in the course of preparing a television documentary in 2001, photocopies of the State papers containing the directive. He reacted sharply. He was instantly struck by the passage in the addendum where Gibbons, referring to requests for arms and ammunition, uses the phrase 'the provision of which the government agreed'. Pointing to that reference, Keating was emphatic:

> There is no escaping from that. I mean this is a very serious document.… I do believe it contradicts flatly the line that there was no Government decision.… We were told it was irrelevant. Now I have seen it, now I know it was relevant.… When he [Minister Jerry Cronin]… instructed the Chief of Staff to tell us there was nothing material in it – that wasn't true, and it wasn't an accidental spreading of something that wasn't true, it was the

deliberate spreading of an untruth. And I'm afraid that's called a lie. And I don't have any way out of the conclusion that very important lies were told by very important people.... It does seem to me inescapable that for almost a third of a century, the apparatus of the State spread and defended a version of events that were untruthful. It [the directive] is quite sensational. It gob-smacked me. I think we have to re-think that third of a century of the most recent Irish history in the light of it.[27]

Keating, from whose extended interview only short extracts have previously been published, concluded that the directive was irreconcilable with the position taken by Lynch and his supporters down the decades since 1970. The prosecution of Haughey had been very incorrect and improper – 'in fact', he said, 'disgraceful'. He felt Blaney too had been unjustly treated. On the alleged conspiracy of Haughey and Blaney against Lynch, Keating said:

It wouldn't be a secret that Haughey and Jack Lynch were not friends. But to leap from that to saying that he set up a conspiracy which would have got Ireland into a war with Britain and would have toppled Jack Lynch, is a leap that the evidence does not warrant people making.

Keating also raised the specific question as to whether Lynch had told Attorney General Colm Condon SC of the directive's existence when he began the prosecution of Haughey, Blaney and their associates. His view was that Condon did not know of the directive; if he had known, Keating felt there could never have been charges: 'There couldn't have been. It was too disgraceful.' In summary, Keating's view of the 6 February 1970 directive was that it suggested the prosecution leading to the arms trials had been false; because of the way the directive's terms were kept from public view, he felt this must have been connived at by the Taoiseach, Jack Lynch, either with, or without, the knowledge and assistance of his Attorney General.

7

Berry's Warning

One of the many unresolved questions in the Arms Crisis concerns the moment when Jack Lynch and Jim Gibbons first learned of Captain Kelly's efforts to provide arms to Northern republicans. Lynch claimed to know nothing before 20 April 1970, while Gibbons denied any real awareness of Captain Kelly throughout the whole of 1969, and any direct knowledge before March 1970. However, the posthumous publication ten years later in *Magill* magazine of Peter Berry's *Diaries* raised the charge that both men were informed as early as October 1969 – six months earlier than Lynch ever acknowledged – and had failed to act on it.

The matter hinged on the meeting between Captain Kelly and the Northern Defence Committees on 4 October 1969 in Bailieboro, Co. Cavan. As indicated earlier, Kelly described that meeting as the genesis of the gun-running plan. At the time, the Special Branch were concerned that Kelly was offering money for guns to men known to be IRA members. Berry stated in *Magill* that he warned Lynch, and through him Gibbons, of Kelly's activities at the meeting, shortly after it took place. This raised doubts about whether Gibbons and Lynch were being truthful, and why, if Berry was correct, they took no action after being warned of an army captain's apparently seditious dealings. The denials from both Lynch and Gibbons that they knew anything at that time of what Captain Kelly was doing elevated the stakes, in historical terms, to issues of fundamental truthfulness.

The Bailieboro meeting first became an issue for Jim Gibbons when he was giving evidence at the arms trials in September–October 1970. Lynch was not a party to the criminal proceedings, so questions about his role did not arise until the Committee of Public Accounts inquiry the following year. Both Kelly and Hefferon testified at the second arms trial about the meeting with the Defence Committees, but Gibbons said he knew nothing of it before it came up at the trials themselves. Tom Finlay SC (for Captain Kelly) asked the former Minister for Defence if he remembered seeking from Colonel Hefferon a full report on the meeting, on foot of a request from the Taoiseach.

> Gibbons: No, I have no recollection of receiving any information about a meeting of defence committees in Bailieboro or taking any action as a result of any information I might have got.

> Finlay: Do you think this is something that may have slipped your memory?

> Gibbons: I say that I have no recollection of any information being conveyed to me by Colonel Hefferon or anyone else of a meeting of defence committees in Bailieboro.[1]

When Hefferon gave his own evidence several days later, he contradicted Gibbons directly. He told Finlay that at the end of October or early November 1969, he was told by Gibbons, his minister, of complaints from the Department of Justice about such a meeting. At this stage, Hefferon did not refer to any involvement of the Taoiseach. He said that Captain Kelly's name had been mentioned generally. After making inquiries, he reported back to the minister that Kelly was meeting members of the Defence Committees there, 'with my authority'.[2] Kelly, in evidence at the second arms trial, said that Gibbons told him the same thing when they met in March 1970. Kelly at that point also testified to the Taoiseach's involvement: he said that Gibbons told him the Taoiseach had been concerned over the Bailieboro meeting. Gibbons had said that the Taoiseach was called to Peter Berry's hospital bedside to hear complaints, and afterwards took up the complaints with him.[3] The shared evidence of Kelly and Hefferon about the Bailieboro meeting and its aftermath generated a straight conflict with the minister. The matter, however, was left unresolved at the trial, as nothing rested on it other than the credibility of those contesting the point.

When the subject of the Bailieboro meeting arose again the following February 1971, at the more expansive proceedings of the Committee of Public Accounts inquiry, Lynch's role became more of an issue. Kelly repeated his claim that Gibbons had told him the Taoiseach had been involved, and Hefferon explained for the first time, from his perspective, how the Taoiseach's involvement had come up:

> Mr. Gibbons, my Minister, asked to see me and told me that the Taoiseach had had a report from Mr. Berry that Captain Kelly had attended a meeting in Bailieboro, or had attended a meeting in Cavan – I do not think he was specific about the place – at which there were IRA people present, that he had there waved a wad of notes around, promising money to them.[4]

Hefferon said that because the complaint came through the Taoiseach, he regarded it as serious. He called Kelly in and questioned him; as a result, he was happy that nothing untoward had happened. He went back to Gibbons and reported that he was satisfied that there was no foundation for the complaints.[5] Gibbons once again claimed to committee member Garret FitzGerald TD (Fine Gael) that he knew nothing about the Bailieboro meeting:

> The meeting was mentioned at the arms trial. As I recall it, I said that I had no recollection of any description of having been told about that meeting. I have thought a good deal about that since; I racked my brains for any detail about it, the purpose of it, the

people who attended it, what was decided, and I am absolutely certain that I was never informed of the Bailieboro meeting, and that the reference to it in the Four Courts is the first reference that I can recall... there was no question of a complaint from the Taoiseach that I can recall – absolutely none.[6]

These assertions from Gibbons that neither he nor the Taoiseach knew anything of complaints about Captain Kelly's activities in Bailieboro ended the discussion in 1971, because again there was no way of resolving the conflict in evidence. Lynch, as Taoiseach, stayed above the fray and said nothing.

However, nine years later, in 1980, there came belated corroboration of Hefferon and Kelly's evidence about Bailieboro, from the unlikely source of the deceased Peter Berry. There was irony in their mutually consistent accounts, because in life, Berry and Hefferon had been long-time antagonists over security matters. Berry was the effective controller of the Garda Special Branch while Hefferon was head of the smaller department of Military Intelligence, and the pair had enjoyed a chilly relationship.[7] The single most remarkable disclosure in Berry's posthumously published *Diaries* was that on 17 October 1969, after the civil servant became very concerned over possible sedition within the Defence Forces, Lynch responded to an urgent request for an audience by coming to Berry's bedside in Mount Carmel Hospital in Dublin to hear of his anxieties. While receiving treatment, Berry said he alerted the Taoiseach to Special Branch reports of Captain Kelly's activities two weeks earlier at Bailieboro. He wrote:

> I am quite certain that I told him of Captain Kelly's prominent part in the Bailieboro meeting with known members of the IRA, of his possession of a wad of money, of his standing drinks and of a sum of money – £50,000 – that would be made available for the purchase of arms. I remember a conjecture of the Taoiseach as to where they could possibly get it and my suggestion that perhaps Mr. Y, or Mr. Z, two millionaires of the Taca group

[*wealthy supporters of Fianna Fáil*], might put up the money, and the Taoiseach's observation that those boys didn't give it up easily.[8]

Berry's account was striking in the way it tallied closely with the complaints that had reached Hefferon nine years earlier, even repeating phraseology such as Kelly displaying a 'wad' of money. Berry wished to emphasize that, despite his warning, Lynch had done nothing about the activities of Captain Kelly. He noted that their meeting was six months *before* the date on which Lynch later claimed that he got his first information about any gun-running.

Such was the force of Berry's account, delivered from the grave, that some months after its publication, in November 1980, Lynch, although retired as Taoiseach, felt it necessary to respond through a statement in Dáil Éireann. He agreed that he had gone to meet Berry in hospital on the date in question, but he denied all recollection of Berry telling him of Captain Kelly at Bailieboro, or of Kelly supposedly offering money to the IRA for guns. Lynch said Berry had not told him what he claimed. He said he must have been confused by the medication he was taking. He said the civil servant had been in the middle of distracting hospital procedures as they spoke, and while he may have *intended* to tell him of Captain Kelly in Bailieboro, he had not done so: 'I have no recollection whatever of his informing me of a meeting in Bailieboro some time previously in which a plot for alleged arms importation was set, and during which a sum of money was alleged to have passed for this purpose.'[9]

A remarkable aspect of Lynch's denial was that it ignored the apparent corroboration between the accounts of Hefferon, Kelly and Berry. Lynch made no reference to the fact that Hefferon had described nine years earlier how Gibbons had told him that the Taoiseach himself had asked him to make inquiries, following complaints from Berry. Berry explicitly cited this in his *Diaries*, giving chapter and verse on Hefferon's evidence from the Committee of Public Accounts' transcript of proceedings.

He particularly noted how Hefferon's evidence tallied with his own claim of having complained personally to Lynch. He concluded emphatically:

> No person with a scrap of intelligence could doubt that the Taoiseach was made aware by me on 17 October – the date of my medical tests is verifiable in the hospital records – of information of a most serious kind in relation to a plot to import arms and that he avoided making any more than a cursory inquiry.[10]

Berry's frustration was evident, and had good cause. The evidence is entirely persuasive not only that he succeeded in explaining to Lynch at Mount Carmel Hospital what he understood Kelly to be engaged in at Bailieboro, but also that Lynch *did* act on the information, and asked Gibbons to investigate. The accounts of the two security chiefs dovetailed convincingly, and in the process explained something that might otherwise appear unlikely: how it was that the Taoiseach ever became involved in processing the complaint Berry was making. Gibbons, it seems clear, had given false evidence to both the arms trials and the Committee of Public Accounts inquiry, and Lynch, on the evidence, was no more truthful when he addressed the Dáil in November 1980. Ryle Dwyer later offered a tongue-in-cheek explanation for the Taoiseach's denial of the conversation with Berry on 17 October 1969: he wrote that Lynch was suffering from 'political amnesia'.[11]

The emphatic nature of Lynch's denial of Berry's claims has generated a familiar conflict of analysis among writers, one in many ways typical of the whole Arms Crisis. Even those such as Ryle Dwyer, Ó Beacháin, Downey and O'Brien, who have accepted that Berry did give Lynch important information,[12] have been slow to draw the appropriate conclusions. Others, in particular Arnold, Keogh and Collins, have been more sympathetic to Lynch in their

analysis, and have advanced a variety of reasons for minimizing
the importance of the issue. The most emphatic in rejecting Berry's
claims to have told Lynch of Captain Kelly's role at Bailieboro has
been Dermot Keogh, in his biography of Lynch. Keogh described
what he saw as a straight clash of evidence between Berry and
Lynch, and judged that 'on the balance of probability, Lynch is more
likely to have had the clearer recollection of what was said', because
Berry was in the middle of a hospital procedure.[13] This conclusion
might have merit if the issue in fact was just a straight conflict
between the recollections of the two men, but Keogh failed to take
into account how Hefferon's entirely separate evidence, nine years
previously, corroborated what Berry had said. Hefferon, backed up
by the evidence of Captain Kelly, described how Gibbons told him
that Lynch had raised with him *precisely the issues* Berry insisted
had caused him to bring the Taoiseach urgently to the hospital.

Bruce Arnold and Stephen Collins have accepted that Lynch
went on to raise the relevant matters with Gibbons, but attach no
great importance to this, although it appears to mean that they
regard Gibbons's evidence to both the Central Criminal Court
and the Committee of Public Accounts inquiry, and Lynch's 1980
statement in Dáil Éireann, as either false or mistaken. Arnold felt
Berry over-estimated the importance of his information, as at the
time he had no evidence of the involvement of ministers. He said
Berry, on 17 October 1969,

> ...had summoned the head of the Government for a meeting
> that was catastrophically unsuccessful, in that it conveyed no
> substantial information for the head of Government. If what
> had happened mattered, it was for the security forces and the
> relevant Ministers to address. What Lynch was told was either
> unsupported by the necessary intelligence or was imperfectly
> explained.... It seemed to involve centrally a junior Army
> officer whose reported behaviour was giving cause for alarm.
> Lynch appears to have seen it like that. Quite properly, he was
> prepared to leave the matter in the hands of the formidable head

of the State's police and intelligence forces, together with the Defence Minister.[14]

This outwardly plausible attempt to explain Lynch's attitude would have more force if Lynch had not denied in the Dáil any memory of being told of Captain Kelly's activities, or of the Bailieboro meeting itself, and thereby left unexplained how he could ever have asked Gibbons to investigate these matters. What was put to Hefferon about Captain Kelly's behaviour had not been, in Arnold's phrase, 'imperfectly explained', but reflected closely what Berry had complained about to Lynch. The idea that there was no substantial or serious issue involved in Kelly's allegedly unauthorized activity in Bailieboro flies in the face of the evidence and appears disingenuous.

Stephen Collins, for his part, argued that Lynch had recalled the meeting with Berry 'only in general terms'.[15] This is contradicted by the record of Lynch's Dáil speech on the matter in November 1980, which contained references that were not at all general, and matched Berry in terms of detailed recall.[16] Collins appeared to accept that Berry may have got his point across effectively in Mount Carmel, but mused, on the basis of 'a private source', that Lynch 'was not sure how seriously to treat Berry's claims', because he was being told the man was 'far too conspiratorial and had an obsession with republicans and reds under the bed, so he was not fully convinced'.[17] The unstated implication here is that Collins and his source accepted that Lynch had received Berry's complaint, and so had lied to or – at best – thoroughly misled the Dáil in November 1980.

Another possibility that merits consideration is whether Gibbons and Lynch, mistaken though their statements appeared to be, could perhaps have forgotten both the substance of, and the sequel to, Berry's complaints in October 1969. Apart from the somewhat memorable details of treasonable activity – an Irish army officer offering money for guns to the IRA – another not easily forgettable aspect was the way Hefferon, Kelly's commanding officer, had debunked the complaint. It seems certain that Lynch, having asked for an investigation, must subsequently have been given some report on the matter; this could only have been to the effect that Hefferon – and Gibbons – had concluded there was no cause for concern. Hefferon had actually said that Kelly was in Bailieboro acting on his instructions. That all this could have escaped Lynch's memory, especially when the term 'Jimmy Kelly of Army Intelligence' appeared in front of him in Garda reports on 20 and 21 April 1970 describing an apparent gun-running attempt, is not credible. It is not realistic to imagine that the Taoiseach failed to recall how an officer with the same name had come to his attention the previous autumn, suspected by Berry of offering money for guns to the IRA. Nor is he likely to have failed to recall that Gibbons, after consulting Hefferon, must have assured him at the time that there was nothing untoward about what Kelly was doing.

If one assumes the Taoiseach was, as he claimed, genuinely opposed to what Captain Kelly was doing, then it is much more likely that he would have recalled Berry's alarm over the army officer, and how he had asked his Minister for Defence to investigate. Looking back, he would have had every reason at that point to suspect not just Hefferon, for his apparently false assurance over Kelly's activities, but also his own minister, Gibbons, for accepting Hefferon's word, when to do so had led to such embarrassment for the government. In other words, he would have had every reason to be suspicious of Gibbons and Hefferon.

So far as Gibbons's memory is concerned, the evidence is, if it were possible, even less in his favour than in Lynch's case. His evidence in the arms trials was that he learned from Hefferon in the course of January–February 1970, and later from Captain Kelly himself, that the junior officer really *was* engaged in providing guns for Northern republicans, and intended to assist the Northern Defence Committees in importing such arms. Kelly said he was even prepared to leave the army so he could help the Northerners. On getting that information – whether in

February, as Hefferon claimed, or March as Gibbons maintained – there seems little or no possibility that Gibbons could have failed to recall either the Taoiseach's concerns about the army captain the previous November, or the reassurance he as minister had received subsequently from Hefferon. In addition, there was the embarrassment of having determined himself that there was nothing for the Taoiseach to be concerned about. Yet still he did not – according to his own evidence – tell Lynch how Kelly later fully confirmed to him that his interest in giving money for guns to republicans had not been a figment of Berry's imagination, but the beginnings of an active and very real plan. All this is to assume, for argument's sake, that Gibbons's disapproval of the arms importation plan was genuine. Were that so, serious recriminations with both Hefferon and Kelly would have been unavoidable by early March at the latest, including an abject *mea culpa* to the Taoiseach, followed by a swift end to the gun-running project. None of this happened.

This question of Lynch's encounter with Berry at Mount Carmel Hospital, and what was or was not communicated, has been extensively considered in the literature on the Arms Crisis, but it is argued here that its fundamental importance for the credibility of Gibbons and Lynch has been inadequately recognized. The Taoiseach and his Minister for Defence not only failed to act at the time, but later pretended that they had never got the warning and therefore had no anxiety over Kelly's arms activity. Their later disowning of Kelly's attempted gun-running is difficult to reconcile with their joint prior awareness about Kelly, or with their *laissez-faire* attitude clearly in evidence as late as the weekend of 18 April 1970. The strategic importance in the Arms Crisis of the encounter between Lynch and Berry at Mount Carmel Hospital is difficult to overstate; it erodes Gibbons's and Lynch's credibility in a manner that appears – just in itself – little short of devastating.

8

Gibbons's Deceits

James Gibbons's importance in the Arms Crisis saga is two-fold. Firstly, it derives from his position as Minister for Defence: this left him in ultimate command of Captain Kelly and his boss in Military Intelligence, Colonel Hefferon; also, as minister, he was the one person in a position to legalize an importation of arms for the Defence Forces. Once a criminal prosecution was launched, the question of legality and illegality became central. The second reason for Gibbons's importance is more oblique: it is that he became Jack Lynch's closest ally sometime after the crisis began to break on 20 April 1970. The bonding between Gibbons and the Taoiseach at that time proved equal to all subsequent shocks, and allowed the government to survive the political turbulence of the period. The issues that surround Gibbons centre on what he knew, and when he knew it – and, by the same token, on what information he did, or did not, pass on to the Taoiseach. His consistent claim, little short of spectacular, was that he passed on nothing.

The reason Gibbons's silence in regard to the Taoiseach should amount to something spectacular is because other ministers suffered for their alleged failure to tell the Taoiseach what was going on, yet he was uniquely spared. In the immediate aftermath of the second arms trial, Lynch's accusation against Haughey was that he had failed to keep him informed,[1] and a similar alleged failure to pass information to the Taoiseach appears to have been a factor in the forced resignation on 4 May 1970 of Mícheál Ó Móráin as Minister for Justice. Gibbons suffered no such disciplining, despite by the end acknowledging a level of acquaintance with Captain Kelly's activities far beyond that of either Haughey or Ó Móráin, and despite never even attempting to deny his failure to inform Lynch. It is hardly coincidental that this almost inexplicable lack of communication from Gibbons also proved the salvation of Lynch; the phenomenon of the mute Gibbons became the Taoiseach's indispensable shield, his insulation from any contaminating knowledge about his ministers' various activities.

Throughout the period, Lynch's support for Gibbons did not waver, even when it was clearly seen that he had been left in the dark by his Minister for Defence. The support held firm on 5 May 1970 in the face of the anonymous message on Garda-headed notepaper that Fine Gael leader Liam Cosgrave brought to him, naming Gibbons as one of the conspirators. It was unaffected just days later on 9 May by a statement from Captain Kelly that his minister had known of and approved of all his actions. And while on 30 May 1970 Lynch must have been disappointed by the statement taken by gardaí from Colonel Michael Hefferon, in which he revealed how much advance knowledge Gibbons had of the attempted gun-running, Lynch's adherence to his former Minister for Defence, since promoted by him to the more senior Agriculture and Fisheries portfolio, remained steadfast.[2]

Gibbons's role in the Arms Crisis was a source of disagreement from the first moments of political turbulence on 6 May 1970, and five decades later it remained equally contested. Despite his becoming Lynch's main bulwark against his critics, few writers sympathetic to Lynch have been able to present a coherent picture of Gibbons's conduct. Even Bruce Arnold, who viewed Lynch as the wronged character in the drama and accepted that Gibbons's role was 'crucial' in the whole affair, described the minister as 'destabilized' and someone who 'floundered'. According to Arnold, Lynch himself identified Gibbons as 'unreliable, and intimidated by colleagues'. Yet Arnold was unable to fill out the picture, and ultimately judged that 'the full story of Gibbons's role will never be told'.[3] Historian Dermot Keogh, another staunch defender of Lynch, lamented the 'weakness' of Gibbons, whom he said 'may have continued to see himself as a junior minister, [and] was simply bullied and intimidated by Blaney and Haughey'.[4] Journalist Stephen Collins, another writer sympathetic to Lynch, found himself unable to resolve the innumerable question marks over Gibbons's behaviour, and could come only to the somewhat limp conclusion that 'there has always been a mystery about the precise role played by Gibbons'.[5] Such conclusions from analysts generally favourably inclined towards Jack Lynch, while neither satisfactory nor convincing, tend at least to confirm indirectly that in the key disputed realm of what the Taoiseach knew or did not know in the lead-up to the Arms Crisis, Gibbons was his point of vulnerability.

The Kilkenny farmer, father of eleven children, is often represented as a junior and vulnerable member of Lynch's cabinet, prone, as Keogh suggested above, to being bullied by more senior colleagues. But Gibbons in 1969 was an experienced politician, intelligent, and not at all short on self-confidence. He was a year older than Charles Haughey, two years younger than Neil Blaney; he had been in the Dáil for thirteen years, and had served as a junior minister for four years in the Department of Finance, first under Lynch as minister, then Haughey. He had qualified to study medicine in University College Dublin before giving it up after two years for politics. The only thing junior about Gibbons in 1969 was the portfolio he held – Defence was one of the more lowly cabinet posts.

Yet the unlikely proposition that Gibbons was being bullied by more senior ministers was not discouraged by the man himself. He told the first arms trial that he had sent rifles to Dundalk in early April 1970 only because he was afraid that if he did not, Blaney might do something 'rash'.[6] His action followed a phone call from Blaney raising alarm over rioting in Ballymurphy in

Belfast, and Gibbons actually encouraged Garret FitzGerald at the Committee of Public Accounts inquiry in 1971 to believe Blaney may have dominated him.[7] The real reason for sending the rifles, he claimed implausibly, 'was the placation of Mr Blaney'.[8] This self-demeaning explanation for his own action as Minister for Defence also hid the fact, confirmed only thirty years later in 2001, that the sending of the rifles so expeditiously was possible only because he, as minister, had ordered two months earlier that weapons be deployed on lorries for instant availability. Gibbons had planned for precisely the emergency circumstances that appeared to have arisen in Ballymurphy on 2 April 1970.

What seems evident is that Gibbons, more than any other figure in the 1970 Arms Crisis excluding Jack Lynch himself, holds the key to unlocking the saga's numerous conflicts of evidence and disputed conspiracies. Unlike in Lynch's case, Gibbons's role is relatively extensively documented through his four sworn witness statements, his evidence and cross-examination at the two arms trials, his further detailed questioning at the Committee of Public Accounts inquiry in 1971, and a variety of contributions from him to Dáil debates during 1970 and 1971.

His role – arguably more closely scrutinized in this book than in any treatment hitherto – has always created difficulties for proponents of the theory of a Haughey–Blaney conspiracy against Lynch. While there is no evidence that he personally instituted the gun-running project, all the documentation suggests that until 20 April 1970, as Minister for Defence, he was intimately connected with government colleagues Haughey and Blaney in preparing for Northern contingencies. The evidence associates him more closely than any other minister with the hidden, more militaristic side of Lynch's policy on Northern Ireland, already documented above. He not only knew of Captain Kelly's plans to import arms, but the evidence is that he was invited at pivotal moments to contribute to the planning. Facts such as these provoked Peter Maguire SC (for Haughey) to outline to the jury at the second arms trial his theory of 'two Mr Gibbons':

It seems to me, gentlemen, that there are really two Mr. Gibbons. There is the Mr. Gibbons up to the time this case started, and the Mr. Gibbons since the case did start. I think it is hard to find anywhere – and I mean anywhere – anything convincing in his actions and his deeds consistent with what he now says was his view of what was happening at the time.[9]

It may even be argued, based on the analysis below, that a *third* Gibbons persona can be detected in the narrative, in the person of the less guarded, more expansive figure who appeared eventually before the Committee of Public Accounts in April 1971, six months after the trials were over.

Both the early Gibbons and the later Gibbons were quite different from the harassed witness who, in between, gave evidence at the arms trials. In the early period, before April 1970, evidence for Gibbons's close working relationship with Neil Blaney lies in the crucial meeting that he had with Captain Kelly on 4 March, arranged, according to Gibbons's own account, at Blaney's specific request. At this encounter Kelly told his minister face-to-face about his efforts to import arms.[10] This transmission of information from army officer to minister obviously happened with Blaney's blessing; in asking Gibbons to meet Kelly, he had to be aware that his government colleague was going to be briefed on the project Lynch's allies would later deem to be illicit, unauthorized and seditious. But quite separately from this meeting with the junior arms officer, Kelly, Gibbons was always likely to hear of the gun-running plans from Hefferon, who advised him on intelligence and who met him regularly for this purpose.

There is no evidence from any source that either Blaney or Haughey ever told Kelly to keep his mouth shut, or to avoid telling either his superior officer or his minister that he was – as his critics claimed – being enlisted to run guns for subversives. It was as a matter of normal routine that Kelly kept his commanding officer informed on what he was doing; Hefferon in turn reported regularly on Kelly's actions to the minister – although Gibbons sought, with little success, to deny that Hefferon did this. The circle of information was complete, and – critically – it included both Gibbons and Hefferon. There are just two possible explanations for the fact that Blaney and Haughey permitted this to happen. One is that both Gibbons and Hefferon were part of the supposed plot to undermine Lynch's policy on Northern Ireland; the other, more likely explanation, is that there was no plot, and no conspiracy against Lynch, and Gibbons and Hefferon were knowledgeable simply because of their positions, and because the project could not proceed without them.

In the witness box at the first arms trial in September 1970, Gibbons conceded that he had been told of the attempted arms importation six to eight weeks before it reached its final manifestation at Dublin Airport in mid-April. He agreed that he had not acted to stop it. This raised the question – which he was never able to answer convincingly – that if he knew something untoward was going on, why did he not tell the Taoiseach, who said he learned nothing before 20 April 1970? Gibbons's response to this charge was, in part, that although Captain Kelly had told him of the importation plans, as minister he knew nothing of the specifics of the operation, and he did not know precisely what Kelly's role was. He claimed it was also his intention to have Kelly transferred to another part of the public service before the importation could happen. It was an unconvincing explanation that still did not explain why he did not tell the Taoiseach what he agreed he *did* know about Kelly. Nor did it explain how the gun-running would be any more acceptable if Kelly was conducting it from a different part of the public service. Given his manifest failure to halt the project, why was he not sacked by the Taoiseach along with Haughey and Blaney? These are serious questions that have been raised repeatedly in various accounts of the Arms Crisis,[11] as Lynch retained Gibbons as a senior minister in each administration he headed thereafter.

★

While lingering doubts over Gibbons's truthfulness have been central to any analysis of the Arms Crisis, the release of the State papers for 1970 in January 2001 has made possible some firmer conclusions about the former Minister for Defence. Ultimately, the verdict is harsh. It is the result of comparing and contrasting some of Gibbons's earliest accounts, as in his four witness statements made to gardaí in May and June 1970 – statements not available publicly before 2001 – with his much later and much franker evidence at the Committee of Public Accounts inquiry almost a year later in April 1971. In between were his various Dáil statements, and his extensive questioning at the arms trials by some of the brightest young barristers of their day, notably Tom Finlay and Niall McCarthy, later Supreme Court judges. A particular question arises over how Gibbons permitted Lynch, in his presence, to give information to the Dáil on 9 May and 14 May 1970 which Gibbons knew was misinformed. On these two occasions, the Taoiseach effectively denied that public money had been used to buy the arms at the centre of the crisis, while his newly promoted Minister for Agriculture and Fisheries sat mute in the chamber nearby, seemingly complicit in Lynch's misleading of the Dáil.

What is striking about Gibbons's utterances generally is how much his memory improved over the eleven-month period from May 1970 to April 1971. A comparison, as is made below, between his witness statements in May and June 1970, and what he told the Committee of Public Accounts inquiry in April 1971, produces startling results. In addition, his extensive evidence at the two arms trials allows researchers to track in time his stumbling attempts at veracity. The analysis presented below relies almost exclusively on Gibbons's and Lynch's own statements; it takes no account of the numerous instances where both Kelly and Hefferon contradicted Gibbons on key facts and conversations. It considers what Gibbons said to the Garda investigators, to the courts and to the Committee of Public Accounts inquiry, and what he did, or more importantly did not, say to the Taoiseach. It makes the assumption, based on the public record, that when he withheld

facts from the gardaí or the Central Criminal Court, that he likewise did not tell Lynch. Lynch's public position was that he knew
nothing until Peter Berry came to him on 20 April 1970. He got no
information from Gibbons, nor, when the facts began to emerge,
did they generate in the Taoiseach's mind even the slightest
suspicion of his colleague.

Gibbons's first two Garda statements were taken on 18 and
22 May 1970, before any charges were issued and when Gibbons,
although already promoted by Lynch within the government,
could not be certain who – if anyone – might eventually face
criminal charges.[12] His own fate had to be uncertain. Although he
would later reveal extensive knowledge of Captain James Kelly's
activities going back to autumn 1969, little of this is evident in his
early statements. Much of what he knew emerged only when the
trials were over and the Committee of Public Accounts inquiry
got under way in 1971.

His first statement on 18 May 1970, in keeping with this, was
short and vague, offering little to the investigating officers; it also,
however, contained a reference to the discredit of Captain Kelly
that was untrue, and known to Gibbons to be untrue. This was
his suggestion that Army Intelligence had been 'very dissatisfied
with Captain Kelly's performance and failure to report over long
periods'.[13] Any such dissatisfaction could have emanated only from
Hefferon, the head of Military Intelligence and the officer to whom
Kelly had been ordered to report personally and exclusively over
the previous six months. But Hefferon had already told Gibbons
he was not dissatisfied with Kelly's reporting. The minister had
telephoned Hefferon on 8 May while preparing his Dáil speech of
that same date, to be told in answer to his query that Hefferon had
no complaints about Kelly, that he got reports from him 'any time
I wanted them'.[14] Gibbons ignored this and stated the contrary.

More seriously, however, Gibbons failed to mention in any of his
first three statements to gardaí in May 1970 what he later admitted:
that he knew early on of at least one trip to the Continent by Kelly
for suspected arms purchases. This began to emerge, significantly

only *after* charges had been preferred on 27 and 28 May, in his fourth statement on 8 June 1970. In none of his four Garda statements did he reveal that he knew from Kelly from at least the first half of March 1970 – and according to Hefferon much earlier – that he intended to resign from the army so that he could help the Northern Defence Committees secure arms for their defence. Gibbons admitted this first in evidence to the first arms trial in September 1970; it was not something he had told Lynch, either in March 1970 or later. Another fact he did not reveal to gardaí before the trials was that the only reason Kelly was still in the army in April 1970 was because he, as minister, had directed Hefferon not to process a resignation form which Kelly had filled out and submitted at least two months earlier, by mid-February.

Gibbons also did not tell gardaí in any of his four witness statements that Captain Kelly had told him – again on 30 April 1970, according to what he told the Committee of Public Accounts on 21 April 1971 – the precise location in Co. Cavan where he intended to store the arms he was bringing in. Gibbons kept this to himself despite extensive cross-examinations in both arms trials, and waited a further four months, until February 1971, before revealing it. At the second trial, Hefferon's evidence was at variance with this: he said that Gibbons was told by him, not by Kelly, where the arms would be stored. Hefferon said he told him around the end of March 1970, and added, in a convincing flourish in the witness box, that the minister, on hearing the location, had 'smiled, and quoted a well-known line of poetry'.[15] Gibbons, who had already given his evidence at the trial when Hefferon said this, chose to deny Hefferon's account when he was questioned under oath six months later at the Committee of Public Accounts. However, he conceded for the first time that he *had* been told where the arms were going to be stored.[16] He claimed he was told by Kelly, not Hefferon, and gave a date that was one month later than Hefferon had said, on 30 April.

The claim of a later date was important, because by the end of April the attempted importation had already failed and was arguably a matter of history; Gibbons appeared to be suggesting that by that stage his knowledge was just a detail, and not worthy of the authorities' attention. Nonetheless, he was admitting, belatedly, that the supposed conspirator, Kelly, had told him of the location at which he intended to store the imported arms. Even if this had happened as late as 30 April 1970, given the context of alleged sedition, it could not be classified as unimportant. It was something Gibbons might have been expected to disclose, but the evidence of his own testimony is that he did not, neither to the gardaí nor to either arms trial. There is nothing to suggest that he told Jack Lynch.

Another important matter not disclosed in Gibbons's first three statements, prior to the prosecution being initiated, was that Kelly had told him, weeks before the crisis broke, that he had already tried and failed in an attempt to bring the arms in through Dublin Port. Had Gibbons mentioned this earlier, it would have raised immediate issues as to why, as Minister for Defence, he did not at that point stop the junior officer in his tracks. The information was partially revealed in Gibbons's 8 June statement to Special Branch officers Detective Inspector Ned O'Dea and Detective Inspector Patrick Doocey; it was greatly developed, to Gibbons's considerable discomfiture, under the pressure of cross-examination in the two arms trials.[17]

Gibbons's second witness statement, made to Chief Superintendent John Fleming on 28 May 1970, contained a further instance where he was economical with the truth. At a meeting on 23 April 1970 in the ministerial office of Neil Blaney, attended by himself, Captain Kelly and Colonel Hefferon, which Gibbons said he attended at Blaney's request, there was some conversation about the breakdown of the importation plan the previous weekend. Gibbons stated: 'I learned nothing about any other participants in the plan or anything about how or by whom it was carried on.' Gibbons, according to his own evidence four months later at the first arms trial, could have told Fleming, but did not, that at that point he already knew quite a lot about the plan. In September 1970 he would reveal that he had discussed it with Kelly at the end of March, when he was told that a planned consignment into Dublin Port had failed. He had also learned at that point that a further sea shipment – probably, he said, from the port of Trieste – was being contemplated. He disclosed none of this to his Taoiseach, according to his own and Lynch's evidence.

Even more strikingly, only when he gave evidence at the Committee of Public Accounts inquiry on 21 April 1971 did a relaxed Gibbons reveal that he knew 'beyond a shadow of a doubt' on Friday evening, 17 April 1970, that it was his own officer, the same Captain Kelly who had told him he intended to assist the Northern Defence Committees to bring in arms, who was in Vienna, and now seeking to fly a consignment of arms into Dublin Airport. This was something else Gibbons had not previously revealed, neither to investigating gardaí, in his evidence to the two arms trials, or to Lynch. The importance of this particular failure to disclose was that, had Gibbons revealed at any point between May and September 1970 that he knew the officer in question, knew his plans, and had discussed those plans with him, once again it would have highlighted the fact that he took no action to stop the importation.

All Gibbons did that Friday evening, 17 April, according to his own evidence, was retire to his Kilkenny farm for the weekend. He did attempt at one point to suggest that he may have gone to see Haughey on the Friday evening, but his own earlier statement in the Book of Evidence contradicted this, and it was discounted by prosecution counsel.[18] Gibbons left Dublin for his Kilkenny home on the Friday knowing 'perfectly well', as he declared the following year, who was involved. His departmental Secretary, Seán Ó Cearnaigh, had told him; Gibbons remembered it as 'a key date', specifically because it was the very moment he realized Kelly was involved.[19] Had this come out before the 1970 arms trials, rather than in April 1971, it would have shown that for the second time in three weeks, at a pivotal moment, he made no attempt to either stop the gun-running or see that someone else under his command did. At that point, the guns and ammunition were due to come in over the weekend. Monday would have been too late.

There is no evidence – and no claim has been made – that Gibbons sought to inform the Taoiseach either on the Friday evening, 17 April, or indeed at any time prior to his public disclosure at the Committee of Public Accounts the following year, that Gibbons knew personally the officer in Vienna trying to bring in arms. Although they both denied it, this of course was the same Captain Kelly he and Lynch had discussed six months earlier, when the officer came under suspicion by Peter Berry and the Special Branch for his activities in Co. Cavan. Even after a weekend on the farm, on the following Monday Gibbons did not go to Lynch, but went instead to Charles Haughey. According to his own account of their meeting, which is dealt with extensively in Chapter 11, Gibbons pleaded with Haughey to have the importation stopped.

Meanwhile, it was left to Berry himself, earlier that same Monday, to inform the Taoiseach of what was going on. Berry brought to Lynch a Garda report on the involvement of Revenue officials at Dublin Airport in the events of the weekend, including evidence linking Haughey to the arms importation. He followed this with another Garda report next day, this time implicating Blaney.[20] In all this time, Gibbons, by his own account and also that of Lynch, appears to have told the Taoiseach nothing. At a critical moment, once again he neither said anything, nor did anything, to intervene. All of this is evident only because of what Gibbons finally admitted knowing a year later, in evidence to the Committee of Public Accounts inquiry that has not hitherto received the attention it deserves.[21]

Gibbons's witness statement on 8 June 1970, given to detectives O'Dea and Doocey, revealed something else that he had failed to volunteer in his three previous statements: this was his meeting with Charles Haughey about the arms importation on Monday, 20 April 1970. This emerged only when gardaí specifically prompted Gibbons on 8 June, asking whether he had had a conversation with Haughey on that day. The relevant exchange in the 8 June statement is as follows:

> Q 5: On Monday the 20th April 70, was Mr. Haughey speaking to you about Captain Kelly being in Vienna. What was the conversation? Did Mr. Haughey or yourself say that the whole thing would have to be called off?

> A: I spoke to Mr. Haughey and told him of the telephone call from Dublin Airport to the Dept. of Defence asking if the Army expected delivery of a consignment of arms, and of other calls to Transport and Power, etc. Mr. Haughey said the dogs in the street are barking it. *I do not remember any reference to Captain Kelly's being in Vienna.* [emphasis added] I asked Mr. Haughey if he could stop the operation. He said: I will stop it for a month. I said: For God's sake stop it altogether.[22]

This account of Gibbons's conversation with Haughey became a major issue at the second arms trial. It is firstly an issue as to why he failed to refer to such an important event in his three earlier statements. He cannot have been unaware that the meeting was highly relevant to the Garda investigation – and of no small interest to the Taoiseach – yet he kept silent about it in his statements on 18 May, on 22 May and again on 28 May 1970. Eventually, it came out when prompted by gardaí on 8 June; this was of course *after* charges had been issued.

When thus forced to deal with the matter, Gibbons made yet another highly questionable statement: this was the seemingly innocuous remark, 'I do not remember any reference to Captain Kelly's being in Vienna.' This reflected Gibbons's stated position at that time, which offered no awareness of precisely who the figure causing ripples in Vienna was. But his words were far from innocuous. In the context of what Gibbons later revealed he knew, it is not credible that there would be no mention of Kelly in his conversation with Haughey on Monday, 20 April. The reason is that Haughey and Gibbons had an agreed plan about Captain Kelly which had just fallen asunder. It had been drawn up to avoid exactly the situation they found themselves in on 20 April. The plan was to find a new job for Kelly elsewhere in the public service, outside the army. Haughey had been helping Gibbons with this, but progress, Gibbons claimed, had been frustratingly slow.[23] The whole intention, in Gibbons's sworn evidence at the arms trials, had been to shift Kelly from the army *before* he could bring in arms.[24] Gibbons had been waiting for about a month for Haughey to come up with this new job, the Minister for Finance having responsibility for the public service. Their joint plan was Gibbons's stated and only reason for not calling a halt sooner to Kelly's activities. Now time had run out.

Kelly was in Vienna doing exactly what he had told Gibbons he would do – seeking to import arms for the Northern Defence Committees – and the balloon had gone up, while he was still an Irish army officer. In these circumstances, the idea that neither minister would make reference to Kelly being in Vienna makes little or no sense. It would of course be plausible if Gibbons was not aware that it *was* Kelly – as appeared to be the situation prior to April 1971. Once again, the evasion in his 8 June statement becomes visible in hindsight only because of the greatly enhanced memory Gibbons had recovered and felt able to display in April 1971.

The Gibbons–Lynch soap opera, whereby the minister repeatedly (by his own account) withheld important information from the Taoiseach yet miraculously retained his full confidence, reached its highest point of visibility in an episode where Gibbons's silence allowed the Taoiseach to mislead the Dáil over the use of public money by Captain Kelly to buy arms. By his own account, Gibbons knew from 30 April 1970 that publicly voted money from the Northern Relief Fund had been used by Kelly to buy guns. Yet twice over the following two weeks, on 9 and 14 May 1970, Gibbons stood by and allowed Lynch to appear to deny this in the

Dáil. Once again this was a situation where another very belated admission came from Gibbons at the time of the Committee of Public Accounts inquiry in 1971, indicating what he had known and when he had known it.

The record suggests that Gibbons expressly misled Garda investigators on the matter of the use of the Northern Relief Fund to buy arms; he then compounded these deceptions with further questionable evidence to the Committee of Public Accounts inquiry. Nine days after Gibbons claimed to learn where the money to buy arms had come from, Lynch told the Dáil on 9 May, with Gibbons present in the chamber, that it had been established for him that all monies spent by the Department of Defence were spent 'as voted for by this House'. 'Therefore,' he said, 'I do not know where the monies came from that paid for these goods, if they were paid for.'[25] Significantly, Lynch appears from this answer to have made inquiries from the Department of Defence as well as the Department of Finance, and Gibbons was still Minister for Defence at this time.[26] On 14 May, in impromptu exchanges at Question Time in the Dáil, Lynch told Labour deputy James Tully that he had made specific inquiries as to the source of the money, and had asked if it had been paid. He was 'absolutely assured' that the money did not come from any State funds, but as to where it did come from, he did not know.[27] Later that day in his closing speech to the Dáil debate, Lynch added:

> I made specific inquiries as to whether any monies could have been voted or could have been paid out of Exchequer funds or out of any public funds in respect of a consignment of arms of the size we have been dealing with and I am assured that there was not nor could not have been.[28]

This statement proved mistaken. Gibbons was in the Dáil chamber on both occasions when Lynch made these various statements, and failed, either publicly or privately, to correct the record or have Lynch correct it.[29]

twice misleading the Dáil, Gibbons himself went on to mislead Garda investigators. His second statement on 22 May, responding to Garda questions, contained two answers which, having regard to what he admitted later, can only be viewed as false. Eighteen questions in total were put to him by Chief Superintendent John Fleming; three of them concerned funding. Two of the questions provided an opportunity for Gibbons to set the record straight:

Q 10: Did you not think it strange that Captain Kelly was going direct to the Dept. of Finance for cash, instead of to your Dept., or to his superiors?

A: I had no knowledge of Captain Kelly having gone to the Department of Finance for funds.

Q 14: Were you aware of the purposes for which the Grant-in-Aid Fund for the North was established?

A: Apart from knowing that this Fund existed, I had no further knowledge of it.[35]

Neither of these responses reflected what Gibbons knew at the time he was being questioned, or what he had known from 30 April onwards, according to his own evidence to the second arms trial, and to the Committee of Public Accounts in 1971. His answers appear to show a further attempt to conceal data from the authorities. Regarding the answer to Question 10, Gibbons had known for at least two weeks at that point that Kelly had used money to buy arms from a fund known to be disbursed through the Department of Finance.

The answer to Question 14 was even more questionable, judging by what Gibbons told the Committee of Public Accounts on 22 April 1971. He said then that when Captain Kelly admitted using money from the fund to buy arms, he knew immediately the significance of this. His reaction was 'extreme shock'; he realized it meant that the money had been 'procured in some illicit manner' from the grant-in-aid.[36] None of this shock or awareness featured in his answer to gardaí questions on 22 May 1970, when he claimed to know nothing of the fund except that it existed. The truth was that he had a special and informed knowledge of the fund and how it was used. He revealed this partially to the second arms trial in October 1970,[37] but failed in the meantime – on the basis of his own account – to tell the truth either to the gardaí or to the Taoiseach.

It seems that Gibbons's reticence over what he knew about the arms funding may also have influenced the charges that led to the arms trials. The files show that, at the time, there was a distinct possibility that extra charges might be laid. Fleming and his Garda colleagues devoted considerable time and attention in the early summer of 1970 to the investigation of funding issues raised in the statements of Department of Finance official Tony Fagan.[38] Peter Berry on 21 May told officials in Allied Irish Bank that criminal charges 'were in contemplation'.[39] It would be difficult to argue that the failure in the end to lay such charges was entirely uninfluenced by Gibbons withholding the information on how the guns were paid for, which he had from Captain Kelly.

The Taoiseach, having misled the Dáil, subsequently failed to correct the record, either in advance of the arms trials or thereafter. While Gibbons, by all appearances, had kept Lynch in the dark, by the time of the Committee of Public Accounts inquiry in 1971, he appeared reluctant to concede this. When directly accused by Justin Keating of failing to inform Lynch, his response was qualified:

I am certain that if the Taoiseach denied any knowledge of the expenditure of the money that Captain Kelly said was expended, I had not told him. In other words, I will accept without reservation what the Taoiseach said as being true so far as he knew it.[40]

As with so much else in his admitted, or stated conduct, Gibbons's failure to prevent the Taoiseach from misleading the Dáil clearly provided grounds for significant recriminations – or worse – between Gibbons and Lynch thereafter. However, the Taoiseach appeared to be exceptionally understanding of Gibbons's persistent, extraordinary and frankly incredible reticence, and in none of these many instances where Gibbons failed, according to his own account, to bring important information to him did such neglect produce even a ripple of public disharmony between the two bonded allies.[41]

The analysis conducted above shows that the evidence of Gibbons is entitled to almost zero credibility. But that is hardly the limit to the deceptions here. When allied to evidence arising from Lynch's meeting with Peter Berry at Mount Carmel Hospital in October 1969, and a context of false and entirely unconvincing joint efforts to deny receipt of Berry's warnings over Captain Kelly and Bailieboro, the behaviour of Lynch and Gibbons strongly suggests that they were colluding to hide the truth.

It is noteworthy that, even if it was true that Gibbons did not tell Lynch that public money had in fact been used to buy arms, which seems unlikely, there is other evidence that Lynch must have been aware of serious problems over what he had told the Dáil. The *Final Report of the Committee of Public Accounts Inquiry* missed this: it could only hint at a potential problem for the Taoiseach, stating that shortly after Lynch's remarks to the Dáil,

> [when] …suspicions were aroused that money for the purchase of arms might have come from the fund, the Taoiseach's attention should have been drawn to the implications of this so far as the assurance given to the Dáil was concerned.[42]

What the committee did not know, and what its members were not told, was that Lynch's attention had indeed been drawn to the matter. Evidence for this is contained in files in the National Archives showing that on 7 May 1970, officials in the Department of the Taoiseach made Lynch aware of a front-page report in the *Evening Herald* of the same day.[43] The newspaper report linked funds which went to the Irish Red Cross with the attempted gun-running that had caused the sacking of Haughey and Blaney from the cabinet on the previous day, 6 May.

And there is further evidence that the 'suspicions' to which the *Committee of Public Accounts Report* referred reached Lynch early on. This arises from communications between Peter Berry and his counterpart, Charles Murray, Secretary of the Department of Finance, on 19 May 1970. Berry, in a phone call which he recorded and later transcribed, told Murray that he believed public monies had in fact been used to buy arms. He spoke of 'an abyss opening under our feet' as a result of a witness statement from Tony Fagan, one of Murray's Department of Finance officials, which had been given to gardaí a few days earlier, on 17 May. Berry thought it was plain from Fagan's statement that 'monies voted for one purpose were devoted to another'.[44] Berry also sent a 'semi-official' follow-up letter to Murray two days later on 21 May 1970, in which he said the file on the matter 'appalled' him, as it appeared money given to the Irish Red Cross 'had been diverted to purchases of a military character'.[45] Berry told Murray that although the chairman of the Irish Red Cross had denied the *Evening Herald* report, 'all the indications point the other way'. The transcript of his phone call to Murray, plus this letter, became publicly available in 2001, and, according to the files, were definitely brought at the time to the Taoiseach's attention. If Berry and the *Evening Herald* were right, what the Dáil had been told less than a week earlier had to be mistaken. Lynch therefore did know it was at least possible that he had misled the Dáil, and yet did nothing about it.

As a caveat, it should be noted that the Department of Finance were much slower than Berry to conclude that public money had been used to buy arms. Murray in fact told Berry shortly afterwards, somewhat testily, that he disagreed with him, and that he (Murray) was the accounting officer, not Berry.[46] It was not until the following year that it was determined conclusively that the information Lynch gave the Dáil was incorrect, and that public money had been used to buy the arms. Gibbons of course, all this time, although he knew the facts from Captain Kelly, appears to have kept mute, while he mysteriously retained Lynch's confidence.

In conclusion on Gibbons, his shared evidence with Lynch was that at no time before 20 April 1970 did he inform the Taoiseach of a subversive plan to import arms, involving two senior government ministers. Lynch told Vincent Browne in 1980 that 'he could take it from me that he [Gibbons] had never informed me about any conspiracy to import arms'.[47] If this statement was true, then given what Gibbons admitted knowing, and when he knew it, his only fully credible basis for not informing Lynch was either that there was no plot, and nothing to tell the Taoiseach about, or, if there was a plot, then he was a part of it, and was hiding this from the Taoiseach.

In general, Gibbons's assertions that he really knew nothing of consequence were fatally undermined by his own evidence to the contrary, and his claims in this regard were seen as threadbare during the arms trials. It may, as a postscript, be of significance that the British establishment, in the years after the Arms Crisis, appears to have concluded that Gibbons was centrally involved. Writing in 1980, then ambassador to Dublin, Robin Hayden, briefed his Secretary of State Lord Carrington that in May 1970 Charles Haughey, 'together with two other ministers, Gibbons and Blaney', was part of 'a conspiracy to import arms for the IRA'.[48]

9

Blaney Reassessed

By the time the Arms Crisis began to come to a head in April 1970, Neil Blaney had a well-honed image as the most militant republican voice within Jack Lynch's cabinet. He had earned this in part through a series of uncompromising speeches on Northern Ireland, delivered throughout 1968 and 1969, which were widely seen as challenging Lynch's leadership. He was memorably described by Tom MacIntyre:

> He whom London, right or wrong, saw as the South's Ian Paisley. Chunky Donegal man, face long as a Lurgan spade, desolation and humour there – the classic Irish mix, the humour losing though, and likely to continue losing through the years. A born politician, and not without charm as a man.[1]

Blaney's political base flanked the border in Co. Donegal, and when pressures from the Northern civil rights campaign mounted from 1968 on, he made no secret of his impatience over how his government had responded to the cross-border turbulence. He wanted action to further his party's aim of a united Ireland, and viewed the unrest among Northern nationalists as an opportunity for the Irish government to push for unification.

Although Blaney shared with Jack Lynch a penchant for pipe smoking, that was where the similarities between the sometimes truculent Donegal man and his easy–going Cork Taoiseach ended. Unlike Lynch, Blaney had a strong family history of republicanism, from the time his father was an IRA commander in the War of Independence. By 1969, Blaney had been twenty-one years in the Dáil and had held several ministries under Seán Lemass as Taoiseach. He was also known for heading up the so-called 'Donegal Mafia'; this was in reference less to any illicit dealings in narcotics across the north-western border, but rather to the meticulous machine politics through which Blaney controlled his political hinterland. He had introduced the phenomenon of victory cavalcades and triumphant bonfires to the Donegal area, and had organized Fianna Fáil's various by-election campaigns throughout the 1950s and 1960s. The June 1969 general election victory that returned Jack Lynch to office as Taoiseach had enhanced Blaney's status as one of the party's most powerful figures; his intimate knowledge of the Fianna Fáil grass-roots was a factor in the defeat of Fine Gael and Labour. Afterwards, he retained the senior position of Minister for Agriculture and Fisheries.

While Blaney was clearly perceived as a thorn in Jack Lynch's side due to his strident nationalist tone, what is less clear is the extent to which he was actually adrift of his government's policy on Northern Ireland in the period from August 1969 to May 1970. Not everything was as it seemed at the time, and the hidden elements in Jack Lynch's approach, as shown in Chapter 5, raise questions over precisely where he and Blaney diverged.

Blaney's influence over the government's Northern Ireland policy, as stated earlier, had grown with the departure from the cabinet after the June 1969 general election of party veteran Frank Aiken, who consistently took a more cautious approach to the North.[2] This chapter will focus on two key aspects of Blaney's record over the following months, and suggest that he may have been more closely aligned to government policy than his loud-mouth, hardline republican image might suggest. One important question here concerns his relationship with Lynch over policy on Northern Ireland; another is the related matter of how, given his self-appointed role as his party's republican conscience, Blaney viewed the IRA.

★

Blaney's largely infamous speech in Letterkenny in December 1969 provides a stunning example of the divergence between image and reality. At the time and since, the Letterkenny speech has been represented as Blaney's very public challenge to Lynch's peaceful approach to partition. The Donegal man invited this response by his explicit public discussion of the possibility of the use of force by the Irish government within Northern Ireland. But since the release of the State papers in January 2001, it has become evident that the language Blaney employed in Letterkenny was very similar to that used privately by Gibbons when delivering his directive to the Defence Forces of 6 February 1970.[3] This comparison has been possible only since the precise terms of the directive were revealed in 2001. That directive was a classic statement in support of the use of force in Northern Ireland, but force for humanitarian purposes only. As discussed in Chapter 5, it contemplated both cross-border army incursions and the distribution of weapons to Northern nationalists, but only in the event of the British army losing control, and only for the defence and protection of the minority population.

Most importantly, the policy was covert, and the orders communicating it were well hidden from public view. They were recorded in Army GHQ on a document stamped 'Top Secret', and accordingly, they brought no accompanying outcry. No one knew. And even when Hefferon revealed the existence of the directive at the first arms trial, while his revelations had a major impact, there was no clarity provided on the full extent of Gibbons's instructions. Hefferon was clear in his recall that Irish army incursions across the border were contemplated, and that surplus arms were to be provided, but he did not remember Gibbons's precise words: that the government had 'agreed' to provide arms to nationalists, and that the minister had ordered arms, ammunition and respirators to be loaded onto army lorries for possible instant delivery across the border. The full story had to wait for another thirty years, and even then, its significance did not immediately fully register.

By contrast with the directive, Blaney's words at Letterkenny were delivered two months earlier in full public spotlight. They caused him to be excoriated for remarks seen as inflammatory. What is now apparent is that at Letterkenny, he was referring to a situation not dissimilar to that contemplated by Minister for Defence Gibbons on 6 February; both statements envisaged cross-border intervention if defenceless Northern nationalists came under sustained and murderous assault, and needed to be protected. These were the circumstances that, in broad terms, both ministers felt warranted the intervention of the Irish army and the use of force in a defensive mode. Gibbons, notably, in the latter event was not speaking just as Minister for Defence, but was carrying out instructions on behalf of the Taoiseach and his cabinet.

The similarities now evident between the two statements make it easier to understand, in retrospect, why Lynch refused to sack Blaney in December 1969. At the time, he was accused of weak leadership.[4] But however much Blaney's public forcefulness brought embarrassment on the Taoiseach, he perhaps had a better understanding of his Donegal colleague's position than did those political and journalistic outsiders baying for Blaney to be sacked. Lynch noted at the time that Blaney 'knows and endorses government policy' on partition, adding 'as he did in his speech in Letterkenny last night'.[5] The episode, as revisited here, is a further indicator of the need to exercise caution on the extent of the divisions within Lynch's cabinet over the winter of 1969–70.

What is undeniable is that by referring in public to the use of force within Northern Ireland, Blaney's Letterkenny speech contained an element of defiance towards Lynch. He may even have intended to create that impression. His impatience with the public policy of the government, especially since Lynch's Tralee speech in September 1969, was palpable. His friend and cabinet colleague, Kevin Boland, was present at the Letterkenny address, and felt that Blaney 'had decided to flush the Taoiseach into the open'.[6] This appears to have been a reference to perceived tensions between Lynch's private and public positions. But Blaney may also have identified something that few others have – that his public show of rebelliousness was not entirely unhelpful to the Taoiseach.

There is evidence in the British State papers for 1969–70 that what officials referred to as 'the Blaney factor', meaning the voice of hardliners within Fianna Fáil, could be useful to the Taoiseach in his dealings with the British. There was an acute awareness in Whitehall of the presence of a republican wing inside the governing party, with officials very conscious of Blaney and Boland's presence at Lynch's shoulder. This is written large in the despatches between the British Embassy in Dublin and the Foreign and Commonwealth Office in London. Ambassador John Peck advised his Foreign Minister, Michael Stewart, in late May 1970 that there was potential for Lynch to use his party dissidents as a form of blackmail:

> It would not take much, in terms of a breakdown in Northern Ireland, to tilt the balance in the party against the Taoiseach. We have to acknowledge and be prepared for an element of blackmail in all this.... I submit, however, that it will be necessary to accept this with forbearance as a necessary part of Lynch's fight for survival.[7]

It has also become apparent that well before the crisis blew up in May 1970, Lynch could see that if he had not had Blaney, he might have had to invent him. He was not slow to use the appearance of party divisions as a lever to seek advantage from the British. An example of this arises in a report to the Foreign and Commonwealth Office in London from Sir Andrew Gilchrist, British ambassador before Peck took over, on a meeting he had with Lynch on the day after the Fianna Fáil Árd Fheis on 20 January 1970. Lynch had made a strong speech in favour of a peaceful approach to the North, and Gilchrist was pleased. He records Lynch as opening up in a seemingly disarming way at their meeting, discussing his ministerial colleagues and the so-called 'Blaney wing' of the party. Lynch thought the challenge from that quarter was serious, and was based on 'an emotional appeal for physical intervention by the Republic in the event of any repetition of the disorders of last August'. Lynch told the ambassador that 'in the event of a renewed conflict on the scale of the previous August, the Blaneyites favoured the creation of an international incident'. He claimed to Gilchrist that he had 'dampened down this enthusiasm (much of it premeditated) as best he could'. Lynch said that 'for a number of reasons' – which he appeared not to have specified to Gilchrist – it would be difficult to see in advance (and thus difficult to forestall) a plan to create an international incident.

Lynch then made his pitch: he put it directly to Gilchrist that a great deal depended on whether or not Ireland could expect 'a general goodwill towards the unity of Ireland' from the British government. The response he got could be described as non-committal.[8] What is particularily striking about this conversation is its date, 20 January 1970; this was just seventeen days before Lynch sent Gibbons to deliver the 6 February directive to the Defence Forces. It seems that the 'dampening down' efforts the Taoiseach was claiming for himself in conversation with the British ambassador were of little consequence.

In this encounter with Gilchrist, Lynch is seen projecting a favoured image of himself to the British: a Taoiseach under serious challenge, trying to hold back his wild men and curb their enthusiasm as best he could. It was the public face of his government, and the one favoured in newspapers; the private face, much closer to the 'Blaney wing' than most commentators have acknowledged, was presented shortly afterwards to the Defence Forces, with secret instructions on potential cross-border army incursions, and a stated agreement to provide arms to Northern nationalists if the need arose. The episode shows the capacity of Lynch to exploit the Blaney rumblings in his dealings with the British. Such behaviour was further in evidence when, at the height of the August 1969 crisis, he somewhat cunningly advised

Gilchrist that he might be, as he said, 'compelled to string along' with the Blaney wing of the party, if the pressure on him got too great.[9]

The perception of Blaney's outspokenness as defiance of Lynch, and as symptomatic of a cabinet deeply fractured on the North, can be seen in historian Mary Daly's otherwise generally balanced account of the Arms Crisis; this reflected, she felt, 'Lynch's lack of control over his cabinet, and at least a tacit willingness to turn a blind eye to defiant ministers, plus a lazy approach to procedures'.[10] Stephen Collins was another who identified a fundamental clash within the government, believing that some ministers viewed chaos in the North as 'the opportunity for a final solution to the partition problem, regardless of the consequences in terms of loss of life and political stability'. Collins took a heroic view of how Lynch and his allies faced up to such perceived divisions: they 'held the line in defence of the rule of law and democratic principles'.

What is suggested here is that the convulsions of May 1970 and the conflicting positions taken up by different sides in the heat of the Arms Crisis may have unhelpfully coloured historical perceptions of the previous nine months, and in particular may have confused where Blaney stood *vis-à-vis* the Taoiseach. The belief that Lynch in May 1970 uncovered a subversive plot within his cabinet encouraged an assumption, made largely if not completely in hindsight, that there had been since August 1969 a stark dichotomy on the North within the government.

It has already been shown that any split between Blaney and Lynch on the North was not over the use of force to end partition, and analysis in this chapter of Blaney's Letterkenny speech in December 1969 also underlines a need for caution. The suggestion, at the least, is that further research may be required on the internal dynamics of the Lynch government pre-May 1970. This is not in any sense to ignore the deep fissures within Lynch's cabinet, fuelled no doubt by personality clashes and mutual dislikes, nor is it to discount the festering, seemingly thwarted, ambitions associated with the presence there of unruly barons such as Blaney and Haughey. The issue is whether, at the time, the Lynch cabinet was as devided over Northern Ireland policy as they are often depicted.

Lynch and his External Affairs Minister Patrick Hillery, judging by their own speeches and actions in August 1969, clearly recognized how the disturbances in the North had brought a united Ireland on to the political agenda. There was no minister – with the possible exception of the moderately inclined Protestant Tánaiste, Erskine Childers – who could not recognize the sense of opportunity presented for Fianna Fáil, *the* republican party – just as, *pace* Kevin Boland, they were all capable of seeing the potentially great dangers for exposed Northern nationalists, especially in Belfast, and for the peace of the island as a whole. As journalist Jim Downey observed pithily, the reaction in the Republic to August 1969 was 'a mixture of horror, apprehension and glee',[11] and to assume any one of these conflicting emotions was foreign to Lynch or any member of his cabinet would be unwarranted.

The second area of interest in Blaney's affairs at this time concerns his view of the IRA. He was involved in significant efforts in the autumn of 1969 to separate the Northern wing of the IRA from the socialist-oriented Goulding leadership in Dublin. These efforts involved officers of the Military Intelligence section of the Defence Forces, including its Director, Colonel Michael Hefferon, and Captain James Kelly. Somehow, despite a lack of real evidence, a whiff of sedition has continued to be attached to this particular project. The suggestion is that it was happening behind Lynch's back, and against his wishes.

Blaney's involvement is not in doubt: he admitted it in subsequent interviews, and it was part of his general close liaison with Captain Kelly throughout this period.[12] Chief Superintendent John Fleming in 1971 told the Committee of Public Accounts inquiry that a recurring feature in Special Branch reports at the time was that money was on offer from the Dublin government if a separate IRA Northern Command was created, free from the control of Goulding's leadership.[13] This Garda intelligence has been independently confirmed in the years since by various writers through personal interviews with republican participants. These further confirm Blaney's involvement, but whether Haughey was directly involved is less clear. But it has already been shown, in Chapter 2, how Peter Berry advised the government in 1969 to move in precisely this direction, and to seek to split the IRA.[14]

In addition, the Army Planning Board reports of September 1969, considered earlier, show that a drive to identify and engage with dependable local republican muscle to help defend nationalist areas of Northern Ireland was in tune with planning going on in Army GHQ. And further again to this, the efforts of Military Intelligence were on a group basis, as Colonel Hefferon was directing not just Captain Kelly but a team of officers in the operation. If Blaney, as has been suggested, was in this exercise manipulating Captain Kelly into subversive activity, he must also have been manipulating and controlling his boss, Hefferon. How Blaney could have achieved this is hard to see, because he did not meet Hefferon before 23 April 1970, when the move against the IRA was long over and the arms importation attempt had already ended in failure.[15]

Whatever involvement Blaney may have had in efforts to split the Goulding IRA, he appears to have been directly responsible, in early December 1969, for a decisive shift in the search to import arms for the Northern Defence Committees. At that time, plans were already well advanced to bring in weapons from the United States, but Blaney, using the power of the purse, halted these in fairly peremptory fashion and insisted that the arms should come from Europe. This intervention has been graphically described in a series of interviews by John Kelly, the Defence Committees' organizer. He was deeply unhappy at Blaney's attitude, having travelled to the US in December with veteran republican Seán

Keenan, co-chairman of the Derry Citizens' Defence Association, to set up the importation that Blaney later caused to be called off.

John Kelly was clear that Blaney's move was a power play; he told Justin O'Brien in 1998–99: 'I think perhaps the feeling from the government... was that they would have more control over weapons coming from the Continent than they would have had over a consignment coming from New York, that was being organized by physical force republicans.'[16] Six years later, in a 2005 interview with journalist Liam Clarke, Kelly was more explicit: 'I think that the reason Blaney cancelled the American operation was that he was afraid that we would take it and that he wouldn't see it.... He thought: we had to have this under our control.'[17] In a further significant interview with political scientist Donnacha Ó Beacháin, John Kelly conceded that his group felt they had no alternative but to accede to Blaney:

> They had the money. They were providing the finances. Again, had the Irish Americans been organised... as two years later, after internment.... That's the reason we had to run with the Irish Government for the arms, for the money for the arms. As I say, if we'd not been in that situation we would have done it ourselves, but that's the way it was. We felt obliged going back. So when Blaney says, 'no, that's not the place to go', we were beggars, we couldn't be choosers. So we had to go by his instructions.[18]

This compelling admission from John Kelly reveals Blaney as a controlling force in the arms importation at that point. He appears to have been emphatically asserting the rights of a paymaster, although the project had been conceived and initiated north of the border by the Defence Committees. Blaney was seeking control, so far as he could, but, with John Kelly in close attendance, it was a limited control, and could never amount to full ownership of the operation.

The reality as to who owned the gun-running plan was complicated, and this is important in assessing the degree of Irish government authorization. This episode in December 1969 also shows Blaney's wariness, as he moved to reorient the whole gun-running plan away from the United States, towards the republicans with whom he and Captain Kelly were now collaborating, and, by the same token, his determination to retain influence by manipulating the purse-strings. It does nothing to strengthen the argument that he and Haughey were using Captain Kelly to rearm and reinvigorate the IRA. Here the history between Fianna Fáil and the IRA is important. August 1969 might have created new circumstances of both opportunity and danger for those seeking a united Ireland, but a bloody history between the Irish State and the IRA could not easily be set aside. Decades of distrust, antipathy and at times deadly enmity between Fianna Fáil governments in the South and the IRA were – perhaps inevitably – in play, and influencing events.

Fianna Fáil itself was a republican grouping that had left the IRA in 1926, choosing under Éamon de Valera to follow a different, constitutional path to Irish unity. Thereafter, Fianna Fáil chose periodically to turn the full power of the twenty-six-county state against its former republican brothers, to suppress them. Blaney's relationship with the IRA in 1969–70 cannot be considered separately from his party's history of dealing with physical force republicanism. The gulf between him and the IRA was in evidence when one of the leaders of the Provisionals, Ruairí Ó Brádaigh, was asked in a 1970 interview for the *This Week* current affairs magazine about claims that Fianna Fáil ministers like Blaney had helped set up the Provisionals. Ó Brádaigh shrugged off the suggestion, reminding the interviewer of how Fianna Fáil governments had twice imprisoned him in the Curragh.[19] Thus, when writer Justin O'Brien observed that at one point Blaney's voice was indistiguishable from that of Ó Brádaigh,[20] he appeared to ignore the deep historical cleavage between the two, based on decades of bloodied animosity as they vied for legitimacy as the true heirs of the republican tradition in Ireland.

If in later years Blaney declared himself reluctant to condemn the Provisionals' militant activity, he defended this on the basis that the Irish government at that stage had, in his view, abdicated on its responsibilities to defend nationalists' rights.[21] At that stage out of office, and out of Fianna Fáil since 1972, Blaney was also giving vent to a traditional ambivalence among nationalists in the South towards republican violence that originated outside the Irish State, from within Northern Ireland.

It is another claim against Blaney that it was his intention, through Captain Kelly's attempted importation, to provide guns for the Provisional IRA. Part of the case in support of this arises from an interview he gave to British journalist Peter Taylor in 1993. Blaney was asked who in the North would have received the rifles despatched to Dundalk by James Gibbons on 2 April 1970 during the Ballymurphy riots in Belfast, had they been distributed as envisaged:

Blaney: They'd have gone into Ballymurphy and to whoever was capable of handling, using and directing their organisation, without name, not because I have the name, but because I just don't know.

Taylor: But they would have gone presumably to the newly emergent Provisionals?

B: Probably, very probably.

T: Because you say they wouldn't have gone to the Officials?

B: Mmm.

T: You say they wouldn't have gone to the Officials?

B: Oh, no way, no way.[22]

This passage has been cited by Justin O'Brien as evidence that Blaney was working to send arms directly to the Provisional

IRA.[23] However, this conclusion appears questionable, since the exchange appears to have been based on a misunderstanding of the situation in Ballymurphy at the time by both Taylor and Blaney. The Belfast historian of those events, Ciarán de Baróid, has shown that in March–April 1970 the Provisionals were neither directing the riots, nor were they even in control in Ballymurphy.[24] It appears the disturbances had emerged spontaneously as a result of heavy-handed British army behaviour; de Baróid indicates that all IRA groupings in Belfast distanced themselves from the unrest and were seeking for their own reasons – eventually successfully – to quell the trouble. De Baróid's account has been backed up by the memoir of Gerry Adams, at the time a young republican leader in Ballymurphy.[25] It is also noteworthy in this context that the weapons Blaney and Taylor believed to be on their way to the Provisionals were *not* the controversial weapons Captain Kelly was seeking to import, but were the Irish army surplus stock set aside for the purpose of distribution on foot of the government's 6 February directive, and despatched northwards by order of the Minister for Defence, James Gibbons.[26]

It is not easy to be definitive about Blaney's attitude to the IRA at that time. In early 1970, the emerging Provisionals certainly appeared to qualify as potential allies in two important respects: they were outside the control of the IRA's Chief of Staff, Cathal Goulding, and in their initial six months at least, they appeared firmly focused on the defence of nationalists within Northern Ireland, rather than on attacking the Stormont regime directly. Yet Blaney had few illusions about those he was dealing with. What he appeared to want in regard to the arms being imported, at least in MacStiofáin's – probably correct – belief, was that the arms would not go to the Goulding-led IRA, nor to the Provisional IRA, but to an entirely independent republican group with no connection to republicans in the twenty-six Counties. The Provisionals' Chief of Staff, anonymously representing the Army Council, told *This Week* in August 1970 that 'Blaney would like to see an independent Northern IRA with no connections with the 26 counties, that is, no connection with the republicans in the 26 counties'.[27] MacStiofáin was sceptical that any republican grouping would have found Blaney's idea acceptable. John Kelly agreed with this view of the Fianna Fáil minister: 'I have no doubt that Blaney and co. wanted to have an IRA that would be solely concerned with Northern affairs.'[28]

The reorganization of republicanism that emerged in January 1970, on this analysis, was not at all what Blaney had sought. The truth is that no leading Fianna Fáil figure, however militant, could have taken anything other than a long spoon to sup with the IRA, whether Officials or Provisionals, because both groups were fundamentally opposed to the government in Dublin and regarded it as illegitimate and illegal. Blaney would have been keenly aware that Fianna Fáil, a twenty-six and not a thirty-two-county organization, was engaged in a nationalist turf war with the IRA; in his view, offering leadership to the Northern minority in the Six Counties was the proper duty of a Fianna Fáil government, not the preserve of IRA gunmen, Provisional or otherwise.

Nonetheless, and whatever their intentions, the claim has been made that Blaney and Haughey's actions during the Arms Crisis played a significant role in the emergence and rise of the Provisional IRA. The claim originated in an Official IRA pamphlet in 1973,[29] and although branded as 'self-serving' by chroniclers of the Provisionals, Bishop and Mallie,[30] and effectively debunked subsequently in every significant account from the leading Provisionals of the period,[31] it still gained a new lease of life from writers O'Brien, Collins and Arnold around 2000–2001.[32] Historian Richard English was more judicious, noting in 2003 that support was given to the emerging Provisionals 'from a section of the Southern establishment at a time when such strengthening was of some value'. But he also said: 'It was important to stress that the new IRA were generated by Northern realities; they would have come into being regardless of Southern backing, and the importance of such backing should not be exaggerated.'[33] Another historian, Thomas Hennessey, was sure that the Provisional IRA 'was nurtured and encouraged, through financial assistance, by elements of the Irish government', which in his view 'sustained the organization at a crucial time'.[34]

Ultimately, however, it is suggested here that, while the money being offered from Dublin by Blaney and Haughey may have contributed in a marginal way to the emergence of the Provisionals, its impact was no more than that, i.e., marginal. The guns in question, it should be recalled, never arrived. Tim Pat Coogan's early judgement, still hard to gainsay, was that the actions by Irish government ministers during the Arms Crisis had done no more than give the Provisionals 'a tiny push along the road'.[35] The overwhelming evidence on the split within the IRA is that it was not caused by Fianna Fáil, nor is it likely that its progress was seriously affected by anything emerging from the Irish government and its representatives; it stemmed from years of internal disaffection over Goulding's attempts to modernize and redefine the Republican Movement, a process that culminated in the perceived failure to protect Belfast nationalists in August 1969.

The tipping point came in December 1969, with the abandonment of the abstentionist policy that had been a core principle of the IRA, and the recognition of the three 'illegitimate' assemblies – Westminster, Leinster House and Stormont.[36] The refusal of the Provisionals to abandon abstentionism in 1969–1970 was a refusal to follow the path taken not just by Goulding and their erstwhile comrades in the Official IRA, but also by Fianna Fáil forty-three years earlier. Nothing could more clearly delineate the gulf between Blaney and Haughey on the one hand, and MacStiofáin and Ó Brádaigh on the other. On the question of government money, so often claimed as a great stimulant to the Provisionals, while some funds may indeed have gone to them, monies also went to the Officials, and there is little evidence that either made a significant difference to events.[37]

★

Despite the tendency in the literature to link Blaney with the Provisional IRA, in 1969–70 the evidence is that Blaney's closest allies on the Northern political landscape, and his natural political soulmates, were not to be found within any IRA, but rather in the conservative and constitutional Nationalist Party, led by Eddie McAteer. McAteer and Blaney were close, as shown by the former's public support for the Donegal minister after his Letterkenny speech in December 1969.[38] Further evidence of Blaney's connection with the Nationalist Party is to be found in his close relationship with Paddy Doherty, otherwise known as Paddy Bogside, the Derry community leader seen by some as the likely successor to McAteer as leader of the party.[39] Doherty was not a member of the IRA, Provisional or otherwise; he described himself rather as a 'right-wing Catholic' who believed the Irish government was 'responsible for people in the North'.[40] Significantly, he was one of the Derry men enrolled in the Fórsa Cosanta Áitiúil (FCA) at Fort Dunree in September 1969 for training in the handling of arms.

Doherty is one of several seemingly peripheral figures in the saga of the Arms Crisis whose importance has been generally overlooked. His visit to Blaney in Government Buildings in the first week of February 1970, accompanied by veteran IRA man Seán Keenan of Derry, provides a prime example of Doherty's unacknowledged role. He appears, through this visit, to have been the catalyst for the issuing of the 6 February directive.

The event was described by Doherty in detail in his memoir, *Paddy Bogside* (2001). He wrote that in February 1970, Blaney telephoned him in Derry to ask him to come urgently to Dublin; the minister was concerned that surplus Irish army rifles were due to be sold on the open market, and could even end up in loyalist paramilitary hands. In Dublin, Blaney told Doherty that his wish was that the guns be withdrawn from sale, and then held for possible future use by Northern nationalists. Doherty and Keenan brought with them alarming reports that UVF assaults on Northern Catholics were imminent; they felt the North was slipping close to civil war.

Blaney included in the meeting with the two Derry men his two government colleagues, Haughey and Gibbons. The government ministers heard from Doherty and Keenan of their fears that nationalists could not depend on the British army for defence. Gibbons told the group that the Irish army was not prepared or equipped to intervene in the North, but added, as Doherty described it, 'I am preparing for the doomsday situation in Northern Ireland, and if the fears expressed here become a reality, we will have to become involved.' Blaney stated that the two Derry men needed to make their case to the Taoiseach; it was time Lynch did something, and a commitment from him to assist was 'vital'. If the Taoiseach would not agree to keep the surplus rifles for possible use by nationalists, as he felt he should, then the delegation should ask for gas masks. Providing them was the least Lynch could do. Haughey picked up the phone and set up a meeting for the Northerners with the Taoiseach.

The following day, Doherty's book records, he and Keenan, having now been joined by Belfast republican Billy Kelly, met Jack Lynch in Government Buildings. They repeated, for the Taoiseach's benefit, their fears for the future. Billy Kelly was particularly insistent on the need for guns in Belfast. 'He said not only were the ghetto Catholics frightened, but many professional and business people were also appealing for guns.' Lynch in response was equivocal; according to Doherty, he 'flinched' in the face of Billy Kelly's demands, saying he could give them gas masks, but guns 'he would have to think about'.[41]

Afterwards, Doherty recorded that the three-man Northern delegation had conflicting reactions to the meeting with the Taoiseach. Keenan and Kelly, the republicans in the group, were euphoric: 'They were sure that Lynch had made a commitment to supply guns.' Doherty described himself as more downbeat; he thought it was clear that Lynch would never get involved, and he could not understand the jubilation of his two companions.

A second perspective on this Doherty/Keenan Dublin visit to Government Buildings in Dublin came from Captain James Kelly

in *The Thimble Riggers* (1999), two years before Doherty's book.
Kelly met the delegation after their meeting with the Taoiseach,
and recalled that they said they had been told by Lynch that gas
masks could be given to them, for humanitarian reasons. Kelly's
version of the Lynch response went on: 'On arms, he assured the
Northerners that his heart was in the right place and that he would
put the arms question to his cabinet.'[42] Henry Patterson, writing
in 2002, cited no source other than Doherty's book when he
claimed – apparently mistakenly – that Lynch 'refused Keenan's
request for weapons'.[43]

Doherty's detailed record is, however, significant, because
of the apparent consequences of his visit. Just two days later,
on 6 February 1970, the State papers show that the government
'informally agreed' to withdraw from sale the surplus rifles Blaney
had been concerned about.[44] Lynch, in a speech the following
year, confirmed that the weapons were held back from sale,
against, he said, 'the possibility of a doomsday situation arising'.[45]
Critically, Lynch left unstated the fact that they were for potential
distribution to Northern civilians, as the military records would
later show. It was directly after that same government meeting, on
6 February, that Gibbons delivered the directive to the Defence
Forces, contemplating cross-border army incursions and the
provision to Northerners of the surplus rifles, should the situation
deteriorate. This probable direct connection between the Doherty
and Keenan delegation and the 6 February directive has not been
previously identified in the literature.

The link between Doherty and Keenan's visit and the 6
February directive was further underscored in 2001, when in
the course of the making of an RTÉ television documentary on
the newly released State papers and the Arms Crisis, Doherty
was shown, by the author, the military records of the directive.
Doherty's memoir had been recently published, but it contained
no reference to the directive, and Doherty appeared unaware of
any link. On inspecting the official records, and noting the dates
involved, Doherty felt certain that the directive was issued as a

result of the meeting between himself, Keenan, Billy Kelly and the Taoiseach. He said that his colleagues had been correct in their reaction at the time, and he had been mistaken. He observed:

I think that conversation [with Lynch] struck home.... I believe that the impact we made on Jack Lynch would have excited him to do some kind of action... to make some definite attempt to deal with it – a doomsday situation – if it arose.... I believe we had quite a serious impact on the Taoiseach.[46]

Billy Kelly, the third member of the group who met Lynch, was also separately shown the directive in 2001. He agreed with Doherty that the delegation's visit had clearly prompted it. He remembered being in very high spirits afterwards. Asked why, he replied:

Because I believed he was going to supply us with what we needed. That he wouldn't let us down. That he would stand by what he said. He wouldn't stand idly by. That he intended to do something about it.

Q: You felt that?

Absolutely...

Q: Are you surprised to see that [the directive]?

No, I am not surprised to see that. That's how I read it at the time and believed that at the time.[46a]

Caution is clearly necessary in relying on the accuracy of Billy Kelly's or Paddy Doherty's recall of events that had occurred thirty years previously, and in *Paddy Bogside* inverted commas are occasionally used to denote direct speech from the time, which has to be problematic.[47] Nonetheless, even in broad terms the memoir seems important in a number of respects. Firstly, for the calendar link between the delegation's visit and the directive, and the strong case now identifiable that there was a cause-and-effect relationship between the two events. Thus understood, Doherty's memoir fills a gap in the literature by explaining the timing of the directive, and why it was issued when it was. Secondly, the behaviour of Blaney and Haughey, as described by Doherty, is not suggestive of two scheming plotters operating behind the Taoiseach's back. While Blaney, as reported, appeared impatient and showed little respect for Lynch, his focus was on getting the Taoiseach's agreement for action; it was he who suggested that the delegation meet Lynch and request military help. Thirdly, the memoir has particular value because it appears to involve Lynch personally in the build-up to the directive; it links the Taoiseach to a Northern delegation requesting arms, something Gibbons, two days later, told the Defence Forces the government had conditionally 'agreed' to. And fourthly, the sequence of events shows that Blaney, however disgruntled he may have been, was nonetheless exercising enormous influence over Lynch in the matter of policy on Northern Ireland.

There is a double postscript to Paddy Doherty's involvement in these events. Firstly, it also emerged from Doherty's interview with the author in 2001 that it was to him Blaney turned on 2 April 1970, when it seemed as though the surplus arms set aside on 6 February might have to be put to use as the riots in Ballymurphy in Belfast continued. Doherty by then was working for a building contractor in the West Indies. He said Blaney contacted him there, through his home in Derry, and asked him to be on standby to return urgently to Derry to receive arms on behalf of the Irish government.[48] This further undermines suggestions that Blaney had any intention of rearming the IRA. It also confirms his alignment with the North's constitutional nationalists, rather than its republican paramilitaries. Several hours later, Doherty got a message from Dublin stating that calm had returned to Ballymurphy and the emergency was over; as a result, he did not leave the West Indies.

The second postscript concerns Doherty's induction, with his Derry colleagues, into the Irish army's territorial reserve, the FCA, in September 1969. Fresh evidence, detailed below in Chapter 16, shows how this development may have later influenced the acquittal of Charles Haughey by the jury at the second arms trial. The claim is that the FCA membership of Paddy Doherty and his Derry colleagues allowed the jury, at a pivotal point, to ensure that the former Minister for Finance avoided a lengthy spell in an Irish jail.

10

Climactic Weekend

The extended weekend from Friday, 17 April to Monday, 20 April 1970 brought an end to Captain Kelly's attempted gun-running, and proved to be a pivotal few days in the development of the subsequent political crisis. From the moment the planned importation came to official notice on Friday, 17 April, it was probably already doomed, but not before Charles Haughey managed to incriminate himself deeply through a fateful telephone call on the Saturday evening to the Secretary of the Department of Justice, Peter Berry.

On a weekend when events moved rapidly, the phone call to Berry was central. It was Haughey's vain attempt to get the senior official to lift a Garda Special Branch cordon, or 'ring of steel', thrown around Dublin Airport, and so permit the arms to be cleared safely through customs on arrival. The weekend's events also gave rise to one of the most noteworthy moments at the second arms trial: this was when Judge Seamus Henchy insisted to the jury that, in his view, perjury had been committed by either Haughey or Gibbons over a conversation they had in Haughey's office on Monday afternoon, 20 April. The issue, again arising from Haughey's phone call to Berry, was about when and how the arms importation attempt was finally called off. These events – Haughey's telephone call to Berry and his later meeting with Gibbons – are prime examples of how controversy and disagreement has persisted around these key figures in the Arms Crisis. Indeed, much of what happened over these four pivotal days has remained uncertain in the decades since.

Four areas where the facts about the weekend's events have been unclear can be identified. In the first instance, when information reached top civil servants and ministers in Dublin on Friday 17 April that an arms consignment was due to arrive in Dublin over the weekend, it has never been entirely clear how the principals, including Minister for Justice Mícheál Ó Móráin, responded in the course of the Saturday, Sunday and Monday. Secondly, although the gun-running was eventually called off, there has been confusion over precisely when this was decided, and after what process of decision-making. Thirdly, regarding Haughey's telephone call to Berry at 6 p.m. on Saturday, 18 April, no analysis has fully explained how Haughey could have made such a schoolboy error as to expect the highly officious and formidable Secretary of the Department of Justice to play along with a gun-running effort that was at best irregular, and at worst appeared illegal and seditious. What was Haughey thinking? By the same token, Berry's conclusion that the minister, in seeking to have the guns let through, was trying to suborn him into an act of sedition against the State, appears so intrinsically unlikely that it has called for a far more searching interrogation than has generally been accorded to it. Fourthly, in relation to the critical meeting on Monday, 20 April between Haughey and Gibbons, in the aftermath of the Haughey–Berry phone call, little of the conflicting evidence about that encounter has ever seemed entirely credible. Judge Seamus Henchy, who considered that evidence at the second arms trial, was patently perplexed. His reluctant conclusion, one he considered inescapable, was that one or the other of Haughey and Gibbons had perjured themselves.

However, a different conclusion is suggested here on the basis of facts that were withheld from the court, and which could have clarified what really transpired between Haughey and Gibbons. The evidence considered below points to the existence of a previous, unacknowledged conversation that day between the two ministers.

The concealment of this important exchange may be symptomatic of the whole Arms Crisis, but also of a pivotal weekend where the narrative has been consciously and unnecessarily jumbled, and writers have been left over-dependent on guesswork.

The weekend's drama began with a telephone query from Captain James Kelly in Vienna to Aer Lingus in Dublin, signalling his intention to fly in a consignment of ammunition and arms on Sunday. This was referred by Aer Lingus to the Department of Transport and Power; from there it passed to the departments of Justice and Defence, to see whether the Garda Síochána or the Defence Forces were expecting such a consignment. Concern was quickly heightened when none of the officials knew anything of it. Additional doubts were raised by calls from a private air freight company, Aer Turas, whose managing director, John Squire, was concerned over the legitimacy of a request to fly in a consignment of pistols, supposedly for the Garda Síochána. There followed discussions in the Department of Justice between the minister, Ó Móráin, and his top officials, including Peter Berry, the Department Secretary. A Garda cordon – what Berry later referred to as 'a ring of steel' – was placed around Dublin Airport and other airports.

With the situation thus poised, on Saturday detectives began questioning officials of the Revenue Commissioners at the airport about their dealings over the proposed consignment. From these interviews it became clear that the Minister for Finance, Haughey, had an interest in the importation, and that Captain James Kelly was involved centrally. Under the effective direction of Berry, the Garda Special Branch prepared to seize the arms on arrival at the airport. On Saturday afternoon, Haughey's assistant Tony Fagan learned of this. He got through to Haughey later on Saturday afternoon to alert him to the difficulties at the airport, telling him that Chief Superintendent Fleming intended to seize the consignment unless Haughey, or some other government minister, contacted him in the meantime.[1]

On being told of this around 6 p.m., Haughey decided his best course was not to ring Fleming, but to telephone Peter Berry at home. Berry was an official with whom he was familiar from his own days as Minister for Justice, and whom he understood to be the effective director of the Special Branch. The civil servant described the phone call that ensued in his short witness statement:

> Without any preliminaries he [Haughey] asked me if I was aware of a certain cargo which was due to arrive at Dublin Airport on Sunday.
>
> I replied: 'Yes, Minister.'
>
> Mr. Haughey then asked if the cargo could be let through if a guarantee were given that it would go direct to the North.
>
> I replied: 'No.'
>
> He then said: 'I think that is a bad decision.'
>
> I made no comment.
>
> After a pause he asked: 'Does the man from Mayo [Micheál Ó Móráin] know about this?'
>
> I replied: 'Yes.'
>
> He then said: 'What will happen to it when it arrives?'
>
> I replied: 'It will be grabbed.'
>
> He then said: 'I had better have it called off.'[2]

All this time Captain Kelly was waiting in Vienna, hoping for the go-ahead to fly in the guns. That evening he got word from Dublin, through his wife, that problems had arisen at Dublin Airport. He spent Sunday trying to get clarification on this through Fagan, Haughey's assistant, but it was not until nearly midday on the Monday that Fagan was able to confirm, by telephone to Vienna, that the importation was cancelled and Kelly could return home.

In Dublin on that Monday afternoon, Gibbons arranged to meet Haughey in the latter's office to discuss the situation. His evidence at the arms trials was that when they met he pleaded with Haughey to terminate the project; in response to this, Gibbons claimed, Haughey offered to call it off, but only for a month. Haughey in evidence denied that their conversation was as Gibbons described, but he did accept that they reached a mutual agreement that the importation should be called off. Meantime, elsewhere in Government Buildings, Berry visited Lynch in his office on Monday, handing him a Garda report on the weekend inquiries, plus his own personal oral report on his phone call from Haughey on Saturday evening. It was, Lynch later claimed, the first he knew of an attempt to bring in arms.

From the start, it has been clear that any attempt to produce a definitive version of what happened over that extended weekend, or even to construct a timeline for the events from Friday to Monday afternoon, are doomed, owing to a severe absence of information. As an example: in the circumstances developing on Friday evening, it is likely that there were a number of informal conversations between members of the government, none of which are documented. Someone – it is not known who – informed Blaney, who it seems had become aware by Saturday afternoon of the Garda operation at Dublin Airport. According to Fagan's evidence, Blaney got in touch with Haughey, but nothing is known of this conversation other than that it happened. It may well have been Gibbons who had alerted Blaney; another possibility is that it was the Minister for Transport and Power, Brian Lenihan, who, according to Captain Kelly's later account, alerted Colonel Hefferon on Saturday to the Garda cordon around the airport.[3]

The absence of records on conversations between these

ministers clearly does not mean that they did not happen; rather, it means that the record, as in much of the Arms Crisis, is no better than fragmentary. There is, however, still much to be gleaned from the known responses of Gibbons in particular, and from the evidence, considered below for the first time, that Gibbons and Haughey concealed information from the court about a second conversation they had had in this immediate period.

The Haughey phone call to Berry appeared to signal the end of the importation, at least for the moment; Haughey, having been rebuffed by the civil servant, had conceded that it had to be called off. However, the outcome was not so straightforward, because Haughey initially did nothing to cancel it. He knew the event was planned for the following day, Sunday.[4] He spoke briefly to Fagan, his assistant, but although he indicated in that conversation that the importation would have to be called off, following the phone call to Berry, he did not ask Fagan to cancel it. Thus, when the next day Fagan received a phone call from Captain Kelly in Vienna, he was unable to instruct him on the project's status.[5] Haughey's evidence was that he himself took no further action, nor spoke to anyone about the matter, until Monday. He told the second arms trial that 'as far as I was concerned, it was Mr Gibbons's business, or at least army business'[6] – yet he specifically denied contacting Gibbons or anyone other than Tony Fagan after his conversation with Berry. What is certain is that he did not instruct Fagan to cancel the operation at any time before Monday.

In regard to Gibbons's behaviour over the weekend, whatever he did in response to the news regarding Vienna on the Friday, his account that he simply went off to his farm in Co. Kilkenny that evening, without consulting any of his colleagues, makes little sense. His own junior army officer was in Vienna seeking to fly arms into Dublin Airport; it was evident that the authorities were lying in wait for him, which meant an imminent potential crisis. The matter was urgent, as the arms were scheduled to arrive

probably on the Sunday.[7] Gibbons had personal knowledge of
the officer at the centre of this developing drama, and also of his
plans, yet strikingly, throughout the whole of 1970, including in
his evidence at both arms trials, he would keep this information
to himself. The extent of what he knew on that Friday evening
would be clarified only six months later, on 21 April 1971, when
he gave extended evidence to the Committee of Public Accounts
inquiry. By any rational standards Gibbons, aware that it was
Captain Kelly, knowing personally of his plans, and, as he later
claimed, being opposed to them, had to be spurred into action. He
had two choices: either to order Kelly to stop, or, if not that, at least
to inform the Taoiseach. Yet, on his own evidence, he did neither.

Gibbons did not halt Kelly, and he did not inform the Taoiseach,
either on the Friday evening or on the following Monday
morning, or indeed at any time prior to his public disclosure at
the Committee of Public Accounts inquiry the following year.
At the arms trials, he made a belated attempt to suggest that his
meeting with Haughey, shown conclusively by other evidence to
have taken place on the following Monday afternoon, may actually
have taken place on the Friday; however, as shown in Chapter 8,
counsel representing the State was not prepared to accept that.[8]
Meanwhile, it was left to Berry himself on the following Monday
to inform Lynch. The Taoiseach got a second report from Berry
the next day, Tuesday, while in all this time Gibbons, by his own
account and that of Lynch, told the Taoiseach nothing.

No greater clarity attaches to the role played by Minister for
Justice, Mícheál Ó Móráin, over this critical weekend. The issue
is whether Ó Móráin knew in advance of the arms consignment,
and whether he consented to the Special Branch seizing it at
Dublin Airport. Ó Móráin was a sick man, and his resulting
incapacity meant that effective control of the Department of
Justice periodically devolved, temporarily, to his permanent
Secretary, Peter Berry. Ó Móráin's ill health somewhat blighted
his evidence at the arms trials, but he did testify that he had heard
of the importation 'at different times' before 18 April 1970. He

added: 'Certainly at one of these stages I thought this was an official importation.' Although this reference is striking, not least because it was misreported in the national newspapers,[9] owing to Ó Móráin's disability it is impossible to be categorical about his views or his true state of knowledge.

The files show that he was present in the office in Dublin on Friday when word of the arms shipment first came through. Berry advised him that the consignment should be seized. Ó Móráin was hesitant; a memo from Andrew Ward, Deputy Secretary of the department, noted his uncertainty.[10] Berry similarly described the minister in his *Diaries* as being 'in a quandary'. Ó Móráin, no doubt sensing the embarrassment for the government that lay ahead, asked his officials why, rather than seizing the consignment on arrival, it should not simply be stopped at Hamburg? Immediately after this meeting, Berry arranged for the Garda Special Branch to place a cordon around several airports, including Dublin Airport, to monitor and control all arriving shipments.

The uncertainty about Ó Móráin here is whether he explicitly sanctioned the seizure of the arms consignment, or whether Berry took unilateral action. Ó Móráin gave evidence at the first arms trial that he was not told of the 'ring of steel' around Dublin Airport until some days *after* the event, and this has led some writers to suggest he did not know of the intention to seize, that it was an effective *coup d'état* by his department Secretary.[11] However, the memo referred to above from Deputy Secretary Ward has information that seems to refute this. Ward's memo describes how, when Berry recommended to Ó Móráin that the opportunity should not be missed to make a major 'seizure', at that point 'the minister agreed'. Ó Móráin appears, on this evidence, at the very least to have *assented* to the seizure, and to have gone along with his official's advice. There is nothing to show that he knew at any point that Haughey had directed Revenue to give the consignment customs clearance.

★

The decisive event of the weekend was undoubtedly Haughey's phone call to Berry on Saturday, 18 April. It was used to very considerable effect against Haughey in the arms trials and thereafter, and merits close scrutiny. The issues that it raises are how Haughey came to make the phone call, how he so seriously miscalculated Berry's response, and whether Berry was correct to draw from it the conclusions he did about Haughey.[12] Particularly damaging to Haughey was his suggestion, as reported by Berry, that the consignment could go directly to the North. If he did say this, it appeared to rule out any argument that the arms, as required under the Firearms Act, were or could have been 'for the use of the Defence Forces'. This would make it almost impossible to prove that the importation was not illegal, as shown in Chapter 16. Although Haughey in court disputed the accuracy of Berry's recall, it appears that the jury broadly accepted Berry's account. Evidence for this lies in the difficulties experienced in the jury room at the second arms trial, before the decision to acquit Haughey.[13]

In Berry's Explanatory Note, addressed to State counsel preparing the case for the arms trial, he gave one of his earliest commentaries on Haughey's phone call:

> It was a matter of great distress to me that on 18th April he had tried to make me a party to his designs to illegally import arms which it was apparent from his very conversation – 'Does the man from Mayo know?' – was not a matter of government policy....[14]

Berry concluded from the conversation not just that it was an attempt to enlist him in criminality, but also that when Haughey asked him if Ó Móráin was aware, he had unintentionally revealed that the project could not be government policy. He elaborated on this in his *Diaries*:

> It was as a result of that call that I came to realise the enormity of the attempts that were being made to suborn the security forces...

it now seemed evident that, at most, a caucus was involved, and that Government *qua Government* were not behind the arms conspiracy.[15]

But it is possible to argue, as writer Angela Clifford has done, that this was a misunderstanding by Berry, one that led to a serious misrepresentation by him of Haughey's approach. These two men knew each other of old; they had worked closely together on security matters less than a decade previously. Given this mutual familiarity, Clifford argues that it is not credible to believe that Haughey would ring such an official to facilitate a criminal and subversive plot:

> Haughey would have got to know him well when he was Minister for Justice. The idea that the Minister would try to implicate such a stickler for proper behaviour in a conspiracy to illegally import arms for the IRA is absolutely laughable.[16]

Haughey, it is worth noting, also had to be aware that anything he suggested or disclosed to Berry would sooner or later be likely to reach the Taoiseach. These are convincing reasons for questioning the conclusions Berry reached about Haughey, yet Clifford has been almost alone in the literature in finding Berry's theory risible. Support for her view, however, came in the address made by Haughey's counsel, Peter Maguire SC, to the jury at the second arms trial:

> Do you think, gentlemen, for one moment, that if Mr Haughey had a guilty conscience, that if he had been involved in a criminal conspiracy to import arms illegally into this country, that he would phone up Mr Berry, Secretary of the Department of Justice, to talk to him in this way? Isn't it, gentlemen, the last thing he would have thought of doing?[17]

One of the main points of detail at issue over the phone call is what Haughey meant when he asked Berry, 'Does the man from

Mayo know?' Was he asking whether Ó Móráin, a TD for Mayo West, knew generally of the consignment in question, or whether he knew that the Special Branch intended to seize it? The balance of evidence, as Clifford claimed, would strongly suggest the latter meaning, but Berry chose the former; this led to his conclusion that Haughey would not have asked such a question if the arms importation was officially sanctioned. Therefore, he reasoned, it had to be the work of a cabinet 'caucus', and not the cabinet as a whole. Clifford argued that Haughey was asking a different question: 'It is clear to me that the minister was asking whether Ó Móráin knew that Berry intended to seize the cargo when it arrived, whether this was being done on the minister's instructions?'[18]

Berry expounded further on the matter in his Explanatory Note to State counsel in the run-up to the first arms trial. Here he wrote that when Haughey suggested that the consignment might go straight to the North:

> I viewed the matter in the light of my earlier knowledge of his meeting with Goulding, the Chief of Staff of the IRA, of [name blanked out] IRA associations and payments to Goulding for the purchase of arms and Captain Kelly's direct negotiations with the Northern Ireland IRA Command. At no time did it enter into my mind that the arms were being imported, not for the IRA, but for the purpose of giving means of self-defence to ordinary people in Northern Ireland and I never heard of the notion until after the public disclosures in relation to the two Ministers' participation in the attempted importation of arms. Ordinary men have no wish to handle firearms.[19]

This passage reveals both Berry's lack of awareness of events outside his immediate purview, and the conflict and confusion at this time within the security forces. Leaving aside how the Department of Justice official relied at this critical moment on the dubious intelligence of Haughey's supposed meeting with Goulding in August 1969,[20] comparison can be made with the contents of the Army GHQ documents, the Interim Report and the Recommendations of the Planning Board on Northern Ireland Operations.[21] Berry's apprehensions about dealings with the IRA get to the heart of the Arms Crisis conundrum: what was afoot? There were clearly plans to run guns – but for whom, and were they directed at the defence of the nationalist minority, or was there an agenda to attack the Northern state? Had Berry stumbled on the scheming of treacherous politicians, bent on sedition and the rearming of the IRA, or had he merely uncovered some semi-official, well-intentioned but risky fore-planning, intended to avert a pending bloodbath across the border?

What the balance of the evidence suggests is that Haughey's focus, like others such as Colonel Hefferon and senior officers in Army GHQ, was not at all on arming the IRA, but on providing what Berry called 'means of self-defence' for Northern nationalists. Berry, again perhaps not surprisingly, had difficulty imagining the operation uncovered as being *bona fide*; to him, it had to involve some liaison with elements of the IRA, the sworn enemies of the Irish State. The awkward and dangerous calculations that were laid out in the Army Planning Board Reports were not something with which Berry was familiar. While he correctly observed that ordinary people had no wish – he might have added no capability – to handle firearms, his anti-IRA mindset left him unable to follow his own logic: if it was correct that ordinary people in Northern Ireland had no wish to handle firearms, then what group of people might do so on their behalf? Lacking a focus on the acute defensive worries of Northern nationalists, Berry had no means of reaching the same difficult conclusions as those arrived at by senior army officers in GHQ the previous autumn. They had realised that if the Irish authorities in Dublin, frozen out by the British government, wished to help physically in the protection of Northern nationalists, they could achieve little without at some point putting guns in the hands of some Northern republicans.

There is further substantial reason to question the proposition that Haughey, in his phone call to Berry, was exposing the existence of a treacherous conspiracy that he had hatched with the assistance of Neil Blaney. This arises from the sequence of events that caused Haughey to make the phone call in the first place, and which had left him responsible for getting the shipment through customs. At the first arms trial, Colonel Hefferon, as head of Military Intelligence, gave uncontested evidence that it was he who had advised Kelly to approach Haughey, as Minister for Finance, to enable the arms consignment to escape customs scrutiny.[22] Explaining why he had suggested Haughey, and not Gibbons, to be consulted at this point, Hefferon said he knew that Kelly had been working with Haughey over the disbursement of the Northern Relief Fund, and he also knew that the Minister for Finance had the power to direct the Revenue Commissioner to have a customs-free inspection in a given instance. What this shows is that the critical choice that caused Haughey's involvement in this way, and so led indirectly to the phone call to Berry, came not from the man himself, nor from Blaney or Captain Kelly, but from Hefferon, the disinterested senior army officer who was Kelly's commander.

The events that followed Hefferon's advice to Captain Kelly are also of significance in relation to the Haughey–Berry phone call. Having received the advice of his commanding officer, Kelly arrived at Haughey's office in Government Buildings on the afternoon of 19 March 1970. The minister was away at a government meeting. In his absence, Kelly told his assistant, Tony Fagan, that he wanted Haughey to provide clearance through customs for an expected consignment of goods, due to arrive at Dublin Port. The minister, he told Fagan, knew all about it. The goods would be labelled as 'mild steel plate', but would be other than that. Kelly did not state that the shipment was of arms, but Fagan took that understanding from him. Fagan said he would consult Haughey when he returned, and would let Kelly know.

In the interval before Haughey returned to his office, Fagan rang Revenue Commissioner Bartholomew Culligan for advice as to the minister's powers in such a matter. Culligan said if the minister issued a direction, Revenue would observe it. When Haughey returned to his office, Fagan initially told him just of Kelly's request. Haughey, he said, 'seemed doubtful about it, and thought for a while, before asking, who in Revenue should be asked about it?'[23] Fagan then told Haughey that he had already consulted Culligan, and the position was that it was open to the minister to direct that the consignment be customs-free. Haughey said to tell Culligan it was OK. According to Fagan, arms were never mentioned by Haughey, then or afterwards.

The significance of Fagan's evidence, coming from a civil servant with no obvious axe to grind is that it showed Haughey was the last person that day to know he was to have a key role in getting the consignment past customs. It was a plan that had originated with Hefferon, and when Captain Kelly found Haughey to be absent from his office, he had no hesitation in telling his assistant, a public servant, about it. Fagan in turn informed the Revenue Commissioners – all of this without Haughey's knowledge. When Haughey returned and was informed of Kelly's request, his first response was to consider whom to consult among the Revenue Commissioners. On hearing that Fagan had already consulted Culligan, there was no reprimand for indiscretion. Nor is there any evidence that Haughey felt it necessary to speak to Culligan directly about the project, then or later. In this whole process, Haughey had neither oversight, control nor initiative; his responses do not appear at all consistent with the image of a ruthless schemer secretly plotting to bring in arms illegally to rearm the IRA. Yet this is the essential background to Haughey's fateful phone call on the evening of Saturday, 18 April.

Whatever Haughey's motives in the matter, he clearly totally miscalculated how Berry, the seasoned civil servant, would respond to his request. In this, Haughey may have had only himself to blame. He had passed up a possible opportunity to brief Berry on Captain Kelly's activities when, in the first days of October 1969, Berry called him to Mount Carmel Hospital in Dublin. This was several weeks before Berry had a similar meeting with Lynch at the same hospital, as documented in Chapter 7. On this earlier occasion, Berry had also been concerned, on the eve of the Bailieboro meeting, by advance intelligence that republicans were gathering. He tried to reach Lynch, as Taoiseach, but failed, and in those circumstances he called Haughey, whom he knew was accustomed to deputizing in Dublin for the Taoiseach over weekends. Haughey, as shown earlier, knew about the Bailieboro meeting and was even partially funding it, but he chose not to reveal this when he met Berry at the hospital. Haughey, according to Berry's account of their meeting, took the opportunity to quiz the Department of Justice official on what he knew of the IRA Chief of Staff, Cathal Goulding.[24] If the occasion offered a chance to inform Berry about Captain Kelly's activities, Haughey did not use it.

What is also noteworthy about the eventual phone call to Berry on 18 April 1970 is Haughey's unusual diffidence. Although no shrinking violet, he nonetheless made no attempt to face down the uncooperative civil servant, or to use his seniority as a minister to overrule or even argue with him. Haughey, very uncharacteristically, backed down. This seems a further indication of the uncertain, semi-official status of Captain Kelly's operation, and in itself constitutes an early indicator of how neither Haughey nor any other minister – and certainly not Lynch – would ever be prepared *officially* and publicly to underwrite the provision of arms to Northern nationalists.

The remaining issue of uncertainty arising in part from the Haughey–Berry phone call concerns the cancellation of the gun-running project. A common perception is that Haughey cancelled it after being rebuffed in his phone call to Berry. The facts, however, suggest a more complicated narrative, because if the decision was Haughey's alone, it would have been communicated to Fagan when they spoke later on the Saturday. In fact, the cancellation happened almost two days later, shortly after midday on Monday, 20 April. And in a further complication, later that Monday afternoon Haughey and Gibbons met, supposedly to take a decision on cancelling the importation that had already been communicated to Captain Kelly! This has never seemed satisfactory or credible, and in fact the trial record contains no fully coherent account of this meeting or its purpose.

Judge Henchy famously concluded that either Haughey or Gibbons must have committed perjury in their evidence before him. He found the differences in their respective accounts to be 'irreconcilable'. Gibbons said that he pleaded with Haughey to stop the importation for good, and Haughey in response offered to stop it for a month. Haughey in his evidence simply asserted that the conversation as related by Gibbons did not happen. The judge, considering this, said it seemed to him,

> ...in regard to the conversation which Mr. Gibbons says took place in Mr. Haughey's office on Friday 17 April or Monday 20 April, it either took place or it did not take place. Either Mr. Gibbons, it seems, had concocted – invented, as Counsel put to him – this conversation, or it had happened in substance. As you will see later, Mr. Haughey denies it and he cannot explain how his former colleague can say it is so. It is not like something said in the course of a conversation that could be misinterpreted. It seems to me, and you are free to dismiss my opinion, either Mr. Gibbons concocted this and has come to court and perjured himself, or it happened. If there is another explanation, please act on it. There does not seem to me to be any way of avoiding the total conflict on this issue between Mr. Haughey and Mr. Gibbons.[25]

It will be argued here, with the benefit of hindsight and access to the State papers issued in 2001, that the conflict between Haughey and Gibbons was more apparent than real, but that the key to this was hidden from the judge. There *was*, it appears, another explanation for the clash of accounts, one that would permit them to be at least partially reconciled. This is not to argue that either of the two

ministers was being fully truthful, as that seems unlikely. Each of
them already had diminished credibility as witnesses, having being
contradicted in their evidence by senior public servants, specifically
Hefferon and Berry, on a number of vital conversations.[26]

In regard to Monday, 20 April, it appears there were at least
two conversations, not one, between Haughey and Gibbons
on that day. The key witness in support of this is Tony Fagan,
Haughey's personal assistant in the Department of Finance, to
whose evidence, arguably, the judge failed to attach appropriate
weight. The difficulty with the evidence heard by the judge is
obvious: it was well before the late afternoon meeting of Haughey
and Gibbons that Fagan telephoned Captain Kelly in Vienna –
in fact, shortly before 12 noon – to tell him that Haughey had
discussed the matter with Gibbons, and they had both agreed that
the importation was off. Fagan in court was emphatic over the
time of his phone call to Vienna.[27] His evidence again tallied with
that of Kelly, and their agreed timing of their conversation was
accepted unequivocally by State counsel.[28]

Haughey was asked in court how was it Fagan had passed on
this message at midday on Monday, 20 April, when he and Gibbons
did not meet till the late afternoon? Haughey agreed he was simply
unable to explain this, but insisted that he met Gibbons later that
afternoon. The judge left the conflict for the jury to resolve. State
counsel sought to argue that the discrepancy did not matter:

> I don't think it matters, gentlemen, when Mr. Haughey met Mr.
> Gibbons, once it is established that this phone call took place
> on the Monday morning. There can be all sorts of reasons to
> reconcile the apparent discrepancy. Maybe Mr. Fagan is in error
> thinking that Mr. Haughey said he had discussed the matter
> with Mr. Gibbons; maybe he did not say it; maybe Mr. Haughey
> had met Mr. Gibbons earlier.[29]

But it did matter. The timing of any meetings between
Haughey and Gibbons mattered both in the context of the

trial, and historically. The issue was the decision to cancel the gun-running – who took it, and in what circumstances? What role, if any, did Gibbons play? Even in open court in 1970, Fagan's evidence seemed to point to a missing conversation between Haughey and Gibbons. The Department of Finance official was the honest broker in the matter, and his evidence was that the actual decision to cancel was made and communicated – by him – well before Haughey and Gibbons's afternoon meeting. Fagan was emphatic and clear in his recollection: Haughey told him at about 10 a.m. on Monday 20 April that he had already had a conversation with Gibbons. No evidence of such an earlier discussion or decision had been heard. It clearly had to have occurred either earlier on Monday morning, or at least at some time after Haughey had spoken to Berry at 6.30 on Saturday evening.[30] But when?

Evidence has now been identified in the files that may confirm that Haughey and Gibbons had two conversations on 20 April, with the hidden one taking place early that morning. This evidence is contained in the earliest documented account by Tony Fagan of the events of these days, in his detailed handwritten statement dated 13 May 1970. This went largely unnoticed when it was released to the National Archives as part of the State papers in January 2001. It contains an important detail that was not part of the typewritten, formal Garda witness statement taken by Detective Inspector Ned O'Dea the following day, 14 May, and as a result did not feature in any trial documents. Fagan described how Captain Kelly rang him from Vienna on Sunday 19 April, looking for instructions from Haughey. He went on:

> I told the Minister of this next day, and he said that he had already consulted the Minister for Defence *that morning* [emphasis added – MH] about it, and they both agreed that the whole project should be abandoned.[31]

This is important because it was Fagan's earliest record of the events in question. It is the only occasion, despite extensive interrogation at both arms trials and at the Committee of Public Accounts inquiry, when Fagan recorded Haughey as having indicated *when* he talked to Gibbons, i.e., 'that morning'. That meant sometime before 10 a.m. on 20 April. Fagan may have simply forgotten that he wrote this; the handwritten statement was given to his superiors at the time, and he may not have kept a copy. It alone contained this detail. The formal witness statement, in which the reference to 'that morning' did not appear, was the less precise version of his record, but the one that he may subsequently have consulted for recollection purposes. As Fagan never even referred to it subsequently, there seems no reason to suggest he had consciously altered his recollection. The following year, at the Committee of Public Accounts inquiry, Fagan was questioned by Justin Keating TD (Labour) about what Haughey had said to him on 20 April:

> Fagan: All I can say is that Mr. Haughey said: 'I have discussed this with Mr. Gibbons.' Now—
>
> Keating (interrupting) '—I have discussed it with Mr. Gibbons'?
>
> Fagan: 'I have'. Past tense. 'I have discussed this with Mr. Gibbons, and arising from it this is called off. Tell Kelly so....' All I can testify is this is what the Minister said. At what stage or state he had been talking to Mr. Gibbons I do not know.[32]

This passage supports the theory that by January of 1971 Fagan had forgotten what he had written down on 13 May 1970, his earliest record.[33] But he remained emphatic he was told of effectively a prior conversation between Haughey and Gibbons on the morning of Monday 20 April. For whatever reason, this was a conversation which neither party had chosen to reveal to the arms trial.[34] The specific indicator that it took place that particular morning has lain buried in the State papers, only to be released in 2001, and highlighted here for the first time. What remains unknown is where and how Haughey talked to Gibbons, but whether it was on the telephone or, more likely, in Haughey's office before the civil servants were at their desks, an acceptance that the two men had a significant conversation earlier in the day completely alters the context in which the second, much-discussed conversation took place later on Monday afternoon.

While the judge could only explain the conflicting evidence of the two men on the afternoon meeting in terms of perjury and irreconcilable accounts, in fact both Gibbons's and Haughey's accounts may have had a semblance of truth. The key was the fact of not one, but two conversations. In their afternoon discussion, one point on which Haughey and Gibbons seemed in agreement was that their focus was on the *longer term*. One may speculate that in the earlier, undisclosed discussion, it had not been clarified whether the arms importation was being called off temporarily or permanently. Seen in this light, Gibbons's account has some credibility. What he did not do, nor did Haughey, was acknowledge that there had been an earlier discussion in which they had already agreed, apparently jointly, to call off the importation.

What may have happened by the mid-afternoon on Monday was that Gibbons had learned from the Taoiseach how Peter Berry earlier that day had gone to his office with a Garda report on the events of the weekend. At that point, with the Taoiseach now fully engaged, it may have seemed necessary to revisit whatever Gibbons and Haughey had agreed earlier. Lynch, forced into a corner by Berry's persistence and the report from Chief Superintendent Fleming, may have simply told Gibbons that the project had to be totally abandoned. Haughey, at the arms trial, agreed their focus in the afternoon meeting had been on the longer term, but sought to turn the story against his former colleague: 'There was a possibility that Mr Gibbons as Minister for Defence might decide to resurrect it again,' he said. 'It was in that context we both agreed that it had been called off, and had better stay called off.'[35]

In conclusion, several points can be made. Judge Henchy did not have all the facts before him when he charged the jury, and the truth was considerably more complicated than his 'one or other of these two men is lying' summation suggested. Both men were shielding the truth, and both were unreliable witnesses; their conflicting accounts of a key conversation were viewed by the judge, correctly, as irreconcilable. The judge's only failure, if such it was, may have been not to assign an appropriate priority to the precise sworn evidence of the one disinterested witness, Tony Fagan. Fagan's evidence, even without the timing of the conversation as 'that morning', clearly pointed to a second unacknowledged conversation between Haughey and Gibbons, which it now seems clear took place at some time before 10 a.m.[36] Gibbons had completely misrepresented the second meeting by failing to mention the first. Haughey's account was already incoherent, as he simply said he could not explain how Fagan called Kelly before midday, when he and Gibbons did not meet until about 5 p.m. The judge had no chance of being able to guide the jury towards a clear finding on the facts. It seems now that the gun-running operation was called off in two stages, both of them on Monday, 20 April. The first phase was a joint early morning decision when Haughey and Gibbons decided to halt the importation; the second phase came that afternoon, when they further agreed that the cancellation had to be final.

11

Hanging Fire

The dramatic events of the weekend of 17–20 April 1970 were followed by a valley period, one that terminated in the political cataclysm of 6 May. In this interval, it was far from inevitable what the outcome would be. For one thing, Jack Lynch was markedly slow to act against his two most senior-ranked ministers, Haughey and Blaney. He was in possession of evidence against them for over two weeks, from 21 April to 6 May, before deciding suddenly to sack them. His evidence against them was far from conclusive; such as it was, it resided in Berry's account of his telephone conversation with Haughey on 18 April, and in the contents of two Garda reports from Chief Superintendent Fleming, brought to the Taoiseach by Peter Berry on successive days, 20 and 21 April. The first report connected Haughey with the gun-running attempt at Dublin Airport, and the second report connected Blaney. In the Haughey–Berry phone call, Haughey was accused of having sought to have the arms consignment admitted through customs, on condition that it went directly to Northern Ireland.

For several weeks Lynch dithered over this information, until suddenly everything changed on the evening of 5 May. The anonymous Garda note that Opposition Leader Liam Cosgrave presented to him on that date may have changed nothing in strict evidential terms, but it changed everything politically. The leader of Fine Gael was now on the case, having been alerted to the fact that government ministers were engaged in gun-running activity. Within hours, Haughey and Blaney were sacked by Lynch and the matter became a public sensation. One consequence of the dramatic sackings of 6 May is that the previous two weeks have become a kind of lost fortnight, given only intermittent attention in the literature on the Arms Crisis. This is unsatisfactory, because in this period different outcomes, with possibly different winners and losers, were all possible; the various parties, and especially Lynch, were tentatively considering how best to manage the shifting ground. It is important historically to pick through the patchy evidence from these days to see, before the Cosgrave thunderbolt arrived, in what direction events were heading. With outcomes far from preordained, important insights can be gained into the mindset of some of the key players. The big change after 20 April was that Lynch, because of Berry's persistence, was now centre stage. Evidence for a gun-running attempt, so long in the shadows, now lay physically on his desk, and he could no longer avoid dealing with it.

Throughout the following two weeks, all parties – Captain Kelly, Gibbons, Haughey and Blaney – were awaiting the Taoiseach's definitive response. The issue at the time, and historically, is whether Lynch would ever have sacked Haughey and Blaney, and risked the political crisis that in fact followed, had Cosgrave not been given leaked information in early May.[1] But it was not just the fate of the two eventually sacked ministers that was in the balance. A closely related matter, as Lynch pondered his options, was Gibbons's position as Minister for Defence. He appears to have been aware of a danger that he too might find himself cut loose, if the government was to survive. As for Captain Kelly, although he had been exposed as a key figure in the gun-running effort, no immediate action was taken against him. He remained an army officer, but with the nagging worry that if he stayed in the army, he might end up being court-martialled. Initially, he was not even questioned about his activities in Vienna. The Garda Special Branch, led by Fleming, were, as always, watching events closely, but were clearly expecting some decisive action from Lynch. Their essential boss, Peter Berry, had been sceptical about the Taoiseach from as far back as the Mount Carmel Hospital meeting the previous October, and in this period after 20 April 1970 he was heading into what would be an increasingly fractious relationship with Lynch.

In the midst of all this, the one decisive action taken by Lynch in the fifteen days before Cosgrave's intervention was the forced resignation of the Minister for Justice, Ó Móráin, on 4 May. This is an event that raises questions of its own. Considering all of this, it seems that outside the public gaze – for none of this had reached the media – a complex of different circumstances and individual expectations was developing. This would be comprehensively jolted into a new situation by Cosgrave's intervention on 5 May.

Insight into Gibbons's state of mind after 20 April can be gleaned from the way he carefully set up and managed an investigation by his new Director of Army Intelligence, Colonel P. J. Delaney (Hefferon having reached retirement age on 9 April 1970). This little-scrutinized investigation of Delaney was ordered by Gibbons.[2] An extraordinary aspect of the inquiry that resulted is that the minister appeared to tell his new Director of Intelligence almost nothing of his own past knowledge of Captain Kelly and their direct contacts. It is evident, on the basis of Delaney's various memos at the time of the arms trials, that Gibbons did not disclose to him how familiar he was with Kelly's intention to help bring in weapons for the Northern Defence Committees, a familiarity that went back certainly as far as mid-February 1970. This reticence was entirely consistent with Gibbons's early statements to the gardaí, made in the latter half of May 1970, in which he revealed little of what he was able to recall freely by the following year. He could hardly be expected to brief Delaney on matters of which, at the time, the minister claimed to know almost nothing.

Even before this investigation was launched, Delaney was under the disability that he had come in as Hefferon's successor on 9 April without having been briefed, by either Hefferon or by

Gibbons, on the role being played by Captain Kelly. This left him smarting in the aftermath; he offered no criticism of his minister's failure to keep him informed, but chose to view Hefferon's failure to brief him as implying some complicity in illegal and subversive activities. Although this appears well short of the mark, Delaney's opinion has been widely recycled in the literature, including by writers Keogh and Arnold.[3] It is not entirely clear why Hefferon failed to brief Delaney. He had been initially totally opposed to Kelly helping the Northern Defence Committees acquire guns, and only relented on this once Gibbons's actions persuaded him that Kelly was acting in line with government policy. It may be that it was this belief by Hefferon, that Kelly was operating under a highly sensitive government-ordained policy, which led him to the view that it was for the minister to brief Delaney on Kelly, not him.[4] But Gibbons, again for whatever reason, also chose to leave Delaney in the dark.The upshot was that when a crisis began to develop over the weekend of 17–20 April, Delaney was hopelessly unprepared to get its measure. His lack of knowledge of the background and context left him vulnerable to being exploited thereafter, as it appears he may have been, by his minister.

Although the arms importation at Dublin Airport began to create alarm on Friday, 17 April, it was not until the following Monday that Gibbons asked Delaney to investigate. At that stage Delaney, as can be seen from one of his early memos on the subject, had already on the previous Friday been told by Garda Chief Superintendent Pat Malone – conspicuously not by Gibbons – that someone called 'Comdt. Kelly' had applied for a licence to import arms. In a 'Top Secret' memo dated 7 May 1970, Delaney wrote, in part:

> Comdt. Kelly now identified as Captain Kelly on Tuesday 21 April, 1970. D. Int. [Director of Intelligence] advised inform Ceann Fóirne [Chief of Staff] as break was imminent – which he did. On Wednesday 22 April 70, D. Int saw an tAire [the Minister] and advised him of Kelly's involvement.[5]

Two days into his investigation, on Wednesday, 22 April, Delaney thus reported back to Gibbons what the minister had in fact known for five days, but had not told Delaney: that the man at the centre of events was his own officer, Captain James Kelly, whom he also knew had been planning to import guns, and who had told him about a similar failed arms importation attempt at Dublin Port just three weeks previously.[6] Nor had Gibbons told Delaney that Kelly had been entirely open with him and with Hefferon about helping the Northern Defence Committees, or that he had offered to retire from the army almost two months previously, before he, Gibbons, as the minister responsible, had personally stalled the retirement. In extraordinary fashion, Delaney went about his work for the minister unaware of all this.

Delaney's ignorance of how his minister had interacted with Kelly is manifest in a document headed 'Top Secret: Verbal Briefing for an tAire' [the Minister], dated Wednesday, 22 April 1970. Here Delaney recorded that he had advised Gibbons as follows:

1.   Captain J. J. Kelly Int [Intelligence] Section has connections with nationalist and Republican elements in Northern Ireland. Since August last he has been acting as a Field Liaison Officer and he has also acted as a link man for these groups....

2.   His activities also brought him into contact with IRA leaders, notably [blacked out]. During these meetings he has always been known as a G2 (int) officer and has openly promised money for the purchase of arms....

3.   From late November 1969 he ceased to have any contact with the Security Sub-Section....

4.   Recently a Comdt. Kelly came to notice as seeking a license [sic] to import six tons of 'goods' from Vienna. He has been identified as Captain Kelly and it is apparent that this is an

attempt to import arms illegally for subversive groups on both
sides of the Border....[7]

Delaney, it seems clear from this memo, was getting his
information from the Special Branch. His briefing, apart from
the innocence it displayed over what the minister already knew
about Kelly, offered Gibbons very largely the same analysis that
had come from Peter Berry the previous autumn over Bailieboro,
which Hefferon had said at the time was of no consequence,
and which Gibbons and Lynch had chosen thereafter not just to
ignore, but to deny ever receiving.

Lynch received Delaney's report on 24 April, along with a verbal
report from Gibbons.[8] At this stage, a full week had passed since
Gibbons had become aware that his own army officer, Captain
James Kelly, had been in Vienna seeking to fly guns into Ireland,
yet this was the first discussion he and Lynch admitted to having
on the matter.[9] While such a delay again seems hardly credible,
at least from this point on Lynch and Gibbons were in confirmed
dialogue on the matter. The similarities between what Delaney
reported and what Berry had warned them of the previous October
cannot have escaped either man. The course chosen then had been
to ignore the alarm bells ringing around Captain Kelly, but in late
April 1970 that was no longer a viable option. The situation had
changed totally. From Tuesday morning, 21 April, two Garda
reports from Chief Superintendent Fleming were on Lynch's desk,
implicating Kelly, Haughey and Blaney in apparent gun-running.
The cat was well and truly out of the bag, and required a very
different response to that taken six months earlier.

So it was that Delaney's ill-informed analysis on 24 April
1970 appears to have been accepted without reservation. As an
investigation it had been a sham, a product of manipulated and
withheld information, and a contrivance of cunning by Delaney's
minister.[10] It could not have been produced without Gibbons
knowingly keeping Delaney in the dark about his own previous
knowledge of Kelly and the Defence Committees. Nor, it seems,

could it have been accepted without collusion between Lynch and Gibbons in pretending they were not alerted by Peter Berry to Captain Kelly's activities six months earlier than Lynch would ever admit.

After the Taoiseach received the Garda reports on 20 and 21 April 1970, there was little urgency about his initial response, despite two of his most senior ministers being implicated in the arms importation. The Taoiseach claimed afterwards that the situation was complicated by the fact that Haughey had suffered a serious accident on 22 April, apparently falling from a horse at his Kinsealy estate in north Dublin. With Haughey hospitalized with significant head injuries, Lynch explained later how he felt he should not confront him with the evidence until his doctors indicated that he had sufficiently recovered. Accordingly, he did not speak to him until 29 April. He only saw Blaney, separately, on that same date. Lynch invited both men to resign. Each declined.[11] Lynch had waited eight days before issuing what turned out to be a half-hearted request for the two ministers to stand down.

As Opposition deputies stressed heavily at the time, while the delay can be partially explained by reference to the Haughey injury, no such excuse could be made over the handling of Blaney. He was able-bodied and healthy, yet in the days after 21 April he was left in his cabinet post, subject to no questioning about the serious allegations that featured in Fleming's second report on 21 April, connecting him with the arms importation.[12] Apart from those initial eight days, Blaney remained in office for a further six days, up to 6 May, during which time he had the full authority of his ministerial position and was free to 'cover his tracks', as Justin Keating stated accusingly in the Dáil on 8 May.[13]

Although he asked for Haughey and Blaney's resignations on 29 April, Lynch did not press the point. Later he would claim that he always intended to continue his investigations. However, that is contradicted by events the following day, 30 April, when

Berry claims he was told by Lynch that nobody was to be sacked. Lynch said he had spoken to both Haughey and Blaney: they had denied any wrong-doing and 'the matter was ended, there would be no repetition'. In his account in the *Diaries* of Lynch's conversation with him that morning, Berry states that he asked despairingly of the Taoiseach what his position *vis-à-vis* Haughey would be, after he had reported to Lynch on their fraught telephone conversation on the evening of 18 April. Lynch's scarcely reassuring response was that he would protect him.[14]

This reported conversation between Berry and Lynch on 30 April 1970 suggests that Lynch had decided not to sack Haughey and Blaney, before he was faced with Cosgrave's dramatic intervention on 5 May. It is an impression that is supported by evidence from a government meeting the following day, 1 May. Here Lynch seemed to draw a line under the matter of taking action against Haughey and Blaney. While no official record of what he said at cabinet exists in the files, several of those present have subsequently set down their memory of it. Kevin Boland, Lynch's Minister for Local Government at that point, but shortly afterwards out of the cabinet, said in a radio interview in November 1970 that Lynch told the cabinet that he had discussed the matter with Haughey and Blaney, that he had accepted their explanations, and that the matter was over.[15] Writing further about it two years later, Boland said that Lynch had dealt with the matter emphatically:

> He said he had got this information, had put it to the two Ministers, and they had both denied having been involved in an illegal attempt to import arms. He said he had decided to accept their denial, that the matter was now closed and warned the members in general that any specific action in relation to the Six Counties should be brought to the government for sanction.[16]

John Walsh, in his authorized biography of Patrick Hillery, cited contemporaneous recordings made by Hillery in 1970 which supported Boland's account:

The government meeting ended with everyone thinking that the case was closed as far as the Blaney Haughey episode, both were mentioned and that was that.... There would be no implications for the two Ministers involved in the attempt to import arms. The Taoiseach gave the impression that it was the end of the matter.... It seemed to be something with which he had dealt and did not want to happen again.[17]

Another minister present that day, P. J. Lalor, in an interview with author Bruce Arnold, had a similar memory of what Lynch said:

When Lynch came into the government meeting, and before the start of business, he said: 'I have something to say. Information has come to me of an attempt to bring in arms. It has been suggested to me that two members of the government were involved, Neil Blaney and Charles Haughey. I have spoken with them, and they have denied all knowledge. I have accepted their assurances they were not involved...[18]

Finally, Blaney himself, twenty years after the events in question, talked about the cabinet meeting on 1 May, and what Lynch had said:

He sat down and finally told the cabinet of the trauma he'd gone through on the day before and how he'd come by information that would indicate that two of his Ministers had been other than loyal subjects and so forth, and how relieved he was that it was all over and done with and closed and now could he get on with his fucking meeting.[19]

Entirely against this weight of first-hand evidence, Lynch insisted to the Dáil later in 1970 that 'I had decided to act before Deputy Cosgrave's hint', and also that 'I did not say at a government meeting that the matter was ended'.[20] Bruce Arnold, without citing any source, wrote in 2001 that what Lynch actually told the cabinet

was that 'the matter is closed for the present'. Arnold disputed that
Cosgrave had forced Lynch to move against Haughey and Blaney;
it was a position 'widely and wrongly believed at the time' because,
he said, the resignation request had never been withdrawn.[21]
Arnold's argument was echoed by Stephen Collins, who concluded
his account of the cabinet meeting in question by stating that 'the
matter was, for the present, closed', again without providing any
reference for this qualification.[22] Dermot Keogh chose to make no
reference to what Lynch told the cabinet on 1 May 1970. Writing in
2016, historian Stephen Kelly also appeared to overlook the various
first-hand accounts of what Lynch said on that occasion.[23]

Despite these various treatments, Vincent Browne was probably
correct in concluding in 1980 that Lynch had no intention of
pursuing the matter against Haughey and Blaney any further.
Browne saw further evidence for this in Lynch's departure from
Dublin on the afternoon of 1 May for a management conference
in Killarney.[24] Lynch insisted repeatedly in the Dáil that he had
been intent on enforcing the resignations before Cosgrave came to
him. And he repeated the claim ten years later in November 1980,
in the aftermath of the publication of the Berry *Diaries*, when he
stated that 'at no stage did I indicate to the government... that
the matter was ended as far as I was concerned'.[25] The evidence,
however, strongly suggests otherwise. Also, the speed with which
he reacted to the anonymous and unchecked note presented to
him by Liam Cosgrave on 5 May 1970 suggests a panicked and
forced response, one more consistent with a sudden change of
plan, and entirely contrary to what he had outlined six days earlier
on 30 April 1970 to a shell-shocked Peter Berry.

The only significant action Lynch is known to have taken between
1 May and 5 May – that is, before Cosgrave came to him – was
to ask Minister for Justice Ó Móráin for his resignation, which
he duly received on 4 May. Lynch said that Ó Móráin had no
involvement in the gun-running, and insisted he had resigned for

health reasons. He later conceded that this was not so, that he had forced his resignation, although on a basis of alleged incapacity rather than any hint of neglect, disloyalty or sedition. But at a later stage, it became clear that privately Lynch did blame Ó Móráin for not having informed him of the concerns emanating from his department Secretary, and from the Special Branch, that an illicit gun-running operation seemed to be in train.[26]

This has remained the outstanding historical issue over Ó Móráin's forced resignation: whatever about Gibbons, can it be reasonably argued that it was the Minister for Justice who was to blame for Lynch's claimed lack of knowledge of an arms importation at any time before 20 April 1970? In the first days of May 1970, as Lynch continued to plot his way out of an already embarrassing situation, there is some evidence that he may have been lining up Ó Móráin as the fall guy for the whole affair, based on this supposed failure to inform him about Special Branch worries over Captain Kelly.

Kevin Boland, Ó Móráin's colleague, who sat beside him at cabinet, wrote later that Ó Móráin was deeply frustrated by having tried and failed on several occasions to get Lynch to raise at cabinet the question of an arms consignment. Boland knew from his cabinet colleague that the matter was causing concern within the Department of Justice – this was presumably a reference to Berry – and Ó Móráin wanted to be able to advise officials. Boland wrote: 'Either the importation was right or wrong.... If it was right, the Minister for Justice should know, so he could direct his department in the matter.... He had asked the Taoiseach, and he wouldn't tell him, nor would he raise the matter at government level.'[27] Boland's view was that Lynch knew of the consignment and, by resisting its formal discussion by the government, was effectively permitting it. At the same time, in an appraisal that carries an impressive honesty, he thought that if the matter came up formally, Lynch would oppose it.

The view that Ó Móráin knew of the pending arms shipment but was unclear about its exact status is one that finds support in the former Minister for Justice's evidence at the first arms trial. There, Ó Móráin stated that he had heard conflicting reports at different stages before 18 April 1970, and 'certainly at one of these stages I thought this was an official importation'.[28] Overall, while, as noted earlier, it is difficult to be categorical about Ó Móráin's situation, there is no doubt that he offered an easy target for the Taoiseach if he was seeking to evade responsibility.

Berry has offered conflicting evidence regarding his minister. While he believed there had been a failure to pass on information to Lynch, his own *Diaries* showed how Ó Móráin authorized the passing of all relevant information to the Taoiseach at least a week before the date Lynch claimed. Berry wrote that on 13 April 1970, Ó Móráin, although in ill health, told him to tell Lynch all he knew of Captain Kelly and any arms dealing. This the Department of Justice Secretary duly did, on that same date.[29] Berry did not specify what he told Lynch on that occasion, but it can only have been substantially what he had sought to bring to Lynch's attention in Mount Carmel Hospital the previous October.

Lynch always claimed that he knew nothing of an arms plot before Berry came to him a week later on 20 April, a position that ignored both his meeting with Berry on 13 April and the Mount Carmel warning given to him six months earlier. On 16 May, after Lynch had forced Ó Móráin to resign and then sacked Haughey and Blaney for operating behind his back, somewhat suspiciously he quizzed Berry as to whether his former minister would be likely to remember the conversation he had with Berry on 13 April. Berry in reply said he thought Ó Móráin would not remember. But the fact that Lynch asked such a question strengthens the impression that, regardless of the facts, his Minister for Justice may have been at risk of carrying the can for the claimed failure to inform the Taoiseach of the arms importation plan.

Meanwhile, Berry was uncertain what he should do next, after he had faced down Charles Haughey over the arms consignment on Saturday 18 April. He did not know to whom he could safely turn, in a delicately poised situation. The arms shipment was still awaiting consignment in Vienna with Captain Kelly in attendance, the Special Branch were *in situ* around Dublin Airport, and Berry had drawn on all the iron in his soul in refusing to yield to one of the most powerful ministers in the government. His own minister was indisposed, or certainly absent. Berry needed to report what had happened, but to whom? He was not immediately inclined to trust the Taoiseach. So far as he could see, Lynch had failed to act, not just after his recent briefing of him on 13 April, but six months earlier, after the Mount Carmel conversation.

Berry turned now to the only senior Fianna Fáil source he felt could be relied on, the elderly founder of the party, President Éamon de Valera. He made a highly irregular telephone call to Áras an Úachtaráin, either late on Saturday or on the Sunday of that weekend, a call clearly designed – at least in part – to put indirect pressure on the Taoiseach finally to take some action. It also appears to have been an attempt to fire-proof his own position in the event of future recriminations over his conduct. But still, in his phone call to de Valera, Berry did not tell the President the real reason why he was contacting him. Hiding behind his minister's incapacity, he basically asked de Valera whether it was permissible for him, having received some vital information, to go over his minister's head and to inform the Taoiseach directly. It was only when de Valera advised him to go to Lynch that Berry did so, on Monday, 20 April.

In contacting de Valera, Berry appeared to be taking out an insurance policy against some unpredictable, perhaps hostile, response from the Taoiseach. Berry saw himself as being in 'a frightful dilemma' over that weekend. In an *aide-mémoire* written later in the summer to assist the arms trial prosecution, he explained that he had been worried that he might embarrass the Taoiseach by raising issues over what could possibly be a secret government policy.[30] He was more forthright when writing his *Diaries* in the mid-1970s; here he reflected on the doubts and suspicions he had about Lynch at the time:

Analysing my motives afterwards in speaking to him [President de Valera], I could only suppose that sub-consciously I retained lingering doubts about the Taoiseach, and that by consulting the President and telling the Taoiseach that I had consulted the President, I would be pushing the Taoiseach towards an enforcement of the rule of law. I had not forgotten that the Taoiseach had taken no effective steps to curb the activities of Captain Kelly of Military Intelligence about whom I had given him very definite information on 17 October 1969 in Mount Carmel Hospital.[31]

Duly advised by de Valera, on 20 and 21 April Berry brought to the Taoiseach Fleming's two reports, plus a verbal report on his telephone conversation with Haughey. Significantly, he also told Lynch that he had spoken to de Valera, because, he admitted, he had qualms about going to him directly as Taoiseach, 'as I might be encroaching on a secret government mission'. Even on Berry's own account, this was at best a half-truth. Just as with de Valera, he baulked at telling the Taoiseach the truth, which was that he did not trust him to enforce the rule of law.

It is noteworthy that in Berry's account of his meetings with Lynch on Monday and Tuesday, 20 and 21 April, neither man referred to their encounter at Mount Carmel Hospital the previous October, though it must have been in both their minds, especially Berry's.[32] It was also strange, in view of the significance of what he was being told, that Lynch made no immediate comment on the information about cabinet ministers being involved in gun-running. However, that changed eight days later; in a meeting with Berry on 29 April, Lynch showed he was aware that his previous silence in the face of startling information from Berry had been highly unusual. He 'suddenly' interrupted a conversation on other matters and referred back to his earlier behaviour. He told Berry that he was so furious at him for thinking the government might be secretly involved in gun-running that he had 'seen red', and had not been able to speak.[33] This, as an explanation by Lynch

for his muted response at the time, reads in print quite unconvincingly; no doubt it appeared likewise to Berry, though he
offered no comment.

The Berry *Diaries* represent the Taoiseach in the days after
21 April as being ill-tempered and slow to act on the information
he had been given. Berry was fretting over the slow pace of
investigation, and found himself getting under Lynch's skin more
than once. His zeal for uncovering the facts did not seem to him
to be shared by the Taoiseach. Their next *tête-à-tête* came only two
days later, when Berry, who believed that Lynch had 'instructed me
to have the matter fully investigated', was carpeted by Lynch over
a heavy-handed attitude to Revenue officials at Dublin Airport
from whom statements were being sought. When the officials
did not respond speedily, Berry threatened the chairman of the
Revenue Commissioners that 'heads would roll' unless there was
more cooperation. Lynch summoned Berry and told him he had
no business or right to talk to the chairman of the Revenue in that
way. He should leave the investigation to the police. Berry wrote
that he was 'dumbfounded':

> I had expected to be praised, not blamed. All my doubts of earlier
> months that the Taoiseach could not have some knowledge of
> what was going on in the background came flooding back; his
> remarks and attitude did not seem to fit a head of government
> who was anxious to bring malefactors to justice.[34]

There was more tetchiness to come. On 29 April Lynch discussed
with Berry what he should do about the apparent involvement of
Haughey and Blaney in the arms importation. Thinking his advice
was being sought, Berry offered that if it were him, he would sack
them immediately. Lynch then 'rounded on me', Berry wrote in
the *Diaries*, angry that he had presumed to give him advice as
Taoiseach. The following day, 30 April, Lynch, as noted earlier,
shocked Berry by telling him he had decided to take no action
against Blaney and Haughey, and that he would protect the Justice

official from Haughey's potential wrath at the way their telephone conversation had been disclosed. Berry later wrote sardonically that he found it 'interesting' to read Lynch's 'very different' account in the Dáil on how he had dealt with Haughey and Blaney in the period 21 April to 5 May. This was a reference to Lynch's insistence, after he sacked the two ministers, that he had always intended to do so, regardless of Cosgrave's intervention.[35]

Later that day, 30 April, Lynch held an evening conference at his home to discuss the Garda investigation. The Attorney General, Colm Condon, and Gibbons, Minister for Defence, were present. Berry – it seems to his chagrin – was not invited to attend. Chief Superintendent Fleming, who appeared to share Berry's view that ministers had been engaging in something close to sedition, was present but not invited to speak. Immediately after the meeting, Fleming visited Berry at his home and told him that neither he nor Colonel Delaney, who was also there, were asked any questions. Fleming wondered why his presence had been required at such a meeting. Berry, probably still smarting from the news earlier in the day that Lynch did not intend to sack Haughey, received a phone call from the Taoiseach while Fleming was still with him. The Taoiseach wanted to update Berry on the conference he had just held, telling him, 'I now have a better understanding of the position.'[36] Berry took it upon himself to tell Lynch of Fleming's dissatisfaction at not being asked to contribute to the meeting; Berry noted that Lynch's voice, in response, was angry on the phone.

On 9 May, Lynch gave the Dáil an account of this conference in his home on 30 April. He said it had been held to coordinate the evidence arising from the investigations by both the Garda Special Branch and Army Intelligence up to that point.[37] Berry wrote in the *Diaries* that when he read these comments by Lynch at the time, 'as a result of the mis-statements already recorded, with more to follow, I lost respect for the Taoiseach's credibility'.[38] He said that Lynch was clearly engaged in 'bridge-building' – an ambiguous phrase, but hardly intended as a compliment.

1. Paddy Bogside Doherty, Derry Citizens Action Committee, controlling a large crowd at junction of Rossville St. and William St., Derry, on the occasion of a visit from Home Secretary James Callaghan, August 1969.

2. Members of the new Irish Cabinet, July 1969:
(seated) Patrick Hillery (External Affairs), Kevin Boland (Local Government), Erskine Childers (Tanaiste and Health), Jack Lynch (Taoiseach), Neil Blaney (Agriculture and Fisheries), Micheál Ó Móráin (Justice), Charles Haughey (Finance);
(standing): Brian Lenihan (Transport and Power), Sean Flanagan (Lands), Padraig Faulkner (Education), Patrick Lalor (Posts and Telegraph), George Colley (Industry and Commerce), James Gibbons (Defence), Joe Brennan (Labour), Colm Condon SC (Attorney General), and Dr. O`Nualláin, Secretary to the Government.

3. Micheál Ó Móráin, Minister for Justice, outside the Four Courts, September 1970.

4. Neil Blaney, sacked Minister for Agriculture and Fisheries, (in the background, to Blaney's right, James Kelly), outside the Bridewell courthouse, July 1970.

5. Taoiseach Jack Lynch addresses the Fianna Fáil Árd Fheis, January 1970.

(Right) 6. Witness for the prosecution and former Minister for Defence, James Gibbons, arrives at the Four Courts for the first arms trial, September 1970.

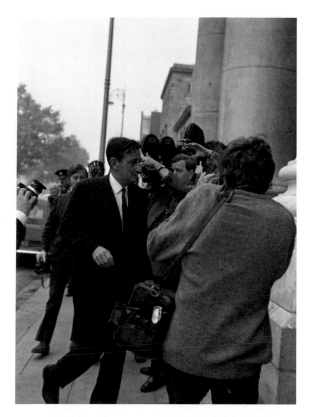

(Below) 7. State Counsel outside the Four Courts, October 1970: (from left) Aiden Browne, Seamus McKenna, S.C., and Eamonn Walsh, S.C.

(*Above*) 8. John Kelly being carried shoulder high after his acquittal at the arms trial, October 1970.

(*Right*) 9. Colonel Michael Hefferon. Director of Military Intelligence, outside the Four Courts, September 1970.

10. Counsel for Charles Haughey, Peter Maguire, SC., and Niall McCarthy, SC., outside the Four Courts, October 1970.

11. Charles Haughey flanked by photographers at a press conference in Dublin, following his acquittal in the arms trial, October 1970.

12. Neil Blaney, James Kelly, John Kelly and Albert Luykx (on right) leaving the Circuit Criminal Court, July 1970.

Berry felt Lynch was constructing an *appearance* of inquiry and investigation, a possible smokescreen to help the government safely out of the crisis. Vincent Browne, publisher of the *Diaries*, wrote of the 30 April conference that Fleming and Berry believed the Taoiseach was simply closing down the inquiry, rather than planning its extension. Browne concurred: 'Certainly... it would appear this was the purpose of the meeting.'[39]

Another perspective on Gibbons's presence in Lynch's house in Rathgar in Dublin at the 30 April 1970 conference emerged in 2001; this suggested it may have marked the watershed moment when Gibbons deserted his former close colleagues, Haughey and Blaney, and entered into a pact with the Taoiseach. Blaney told an interviewer that Gibbons said to him, earlier on that same day, that he was on his way to Lynch's house in Rathgar, where he believed he was going to be sacked. At the time, Lynch had just requested resignations from Haughey and Blaney. 'I'm for the high jump too,' Gibbons had said. Blaney said this conversation was the last 'normal' one he ever had with Gibbons. His belief was that, while in Rathgar, Gibbons's status was transformed from that of a potential co-defendant in a criminal prosecution to that of 'prime chief prosecution witness'.[40] Gibbons's remark to Blaney suggests that Lynch had waited some ten days after 20 April before reassuring his former Minister for Defence that his position was, at least to a degree, safe; perhaps it took this long for Lynch to appreciate that the insulation of his Minister for Defence from complicity in the gun-running was an effective *sine qua non* for the government's survival in office.[41]

It was also about ten days after the cancellation of the project that Captain Kelly was arrested and questioned over his part in it. In that time, Kelly became suspicious that Gibbons intended to get him court-martialled. To avoid this, he forced through his early retirement from the army. Kelly has provided an exceptionally detailed and useful record of his affairs in this period in both

Orders for the Captain? (1971) and *The Thimble Riggers* (1999), including a blow-by-blow account of his arrest and questioning on 1 May 1970.[42] Some writers have suggested that the decision to question him after such a delay may have been a unilateral move by the Special Branch and Berry, driven by impatience over government inaction. While the dissatisfaction of both Berry and Fleming over the previous evening's conference at Lynch's house lends circumstantial support to this theory, the involvement of both Gibbons and Lynch in the questioning of Kelly on 1 May, as described by Kelly himself, suggests that the arrest is more likely to have been coordinated. The main purpose of the questioning appears to have been to find out if the arrested army officer could, or would, provide further incriminating evidence against Haughey or Blaney. Kelly declined to do so, in robust fashion, and refused to make a prepared statement, even after Lynch, unusually, had made himself available to help in the acquisition of one.

The most striking part of Kelly's account of his forty-eight-hour detention in Bridewell Garda Station in Dublin concerns the expression of views he attributed to Chief Superintendent Fleming. Kelly said Fleming named three ministers to him as having been complicit in the gun-running – Haughey, Blaney and Gibbons – and went on to tell Kelly that he believed Lynch, as Taoiseach, also knew of it.[43] Fleming, when he gave evidence at the Committee of Public Accounts inquiry a year later, denied saying this. He agreed that he named three ministers to Kelly, but denied that Gibbons was one of them; he said the third minister he named, after Haughey and Blaney, was Boland.[44] The questioning of Kelly on 1 May 1970 was inconclusive and produced no statement; its most significant effect was probably to add to the sense of impatience building up in this period, in Garda Síochána and Department of Justice circles.

The circumstantial evidence suggests strongly that it was this growing neurosis within the security forces that brought about the leak of information to Cosgrave which in turn led to Lynch's drastic response on 6 May 1970. The only semi-credible alternative theory of the source of the leak has laid the blame on the British intelligence services.[45] But British officials appeared surprised, above all, by Lynch's sudden dismissal of his ministers. One official, on the morning of 6 May, told London: 'We have no idea what precipitated the crisis.'[46] A 'speaking note' from officials briefing Foreign Secretary Michael Stewart for a cabinet meeting on 7 May stated: 'No one expected the announcement of 6 May,'[47] while at the end of May 1970 Peck described the sacking as having 'burst like a bomb', with nobody prepared for it.[48] None of this is suggestive of a British role in instigating the crisis. Some days later, Foreign Secretary Stewart advised British Embassy officials in Dublin that there was no truth in rumours of British involvement. He advised officials they should not volunteer comment on the issue, but, if asked about it, they could deny any British role in the leak and say that the matter was seen as 'essentially a domestic problem for the Irish Republic'.[49]

On balance, the evidence favours a Garda Special Branch source for the leak, possibly with Peter Berry's covert approval. Collins, in *The Power Game,* specifically named retired head of the Special Branch, Chief Superintendent Phil McMahon, as the person responsible, though he cited only a 'private source' for this information.[50] In further support of this view, it is arguable that the leak had a purpose contrary to any identifiable British interest in the matter. The British were anxious to assist Lynch against his more militant colleagues within Fianna Fáil, but by including the Minister for Defence, Gibbons, and the Director of Military Intelligence, Hefferon, as part of the reported conspiracy, the information implicated Lynch's government officially in the importation, and not just Haughey and Blaney. This was far from helpful to the Taoiseach. Its obvious purpose was to spur him into action, in which respect it was spectacularly successful; at the same time, as described earlier, it was only due to some nimble footwork from Lynch, and a compliant Leader of the Opposition, that the names of Gibbons and Hefferon were kept out of Liam Cosgrave's report to the Dáil on the matter.

12
Hefferon's Defiance

His widow Peggy once remarked that Michael Hefferon was 'a great man to keep a secret'.[1] As a quality, this had to be invaluable to any holder of the office of Director of Military Intelligence, but, if anything, Hefferon took it to excess. There are times when charting the unfolding of the Arms Crisis through 1970 and 1971 that a disinterested observer can only throw his or her eyes heavenwards and wonder why Hefferon was unable to share important data with his Chief of Staff, Lieutenant General MacEoin. His closeness with information was extraordinary. Yet it was consistent with an officer moored to extreme discretion, and one who has remained one of the least known figures in this drama. Tom MacIntyre described the colonel's appearance in the witness box at the first arms trial:

> Colonel Hefferon is stern, forthright; the jut of jaw under moustache and spectacles, the parade of the shoulders, say, This is how I am, how I have disciplined myself to be, take or leave – and the jury take to him at once. A good witness.[2]

Hefferon's misfortune was that the last eight months of his forty-year unblemished career in the Defence Forces coincided with the turbulence that eventually generated the Arms Crisis. Once the State moved to prosecute Captain Kelly, his own staff officer in Military Intelligence, Hefferon could hardly avoid being engulfed in the controversy and the criminal trial that followed.

Apart from his supervisory role over Kelly, Hefferon had another role that made him a pivotal figure in the affair: that of direct adviser on intelligence matters to James Gibbons, the recently appointed (July 1969) Minister for Defence. That meant that at the relevant period he was directly connected both to one of the accused and to his principal accuser, and this triangular relationship between Kelly, Hefferon and Gibbons was a constant factor not just in the trials but also in the subsequent fifty-year argument over the Arms Crisis.

Although their relationship would later sour, Hefferon appears to have established a friendship with his minister, Gibbons, in the short period from July 1969 to May 1970 in which they worked together. They were both intelligent and literate men, and Gibbons came to rely on Hefferon's military know-how as he learned the ropes in his first full cabinet ministry. Given the serious deterioration later in their relationship, it is interesting to observe how Hefferon's widow saw their friendship:

> Mr. Gibbons was a great friend of my husband. All the years... he was Director of Intelligence, they were great friends. And Mr. Gibbons was a friendly and jovial man. They got on very well. Until the arms trial. That was the end of it. But I think you see, Mr. Gibbons was quite sure that Michael was going to support him.... He didn't know Michael was going to tell the truth. Which he emphasised all through his life, that he told the truth.[3]

Hefferon by 1970 had been in charge of the military branch of the intelligence services of the Irish State for eight years. His department of the army was, in intelligence terms, very much the junior partner; the more senior agency, the section of the Garda Síochána known as S Branch, or Special Branch, was, as part of the civil power, larger and better resourced. It is one of the ironies of this story that Hefferon, who had a fraught and rather testy relationship in his life and career with his rival intelligence 'chief', Secretary of the Department of Justice Peter Berry, still forged from the grave a bond of agreed evidence with his old adversary that illuminates in a special way understanding of the period (see Chapter 7).

But it was as a witness in the arms trials that Hefferon made the choice that came to define him, and which appears to have brought him grief in his years of retirement from the army. That choice was to refuse to disassociate himself from the arms importation scheme of his subordinate officer, Kelly. In taking such a position, it must have been clear to Hefferon that he risked bringing similar criminal charges against himself, sometime in the future. It was a choice that involved him in a serious conflict of evidence with his minister, and which might even have threatened to collapse the Lynch government at a time of national crisis. This cannot have been easy for a military man accustomed to loyal service of the State and to obeying orders from his Commander-in-Chief. The effect was to bring on Hefferon much of the same suspicion and obloquy that Captain Kelly incurred, and to earn for him an official disfavour that lingered throughout his retirement.[4]

Hefferon and Gibbons met regularly in the period 1969–70; the Director of Military Intelligence had, by custom and usage, a well-established channel of communication directly to the Minister for Defence. This meant, in effect, bypassing the Chief of Staff, Lieutenant General MacEoin. Hefferon was a widely experienced officer; he had been in charge of the Defence Forces Infantry School, had been *aide-de-camp* to President Seán T. O'Ceallaigh, and had been assigned as personal *aide-de-camp* to US President John F. Kennedy during his Irish visit in June 1963. In his eight years in charge of military intelligence, Hefferon had a record of defending his patch; he sternly resisted efforts by Peter Berry, the effective controller of the Garda Special Branch, to control and limit his right of direct access on intelligence matters to the Minister for Justice. One encounter, in which Hefferon refused to bow the knee to Berry, had ended with the civil servant 'storming out of the room in a very bad temper indeed'.[5]

Although he became a major witness in the two arms trials, in the overall literature on the Arms Crisis Hefferon has been treated almost as a peripheral figure, with little direct focus on his role. Some writers have depicted him as an honourable officer who was nonetheless neglectful in allowing himself to be undermined by a supposedly wayward subordinate – Kelly – and by two conspiring cabinet ministers, Haughey and Blaney. This supposed neglect has been an essential component in the Haughey–Blaney conspiracy theory.[6] It will be evident in Chapters 14 and 15 that Hefferon, although he was a pivotal witness in the case, was handled in a most irregular fashion by the Attorney General in the course of both the Garda investigation and the preliminaries to the trials. That he was a major and possibly decisive figure in the two arms trials is evident, but on the broader canvas of the Arms Crisis, relatively little attention has been given to the vital part Hefferon played not just in divulging and confirming the existence of the 6 February directive, but also in connecting the directive to Kelly's plans to import arms. Just as the historical significance of the directive has been often either underplayed, or even ignored, so the officer who more than anyone ensured it came to public notice has escaped the attention he deserves. This has left Hefferon occupying an ill-defined space in the narrative of the Arms Crisis, and may have indirectly facilitated the avoidance of some uncomfortable truths associated with his role.

Chief among the awkward facts about Hefferon is the way in which, as Kelly's immediate superior, he associated himself with activities that the State deemed conspiratorial, illicit and subversive of the Lynch government's approach to Northern Ireland. When it came time for him to make a witness statement, Hefferon chose for himself a role that, from the State's malign perspective, could be represented as that of a self-confessed co-conspirator.[7] He accepted without qualification that he knew of and had even contributed to Captain Kelly's gun-running project. It was an acceptance of involvement that could, as noted, have brought charges against himself; but that course of action, in reality, was one of the last options the State would have chosen. To prosecute Hefferon would have meant conceding that the gun-running had a level of official army sanction much higher than that of a junior officer such as Kelly.[8]

Nor was that the only problem with prosecuting Hefferon. His account of what had happened directly implicated the minister, Jim Gibbons; the Attorney General, in his role as State prosecutor, must, from the moment Hefferon's statement of evidence came in, have feared that it could cause the whole prosecution case to unravel. Because of these simple facts, Hefferon's role has represented a challenge to writers sympathetic to the Lynch view of the Arms Crisis. If it was true that a conspiracy by disloyal cabinet ministers against Lynch was driving the gun-running attempt, then it would be logical that Hefferon, given his self-confessed involvement in the planning, was part of the conspiracy. This logic commended itself to Hefferon's hapless successor, Colonel P. J. Delaney, who advanced it at the time. That would have made Hefferon an unlikely servant of the alleged 'government within a government' supposedly operated by Haughey and Blaney,[9] and would have given him a central role in a supposed subversive plot to rearm the IRA. Hefferon in turn linked Gibbons to the plotting, as Gibbons was the minister he was briefing regularly, and was his guide to the government's approach on such matters.

Yet few of those writers who have favoured Jack Lynch's position in the Arms Crisis have been prepared to implicate Hefferon – or Gibbons – directly in the supposed plot. The effect has been to leave Hefferon's involvement in the gun-running, as well as in the Bailieboro meeting in October 1969, as difficulties for those such as Collins, Keogh and Arnold – even O'Brien, who had a more nuanced view of Lynch – all of whom have identified an illegal plot by renegade ministers against a sitting Taoiseach.[10] Apart from the fact that Hefferon never met Blaney before 23 April 1970, when the gun-running was effectively over, and had minimal dealings with Haughey either before or after that point, little in the evidence ascribes extreme republican views to him.

He was manifestly neither a subversive nor a criminal, and there is nothing to place him within any political cabal dedicated to elevating the careers of either Charles Haughey or Neil Blaney.

The evidence, on the contrary, is that Hefferon was an experienced and trusted soldier at the very top of the Defence Forces, tasked in 1969–70 with helping prepare the Defence Forces for crisis contingency activity across the border, inside Northern Ireland. Hefferon shared the continuing anxiety inside Irish government circles at the time over the possibility of further sectarian pogroms over the border, after what he called 'the thunderclap' of 13 August 1969.[11] These concerns are fully evidenced in Irish diplomatic files through April and May 1970,[12] and contrary to some accounts, the doubts that British forces could or would provide adequate safeguards against possible Ulster Volunteer Force assaults on Catholics persisted well after the arrival of the British army on the streets of the North in August 1969.[13] Hefferon, in his *Papers*, described how the situation was seen in Dublin: 'With bloody civil war looming dangerously close… it was common prudence for us here to prepare for the worst – disagreeable though that prospect might be.'[14]

These preparations for the worst, as Hefferon termed them, were focused on defending nationalist lives, and not on the destruction of partition. While the authorization for the arms importation of Captain Kelly would later, after 6 May 1970, become strongly contested, Hefferon's actions at the time were as a high-level public servant, and one who was in close communication with the Minister for Defence. Gibbons was ideally placed to inform his Director of Military Intelligence on the realities of government policy on Northern Ireland, and appears to have done exactly this, particularly on 6 February 1970.

Pivotal to understanding Hefferon's position – and much of the Arms Crisis – is the directive of 6 February 1970. The instructions from the government that day envisaged the use of force within

Northern Ireland, but force only for humanitarian and defensive purposes. The distinction between a use of force to protect – *in extremis* – nationalist lives and property in the North, and a more aggressive use of force to attack partition and create a united Ireland, is, as was argued in Chapter 5, fundamental to the Arms Crisis. Hefferon sought to explain his view of the distinction in a fascinating exchange with Deputy Justin Keating at the Committee of Public Accounts inquiry in 1971:

> Keating: You are now saying you were not quite clear as to what government policy was. Would you indicate to us what raised any possible confusion in your mind?
>
> Hefferon: I was aware of this, but there is a difference between force which I think nobody – the use of force or the using of the Army or the armed forces to go into the North and to take over the Six Counties by force, and the situation in which the government here are forced to take some action owing to a breakdown of law and order in the North, or a similar situation, a worse situation perhaps arising in Northern Ireland than the one that arose in August – I think there is a difference between the two.
>
> Keating: I agree there is and I do not propose to tease out the difference, because incursions by an Army in the context of a breakdown of law and order is one thing, and the arming of the civilian population in the Six Counties is a different thing....[15]

What is fascinating about this exchange, apart from Hefferon explaining the alternative view on the use of force, is that it shows how, within the Committee of Public Accounts in 1971, and probably at large, there was little understanding of how the directive combined *both* the arming of the Northern nationalist civilian population with possible Irish army incursions on a mercy-mission basis. This clarity emerged only in the documents released in 2001. Without Hefferon's evidence at the first and second arms trials, it is likely that the existence of the 6 February directive would have remained a secret in the thirty years before the State papers were released in 2001 – and perhaps even beyond that.

Hefferon's presence at the critical moment when Gibbons issued the directive to his Chief of Staff, Lieutenant General MacEoin, was partly accidental, but also partly deliberate on Gibbons's behalf. Hefferon has recorded how he was in the minister's office that day on other prearranged business; but when he rose to leave after Gibbons summoned the Chief of Staff, the minister waved him back into his seat, saying, 'You will have an interest in this too, Colonel.'[16] He then proceeded to issue the directive in the presence of both men. Hefferon's revelation that he had personally attended in this way at the issuing of the instructions appeared to leave Seamus McKenna SC (for the State) nonplussed, and without any effective come-back[17] after the witness had surprised the prosecution at the first arms trial with his sensational evidence about the government plans for cross-border incursions, and the setting aside of surplus arms for Northern nationalists.

The other critical aspect of Hefferon's dealings *vis-à-vis* the directive is his evidence on how it directly affected *him*, and altered his view of Captain Kelly's gun-buying activities. Previously, Hefferon had been strongly opposed to Kelly's wish, as an Irish army officer, to assist Northern nationalists in acquiring arms for their self-defence; he had insisted that Kelly retire from the army before proceeding with any such plan.[18] Gibbons, as minister, initially agreed with this, and Kelly duly submitted a resignation form around early February. But then – it seems shortly after the directive was issued – Gibbons told Hefferon not to proceed with Kelly's retirement. Gibbons claimed later in court that he was waiting, in growing frustration, for his cabinet colleagues Haughey and Blaney to come up with an alternative job for Kelly within the public service. He argued that he did not wish such an intelligence officer to leave the Defence Forces in a disgruntled state of mind. Regardless of the credibility of this explanation for Gibbons leaving

Kelly inside the army, which is questionable, what is clear is that his decision that Kelly should remain within military ranks caused Hefferon to reassess his own attitude.

Hefferon, having witnessed the minister set out government policy of 6 February, then drop the insistence that the junior officer retire before his arms-buying trips to Germany, concluded, not unreasonably, that Kelly's efforts to help the Defence Committees acquire guns for their defence was in line with government policy. He knew that the policy involved providing arms, ammunition and gas masks to Northern nationalists, if the situation deteriorated sufficiently. He even told Kelly at the time that the directive might mean arms being made available to people in Northern Ireland.[19] The later claims by the State – including by Jack Lynch – that the directive had no relevance to the gun-running attempts of Captain Kelly are historically difficult to sustain in the face of Hefferon's own evidence that, as one of the principals, it had caused him to change his approach to what Kelly was doing.

Although Hefferon never said as much, it may be speculated that the real reason Gibbons dropped the requirement for Kelly to retire from the army in mid-February 1970 was because the junior officer was essential to the contingency plans he had announced to the army on 6 February. Who, other than Kelly, would be able to advise on the delicate matter of which Northern nationalists/republicans were to be entrusted with guns? Eamonn Gallagher, an official in the Department of External Affairs, was an informed diplomatic presence on the ground in Northern Ireland and could advise generally; but undoubtedly Kelly, who had been in close contact with the Northern Defence Committees, was indispensable to the policy set out in the directive. Hefferon knew this, and probably Gibbons knew it also. The minister admitted to MacEoin that he personally had no idea to whom in the North the surplus rifles that he withdrew from sale on 6 February 1970 might be given. Kelly was better versed than anyone else to answer this question.

★

After the first week of February 1970, Hefferon could see that there were now in existence two schemes by which arms could be provided to Northern nationalists. Although they had separate origins they were also linked, through Hefferon and Kelly, and through the two government ministers, Gibbons and Blaney. One plan arose from the 6 February directive, the other had originated earlier with the Defence Committees. For historians, a key question is the extent to which these two schemes can be connected. Hefferon judged them to be all part of the same government policy. Was he correct? Lynch denied there was any link when he met the chairman of the Public Accounts Committee in 1971, as shown above; he effectively contradicted what Hefferon had told the committee.[20]

Clearly, there were important differences between the two schemes. Kelly's plan to help arm the Northern Defence Committees was the earlier of the two: it had begun in early October 1969, four months before the directive. Although it was largely being financed from the government-established Northern Ireland Relief Fund, it belonged ultimately to the Northerners. There was no question of a formal government authorization, unlike the 6 February directive to the Defence Forces; ownership lay elsewhere, north of the border with the Defence Committees. That scheme was also different in that it involved the purchase of new weapons abroad, with money that had been given to the account holders and with a junior Irish army officer, Kelly, assisting. Hefferon's understanding, which he communicated to the Minister for Defence, was that Kelly intended to retain control of the weaponry, and to store it in a monastery in Co. Cavan under lock and key, until the government decided the weapons should be released. By contrast, the scheme laid out in the directive did not involve any importation of arms, because the surplus stock was already in army hands. It was a projected operation that, at least initially, would be totally under State control.

Each of the schemes brought their own separate difficulties; neither was anywhere near perfect. Hefferon did not believe it was practicable, as the directive envisaged, to plan to distribute identifiable Irish army-issue rifles to Northern nationalists. Given the policy outlined, newly purchased and untraceable weapons seemed to him a more practicable option. So far as the scheme to help the Defence Committees was concerned, it must always have seemed questionable whether Captain Kelly's control of the imported guns could be guaranteed, however good his intentions, in any interval pending a government decision to release the weapons.

To Hefferon, however, the differences between the two schemes were dwarfed by the similarities. The Defence Forces had been told by the government to make provision for giving weapons to a threatened community across the border, and both plans fitted within such a policy. Each was top secret, and each was deniable. Indeed, in the end both of them *were* denied. Each depended on Hefferon and Military Intelligence identifying appropriate potential recipients across the border. In each case, that involved Captain Kelly, Hefferon's assistant, and the only person with the necessary contacts with Northern republicans. Each of the schemes, so far as Hefferon understood them, involved retaining the arms in military hands until there was a government decision to release them. Each of the plans, certainly in the later stages, was known to government ministers Gibbons, Blaney and Haughey.

It may also be significant that the jury in the second arms trial, in reaching its verdict of acquittal, appear to have seen the two schemes as linked. After having retired to consider their verdict, the jury returned to ask the judge for clarification on an issue of importance to them: had Colonel Hefferon said that the 6 February directive to the Defence Forces ordered the provision of arms against the contingency of possibly distributing them to civilians in Northern Ireland? The answer the judge gave, after reading Hefferon's evidence back to the court, was yes, that was the evidence. Shortly after that, the jury came back with its verdict of acquittal. The former Minister for Justice, Mícheál Ó Móráin, himself a solicitor, commented after the trial on the question the jury had sought clarification on:

That indicated to people experienced with juries and with trials
that the jury had accepted the Colonel's evidence, and that
their line of thought was, if this was part of the overall official
government plan, to have arms for distribution in the North, that
this whole business was an official job, in plain man's language.[21]

It might be further claimed that if Hefferon – and indeed the jury
– were mistaken in seeing a single government policy at play here,
and if the two arms provision schemes were really different from
one another, in the sense that one was seditious and the other
was State policy, that would have become a lot clearer had Lynch
ever acknowledged the existence of *either of them*. But Lynch did
not do this. He never accepted ownership publicly of any scheme
that envisaged, even as a matter of extreme contingency, the
distribution of arms to Northern nationalists.

Finally, what may also vindicate Hefferon's attitude is the
extraordinary coincidence that when Haughey and Blaney were
cut adrift on 6 May for breach of government policy in regard to
Captain Kelly's gun-running, the 6 February scheme involving
surplus army rifles also seemed to vanish without trace. This
is part of the import of the minutes of Lynch's meeting with
Lieutenant General MacEoin on 9 June 1970. Had the 6 February
scheme been of a different order, it would presumably still have
been policy, and still under discussion in early June. Ultimately
therefore it seems that Hefferon was correct in his judgement
that the two schemes were connected; they were consistent with
a covert government policy that was dropped, finally, on 6 May
1970, when Captain Kelly's arms-buying operation became
public and had to be disowned. Part of that process involved the
identification of appropriate scapegoats, which included Kelly and
– if only indirectly – his boss Hefferon.

Perception of Hefferon's role in the Arms Crisis has been significantly influenced by criticisms of him made by his successor as

head of Military Intelligence, Colonel P. J. Delaney. Delaney is a curious presence in the Arms Crisis narrative. It has already been shown how he was misused by his minister, Gibbons, resulting in his sham investigation into Captain Kelly's activities.[22] However, Delaney's general disparagement of Hefferon has been recycled without query by so many writers that it requires consideration here.

There are in fact significant reasons to question the basis for many of Delaney's criticisms. He appears to have allowed himself to be enlisted by the State, in the aftermath of Hefferon's bruising evidence in the first arms trial, to undermine his predecessor's authority and reduce the damage from his revelations about the 6 February directive. To this end, he prepared a series of memos criticising Hefferon, memos that feature strongly in the historiography.[23] Nor has Delaney been alone in criticizing Hefferon; other trenchant critics have included Gibbons, who took the brunt of the damage from Hefferon's court evidence, and Desmond O'Malley, former Minister for Justice, who became particularly voluble after Delaney's various memoranda were released in the State papers in 2001. O'Malley drew on Delaney's memos in a Dáil speech on 6 July 2001, making oblique criticism of Hefferon.[24]

Other writers, including some broadly sympathetic to Lynch, have side-stepped the difficulties presented by Hefferon's endorsement of Captain Kelly's conduct, largely by ignoring him. Hefferon is not mentioned in the memoir of former minister Padraig Faulkner (2005), nor by Patrick Hillery's official biographer John Walsh (2008), nor by historian Stephen Kelly in his analysis of Fianna Fáil and partition (2013). Eunan O'Halpin (2008) also fails to mention Hefferon by name, only making reference to Kelly's boss as being 'a man close to retirement'.[25] Arnold (2001), Collins (2001) and O'Brien (2000) in their various books characterize Hefferon's section of the army, Military Intelligence, as a mere tool in the hands of Blaney and Haughey in their supposed conspiracy against Jack Lynch, and make little personal mention of Hefferon.

Dermot Keogh (2008) describes Hefferon as 'an honourable man',[26] but nonetheless judged that the evidence 'pointed firmly' towards the possibility advanced by Colonel Delaney, that he was 'party to a plot unknown to the General Staff'.[27] Henry Patterson (2006), like Keogh, recycles without qualification Delaney's criticisms of Hefferon.[28] The memoirs of Desmond O'Malley (2014) and political correspondent Michael Mills (2005) likewise rely in part on Delaney's analysis, although they avoid any explicit criticism of Hefferon. Mills refers to 'the reliable and very impressive Michael Hefferon',[29] but also felt that he 'undoubtedly gave a great deal of latitude to Captain Kelly', suggesting an absence of proper supervision. Only Angela Clifford (2009) in the literature is unequivocal in seeing Hefferon as 'the personification of an honourable and disciplined army officer', a man 'whose refusal to perjure himself probably saved Captain Kelly and the other defendants',[30] but at a significant personal cost to Hefferon himself.

While Delaney appears to have received effectively no briefing about Kelly from Gibbons, perhaps not surprisingly he made no recorded complaint about his political boss and Commander in Chief. By contrast, he was deeply suspicious of Hefferon's failure to inform him about Kelly's activities. He took issue with Hefferon's assertions that Kelly was part of a government mission in which at times he reported directly to ministers Gibbons, Haughey and Blaney, rather than to his army superior. Delaney argued that Hefferon was the only person authorized to command Kelly. He also said that the Director of Intelligence should have no role in arms procurement for the army; he saw no justification for the unorthodox importation procedures, outside the army's normal procurement protocols, which Hefferon had seemed to endorse.

In response to this, Hefferon did not dispute that he had not confided in Delaney, nor had he informed MacEoin as Chief of Staff. He said that, given the top secret nature of the contingency planning, it was the responsibility of the minister, not him, to brief appropriate persons. He defended his bypassing of the Chief of Staff by stating that the Director of Military Intelligence had a thirty-year tradition of reporting directly to the minister, and was not required necessarily to go through the Chief of Staff. He said the Director of Military Intelligence had 'the right, but also the obligation' to report direct to the Minister for Defence 'without benefit of intermediary'.[31] (While MacEoin never spoke publicly about this, or any other aspect of the Arms Crisis, there is some evidence that he felt Hefferon should have kept him better informed.)[32]

On Delaney's charge that Hefferon had endorsed an arms acquisition operation that was outside of any normal army procedures, Hefferon said the circumstances were far from normal, and that they demanded a high degree of secrecy. He had informed Gibbons more than once of Captain Kelly's plan to import arms, and when the minister accepted this, he regarded the activities as in line with government policy. It was on foot of that belief that he told Kelly that the arms coming in should not be checked into Cathal Brúgha Barracks in Dublin, but should be brought in and stored *outside of* an army barracks or normal systems of storage.[33] Hefferon felt this would facilitate the secrecy and efficiency of an operation that the minister knew of and accepted, though it was clearly *sub rosa*; in his view, if arms were to be provided as the directive ordered, newly acquired ones would be more suitable, since they would be untraceable and so protect the government from future embarrassment. Even if this judgement was open to query, Hefferon based it on plausible operational considerations. He also explained why he had advised Kelly to approach Haughey to arrange customs clearance for the arms consignment. It was because he knew Kelly had already dealt with Haughey over the disbursement of money from the Northern Relief Fund; more importantly, it was also because he knew the Minister for Finance had the power to instruct the Revenue Commissioners to allow the consignment in without customs inspection.

Delaney also criticized Hefferon in relation to the Dundalk rifles episode of 2 April 1970; he asked, with a touch of venom, whether Hefferon had been 'party to a plot unknown to the General Staff'.[34] Hefferon's evidence on this was that he sought urgently to get Captain Kelly home from the Continent in case the rifles being sent to Dundalk needed to be distributed north of the border.[35] Delaney, revealingly, asked: who said the rifles were to be distributed? This question showed he was unfamiliar with the official documentation on the directive, as he clearly had either not read, or had not understood, the memorandum in the army files from 9 June 1970, Brief for the Ceann Fóirne. This identified the 500 rifles and the 80,000 rounds of ammunition transferred to Dundalk in early April as the same surplus arms set aside after 6 February, intended for immediate 'readiness' in the event of an emergency, and loaded at the time onto trucks in Dublin and Athlone.[36] Gibbons had confirmed to the Chief of Staff later in February, if it was in any doubt, that the rifles were for distribution, though to which individuals the minister could not say. Hefferon's evidence was that potential distribution was the only logical reason for sending the rifles northwards.[37] Although Gibbons in court sought to avoid the point,[38] the documents released in 2001 supported Hefferon's view.

Desmond O'Malley, in a Dáil speech on 6 July 2001, indirectly queried Hefferon's supervision of Kelly in 1969–70, though he did not mention Hefferon by name, nor make any reference to Hefferon's lengthy 1971 rebuttal of Delaney's criticisms.[39] O'Malley queried whether Kelly was being adequately controlled by his superior; why, he asked, was Kelly, by his own admission, reporting to the Minister for Agriculture (Blaney) rather than to the Minister for Defence, regarding his activities? This supposed lack of proper supervision of Kelly had been widely voiced at the Committee of Public Accounts inquiry in 1971, the suggestion being that there was a 'breach in the chain of command' over Kelly.[40] While Hefferon denied that there was any such breach, he may have been on less solid ground here. On his own admission, he did not feel responsible for those activities of Kelly that were unrelated to intelligence, especially when they arose at the behest of government ministers.[41] Whenever Kelly was working directly with ministers on matters not related to intelligence, Hefferon's view was that this was above his authority, and outside his particular responsibility. His own position was that he had opposed Kelly's engaging in arms-buying activities while an army officer.[42] While he did not waver in his trust of his subordinate officer, and he believed that he reported to him fully, whenever he was asked, and whenever it was appropriate,[43] he also made it clear that he did not question Kelly about his handling of the Northern bank accounts, or about his dealings with Haughey and the Northern Relief Fund, because he felt they had nothing to do with intelligence. This position was sufficiently open to allow writers O'Brien, Arnold, Keogh and others to suggest that Blaney and Haughey were directing Military Intelligence through their involvement with Kelly.[44]

Hefferon rejected any claim that, in regard to the arms importation plan, his section was being manipulated by outside ministers; he took responsibility, saying Kelly was at all times either under his direction or that of his minister, Jim Gibbons. But in relation to the bank accounts used to purchase arms, he did not claim a similar control. What he saw was Kelly liaising with the Minister for Finance, in line, Hefferon felt, with the government's wishes. But he viewed the arms-buying plan as having originated with the Northern Defence Committees, not with Haughey or Blaney, and as being financed by money under the Northerners' control. He saw Kelly as representing the Defence Committees when he helped operate the accounts; in his view Kelly was acting, just as he claimed, under the instructions of the account holders, and not those of Haughey or Blaney.[45]

Above all, Hefferon believed, because he was briefing Gibbons personally, that Kelly's own minister knew what he was doing as regards the purchasing of arms, and approved of it. He appears to have believed that Kelly's dealings with Blaney, the Minister for Agriculture and Fisheries, arose simply because of Blaney's knowledge of the North – unique within the cabinet – and his position on a

cabinet sub-committee set up to coordinate information *vis-à-vis* the
North. Critical to Hefferon's stance was his reliance on his own
direct communications with Gibbons, the Minister for Defence,
which he said confirmed to him that Kelly's activities were known
of and were in order. Gibbons of course disputed Hefferon's
evidence, but he never offered a reason why his Director of Military
Intelligence would lie repeatedly about their discussions.

On close inspection, Delaney cuts a sad figure in the records
of the Arms Crisis. His minister, Gibbons, kept him in the dark
over the extent of his own involvement with Captain Kelly, and so
undermined his supposed investigation. He had also been denied
the confidence of Hefferon regarding Kelly's engagement with
the Northern Defence Committees. In the interval between the
two arms trials, clearly smarting from this exclusion, he took on
the task of gathering data to blacken his predecessor. The energy
Delaney displayed in performing this role hardly went unnoticed
in government circles, for he became the next Defence Forces Chief
of Staff. While Hefferon's performance in extremely abnormal
times appears to have been, by and large, exemplary, Delaney's
various memoranda have succeeded in leaving an unwarranted
shadow over his predecessor's reputation, one that writers on the
period have been lamentably slow to query.

Hefferon has also been criticized over remarks seemingly from
Kelly in an early intelligence report received on 23 August 1969.
Kelly made a reference to 'accepting the possibility of armed action
of some sort as the ultimate solution' to the issue of unification.[46]
Arnold commented that this remark appeared contrary to the
government policy of opposition to the use of force, and that it
raised questions about the direction Kelly was receiving from
Hefferon.[47] Hefferon's view of the particular remark complained
of is not known, but he did, early on, insist that Kelly confine
himself to reporting by word of mouth only. There is nothing in
the written or spoken record to suggest that at any point he felt
Kelly's actions breached government or army policy on Northern
Ireland.

★

The controversy over Hefferon's statement of evidence in May 1970, and its subsequent editing for the arms trial Book of Evidence, is considered in Chapters 14 and 15, but one aspect worth considering here concerns an event that took place in the Round Hall of the Four Courts in Dublin in September 1970, on the opening morning of the first arms trial. The context was that Hefferon had made a strong witness statement supportive of Captain Kelly, and had acknowledged how both he and James Gibbons knew in advance of all Kelly's arms-buying adventures. However, the editing for the Book of Evidence removed almost all references to the minister's foreknowledge. Hefferon, listed as a witness for the prosecution, felt under pressure as the trial began. He seems to have seen the truncated version of his statement in the Book of Evidence as a silent invitation to change his story, a sign that, when he came to give evidence, he should avoid incriminating his minister. He saw it as an invitation to commit perjury.

Frank Fitzpatrick, solicitor for Captain Kelly, was in the Round Hall on that morning, awaiting the opening of the trial, and Hefferon sought him out. He told Fitzpatrick that he had been in a local church for two hours that morning, contemplating and praying. He wanted now to tell Fitzpatrick that his client, James Kelly, was an innocent man, and that he – Hefferon – was not prepared to commit perjury. The conversation was brief. Fitzpatrick, struck by the force of conviction and depth of feeling Hefferon expressed, went straight to Seamus McKenna SC, the leading State barrister in the case, who was nearby. He told him of the encounter, adding, 'He is my witness now.' McKenna, in Fitzpatrick's recall, did not respond.[48] In the event, Hefferon remained as a prosecution witness, but only until he gave his evidence in the first trial. The prosecution at that point had to endure the spectacle of its own witness buttressing the defence case, a development that left the State in significant disarray. The trial collapsed after six days, ostensibly for other reasons, and a retrial was hastily arranged.[49] The State refused to call Hefferon as its witness in the second trial, and as a compromise, he was called by Judge Seamus Henchy.

The significance of Hefferon's conversation with Fitzpatrick in the Round Hall is that, as the trial began, he considered himself under great pressure to disown the statement of evidence he had given to the gardaí. He believed he was being invited not to tell the truth about Captain Kelly. But the conversation showed that Hefferon was not about to be deterred; he went on to astonish the prosecution lawyers and the country with his detailed evidence. This had the appearance of self-incrimination, but more particularly it meant the incrimination of Kelly's minister, Gibbons; it won for Hefferon a *persona non grata* label in the eyes of the State, which he apparently carried to his grave.[50]

From his retirement in 1970 until his death in 1985, Hefferon, in the view of his family, was ostracized and shunned by the Defence Forces and the political establishment.[51] One of his worst moments came when, under Dáil privilege on 9 November 1971, Gibbons launched a bitter personal attack on him. He accused Hefferon of standing in line with Iago, the 'false friend' of Othello; he said that he had betrayed the minister's trust and did not deserve to hold high office in the army.[52] It was a cruel assault from a damaged politician against an officer who had served his country with distinction over many decades, but who at the end found himself caught up in an unfamiliar swirl of high level political intrigue. Hefferon did not buckle, but remained throughout, under the most testing legal scrutiny, a strong and dignified character, and one who never sought to evade responsibility for activities that had taken place on his watch.

13

Honest Jack?

Jack Lynch, the amiable Corkman, eternally smoking his pipe and looking for all the world as if butter would not melt in his mouth, lies at the centre of the long-standing mysteries of the Arms Crisis. Lynch was a charmer, a Gaelic football and hurling hero for his native county, and an intelligent man who showed no animus against even his most hostile critics. His friend, adviser and speechwriter during the tumultuous times of 1969–70, T. K. Whitaker, wrote of him: 'Softness of speech and manner, consideration for others, readiness to listen, absence of pomp, a sense of humour, were elements of a most attractive personality, which combined modesty and unpretentiousness with good judgement and a deep sense of responsibility and firmness of purpose. I never saw him in a rage, or heard him say anything disparaging or hurtful about others.'[1]

But the question about Lynch is where did the niceness end, and where did the necessarily tougher, more devious side of this successful fourteen-year leader of Fianna Fáil kick in? A somewhat one-dimensional picture of the 'good Jack' has dominated historical perceptions of the years of the Arms Crisis. Then came the point when he became supposedly transformed on 6 May 1970, from the supposedly weak-willed and indecisive politician of the previous months to one who had discovered a hidden steel within, now able to scatter his enemies with one majestic blow of his hurley. Lynch before the crisis, and Lynch after the crisis: it is a story of the dramatic reinvention of a politician, one that carries echoes of his close ally Jim Gibbons, who appears in one light before 20 April 1970, and then entirely differently afterwards. Just as Peter Maguire SC found 'two Mr Gibbons' in that story, could it be that there were 'two Jack Lynchs' also at work? Lynch never had to submit to the brutal interrogators of the Central Criminal Court – that task he left to Gibbons – but had those distinguished members of the Bar, Messrs Finlay, Sorahan and McCarthy, set about him in a closed arena, it is not clear how much of the benevolent and blameless image would have survived. It has always been a question for historians whether this Taoiseach, at least as regards 1970 and its aftermath, was entirely the gentleman that he has seemed. While Lynch played a central role in the 1970 Arms Crisis, the precise nature of that role has remained stubbornly elusive. The issue central to this book's inquiry is whether he was a victim of events, or the essential cause of the crisis that arose.

When he succeeded Seán Lemass as Taoiseach and leader of Fianna Fáil in 1966, the Corkman had been only a compromise choice and was expected to have no more than a caretaker role in that position. But by autumn 1969, much had changed for him. In the June general election of that year, Lynch secured his own mandate as Taoiseach. This gave him an enhanced authority over his cabinet colleagues; ambitious rivals for the party leadership, such as Charles Haughey and Neil Blaney, appeared to be obliged for the foreseeable future to place their ambitions on ice.

Yet Northern Ireland was something of an x-factor facing Lynch's newly constituted cabinet in July 1969. For several years there had been the stirrings there of a fresh civil rights campaign, a development set to challenge the traditional Fianna Fáil approach to partition. A civil rights campaign that succeeded in reforming the partitionist Stormont regime from within, rather than simply seeking its abolition, could have the effect of strengthening partition, not weakening it. This was hardly something Fianna Fáil, a party dedicated to ending partition, would welcome, and its leaders were accordingly uncertain on how to embrace the civil rights movement. Nor was Lynch, a politician from the south of the country without any republican family pedigree, ideally placed to take a strong lead in this, or even to identify with the developing unrest among Northern nationalists. With the North bubbling ominously, how much of the initiative would Lynch yield to Neil Blaney? The answer, it appears now, was quite a lot.

While the term 'honest Jack' was originally coined in the newspapers as a term of derision for Lynch, it came later to be employed in a less sarcastic, more complimentary sense. Yet the issue of Lynch's honesty has remained a central historical question about 1970. The core question – did Jack know? (of the gun-running) – has proved frustratingly difficult to answer. On Lynch's behalf, the case has frequently been made that no evidence has been unearthed of any government decision to import arms; short of such evidence, it is argued, the attempted gun-running has to be seen as illicit and unauthorized, as Lynch always claimed. This view appears to have held sway since, although it has never been short of challengers.

As is clear from previous chapters, Lynch cannot be fully trusted in his claims to have known nothing of an arms plan before 20 April 1970. His critics can point to evidence that he knew a project was under way as far back as October 1969, and chose neither to intervene nor to acknowledge that he ever got such information. Moreover, so many of his cabinet colleagues appear to have known, well before May 1970, about an arms shipment. Arising from this clash of perspectives on the Arms Crisis, a compromise view offers itself: it is that the arms importation attempt was part of an unofficial project, not one ever formally ratified by Lynch or his government, and yet one that operated before 18–20 April 1970 with a high degree of ministerial approval. With many loose ends hanging from this theory, it has nonetheless permitted both the pro- and anti-Lynch sides of the argument to feel secure in their positions. But still the question hangs: did Jack know?

The complexity of the 'did Jack know?' approach can be seen from the comments of Kevin Boland, Lynch's one-time colleague and eventual adversary. Boland wrote very honestly in 1977 that he felt Lynch would not have agreed to the importation 'if it came up for specific government decision', and yet he was certain Lynch knew it was happening, that he avoided efforts to have it discussed formally and 'deliberately refrained from taking any action' to halt it.[2] This perspective from Boland neatly illustrates the difficulties in arriving at definite, uncontested answers about the status of the arms importation plan, and about what Lynch knew or did not know.

To escape, therefore, an inconclusive focus on Lynch, a different question presents itself: was the intended gun-running in conflict with Lynch government policy at the time? Such a question immediately has the effect of highlighting the historical importance of the 6 February directive. This was issued on behalf of Lynch and his cabinet by Jim Gibbons, and threw a powerful beam of light on the most sensitive aspect of the government's Northern Ireland policy – its approach to any cross-border military involvement. At the time, the instructions in the directive were hidden from public view, a fact that, as seen earlier, posed difficulties for the Taoiseach's truthfulness in both the public and private spheres. Secrecy, and where necessary denial, were essential components of the policy. This was not because the directive contradicted Lynch's essentially peaceful approach to Northern Ireland, which it indisputably did not, but because of its implications for Anglo-Irish relations.[3]

Lynch never discussed the directive and the reasoning behind it in public, either before or after the Arms Crisis. Even though it arose from a genuine concern simply to protect Northern nationalists, rather than to wage war, Lynch was not prepared to admit publicly that he was prepared, if the worst came to the worst, to send the Irish army over the border. Even less could he admit that his government had instructed the Defence Forces that it was willing, if necessary, to provide arms to nationalists for their self-defence. Lynch felt obliged to dissimulate, and ultimately he engaged in a cover-up of the directive's full contents.

It is the revealed full terms of the directive that, more than anything else, invite historians to change the question that has governed research on the Arms Crisis for much of the past half–century. The directive shifts the focus away from whether Lynch knew of, and authorized, an importation of arms, to a larger question: his government's policy on *providing* arms. If it was agreed policy that arms be made available, the question of whether this happened by importing them or acquiring them by other means becomes distinctly secondary.

The directive is evidence that Lynch knew of, and had approved in principle, the planned provision of arms. Was this a fundamentally different policy to that embodied in Captain Kelly's gun-running attempt? A full-blooded discussion on this issue, a matter considered in the previous chapter, has never been possible because of Lynch's failure ever to acknowledge either scheme. Both were taken off the table around the same time in May–June 1970 – one in a blaze of public controversy, the other silently, in the dark. It seems significant that just eight months later Lynch can be observed hiding from the chairman of the Committee of Public Accounts inquiry, Patrick Hogan TD (Fine Gael), the fact that the 'agreed' provision of arms to Northerners was an important element in the 6 February directive.

Some unique insights into Lynch's behaviour behind closed doors in the critical period of April–May 1970 have come from the civil servant Peter Berry. He was Charles Haughey's accuser-in-chief at the arms trials, providing the State with some of its most damaging evidence against his former minister, but ten years later, speaking from the grave, he took on a similar accusatory role in relation to Jack Lynch. Berry documented in his posthumously published *Diaries* a pattern of what he believed were prevarications and misstatements from the Taoiseach during the Arms Crisis. Despite being burdened with strong *a priori* assumptions, and a selective, sometimes self-serving approach to the facts,[4] Berry has provided a unique window on Lynch's private discussions within government in 1969–70. His insider view offers a dimension to the historical record that no collection of Dáil speeches could ever yield. Focusing closely on Lynch, Berry's *Diaries* offer historians a fascinating challenge: how to distinguish the wheat from the undoubted chaff? This is an account written in opinionated fashion several years after the fact, but also from a uniquely intimate vantage point. It is not, in any conventional sense of the word, a diary of the times. It is the work of a calculating official whose writings need to be read with discrimination,[5] but the accumulation of data he has provided about Lynch's conduct and demeanour in the important period from 20 April to 6 May, some of which was detailed in Chapter 11, remains exceptionally valuable.

It was never in Berry's interest to find himself clashing with Lynch. Unsettled by what he had learned about a seeming collaboration by agents of the State with the IRA, the Taoiseach was an ally he sorely needed. Berry had every reason to resist coming to distrust the Taoiseach, and the persistent thread of criticism in the *Diaries* came with a somewhat rueful tinge. His ultimate disillusionment with Lynch arose from many perceived private disappointments. It seems to have been this that drove him, in retirement, to write his *Diaries*, with a manifest impulse for self-justification. Accounts of the events he described were supplemented in 2000 and 2001 by the release of official Department of Justice files from 1969 and 1970, including many notes and contemporaneous memos from Berry himself. Together, these State papers and the *Diaries* show that Berry had not become one of the most powerful figures in the Irish public service for nothing; they reveal an official with a meticulous attention to detail, a special access to the highest levels of government, including the Taoiseach's office, and possessing an exceptional authority over the Garda Síochána.

Berry, by the time he wrote the *Diaries*, had concluded that Lynch was a far from truthful politician. While he hardly mentioned Gibbons, several glancing references suggest that Berry had little confidence in him either. His writings reveal a hardening concern over Lynch's tolerance of Captain Kelly's arms-related activities. He believed his views on this were shared by the head of the Special Branch, Chief Superintendent Fleming. In the first instance, Berry was certain that on 17 October 1969, at Mount Carmel Hospital in Dublin, he had given Lynch information that Captain Kelly, an Irish army officer, had been observed offering money to republicans for arms, and that Lynch had taken no action.[6] He believed Lynch demonstrated the same reluctance to act six months later in April 1970, when Berry brought him evidence that several of his ministers were involved with Kelly in actual gun-running. Lynch appeared to Berry to sit on his hands for three weeks after 20 April 1970, before Liam Cosgrave confronted him with the facts on the evening of 5 May 1970.

Apart from what he saw as Lynch's prevarications at this time, Berry identified at least six statements to the Dáil where he felt the Taoiseach deviated from the truth. The instances in question were: when Lynch said he knew nothing before 20 April 1970; when he said he acted immediately after that information came to him on 20 April; when he claimed to have always intended to sack Haughey and Blaney; when he described the conference in his house on 30 April 1970 as one to 'coordinate evidence'; when he denied that some ministers knew of an arms plan involving members of the government months before he claimed to know; and when he led the Dáil to believe on several occasions that no public money went, or could have gone, to buy arms. In each of these instances, Berry believed Lynch did not speak the truth.

In the period after charges were laid by the Attorney General, Berry, whose scepticism over the Taoiseach's conduct must have been apparent, described in his *Diaries* how he felt he was being kept at a distance from Lynch, by what he identified as a kind of Fianna Fáil Praetorian Guard. In a particularly cynical passage, Berry noted that at a conference on 20 May, one minister 'was not pleased with my intimacy with the Taoiseach'. He went on:

This was a curious phenomenon which I was to observe again and again in the coming months: the desire of the Centurion

Imperial Caesar's Bodyguard, in the persons of a caucus in the cabinet, to keep access to the Taoiseach within a chosen circle and resentment against anyone who breached it. It was very necessary of course, in order that a prepared story should stand up, that persons with a knowledge of contradictions should be isolated and, as far as possible, kept in ignorance of the developing theme. The necessity to keep the Fianna Fáil government in power at all costs was the over-riding consideration, and I had shown an independence of thought in recent years which, while not mak- ing me suspect of anti-Fianna Fáil leanings, did not make for certainty that I would go with them all the way.... The naked face of self-interest in Ministerial circles was on exhibition without any attempts at concealment from the serving civil servants.[7]

Looking with hindsight on the Taoiseach's behaviour over the months afterwards, Berry wrote: 'I formed the impression from time to time that he was consulting me to find out how much I did not know, and that he was not thankful to me for bringing awkward facts to his notice.'[8] Later still, Berry was disturbed by what he said was Lynch's refusal of a request from the Garda Commissioner to allow the wire-tapping of someone he described as 'a public servant (not a Member of Parliament) who was deeply involved' with the attempted arms importation. He wrote that this again led him and the Garda authorities to 'have doubts as to whether the Taoiseach was in earnest in directing on April 20 that the matter be fully investigated'.[9]

Despite comments such as these, laced with suspicion, Berry's *Diaries* present no coherent sense of *why* Lynch was behaving in this way. He had clearly decided that the Taoiseach was dissim- ulating, even lying, though he resisted using that word; but he left unaddressed the question of why the Taoiseach appeared so evasive, so unwilling to act against what Berry felt was evident subversion. Berry came to the view, as his jaundiced comments above indicate, that the principal issue for Lynch had become the survival of the Fianna Fáil government. Yet in the critical holding period between mid-April and the first week of May 1970, Berry appears to have felt it necessary to cling to the Taoiseach for protection. To him, in the face of ministers seemingly collaborating with the IRA, Lynch's ambivalence may have seemed a lesser evil. Berry did not trust him, but only the Taoiseach had the power to thwart those ministers Berry saw as operating hand-in-glove with the IRA.

Berry's difficulty may have been that he lacked important points of reference which might have allowed him to understand Lynch's puzzling prevarications. In particular, he was unaware of the 6 February directive and had difficulty grasping the difference between engaging with republicans to assist in the defence of Northern nationalists – as shown in the Army Planning Board reports discussed in Chapter 2 – and being part of a subversive collaboration with the IRA, designed to end the Northern State. Had the 6 February directive been disclosed to him, the distinction might have been clearer. He could see that Lynch had ignored, pretended not to have heard, dragged his feet and/or just generally displayed a lack of enthusiasm for the information placed in front of him between October 1969 and the end of April 1970; but why that should be, Berry never seemed able to work out.

Berry's list of Lynch's false statements detailed above is far from comprehensive. Overall, it is possible to identify at least thirty specific instances when Jack Lynch either made demonstrably false statements, was deliberately misleading or chose to side-step the facts. Most, but not all, of his misstatements were to Dáil Éireann. The examples span the period from 5 May 1970 to the moment when Lynch, recently retired from the office of Taoiseach, attempted on 25 November 1980 to defend himself against some of the more serious barbs directed against him by Peter Berry in his posthumous *Diaries*. At the top of the list are the occasions on 9 May 1970 and 4 November 1970, when he told the Dáil that all the Northern delegations he met were told the same thing by him: that there would be no troops sent across the border, and no arms provided for their defence.[10] All the evidence from the various delegations he met contradicts this definitive claim; and if indeed he had told them this, it would have been a false assurance, as shown by the terms of the 6 February directive, revealed in 2001. On 19 May 1970, he told Owen Hickey, a *Times* correspondent, that even if the British army lost control in the North, no arms or troops would be provided by the Irish government to protect nationalists.[11] Even as late as 9 June 1970, Lynch confirmed to the Chief of Staff that cross-border army incursions were still contemplated, on a mercy-mission basis. On 10 November 1970, he told the *7 Days* television programme that the only circumstances in which Irish troops would have crossed the border were with British agreement.[12] This was also not true, according to the directive and related military records.

On 2 February 1971, in a private meeting, Lynch seems to have deliberately misrepresented the contents of the directive of 6 February 1970 to the chairman of the Committee of Public Accounts, Patrick Hogan TD (Fine Gael).[13] On 25 November 1980, he claimed to the Dáil that he had no recollection of being told by Peter Berry at Mount Carmel Hospital of Captain Kelly's meeting in Bailieboro or of a plot to provide arms.[14] On 7 May, 9 May and 14 May 1970, he misrepresented to the Dáil the circumstances in which he had effectively fired Mícheál O'Móráin as Minister for Justice.[15] On those three same days, 7, 9 and 14 May, he falsely insisted to the Dáil that he had already decided to fire Haughey and Blaney from the cabinet, regardless of Liam Cosgrave's intervention.[16] This is contradicted by his conversation with Berry on 30 April, and by his remarks to cabinet on 1 May. When on 7 May he told the Dáil that Cosgrave had brought information to him about Haughey and Blaney being involved in a gun-running plot, he omitted to say that Gibbons's name was also on Cosgrave's list.[17] He misled the Dáil on 9 May and 14 May about the fact that public money had been spent on Captain Kelly's notorious arms consignment; although he was shortly afterwards alerted to his mistake, as shown above, he never corrected the record.[18]

Again on 7, 9 and 14 May, as well as on 4 November 1970, Lynch claimed to have conducted a thorough investigation into Gibbons's conduct, to establish whether he had been involved in the arms importation attempt; he would not have promoted him thereafter, he said, if the slightest suspicion of being involved attached to him.[19] There is no evidence in the files of any such investigation. It certainly could not have been effected without talking to Colonel Hefferon – a course Department of Finance official Tony Fagan urged on Lynch on 4 May, but to no avail. Hefferon was aware, because he had briefed him personally, that Gibbons knew a great deal about Captain Kelly's activities prior to April 1970, yet the minister had permitted him to continue. Had Lynch talked to Chief Superintendent Fleming, he was in danger of hearing from him how Fleming shared Berry's long-standing suspicion of Gibbons, going back to the previous October. The only remaining source Lynch could have consulted before giving Gibbons a clean bill of health was Hefferon's successor, Colonel P. J. Delaney, an officer who had complained about being kept in the dark over Kelly's activities[20] and had been briefed by neither Gibbons nor Hefferon. There is a surprising absence in the literature on the Arms Crisis of any systematic interrogation of the truthfulness of Lynch's assertion that he had investigated Gibbons's role before promoting him. The claim appears essentially threadbare, little more than a convenient fiction.

In the context of what Lynch claimed to know or not know before 20 April 1970, the State papers contain additional evidence of questionable statements from him. This is to be found in the initial handwritten statement of Tony Fagan, Haughey's assistant in the Department of Finance, dated 13 May 1970 and previously cited in a different context in Chapter 10. Among several important references not included in the subsequent witness statements taken by gardaí was an account of two meetings Fagan had with Jack Lynch in April–May 1970, in the aftermath of the failed gun-running attempt. His first meeting with the Taoiseach was at his own request on 28 April; the second was on 4 May, at Lynch's request. This second meeting was just one day before the intervention by Cosgrave which led to the sacking of Haughey and Blaney. The relevant section of Fagan's account of this 4 May meeting with Lynch is as follows:

> He [Lynch] spoke again about Captain Kelly, and I said that Colonel Hefferon, Chief of Intelligence (he retired from the Army in April) had always spoken highly of Kelly. I suggested to the Taoiseach that he might like to have a word with the Colonel about him. The Taoiseach said that he had spoken to the Minister for Defence, who told him that he knew nothing about the involvement of Army Intelligence in all of this.[21]

Although this is only a second-hand record of what Gibbons had told Lynch, it is a first-hand account of what Lynch told Fagan. It is important historically – firstly, because of its source, a public servant with no obvious reason to lie; secondly, it is important because Fagan documented it relatively soon afterwards, after just nine days; and thirdly, most of all, because Lynch stated here that Gibbons had told him privately he knew nothing of Army Intelligence being involved in any arms importation.

To parse and analyse this: if Gibbons *did* say this to Lynch, then he clearly was not being truthful to him, because in fact he knew a great deal at this stage about how Kelly, an Army Intelligence officer, had been trying to bring arms into the country for the Northern Defence Committees.[22] But what is more significant is that Lynch himself must have known that what he was telling Fagan about Gibbons's level of knowledge could not be true, and was a lie. As detailed previously, the separate evidence of Hefferon and of Berry about the conversation in Mount Carmel Hospital in October 1969 leaves no room for doubt that Lynch – and through him, Gibbons – had been informed six months earlier of an alleged involvement of intelligence officer Kelly with republicans, promising them £50,000 for guns.

In other words, Lynch knew that Gibbons knew, because Lynch had personally brought it to the attention of his Minister for Defence after meeting Berry in Mount Carmel Hospital. This situation was therefore different – and was *known* to Lynch to be different – to what he was seemingly describing to Fagan. Assuming that Fagan's account of what Lynch had said to him was accurate, this record seems to offer further evidence of Lynch colluding with Gibbons in a false representation of the facts.

Lynch's sacking of Haughey and Blaney from the cabinet removed, at a stroke, his two main rivals inside the Fianna Fáil party. An immediate result was that he gained greater control of his cabinet. But what is far from proven, though frequently alleged, is that it was for precisely that purpose that he acted against the two ministers. After the sackings, Lynch described himself as 'heartbroken' by the decision. While this can easily look like crocodile tears, the words may have been less insincere than they appear. Lynch accompanied them with some remarkably fulsome tributes, given the circumstances, to the abilities of Haughey and Blaney. He described them as men of outstanding ability, persons of great intellect, able and brilliant, who had given great service to the State.[23] However one reads these words, it is possible to argue that Lynch simply did what, in Fianna Fáil terms, he had to do. In the circumstances in which he found himself on 5 May, and on an entirely pragmatic basis, it is difficult to see what other action, short of giving Cosgrave the two ministerial heads the Opposition parties most eagerly sought, could have so adroitly secured the survival of his government. Lynch's decision to sack them may simply have been in the best interests of his party at that point.

The grey area in all this is the exact status of the arms importation in Lynch's eyes. That Gibbons told him nothing in the period leading up to the events of 18–20 April does not seem credible, especially given their shared awareness of the concerns Berry had expressed in October 1969. The two men appear to have acted in collusion over this and later events, and the Taoiseach, as was his wont, appears to have taken, at the very least, a *laissez-faire* approach; this tolerated Captain Kelly's activities and the fact that his Minister for Defence did nothing to stop what was happening. If Lynch did not specifically authorize the gun-running – so far as is known – like Gibbons, he certainly allowed it to happen.

There can, in truth, be nothing surprising about his ultimate refusal to take responsibility for the project, in circumstances where the survival of the government was at stake. Government involvement in the affair was probably always going to be denied – although no one seems to have explained this in advance to Captain Kelly. It is significant that neither Haughey, Gibbons nor Lynch were prepared to stand publicly over the attempted gun-running. Realistically, Lynch's political options were very limited once Liam Cosgrave confronted him on 5 May. Ó Beacháin speculated that the Taoiseach could have called in Gibbons and had him explain to Cosgrave 'that the operation was official, conducted by the Department of Defence with a view to providing Northern nationalists with weapons should the situation in the North deteriorate further. Instead he chose to take the line… that the arms importation had no authority'.[24] The problem with Ó Beacháin's view is that there is no evidence that the importation had anything more than unofficial approval. J. J. Lee also considered whether Lynch, when faced with Cosgrave's accusations, might have stood over the importation; in Lee's view, this would have opened 'a Pandora's box in terms of Anglo-Irish relations' while also reversing a policy of Lynch on Northern Ireland, which was 'to convey a feeling of deep concern while resisting pressure for any action'.[25]

It can be argued that Lynch's real failure had come earlier, at a point when he might still have averted the looming political crisis. This was when Berry came to him with a Garda report on 20 April. At that point he could have moved decisively to take ownership of the situation, but did not. Action then would have involved some straight talking – to Berry, to Fleming and to several of his ministers – and conceivably might even have led to the same change of policy he eventually made hurriedly on 6 May. But confronting difficulties in that way was not Lynch's style. Instead, he allowed events to drift for three weeks, no doubt making Berry and the Special Branch further agitated that some deal with republicans was afoot. As a consequence, the climax, provoked by Cosgrave's intervention, arrived with maximum drama and an unnecessary sense of crisis on 6 May.

Having persistently over six months turned a blind eye to what was going on, Lynch's delayed and indecisive response after 20 April does not suggest, contrary to much that has been written, that this was a politician seizing an opportunity to eliminate political rivals. Nor are the claims of Arnold and others persuasive that Lynch was just biding his time between then and Cosgrave's intervention fifteen days later, waiting for a stronger hand against the two ministers.[26] In explaining how events unfolded, it appears more relevant that Lynch, Haughey, Blaney and Gibbons knew that a secret government policy was in place concerning the possible provision of guns to Northern nationalists for their own defence.

Lynch retained throughout his career the image of something of an innocent, but this was not the view of him shared – in an un-likely harmony – by either Kevin Boland or Peter Berry. These two men viewed the Taoiseach from very different, but close vantage–points: one was a government colleague and fellow member of Fianna Fáil, the other was one of the government's longest-standing and most important civil service advisers. Despite their very differing perspectives, each saw in Lynch a devious, hard-to-read political operator. Boland seemed scarcely able to credit the levels of cunning he identified in Lynch's make-up.[27] Both felt that Lynch knew of the arms importation in advance, but did not intervene to stop it.

The perception of Lynch as devious and calculating was not shared by Minister for External Affairs Patrick Hillery; according to John Walsh in his official biography, he detected in Lynch 'a kind of innocence'.[28] Hillery 'was convinced that the Taoiseach did not know of the effort to import arms for the Provisional IRA', and further believed he was 'deeply shocked when the details of involvement by ministers were brought to his attention'.[29] This sense of a trusting leader who felt let down by close colleagues also emerges in Dick Walsh's book *The Party*. Walsh, normally a sceptical observer of the politics of the time, said that Lynch's reaction when Berry came to him on 20 April was to feel 'betrayed, angry and at first reluctant to believe what he had heard'.[30] Walsh put all cynicism aside, choosing to take Lynch exactly at his word. His book went on to develop a poignant image of an isolated, even lonely, leader of Fianna Fáil, 'regarded as an outsider by an important section of the party', a man who now felt betrayed by those to whom he had thought he was becoming more acceptable. Walsh, like Hillery, took the conventional view that Haughey and Blaney had been conspiring against Lynch; he too made light of the Taoiseach's hesitation in acting against his two colleagues after 20 April, arguing that he was simply waiting to be sure of his ground, and that the confrontation with Haughey and Blaney had been 'inevitable'.[31] Michael Mills was less sure; he struggled in his 2005 memoir to explain Lynch's behaviour, and was not convinced by the theory that Lynch had been dealing out enough rope to enable Haughey and Blaney to hang themselves.[32] Jim Downey, another contemporary journalistic observer of Lynch, also found explanation of his conduct difficult, but was inclined to believe, on balance, that Lynch did set a trap for his cabinet rivals, with Gibbons being used as a kind of bait.[33]

While there is ample evidence that Jack Lynch had a charismatic and engaging personality, some archival documents also provide support for the less generally stated view of him as devious and calculating. An example of this, noted in Chapter 9, arises in British State papers in a report from Sir Anthony Gilchrist, British ambassador in Dublin, to the Foreign and Commonwealth Office in London, detailing a meeting he had with Lynch on the day after the Fianna Fáil Árd Fheis. In this encounter, on 20 January 1970, Lynch is seen projecting a favoured image of himself to the British: a Taoiseach under serious challenge from the so-called 'Blaney wing', trying to hold back his wild men and dampen their enthusiasm as best he could. But a little over two weeks later, on 6 February, Lynch sent his Minister for Defence to instruct the Defence Forces on radical contingency plans straight from Blaney's hymn sheet. Another indication of Lynch's capacity for deviousness came when he apparently advised Ambassador Gilchrist at the height of the August 1969 crisis how he might be 'compelled to string along' with the Blaney wing of the party, if the pressure got too great.[34]

Deviousness was again evident in comments Lynch made about Haughey to Gilchrist's successor as ambassador, Sir John Peck, in the run-up to the arms trial verdict in 1970. Peck recorded Lynch as telling him he hoped Haughey would be acquitted; he said that he was sorry that 'Charlie' had the extra pressure of having just had the criminal proceedings against him deferred until the autumn. Peck offered no comment on these somewhat surprising remarks when transmitting them to the Foreign and Commonwealth Office in London, but his private opinion may perhaps be gauged by the fact that elsewhere in the same report he noted 'speculation that the Taoiseach hopes to use the further scandal to destroy him' [Haughey], in reference to Haughey's pending appearance before the Committee of Public Accounts inquiry. Later, in the aftermath of the arms trials, Peck came to the view that 'there is a feeling that the whole truth has not been allowed to come out, and that "honest Jack Lynch" is perhaps a more devious character than his popular image suggests'.[35]

A close observer who had access to both Lynch's and Gibbons's thoughts in the course of the 1970s, and who documented it, was Frank Dunlop, former government press Secretary to both Lynch and his successor in 1980, Charles Haughey.[36] Dunlop later fell from grace when he admitted bribing Dublin County councillors over planning applications in the 1990s, but has nonetheless written tellingly of relations, as he perceived them, between Lynch and Gibbons in the decade after 1970. Dunlop accorded to Lynch contradictory qualities: he agreed with Hillery that Lynch 'was innocent, perhaps naïve, in many ways',[37] but Dunlop also saw in him a trait of 'cuteness'. He wrote: 'Others might be less kind and call it cunning… he did not mind going against the rules as long as he was not caught.'[38] Dunlop described Haughey as being 'stitched up',[39] meaning he was made a scapegoat for the activities of others; he said that everyone at the top of the party knew this. Dunlop's soundings told him that all senior figures in Fianna Fáil knew that 'certain actions' were being taken at the time to help Northern nationalists, the details of which were never alluded to – and that suited Lynch.[40] But Dunlop's most interesting remarks concern relations between Lynch and Gibbons in the years after the crisis had passed:

> At first I imagined that because of the events of 1970, Lynch and Gibbons would be close friends, or at the least something approaching political allies. In fact the opposite was the case, and I was amazed on one or two occasions to discover that their attitude to one another was distinctly chilly, even glacial. Underneath Gibbons's antipathy to Haughey there lay an animus, bordering on contempt, against Lynch. Again, it clearly went back to the events of the Arms Crisis. Gibbons did not trust him and was downright dismissive of him in many of the conversations I had with him. This seems extraordinary in circumstances where Lynch, to all intents and purposes, stood by Gibbons in the white heat of the controversy. Sometimes Gibbons could show chilling disdain for his colleagues and Lynch did not escape his sharp tongue.[41]

This insight into Gibbons's view of the two men's relationship can be read in several ways. It is certainly open to the interpretation that Gibbons, in line with Vincent Browne's characterization of him as 'principal victim of the Arms Crisis', felt aggrieved that he had, in his own mind at least, been made the fall guy by Lynch for the government's troubles in 1970. Such resentments would be understandable, since the discrepancies, fumblings and clear lies that littered Gibbons's sworn evidence and provided so much ammunition for the barristers at the arms trials, had also served to keep the Lynch government in power for a further three years, with Gibbons himself left to nurse an irremediably shattered personal reputation.

While Lynch's commitment to peaceful means of ending partition has never been in dispute, he was at the same time obliged to plan for contingencies; such plans had to be kept secret, even – as it appears from the evidence – from key advisers on Northern policy such as T. K. Whitaker.[42] The Taoiseach was not blind to the dangers to the Irish State if his government proved once again incapable of defending Northern nationalists from assault; even a stable democracy was not invulnerable to the IRA presenting itself in time of crisis as the only true defender of threatened kinsmen. Here it is significant as noted earlier that in the autumn of 1969 the Taoiseach warned British Ambassador Gilchrist privately of the danger that, as Gilchrist described his words at the time, the IRA might 'by some traditionally violent intervention, recapture the moral leadership of Ireland'.[43]

Overall, the provision of arms to Northern nationalists, if the worst came to the worst, seemed to those involved not just necessary contingency planning, but a necessary positioning of the Irish State after finding itself sidelined and impotent during the Northern convulsions of the previous August. If an indecisive and hesitant Lynch had a different view, his actions, certainly before 20 April 1970, did little to bear this out. Above all, the persistent evidence of his subsequent double-talk and false statements are convincing proof that, on Northern Ireland, Lynch felt afterwards he had something to hide.

14

The Arms Trial Prosecution (1)

Although the arms trials were just one component in the overall Arms Crisis, they provided, through their extended set-piece legal confrontations, some of the highest points of the drama. In the dock in the autumn of 1970, and carrying a whiff of cordite, was the long-time golden boy of Irish politics, Charles Haughey. Haughey's career seemed, at the time of the trial, in ruins; he had been dismissed from the government in apparent disgrace, and if the trial went against him, the net result could be a spell in jail. Alongside him, an Irish army officer, James Kelly, stood accused, like Haughey, of conspiracy to import arms illegally. In the air was the taint of sedition. A gun-running attempt had been uncovered, involving suspected collusion with the IRA and a plot supposedly to bring down Lynch as Taoiseach.

Rumours abounded in advance of the trials: rumours of an attempted army coup, of a real threat to the country's democratic systems, of a desire to go to war over Northern Ireland. From the opening salvoes in Dublin's Four Courts, when State counsel singled out Haughey as a prime target in the proceedings, tension remained at an elevated level right up to the point of the jury's brisk verdict of 'not guilty' just over a month later. The intense atmosphere of the arms trial courtroom was well captured by Tom MacIntyre when he described State counsel Seamus McKenna SC facing into cross-examining Colonel Hefferon in the second trial:

Break this witness, and preferment is his for the asking; he
knows it, the witness knows it, all know it. Counsel – knuckles
on parade – grips his sheaf of papers. Very well, *With the shield
or on it,* says the Colonel's jaw. And it begins.[1]

The claim that the arms trial prosecutions should never
have been brought was first aired – and extensively so – at the
second trial in October 1970, and has remained an issue ever
since. Almost every barrister on the defence side argued to Judge
Seamus Henchy that the prosecutions were improper. Peter
Maguire SC (for Haughey) said: 'I say there should never have
been a prosecution, because there was not the evidence to justify
a prosecution.'[2] Seamus Sorahan BL (for John Kelly) described
the prosecution to the jury as 'smelly, shameful, disgraceful'.[3]
Ernest Wood SC (for Luykx) said the proceedings were 'an asinine
pantomime… a waste of time'.[4] Niall McCarthy SC (for Haughey)
said that, in his opinion, 'it was a prosecution which ought never
to have seen the light of day… a prosecution conceived in panic,
nurtured in rumour, born in malice and brought in spite'.[5] After
the trial, former Minister for Justice Mícheál Ó Móráin, himself
a solicitor, said it had been 'more of a political prosecution than
a criminal prosecution'.[6] Haughey himself, immediately after the
verdict was handed down, described it as 'a political trial'.[7]

Such was the level of protest from counsel at the second trial
that Judge Henchy felt obliged to address their complaints directly.
In the course of his charge to the jury, Henchy said that while it
was open to them to decide otherwise, his own opinion was that
the prosecution had been properly brought. Not only, he said,
was the Attorney General justified in bringing the prosecution,
he thought he would have been unjustified in *not* doing so.[8] This
firm opinion from the bench has been much quoted by writers
and historians since, and may explain why the issue has so often
been treated as closed.[9] However, since the release of the State
files in 2001, Henchy's statement may no longer appear entirely
well-grounded.

In justifying his view that the prosecution was properly brought, the judge said that when the Attorney General decided to institute charges, he had before him three particular statements supporting such a decision. He listed these as one from Tony Fagan, personal assistant to Haughey in the Department of Finance; another from Peter Berry, Secretary of the Department of Justice; and a third from Minister for Defence Jim Gibbons, about a conversation with Haughey on 20 April 1970. However, the judge was misinformed over one of these statements. Gibbons's account of his conversation with Haughey on 20 April 1970 was not taken until 8 June, almost two weeks after charges were issued.

Another problem with Henchy's opinion, on the evidence of the trial and of the State files, is that he did not know when he offered it that controversial deletions had been made from the original witness statement of Colonel Hefferon before it reached the Book of Evidence.[10] Hefferon's statement initially implicated both Gibbons and Hefferon in Kelly's arms importation plans; the editing removed almost all of its incriminating references to Gibbons. Henchy did not know this. He was not aware that Hefferon's likely evidence had been strangely misrepresented by what appeared in the Book of Evidence. Nor could he have been aware that similar questions arose over the editing of witness statements taken from Gibbons, as will be shown and discussed below. These facts became evident only after 2001. With the value of hindsight, they invite significant reservations over the weight of Henchy's opinion that the charges were properly brought.

The doubts about the arms trial prosecutions all relate to the former Minister for Defence, Jim Gibbons. What Gibbons knew, or did not know, of the gun-running attempt that led to the sacking of Haughey and Blaney was from the beginning a matter of controversy. Evidence for this can be seen in the three major debates on the Arms Crisis held in Dáil Éireann during May 1970. Many Fine Gael and Labour deputies focused on Gibbons's oversight of the army captain implicated in the gun-running, and suggested that Kelly's minister was, or should be, a suspect in any criminal investigation. By mid-May that investigation was already well under way, with Attorney General Colm Condon SC directing the Special Branch of the Garda Síochána in the gathering of witness statements.

The Taoiseach's position on Gibbons had already been made known: contrary to those TDs calling for Gibbons to be investigated, he had wasted no time in promoting the former Defence Minister to the more senior portfolio of Agriculture and Fisheries, the position from which Lynch had just ousted Blaney. Lynch in fact had felt able to assure the Dáil on 9 May 1970 that allegations against Gibbons had already been thoroughly investigated, and, as a result, he had no suspicion about him.[11] This supposed investigation of Gibbons was a matter on which Lynch never elaborated. It had, however, marked out his position clearly, whether for the benefit of his Attorney General, his divided party or the Opposition leaders. Gibbons, it seems, was not to be touched.

Still, Opposition Dáil deputies demanded that the Taoiseach justify his early claim that no suspicion attached to Gibbons. A general political assault along these lines culminated on 14 May 1970 with Deputy Garret FitzGerald of Fine Gael demanding to know from the Taoiseach whether or not Gibbons was part of the Garda investigation. Was it the case, he asked, 'that the police have been told by the Taoiseach that he is satisfied with this man, that he has thrown his mantle of protection around him, and that he is outside this investigation?'[12]

Lynch, concluding the debate, gave FitzGerald only a general answer: he said it was up to the Attorney General, not him, to decide what action should be taken in relation to any individual.[13] But the question was prescient. The Taoiseach did not need to remind the Dáil on 9 May that in the most public fashion he had already judged Gibbons to be in the clear. FitzGerald's question had got close to the heart of the historical problems

Lynch would face over the Arms Crisis. These all stemmed from Gibbons, as would become very clear when the case came to trial in September–October 1970.

The issue to be explored in this chapter is whether the Gibbons problem had been clear all along to the Attorney General. Certainly, when Gibbons finally reached the witness box, the fragility of his position was remorselessly exposed. At that point, whatever protection the Taoiseach could afford him at large – which was substantial – could not extend beyond the courtroom door. Inside the two criminal trials, Gibbons was on his own, burdened with the task of sustaining a credible government position under intense questioning from some of the brightest barristers in the Law Library. But while the difficulties Gibbons experienced as a witness were due partly to his own inept performance, they may have owed even more to the way he had been shielded from prosecution by the Attorney General in the lead-up to the trial.

Although it is common in the literature to refer to the criminal proceedings as having been instituted by Lynch himself, in law they were at the direction of the Attorney General. No consideration of the propriety of the 1970 arms trial prosecution can ignore the ambiguous central role played by Condon. Like all Attorney Generals before and since, he was a political appointee; previous to his appointment, he had been an active member of Fianna Fáil.[14] He had a seat at cabinet, where he acted as the government's legal adviser, but he also carried the important role of public prosecutor. This was a position that required of him an absolute independence from any taint of politics.[15] Consistent with this, Lynch always insisted that the decision to prosecute Haughey and the other defendants was taken not by him, but by the Attorney General; he even stated at one point that it had been against his wishes.[16] It was certainly vital for Lynch to dispel suggestions that he had in some way directed Condon to bring a criminal prosecution. As Taoiseach, he said he did not interfere, and he felt certain that if he had done so, he would immediately have had the Attorney General's resignation on his desk.[17] Condon himself insisted in January 1991 on a local radio station in Mallow, Co. Cork, that it was he who decided that Charles Haughey would be prosecuted: 'Jack Lynch had nothing whatsoever to do with it.'[18]

While no evidence has ever been found to contradict these assertions from Lynch and Condon, the Attorney General faced a practical, but unavoidable, dilemma, stemming from the combined political and legal responsibilities of his office. In this particular case, his cabinet colleagues were possible or actual suspects; this made it very difficult for a decision to prosecute ever to be a purely legal one. Was it conceivable that Condon, who sat at cabinet, could prosecute one of his sitting colleagues? How could the government survive such a moment?

Once Lynch handed the various papers in his possession to him, the practical political and legal challenge faced by Condon was whether he could mount a prosecution that did not include serving cabinet member Jim Gibbons. And one of the immediate issues he would have to resolve, basic to the investigation, risked bringing Gibbons directly into the frame: what level of authorization did Kelly have for his gun-running attempt? He was an army officer – was he under orders from his army superiors?

While it is noteworthy that no one in an official position appears in the years since 1970 to have taken issue with Condon's handling of the arms trial prosecutions,[19] it is not clear that such reticence is any longer sustainable. It is certainly important for historians, in the light of available documentation, to question whether or not political calculations could have improperly influenced the prosecution; and if so, at what point, and how? The context for the Attorney General's prosecution, it need scarcely be said, was a convulsion that threatened the survival of the Lynch government and, as it seemed at the time, possibly also threatened the stability of the State. The pressure on Condon was immense.

The eminent historian Ronan Fanning, in a possibly unguarded moment, wrote in 2001 that had Charles Haughey and Neil Blaney not been earlier sacked from the government, it was 'inconceivable' that they would ever have been prosecuted.[20] Fanning, an admirer of Jack Lynch's performance during the Arms Crisis, said it was 'indisputable' that the 1970 arms trials were, in certain respects, political trials. Although it is unlikely this remark was intended in any way to undermine or disparage Lynch's record, the logic of Fanning's position was that Gibbons, who had not been sacked but rather promoted within the cabinet, could not be prosecuted because of his cabinet position. Was Fanning correct in this? Was this the answer to the question Garret FitzGerald had posed rhetorically at the height of the crisis in May 1970, asking if Gibbons could not be prosecuted?

The core issues requiring consideration are, how the Attorney General conducted the criminal investigation, whether it provided for him evidence that rendered Gibbons suspect for involvement in a crime, and, if so, how the Attorney handled that evidence? Can it be shown, from a consideration of the investigation's progress, that Condon acted with absolute propriety? Before the release of the 1970 State papers in 2001, there was no prospect of being able to answer such questions; since then, however, the released documents have opened up a wealth of information that alters this situation. It is now possible, as demonstrated in research for this book, to identify not just how much the Attorney General knew as his Garda investigation proceeded, but also when he knew it. This includes what he knew on the day that he issued criminal charges. Of particular value in this regard are the files from the Department of Justice and from the Attorney General's Office, papers that hitherto appear to have been underused in researching these matters.

There was initially some pessimism about how much the State papers could reveal, because of a perceived absence of some key prosecution files. Thus former Attorney General Michael McDowell SC, in his 2001 *Report of the Attorney General on Questions Concerning the Prosecution of the Arms Trial in 1970*, concluded that there was 'simply no prospect of an official, authoritative, objective and generally accepted history of these events being written now'.[21] On this basis, McDowell, a skilled lawyer and politician, but without a historian's background, saw no need for any form of official public inquiry, or, it appears, for interviews with surviving principals such as Condon or McKenna, He found further support for his gloomy prognosis in the perception that neither 'a prosecution file, nor a Garda file' could be found in the 2001 documentation.

However, the material in the archives may have been more substantial than McDowell realized. Some key documents from the files believed to be missing have, more recently, been located by this writer within the archives, at times dispersed through other files. This includes the bulk of the original witness statements, which are to be found in the files of the Department of Justice.[22] Other valuable documents, including important material on the editing of Hefferon's statement by a senior official in the Attorney General's Office, Declan Quigley, understandably escaped McDowell's scrutiny in his report because they had been mislaid or misfiled, only forming part of a delayed release to the National Archives in January 2003.[23]

Additionally, the final report by Chief Superintendent John Fleming on the results of his Garda investigation, a central document in any decision to prosecute, has also been unearthed by the author within these files, having been misplaced within the misfiled material. Fleming's report is a document of major historical importance, and is assessed below.[24] These various discoveries have meant that much fuller documentation has been available for research on the 1970 prosecution than had appeared to be the case. This has made it possible to probe more deeply into how the arms trials came about than anything attempted before.

The material available since 2001 has enabled the identification, for the first time, of a clear basic chronology, or timeline, for the development of the Attorney General's prosecution.[25] This, in part, has been accomplished by the simple device of assembling, in order, all the original, dated, witness statements taken by the gardaí from the end of April to early June 1970.[26] When cross-referenced with the content of other State papers from the period, it becomes possible to make some appropriate but cautious deductions about the tactics and strategy underlying the prosecution approach. The bulk of the statements were taken in May 1970 by the Special Detective Unit, or Special Branch, the unit responsible for State security, and headed by Fleming.

The Garda investigation began, as shown above, with two reports from Fleming himself, on 19 and 20 April, delivered to his Garda superiors, with a copy to Peter Berry, Secretary in the Department of Justice.[27] In these, Fleming recounted what he had discovered about the events of the weekend, when his officers had foiled Captain Kelly's attempted importation into Dublin Airport. Within twenty-four hours Berry delivered the reports personally to Jack Lynch. That sparked an initial phase of investigation, in which Special Branch officers took statements from Revenue officials in Customs and Excise, and from others connected with the arms importation attempt.

These inquiries appear to have been driven by Berry himself. He believed, probably correctly, that Lynch had directed him to make some level of investigation, but there appears to have been a difference of approach between the two men on how zealously it was to be conducted. Shortly afterwards, Lynch shocked Berry by upbraiding him for an excessively heavy-handed approach to the Revenue Commissioners over their degree of urgency in the taking of statements. The Taoiseach appeared angry that Berry was involving himself so much in the Garda investigation.[28] A chastened Berry concluded that Lynch knew more of the events under investigation than he was admitting.

Matters went quiet for some days thereafter, until a flurry of activity on 1 May. Captain Kelly was arrested for questioning, but after face-to-face separate encounters with both Gibbons and the Taoiseach, he refused to make a statement and was released without charge. Another of the accused, Albert Luykx, did make a lengthy statement on the same date. Luykx's involvement had been simply to act as an interpreter for Captain Kelly on his Continental trips. He had however been recruited for that task by Neil Blaney, who was a friend, and his witness statement inevitably implicated Blaney in the gun-running project.

After the Cosgrave intervention on 5 May and the resulting cabinet upheaval, Lynch announced in the Dáil that he was turning matters over to his Attorney General and stepping back himself. Criminal investigations resumed in mid-May, now under the aegis of Condon. Gardaí further questioned Revenue officials, some of whom had featured in Fleming's reports of 19 and 20 April, about the involvement of customs officers in the attempted airport importation. The questioning was from commissioner level down to staff officers on the ground. Statements were taken from staff in Aer Lingus who had been involved in dealings regarding the arms shipment.

Later in May, Tony Fagan, a principal officer in the Department of Finance, who was Haughey's personal assistant, made a total of eight statements. It is noteworthy that two of these were produced by Fagan independently of the gardaí; these were handwritten, and probably for his superiors in the Department of Finance. They were followed by six formal typed statements given to the gardaí over a period of six weeks. Three separate statements were taken from Minister Jim Gibbons during May, and there was also a short formal statement from Peter Berry about his telephone call with Haughey. Various customs officials in Dublin Port gave statements describing an earlier failed attempt to bring in the arms and ammunition by sea, three weeks before the Dublin Airport events. A statement was taken from Hefferon's successor as Director of Military Intelligence, Colonel P. J. Delaney.

Charges were issued and arrests made between 27 and 29 May. Only after those decisive steps was a statement taken on 29 May from Diarmaid Ó Ríordáin, a Customs and Excise surveyor at Dublin Port. One day later, on 30 May 1970, a first statement was taken from Colonel Hefferon himself. Almost a month had passed since his subordinate Kelly had first been arrested and questioned. Although in the meantime, charges had been issued against Kelly, this was the first attempt by the authorities to elicit Hefferon's views. Several days later on 2 June, almost a week after Captain Kelly had been charged, Fleming submitted his formal and concluding report on the investigation. When a fourth statement was taken from Gibbons on 8 June, it brought the Garda investigation effectively to an end.[29]

This chronology is revealing. It shows firstly that the Garda investigation, unusually, was still ongoing when charges were issued. Inquiries had not been concluded, important witnesses had not been approached, and no formal report on the investigation had been received by the Attorney General. Secondly, one of those who conspicuously had still not been approached for a witness statement when charges were issued was Colonel Hefferon, Captain Kelly's commanding officer. Thirdly, Hefferon was actually one of the last witnesses to be consulted, at the tail-end of an investigation that had been running for five weeks.[30]

Hefferon himself was very conscious of the lateness of the approach to him, and made this known when he was first visited by Garda Detective Inspectors Edward O'Dea and Patrick Doocey. This was on the evening of 28 May, just after charges had been instituted. O'Dea described the greeting they received: 'Colonel Hefferon... stated that he was surprised that, because of his high position, he was not approached before now by some person in high authority.'[31] At that stage it was twenty-nine days since his immediate assistant, Captain Kelly, had been first arrested and questioned. Garda Inspector O'Dea asked Hefferon who was the person 'in high authority' he thought should have approached him earlier. Hefferon would not be drawn. O'Dea thought that he was referring to Gibbons, but it seems equally likely that he was referring to the Attorney General, who had brought charges without contacting him.[32]

Hefferon, it is evident, was surprised that, in a criminal investigation into an army officer's conduct, neither the Attorney General, his investigators nor indeed the relevant minister had been concerned to establish as a matter of priority whether or not that officer was acting under orders. It was a question that could *only* be answered by Colonel Hefferon; he was Kelly's immediate superior, and the officer to whom he reported exclusively. Yet charges had been issued against Kelly three days before Hefferon's first statement. Although the die was already cast, Hefferon in his statement strongly supported Captain Kelly. He provided details of how both he and Kelly's minister, Jim Gibbons, had been kept fully informed about Kelly's attempts to import guns for the Northern Defence Committees throughout February, March and April 1970. His statement raised the question as to whether, had charges been preferred in the normal way – i.e., *after* the conclusion of the Garda investigation, and after the taking of Hefferon's statement, which amounted to a defence of the charged officer – would, or could, the prosecution have developed as it did?

The delay by the Attorney General and his Garda investigators in approaching Hefferon for a witness statement was so marked that it requires explanation. The possibility of a *bona fide* reason for the delay, an explanation that might perhaps lie hidden elsewhere in the files, demands consideration. Here it may be relevant that at least some elements within the prosecution had some idea of what evidence was to be expected of Hefferon. This harked back to the aftermath of the meeting at Bailieboro the previous autumn, when Hefferon had defended his junior officer Kelly. When Peter Berry raised serious queries about money being offered to IRA men to buy arms, it was Hefferon's robust defence of Kelly that defused the matter and caused no action to be taken. Hefferon had not only stood up for Kelly, but had described the complaints as 'pure poppycock'. Berry recorded in his *Diaries* that when he informed the Special Branch of this rebuff, he received the response: 'Christ, Hefferon must be in the swim too.'[33] This barbed but unattributed comment is likely to have come from Fleming; he was head of the Special Branch and Berry's point of contact there, and seemingly had early suspicions of Hefferon. So, whatever the Attorney General, Condon, knew of these events

when he initiated investigating Kelly in May 1970, the head of the
Garda investigation, Fleming, had reason to believe that Hefferon
would take Kelly's side and was a witness unlikely to support
his prosecution.[34] Other evidence considered elsewhere in this
chapter suggests that Fleming also suspected Gibbons was party
to the gun-running.

   What seems clear from all this is that there were conflicting
currents within the prosecution, possibly hinging on different
perspectives on Gibbons and Lynch. The Attorney General, who
was directing the investigation, did not necessarily have the same
mindset or approach as the Special Branch, which was conducting
the actual inquiries. A glimpse of tensions within the prosecution
is provided by an entry in the Berry *Diaries* for September 1970.
Here Berry noted that in the run-up to the arms trials, Garda
witnesses complained to him of 'great difficulty' in getting access
to prosecution lawyers and of being restricted to short conversations, 'much shorter than was usual in police experience'.[35]
The amount of Garda evidence in the trials themselves proved
minimal, and the impression is of some disharmony within the
prosecution team. The Attorney General may have been directing
the investigation and subsequent prosecution, but the gardaí, in
the person of Chief Superintendent Fleming and his officers, were
pulling hard at his handling.

The kind of evidence Hefferon might provide on Gibbons had
been signalled early on in handwritten accounts provided
by Haughey's personal assistant Tony Fagan. In these two
comprehensive documents, Fagan described his early involvement
with Kelly and Hefferon, dating from October 1969, particularly
over the distribution of the Northern Ireland Relief Fund. He
wrote that Hefferon had often referred to Kelly as 'one of his best
officers', someone who was doing 'very valuable work in connection
with the Northern Ireland situation'. As early as 9 May 1970,
Fagan wrote that Hefferon and Captain Kelly 'always gave me

to understand that the Minister for Defence was fully informed on Captain Kelly's activities'.[36] This appeared to support what Kelly said when he was arrested: that his minister was aware of all he was doing. The obvious suggestion was that Gibbons had been party to the gun-running, which if true, would make him a possible suspect. Hefferon was the obvious person to approach to clarify the reference – assuming, that is, that the Attorney General wished to know why Hefferon might have believed this, and assuming also that the Attorney was interested in how much Gibbons knew in advance of the supposed crime. Nothing in the files suggests any effort was in fact made to clarify these matters. Fagan's account pointed the authorities towards Colonel Hefferon as a potentially vital witness in the case, but the army officer was not approached for another three weeks, and not until after Kelly had been charged. These facts speak for themselves.

Other early indicators of the importance of acquiring Hefferon's testimony came, ironically, from Gibbons himself. In his first Garda witness statement, on 18 May, Gibbons said that he had his 'suspicions' about Kelly and his own cabinet colleagues Blaney and Haughey, based on remarks made to him by Colonel Hefferon. This reliance on Hefferon for information was a continuing feature of Gibbons's witness statements. Once again, the importance of taking a statement from Hefferon could scarcely have been clearer. If it needed any extra emphasis, this too came in the advice of the Chief State Solicitor, Diarmaid O'Donovan, who pointed out to Chief Superintendent Fleming on 22 May, before any charges had been issued, that Hefferon was one of several witnesses whose statement was required, but had not yet been taken. This advice was passed on to the Attorney General in a memo from O'Donovan the same day.[37] Still, Hefferon was not approached. Of the several witness statements that O'Donovan specified were not to hand, but were required, Hefferon's was the only one still not taken by the time charges were issued. This failure, and the associated failure even to consult with Hefferon, has to be regarded as highly unusual.

When one takes into account the exclusions eventually made to Hefferon's witness statement when it *was* finally taken on 30 May,[38] the conduct of Condon becomes even more striking.

Nor was the Attorney General in any rush to take a statement from Gibbons himself. It was not until after the two Dáil debates of 8–9 May and 13–14 May, where so many deputies, in particular Fine Gael's Garret FitzGerald, made a public issue of Gibbons as a possible suspect, that he was approached for a statement by the gardaí. Judging by his first bland statement on 18 May, Gibbons came under no great pressure to explain himself. In relation to Captain Kelly, he stuck to the general line he had taken in the Dáil on 8 May,[39] which was to deny any specific knowledge of the officer's activities; he said, however, that, based on information from Hefferon, he had come to harbour 'suspicions' of Kelly, and also of his two cabinet colleagues, Blaney and Haughey. Each of Gibbons's statements to the gardaí, taken on 18 May, 22 May and 28 May, were imprecise and vague, with dates and times qualified and uncertain. This culminated in a remark made at the conclusion of Gibbons's fourth and most specific statement on 8 June, to the effect that 'there may well be items which I cannot now recall which I may remember later'.[40] This proved prescient, because Gibbons's memory, as shown in Chapter 8, improved greatly after the arms trials were over. Initially, none of his statements reflected any detailed involvement by him with Kelly, Haughey or Blaney on an arms project, and he did not appear to be a witness who could greatly help a prosecution.

The State papers released in 2001 have also thrown new light on the circumstances in which charges were issued on 27 and 28 May. This has the appearance of a hurried and unplanned event. Part of the evidence for this, as noted, is that the Garda investigation on which such a decision might be expected to hinge was not yet complete, and the Attorney General had no formal report from Fleming advising on the facts he had found and what charges the evidence might support. Several significant statements – among them Hefferon's – remained to be taken. Others which were in the process of acquisition had been interrupted midway through. There is some evidence that in all this, the Attorney General had to contend with a continuing suspicion from Chief Superintendent Fleming that both Gibbons and Hefferon knew in advance of the gun-running. Fleming's suspicions in this regard were in evidence on 25 May, as he made plans for some sharp questioning of Charles Haughey about Gibbons's and Hefferon's role. His questioning of the sacked Minister for Finance was due to take place that day at his home in Kinsealy in north Dublin. However, on Fleming's arrival there, Haughey insisted that any questions should be given to him in writing, forcing Fleming to retire with no questions either put or replied to. The Chief Superintendent consulted thereafter with Attorney General Colm Condon, in the process listing for him the questions he had proposed to ask of Haughey. Four of his intended questions stand out:

Q 15: Was Mr. Gibbons, to your knowledge, aware of the proposed illegal importation of this cargo of firearms and ammunition?

Q 16: If he was not a party to it, why did you discuss the matter with him at any stage?

Q 26: Was the ex-Minister for Defence, James Gibbons, aware of the fact that Captain Kelly had large sums of money from you [as Minister for Finance] at his disposal?

Q 30: Can you state whether Col. Michael Hefferon played a part in the transaction to import arms illegally?[41]

However, these questions were never asked of Haughey, because it was at precisely this point that the Attorney General, for whatever reason, suddenly decided to issue charges. Fleming, who was effectively in mid-interview, was stopped in his tracks.

The files show that, before Fleming had departed Kinsealy, he had specifically informed Haughey that the investigation was not yet complete. He appears to have left Haughey's home with every intention of returning with written questions after clearance by the Attorney General.[42] Instead, an apparently abrupt decision to issue charges was made by Colm Condon. This short-circuited the questioning of Haughey and simultaneously – on a different plane – pre-empted whatever conclusions or recommendations on prosecution Fleming might have contemplated making in his as-yet-unwritten investigation report.

It is hardly surprising that there are no papers among those released in 2001 which set down why the Attorney General decided to issue charges when he did. The circumstances, however, point to one possible or even likely answer. They suggest that Condon may have seen a need to intervene before Fleming went too far. The Attorney General's eye can be assumed to have fallen on Question 15 on the list for Haughey to answer. The Taoiseach had already promoted Gibbons within the cabinet, and had determined that he was under no suspicion of knowing about the importation. Fleming was obviously unconvinced, and in this question he invited Haughey to implicate Gibbons in advance knowledge of the gun-running. The answer was unlikely to enhance the prospects of a successful prosecution. The same applied to Question 30 about Hefferon. Any prospect of charges against Gibbons or Hefferon, because of their seniority, would greatly complicate the government's situation; both were likely to be essential prosecution witnesses in any putative case involving Captain Kelly.

In short, Fleming appeared to have crossed a red line in the investigation, a line that the evidence suggests the Attorney General had drawn around Gibbons. As Minister for Defence, he was the one person with the authority to make the importation legal, under the terms of the 1925 Firearms Act,[43] and anything that incriminated him at this juncture would have been a seismic blow to any prospective prosecution, and probably to Lynch's hold on power. It would have threatened the government's political survival.

In the investigation, it seems clear that the Attorney General, outside public scrutiny, was picking his steps carefully. He had to contend with tensions between his own view and that of the senior Special Branch officer leading the investigation. Evidence for this can be tracked, to a degree, using data from the State papers and revelations in Berry's *Diaries*. The tension appears to have been building, to the point where on 25 May two different approaches appeared ready to collide. It seems likely that Condon saw this, and took remedial action. The manner in which he pre-empted Chief Superintendent Fleming's final investigation report by deciding on the charges to be issued had consequences, which will be apparent below. Hefferon in the meantime seems to have been treated almost as if he was radioactive; but the taking of his witness statement was not something that could be avoided indefinitely.

When Hefferon's statement was eventually taken on 30 May 1970, it proved to be a remarkable document. Although its contents may not have been entirely unexpected, particularly by Fleming, it still must have transformed the prosecution team's knowledge of the arms importation plan.[44] In it, Hefferon effectively set out his full support for his already charged junior officer. He explained that Kelly had kept him informed over many months on his efforts to import guns and ammunition, and how he himself, on a number of occasions, had made sure that Gibbons, as Minister, knew what Kelly was doing. He said that the army captain had also met Gibbons personally, and had told him about his plans to bring in arms. His statement made clear that Gibbons knew long before mid-April 1970 that Kelly was seeking to import arms for the Northern minority. It contradicted and challenged the evidence taken from Gibbons earlier in May, when the minister had claimed to know very little of Captain Kelly or of any plan to bring arms into Ireland. Hefferon, by contrast, said that both he and Gibbons had known of, and permitted, the gun-running activities.

The statement also raised questions about Gibbons's role in keeping Kelly within army ranks. The junior officer's retirement had been mooted, and planned, but had not happened. Gibbons's own various witness statements had been characteristically vague about why Kelly was due to retire. Hefferon explained that the retirement was not of Kelly's own volition, as Gibbons suggested, but because he, Hefferon, had insisted on it. He had told both Gibbons and Kelly that it was unacceptable for an army officer to be assisting the Northern Defence Committees in bringing in arms, and he would have to resign. But when Kelly, as a result, submitted his resignation, Hefferon described how Gibbons himself had decided the resignation should not be put through.[45] His statement indicated that the only reason Kelly was still in the army in mid-April, planning to bring in guns for Northerners, was because the minister had kept him there.

In many respects, Hefferon's statement was heavily self-incriminating. While he implicated Gibbons in the gun-running, he also implicated himself, and the statement clearly offered a basis for further charges to be brought, this time against its author, if the State was so minded. This of course added to its credibility. But its import regarding Gibbons could hardly have been clearer: so far as his superior officer was concerned, Kelly had been entirely correct in his claim on 8 May that Gibbons was aware of the gun-running and its planning. This was geared to cause consternation, not just within the prosecution, but in wider government circles. The two detectives who took the statement, Inspector Ned O'Dea and Inspector Patrick Doocey, had to be fully aware of how it would be received.

The instant impact that Hefferon's witness statement had can be seen in the excessive annotation made in its margins when it was read the following day by Department of Justice Secretary Peter Berry. These included exclamation marks from Berry, several instances of 'N.B.' drawing attention to certain references, and double or even triple underlining against many sections. Although the factual content of Hefferon's statement would be contested at the arms trials, most particularly by Gibbons himself, on face value it repudiated and contradicted what Gibbons had said several times to the gardaí, and placed question marks against each of his three statements to date, the latest just two days earlier on 28 May.

Just three days after Hefferon made his statement, Chief Superintendent Fleming submitted his final report on the investigation. This was dated 2 June 1970; a ten-page document, it was sent on that date to the Chief State Solicitor's Office. This report has hitherto escaped public notice, having been apparently unnoticed until discovered by the author within the 1970 files of the Attorney General's Office. It appears to have been initially misfiled and then sent belatedly to the National Archives in 2003, two years late. This irregularity in procedure perhaps explains why it has been so late coming to light. The report by Fleming contains analysis and conclusions on which charges might normally have been based; however, in this case the Attorney General had already decided to bring charges on 27 and 28 May. Nonetheless, its discovery and identification is historically significant, not just because such Garda reports on a criminal investigation are important in any decision to prosecute, and may provide core briefing material for solicitors and barristers concerned with any resulting prosecution, but most particularly, because of the exceptional approach taken in it by Fleming to the facts of the case.[46]

In the report's preamble, Fleming set out briefly the events of 17–20 April which caused the alarm to be raised over the arms importation, and precipitated the Garda operation at Dublin Airport. He then stated, following the normal pattern of such reports: 'The matter was fully investigated and written statements

taken from all concerned. *It now appears the facts are as follows...'*
(emphasis added). There followed Fleming's considered assessment of what had been uncovered by the Garda investigation he
had led since the last week of April.

The report used extracts from the various witness statements to
build up a narrative that was seemingly designed to support the
charges already brought against the two Kellys, Luykx, Haughey
and Blaney. Fleming quoted statements from Revenue officials
and Aer Lingus employees to establish that the two Kellys and
Albert Luykx attempted unsuccessfully to import arms and
ammunition, first at Dublin docks on 25 March 1970, then at
Dublin Airport in the week leading up to 18 April 1970. He used
statements from Gibbons and Berry to show that Blaney and
Haughey were involved in the importation. However, Fleming
made no reference to the substance of what Hefferon had told
detectives O'Dea and Doocey; he ignored the fact that Captain
Kelly had kept his superior officer informed about his arms-
buying activities; he said nothing of how Hefferon on more than
one occasion had informed Gibbons about the operation to bring
in guns; and he was silent on how Gibbons had agreed to assist
Kelly in getting to the Continent.

There were other omissions. Fleming excluded how Hefferon
kept Minister Gibbons informed on a failed importation
attempt at Dublin Port on 25 March 1970, though he used other
statements to provide a detailed account of Captain Kelly's role
in this.[47] Various statements described how Kelly went to the
Continent shortly after the failed port attempt, to sort out the
administrative snags responsible for that failure, but Fleming
found no place for Hefferon's account of how he told the minister
of this trip, or how Gibbons offered to free Kelly from army
duties to allow him to travel. Statements were used by Fleming
to illustrate how Kelly was told early on that if he wanted to
help in the purchase of guns he would have to resign from the
army, but excluded was Hefferon's account of how Gibbons had
personally halted the resignation. The Chief Superintendent's

report drew directly on Hefferon's statement to incriminate Haughey and Blaney, noting, for example, how 'during the many conversations Colonel Hefferon had with Captain Kelly, he had become aware that Kelly had direct contact with Mr Haughey and Mr Blaney about aid for the Defence Committees'; but then ignored Hefferon's account of the many conversations he had with his own minister, Gibbons, to the same effect. Overall, the use of Hefferon's statement was minimal; it was quoted only in the report's first two paragraphs, essentially to provide background on Captain Kelly.

Fleming's disregard for the substance of what Hefferon had said was not due to any lack of awareness on his part. He was fully acquainted with the original statement. At the Committee of Public Accounts hearings in November 1971, he accepted that he knew what Hefferon had said, telling barrister Peter Sutherland (for Captain Kelly) flatly: 'I read his statement at the time.'[48] He also said he knew it had been edited, but said he could not recall in what respect.

What is particularly intriguing about the way Fleming's report so seriously misrepresented what his Garda colleagues had been told about 'the facts' of the case is the other evidence, as indicated previously, that suggests his own professional view was that Gibbons was complicit in the gun-running. Peter Berry, a close confidante of Fleming, believed that in early May 1970 the head of the Garda Special Branch 'strongly suspected from all his inquiries that Mr Gibbons had pre-knowledge of the attempt to import arms'.[49] Berry's view finds support in James Kelly's *The Thimble Riggers*, where Fleming is reported as having named Gibbons to him on 1 May 1970 as one of three ministers involved in the arms importation (the others being Haughey and Blaney).[50] The occasion for this comment was during Kelly's questioning in Bridewell Garda Station. Fleming disputed this later; he agreed that he named three ministers to Kelly, but claimed the three were Haughey, Blaney and Kevin Boland, former Minister for Local Government.[51] This claim would be more convincing had Boland ever been named as a suspect anywhere else, or ever implicated in the arms importation by other evidence.

So why did Fleming produce a report on his investigation that seemed to contradict his own beliefs? The reality appears to be that when he sat down to write, his position was already severely circumscribed. The Attorney General had moved on, and days earlier had brought charges against Captain Kelly, John Kelly, Albert Luykx, Charles Haughey and Neil Blaney. Gibbons was not included, and in fact, he and Hefferon would likely be required as witnesses for the prosecution. A report that made a case for the prosecution of either Gibbons or Hefferon, even it that was what the facts indicated, would hardly serve the interests of the Attorney General, or of a prosecution already begun. Fleming may have felt he had little option but to turn a blind eye to 'the facts' on the possible involvement of the Minister for Defence. If this looks uncomfortably like a capitulation on his part and an abdication of a Garda officer's responsibility to follow the evidence wherever it led, it might also be viewed as simply a hard-headed acknowledgement by Fleming of his perceived responsibility to assist, rather than undermine, the prosecution already under way. Whichever view is taken on that, what is not in doubt is that Fleming's concluding report on the Garda investigation he had led contained a view of the facts that was distorted and seriously misleading.

The final important event in the investigation leading to the arms trial prosecution came just days after Fleming had submitted his report, when a fourth statement was taken from Gibbons, on 8 June 1970. The return to the former Minister for Defence for this statement, on this occasion by Detective Inspectors O'Dea and Doocey, appears to have had nothing to do with Hefferon's statement on 30 May, or to any doubts it might have raised over whether Gibbons had been fully truthful in his first three statements. None of the questions put to Gibbons on 8 June appear to have been designed to reconcile the two contradictory accounts, nor was there any evident effort to probe Gibbons's truthfulness. The questions asked were not based on Hefferon's damaging assertions eight days earlier.[52]

Despite this, on 8 June 1970 Gibbons volunteered some new and somewhat startling information about his level of knowledge of the gun-running. These revelations, which would have a devastating effect in the arms trials later that year, came when he was asked to deal with an unrelated issue – why, in an earlier statement, he had said that he had asked Haughey if he knew anything about a gun project? In his reply, Gibbons made the startling declaration that Captain Kelly had told him in early April of an abortive attempt to bring in a quantity of arms by sea. 'This consignment', Gibbons's statement read, 'was to be met at Dublin docks, and when those who were to meet it arrived there, they found Irish army troops taking delivery of army materials. I understood from Captain Kelly that this illegal consignment never left Europe (Belgium).' Later in his statement, Gibbons elaborated: he told how he had said to Captain Kelly, when he told him about the failed consignment at Dublin docks, 'I suppose that is the end of that.' Kelly had replied: 'No, it will be all right.'

Although it came very late, this was another extraordinary moment in the investigation. Gibbons, under no apparent pressure, had suddenly revealed that Kelly had told him about an attempt to import arms at Dublin docks sometime before early April. The attempt had failed because the arms were not despatched. But Gibbons had learned that was not to be the end of the matter, as Kelly had told him it would be 'all right'. This was the first the prosecution had heard of such a conversation between Kelly and Gibbons. The date of the conversation was two to three weeks before the final gun-running attempt at Dublin Airport.

Gibbons, in offering this new information, appeared not to realize that he was revealing that Kelly had presented him with another, surely unmissable, opportunity to put an end to the gun-running, weeks before the final attempt. Gibbons, it may be speculated, believed this new information would further incriminate Kelly, but if so, it was a serious miscalculation on his behalf. He overlooked how it could rebound against himself – if not immediately, then when the case came to trial.

What is also remarkable – on the evidence of the documents – is that when this statement was taken from Gibbons on 8 June, explaining what Kelly had told him, no attempt was made afterwards by the Attorney General to establish whether Gibbons had made the seemingly obvious response, i.e., telling Kelly to stop the whole project. It appears likely that Gibbons on 8 June was responding to submitted written questions, with no opportunity for the Garda officers to ask supplementaries. The professional view of the two gardaí can be gauged from what their superior officer, Fleming, two weeks earlier had wanted to ask Haughey, but was unable to, because of the Attorney General's decision to bring charges. Fleming on that occasion intended to ask Haughey if Gibbons knew in advance about the gun-running. Now, on 8 June, the answer was coming from Gibbons himself, almost accidentally: he said he *did* know. Captain Kelly had told him personally. For the Attorney General, reading this statement at the time, further questions for Gibbons arose automatically – did he tell Kelly to stop? And if he didn't, then why not?

At this point, 8 June 1970, the accumulation of doubt about Gibbons's role would appear to have been irresistible – except there had been a persistent lack of interest by the Attorney General over what Gibbons knew of the gun-running. This by June 1970 must have been clear to Fleming and all his team. It appears obvious that had the issue of Gibbons's failure to stop Captain Kelly been of interest to the Attorney General, these questions would have been put to Gibbons – if not on 8 June 1970, then at some time shortly afterwards. They could have been put to him, in fact, at any time after 30 May, when Hefferon's statement first laid out the extent of Gibbons's foreknowledge. But they were not.

In the end, the truth eventually came out in court: although Gibbons knew of the gun-running, he never told Kelly to stop.

Despite Gibbons making four separate witness statements, this became explicit only at the arms trials themselves. Gibbons in the witness box undermined the State case, perhaps fatally, by clarifying that *at no point* did he tell Kelly to stop what he was doing.[53] He also confirmed something that was implicit rather than explicit in his 8 June statement: that Kelly had been there *in person* to collect the arms at Dublin Port which did not arrive.

When confronted by defence counsel about all this, Gibbons sought to argue that he did not know what Kelly's actual involvement was, that it appeared to be possibly a small affair, and that he basically knew nothing of substance. But this evidence was met with extreme scepticism, not least among jury members at the second trial. One juror recalled thirty years later how Gibbons's revelation was a turning point in the trial:

> I think the feeling was, that it was a done thing for quite a period of the trial, that the lads were all going to be found guilty. And it changed completely.... When he [Gibbons] did admit eventually that he was aware of the arms coming in, you could actually sense the reaction in the jury box, because that was a turning point for the whole thing.[54]

What is important here, in the context of the development of the prosecution in early June, is that the files show that although the Attorney General was aware since the early summer of the problems over Gibbons's state of knowledge, he chose not to pursue the matter. Nor was there any possibility that Condon perhaps missed the full significance of what Gibbons had said on 8 June. He was already at that stage in possession of several relevant witness statements taken during May, specifically from Department of Finance official Tony Fagan, from Revenue Commissioner Bartholomew Culligan,[55] and from Revenue officials Tom Tobin[56] and Diarmaid Ó Ríordáin[57] (leaving out Hefferon for the moment); all these showed to him that what Kelly was telling Gibbons about on 8 June concerned a major operation, one in which Captain Kelly was a central player. Those statements variously showed that a direction had come from the Minister for Finance, after which James Kelly was specifically mandated by the Revenue Commissioners to receive and take away, without interference from customs, an arms consignment due on 25 March at Dublin Port.

Ó Ríordáin's statement had described how Kelly told him on 25 March 1970 that the arms were 'for the defence of Catholics in the North', and that it was 'secret, but had top level approval'. This claimed approval seemed to be confirmed when, on 8 June, the Attorney General and his team learned from Gibbons's own mouth how he and Kelly had discussed the plan, and how Kelly had *volunteered* to his minister information about the operation. That nothing further was done to clarify Gibbons's role at this point speaks volumes about the prosecution attitude to him.

Nor can it have escaped the Attorney General's attention that Gibbons, when he made the statement on 8 June, was contradicting what he had told the Dáil exactly a month earlier, on 8 May. On that occasion he said that, while he had suspicions over Captain Kelly, 'nothing concrete emerged'.[58] Now he was describing a very concrete event – an incriminating conversation with Kelly, just weeks before the alleged crime itself. This undermined Gibbons's three earlier witness statements, and further implicated him in the gun-running. If all this appeared to make Gibbons into a definite suspect, that was not how the Attorney General chose to view it.

15

The Arms Trial Prosecution (2)

Presented with two bombshell witness statements, one from Hefferon, the other from Gibbons, the Attorney General and his team next had to determine how these should be accommodated in the trial Book of Evidence. In any criminal trial, the Book fulfils an important statutory obligation on the prosecution, to furnish the accused with a statement 'of the evidence that a witness is to give'.[1] But after the State papers were made public in 2001, it became apparent that there were issues over how Hefferon's statement was edited for the Book of Evidence in the arms trials. It also became evident, as will be shown below, that a similar problem arose over statements of James Gibbons himself. In the intense public controversy that took place in 2001, when the editing of Hefferon's statement was revealed for the first time, these latter exclusions from Gibbons's statements were overlooked, and received practically no attention. But they involved exclusions from the Book of Evidence of important details that Kelly had given the minister weeks before the final gun-running attempt.

Although editing of witness statements is a necessary and regular occurrence, and usually non-controversial, in these two instances concerning Hefferon and Gibbons it appears to have been problematic. The exclusions can be shown to follow a pattern in the treatment of evidence linking Gibbons to the gun-running, a pattern identifiable throughout the Attorney General's investigation, as documented in the previous chapter. Also, because of the way the statements from Hefferon and from Gibbons were edited, it is argued below that the Book of Evidence in the arms trials failed to fulfil its statutory requirement. Overall, the issues raised by the editing of these statements are as follows: whether the exclusions were justifiable, their effect on the arms trial prosecution, and whether the Attorney General failed to meet an obligation to disclose them to the defence lawyers before the trials.

Arising from a television documentary on RTÉ in 2001, two official reports, one from then Minister for Justice John O'Donoghue TD and another from then Attorney General Michael McDowell SC, considered some but not all of these issues, and only in regard to Hefferon's statement. There was no consideration of the exclusions from Gibbons's various statements. The reports also focused on a somewhat skewed question: whether the editing of Hefferon's initial statement showed an attempt to suppress evidence and pervert the course of justice.[2] Each report concluded this was unlikely. However, it seems now that the real issues raised by the editing were less about any potential criminal conspiracy, and more about what the exclusions revealed about the Attorney General's approach to the case. Although the two official reports received almost no critical appraisal at the time, they merit and reward closer attention, as do the edits themselves.

The material edited from Hefferon's statement included all references from him stating how Gibbons knew of Kelly's activities, what, as minister, he was told about the arms importation plan, and what he knew about Kelly's mooted resignation from the army. Hefferon had told how, on three separate occasions over the autumn and winter of 1969–70, he informed the minister that Kelly was involved in an arms importation plan for the Northern Defence Committees. In the first of these, he stated: 'I told Mr Gibbons at this time about Captain Kelly's involvement with the Defence Committees in the North regarding the procuring of arms and ammunition for their defence.'[3] This was all deleted in the Book of Evidence. In the second reference, having stated that Kelly had gone to the Continent to negotiate for arms, Hefferon added: 'I believe I told the Minister for Defence, Mr Gibbons, about this problem.'[4] This too was deleted. In the third reference, having stated that he saw Gibbons in his office, he added: 'I told him that Captain Kelly intended travelling to the Continent again in connection with this arms deal.'[5] This was excluded.

Elsewhere in his statement, Hefferon, having told the minister how regimental duties could interfere with one of Kelly's trips to negotiate for arms, said: 'Gibbons was prepared to take the necessary steps to have him relieved of duty in order that he could travel to the Continent.'[6] This too was excluded. The following sentence in the Book of Evidence, referring to Gibbons, was altered from 'Around this particular time Captain Kelly told *him* [emphasis added] that he might have to go to Germany again in connection with the arms and ammunition for the North....' to 'Around this particular time Captain Kelly told *me* that he might have to go to Germany again in connection with the arms and ammunition for the North...'.[7] Also deleted for the Book of Evidence, towards the end of his statement, was Hefferon's observation: 'It is my opinion that Mr Gibbons knew that Captain Kelly was involved in assisting the Defence Committee in the North to procure arms.'[8] There were a number of other exclusions also, but those quoted are the main ones in question.

Writers on the subject have since proved strangely unable to agree whether the editing was proper or not.[9] This is partly because, as argued in 2001 by Desmond O'Malley TD[10] and to a lesser extent by former Attorney General McDowell,[11] some of the deleted material may have been excluded on the grounds of hearsay. But this, as McDowell partly conceded, cannot explain all the deletions. Their effect, beyond question, was to transform the meaning of the statement. Whereas Hefferon had originally linked Minister for Defence Gibbons to Captain Kelly's alleged crimes, this link is not apparent in the edited version.

There seems little doubt that, on various grounds, key sections of the excluded matter were relevant and material to the defence case, even allowing for the limited extent to which such a case was identifiable before the first arms trial. In the first instance, this is because the deletions challenged the accuracy of statements already taken from a principal prosecution witness, Jim Gibbons. The excluded references not only undermined Gibbons's credibility, they also suggested that the minister was complicit in the allegedly illegal importation. It was, in that sense, evidence against Gibbons, rather than evidence for Kelly, but it also supported a defence argument that even then, at the beginning of June, was evident to the prosecution – that Gibbons knew of and had approved the importation, and that it was authorized. By the end of May 1970, the Attorney General could see this emergent defence case from a variety of sources: the detailed statement taken on 1 May from one of the other accused, Albert Luykx; Captain Kelly's public statement on 8 May; and Kelly's statement on being arrested on 27 May. The full Hefferon statement supported the case that the importation was known of by the minister, and approved.[12]

After an inconclusive public discussion in 2001, the official responsible for making the exclusions from Hefferon's statement was finally identified almost two years later, in January 2003. Files from the Office of the Attorney General, initially mislaid then discovered and belatedly released to the National Archives, showed that the editing was done within the Office of the Attorney General by a senior official there, the already deceased Declan Quigley.[13] This was a highly significant discovery, because Condon had denied in 2001 that the full statement had ever reached his office, or that he knew anything about it. He had described Hefferon's statement as a mystery; he said its discovery was completely unexpected, and he had not got the remotest idea who might have altered it.[14]

Clearly, Condon's claim that the document did not reach his office was untrue, since two years later it was seen to have reached the attention of Condon's most senior criminal law expert, Declan Quigley. In regard to his claim to have known nothing of it, that too has to appear questionable, given that it was his senior official who physically made the exclusions. It seems not credible to imagine that a highly regarded public servant such as Quigley, with no skin in the game so far as Gibbons was concerned, would have kept his superior in the dark on such significant adjustments to the text, from a witness so central as Hefferon, and in such a high-profile case.

The taking of Hefferon's witness statement had been no routine affair. It was, first of all, suspiciously delayed until after charges had already been issued. When it was in the process of being sought, the files show that Condon was personally involved, being required to sign a form exempting Hefferon from the constraints of the Official Secrets Act, so that he could speak freely.[15] The contents of the statement must have been awaited with some trepidation, as indicated in the previous chapter, and Hefferon did not disappoint. In all these circumstances, it is impossible to imagine the editing was not done under direction. What is certain is that when the exclusions became public in 2001, Condon was not prepared to stand over them. His position then was that he never saw the full original statement, that it never reached his office, and that if it had reached him, he would have gone to Gibbons about it.[16]

One effect of the editing of Hefferon's statement for the Book of Evidence, and probably part of the object of the exercise, was to allow the army officer to be produced seamlessly as a principal witness for the prosecution in the Central Criminal Court in September 1970. The editing disguised some fundamental, unresolved differences between the two key State witnesses, Hefferon and Gibbons. One said he had kept the minister fully informed, while the minister claimed to have known almost nothing. These differences were obviously fully evident to Quigley as he made the edits – and therefore, it is assumed, to the Attorney General – and heralded serious difficulties ahead when the case came to court. Yet they brought no corrective action; the conflict in evidence between these prosecution witnesses was not addressed by either the Attorney General or his investigating gardaí. At the time of going to court, they simply did not know whether Gibbons could rebut the substantial charges against him, because he had never been asked.

Unsurprisingly, when these differences came into public view in the first arms trial in September 1970, the circumstances proved deeply embarrassing to the State. Hefferon in the witness box decided simply to ignore the exclusions, and gave evidence substantially in line with what he had said in his 30 May statement. Gibbons found himself ambushed in open court, and effectively in the dock. Since both he and Hefferon were at that stage prosecution witnesses, under rules of evidence they could not be cross-examined by their own side. McKenna appeared surprised and completely unprepared for the evidence he got from his own witness. Tom MacIntyre, in his sharply observed diary of the two trials, *Through the Bridewell Gate*, described how Hefferon's broadside left the prosecution case 'in tatters'. He described McKenna's condition by the time the witness had completed his evidence-in-chief as 'concussed, suffering from multiple fractures, and bleeding like a stuck pig'.[17] In fact, Hefferon's evidence, given in line with his full original statement, appears to have been a significant factor in the eventual acquittals of all four accused.

When, thirty years later in 2001, the State papers for 1970 were released, they brought a further twist to this story. After the discovery in the Department of Justice files of Hefferon's full unedited statement, Seamus McKenna indicated that he had never seen this document before. It appeared to have been kept from him and from other State counsel in 1970. McKenna revealed this initially, informally, to the author, then a journalist. When asked to make a formal public statement to this effect, McKenna, rather than simply avoid answering on grounds of strict legal protocol – a course open to him and, from the author's experience, normally taken by barristers in such a situation – sought and received special dispensation from the Professional Practices Committee of the Irish Bar Council to break protocol, and to speak publicly about a case in which he was involved. He declined to deal with a series of other questions about the exclusions, but participated in the following written question-and-answer exchange:

Question:

Can you state that neither you, nor, to the best of your knowledge, any of your fellow prosecuting counsel, ever saw the longer version of the statement of Hefferon in advance of the trial?

Answer:

a) I am as certain as one can be at a remove of some 30 years, that I did not see the longer version of the statement of Colonel Hefferon in advance of, or during the trial, and

b) in relation to my colleagues for the prosecution at the time (Eamonn Walshe SC and Aidan Browne BL, both now deceased), all I can say is, that nothing they said or did in relation to the trial, ever suggested to me they had seen the longer version of the statement.[18]

A review by the author of the proceedings of the two arms trials tends to support McKenna's contention that the full original Hefferon statement was not familiar to him, certainly before the first trial. Had it been excluded from the Book of Evidence on the grounds of hearsay, or of irrelevance, that argument would inevitably have been offered in court when Hefferon ignored the exclusions. On the contrary, however; in giving his full evidence, Hefferon met no resistance from McKenna. The State counsel's only reaction appeared to be surprise.

Nothing in the court record suggests advance knowledge by McKenna or his colleagues of the evidence Hefferon would give, or preparedness for the destructive effect it would have on the credibility of Gibbons and on the integrity of the prosecution case. As it transpired, the State case had been effectively booby-trapped from within, and was simply waiting, if not to fall asunder, then at least to inflict serious internal damage on itself. Had McKenna, as the leading counsel for the State, been acquainted with Hefferon's full statement, there seems little likelihood that he would have left himself open to the embarrassment, in open court, of having his two principal witnesses contradicting each other on central issues.

Serious questions are unavoidably raised here regarding the Attorney General's role. There is no doubt that Condon's senior official, Declan Quigley, was familiar with the evidence Hefferon had offered in his statement and intended giving in the witness box; he could anticipate what lay ahead once the case reached open court. It seems not realistic to assume that his boss was not equally aware. But what could have been in Condon's mind? And why was State counsel not informed on Hefferon's full intended evidence? Here, unfortunately, one is in the realm of speculation. The mystery is that the Attorney General's Office, familiar as it was with Hefferon's full statement and knowing what he clearly intended to say in the witness box, still allowed him to be presented as a State witness. In all of this, State counsel McKenna and his colleague Eamonn Walsh SC would be left almost hopelessly exposed – which is precisely what transpired in the first trial. The State gained a temporary reprieve from the resulting shambles when defence counsel Ernest Wood SC (for Albert Luykx) caused the first trial's sudden abandonment by accusing Judge Aindrias O'Caoimh of bias and the judge walked off the case.[19]

One way to explain how the State managed to get itself into such a legal morass in the arms trials is to speculate that the Attorney General (and Quigley) hoped that Hefferon would relent, and would not implicate his own minister, Gibbons, in the affair. Although now retired, he had been a high-ranking army officer and a loyal public servant, someone who might think twice about giving evidence that, at a time of turbulence and insecurity on the island, could potentially bring down the government and deepen a political crisis that was already shaking the State. Certainly Hefferon, judging by his conversation with solicitor Frank Fitzpatrick, described earlier in Chapter 12, appears to have seen his edited statement in the Book of Evidence as a silent invitation to change his story and leave out incriminating references to his minister. He clearly viewed it as an invitation to perjure himself, and this he was not prepared to do. There may have been a serious miscalculation as to how Hefferon would behave. It is worth noting that had he not retired from the army in early April 1970, Hefferon may not have had the freedom to contradict his minister.

As noted, the problems over the Book of Evidence in the arms trials were not confined to Hefferon's statement. The editing of Gibbons's various statements, in particular that of 8 June, raised similar issues. A part of this statement included in the Book of Evidence described how Kelly told his minister of his failed attempt to import arms by sea, and how, although the consignment was being met at Dublin docks, the weapons in fact never arrived. But excluded from the Book was the section that followed, the content of which proved a major issue when the case later came to court. Gibbons said he had asked Kelly if the failed attempt to bring the guns in was the end of the matter, stating 'I suppose that is the end of that?' But in reply, Kelly had stated: 'No, it will be all right.'[20] As argued above, the Attorney General and his colleagues were in a position to understand the significance of this reply from Kelly. It was information that Kelly, remarkably, was volunteering to his minister, and showed his intention to persist with the supposedly criminal gun-running project. Condon knew, from other statements he had received, that Kelly's role was central to the project, and yet here he was, assuring his minister that he would get the job done.

These important details about what Kelly – who was *one of the accused* – had told Gibbons, were unaccountably, and almost certainly improperly, excluded from the Book of Evidence. These exclusions from Gibbons's statement are at least as difficult to explain, or to justify, as the exclusions from that of Hefferon. Their effect was once again to leave the Book of Evidence unrepresentative of important testimony; when that testimony was revealed in court, it would prove of great significance for the defence case.

★

One direct effect of this editing of Gibbons's and Hefferon's statements was that their likely evidence about what Gibbons knew of the gun-running was hidden from the District Justice who conducted the preliminary examination on the case on 2 July 1970. Judge Kearney had in front of him a Book of Evidence that, unbeknownst to him, contained a misleading and arguably false picture of both Hefferon's and Gibbons's likely evidence. The function of the preliminary hearing was essentially to allow the judge to assess from the Book of Evidence, and from counsels' submissions, whether the evidence in the case was capable of permitting a jury properly to convict the accused. The hearing proved far from routine, because the case against Neil Blaney in it was dismissed for lack of evidence. This came after what one source described as 'an onslaught' from Liam Hamilton SC, representing Blaney.[21] The State solicitor attending the case was, it seems, totally unprepared to counter Hamilton's arguments. However, so far as the other accused were concerned, defence counsel had no idea that the Book of Evidence before them seriously misrepresented what Hefferon – and to a lesser degree, Gibbons – would actually say in the witness box.

When the discrepancy between Hefferon's original statement and the version in the Book of Evidence became apparent in 2001 – the argument regarding the editing of Gibbons's statement only being advanced here for the first time – noted criminal lawyer Patrick MacEntee SC in an RTÉ television documentary, saw it as a matter of great significance. After considering the documentation on the matter, and claims from Seamus McKenna SC that he had not been shown Hefferon's full, unedited statement, MacEntee was asked how the full statement might have altered the arms trials, had it been available to the prosecution in advance:

MacEntee: It's very difficult to be categorical about this, but it would have put a totally different complexion on the appropriateness of charging Captain Kelly. And similarly on the appropriateness of not charging Mr. Gibbons.

Q: Are you saying that it's likely on the basis of this statement that Mr. Gibbons would have been charged with conspiracy to import arms?

A: I think that is a likelihood. Yes. Can't be definite about it. Yes, I think it is likely.

Q: And Captain Kelly would not have been charged?

A: I think he probably would not have been. If he had been, just as the District Justice at preliminary examination refused informations against Mr. Blaney, I think there is a probability, certainly a possibility, that informations would have been refused in respect of Captain Kelly....

Q: And is it possible that there would have been no prosecution – at all, in fact?

A: Yes. That is a possibility. I can't put it further than saying, it is a possibility there would have been no trial at all.[22]

Michael McDowell's *Report of the Attorney General* in 2001 took issue with this opinion from MacEntee, but his reasons for so doing may not seem fully convincing. McDowell said he was 'not satisfied that there would have been no basis of a return for trial had the original statement been reproduced in its entirety in the Book of Evidence'. His reasoning was that when Colonel Hefferon went on to testify in the Central Criminal Court in line with his original statement, it did not cause Judge Henchy to direct the jury to acquit. 'This', said McDowell, 'would suggest that the original statement (even if more embarrassing politically) would not have been fatal to the State case had it been included in the

Book of Evidence.'[23] Given Judge Henchy's attitude, McDowell saw no reason to assume the District Justice would have felt differently.

Yet despite McDowell's undoubted legal expertise, it seems possible that he misunderstood MacEntee's argument. The point was not that there was no case for Kelly to answer, but that Hefferon's statement 'put a totally different complexion on the appropriateness of charging Captain Kelly, and similarly on the appropriateness of *not* charging Mr Gibbons'.[24] If there was an identifiable prior case against his boss, the Minister for Defence, how appropriate was it to charge the junior officer? Besides, two very different stages of the prosecution were involved here. When Henchy considered the matter, the prosecution had reached trial stage; Kelly had been charged, Gibbons was just a prosecution witness, and it appears unarguable that in the trial at that point, Kelly had a case to answer. MacEntee's question was whether, at an earlier stage, District Judge Kearney would have considered it appropriate to charge *only* Kelly, when evidence (that should have been before the court, but was not) demonstrated that Kelly's minister knew of and had seemingly approved his activities. Had the full statement been available to lawyers and to the District Court, MacEntee said, it was 'likely' that Gibbons would have been charged, and 'probable' that Kelly would not have been. In any event, he felt the arms trial would have been 'a totally different affair'. Despite McDowell's apparent rejoinder, MacEntee's opinion has yet to receive any effective rebuttal.

The proposition arising from Hefferon's statement, that Gibbons might reasonably be regarded as complicit in the gun-running operation, was discussed in 2001 in a sister report to that of McDowell, from Minister for Justice John O'Donoghue TD (Fianna Fáil). While he agreed with McDowell that it was unlikely there had been an attempt to suppress evidence in the editing of Hefferon's statement, he also made a remarkable observation that appeared closely aligned with the opinion given by Patrick MacEntee. O'Donoghue stated:

If it were established, as a reasonable possibility, that the Minister for Defence was in effect also a conspirator, then it is difficult to imagine that this would not have been seen as a sensational development, or that it would have had no bearing at all on the trial. While it cannot be said that it would, in itself, have had the effect of undermining the specific charges against the accused, it seems reasonable to recognise that the impact of such a development in itself could have led to that result.[25]

This observation from the Minister for Justice attracted little attention at the time, perhaps because of O'Donoghue's convoluted prose; also greater attention was being paid to McDowell's report, released simultaneously. Yet O'Donoghue was making a point not dissimilar to that of MacEntee: that if there appeared to be a reasonable possibility that Gibbons was involved, it could – he did not feel one could say it *would* – have had the effect of undercutting the charges against a junior army officer under his command. O'Donoghue's observation effectively described why the State case at the arms trials ultimately failed to convince the jury. What he was unable to see was the extent of the evidence that had been available to the Attorney General from at least the end of May 1970; this indicated that Gibbons knew of, and, so far as could be judged, had assented to the attempted gun-running. Condon had such information, but manifestly had no intention of acting on it.

There is nothing to suggest that the excluded sections from either Gibbons's or Hefferon's statements were disclosed to the defence lawyers in June 1970, or at any time prior to the trials. Legally, no issue would arise from this if the exclusions were not material, i.e., if they were not relevant or significant to the case as it was developing at that stage. However, some of the exclusions appear highly material, and highly relevant. Hefferon's original statement arguably not only undermined Gibbons's credibility as a witness, but also implied that he was complicit in the allegedly illegal importation. In the same way, the statement supported the core defence argument, that Gibbons knew of and approved the importation. It seems evident therefore, that some of the deletions – not necessarily all of them – should have been disclosed. The same applies to the exclusions from Gibbons's statement; these were also important, and relevant to the defence case.

Another critical legal question is whether in the early 1970s there was an obligation on the prosecution to inform the defence of these exclusions, whether informally or otherwise. The relevant authority for this is J. H. Archbold: *Criminal Pleading – Evidence and Practice*, whose regularly updated volumes have been for almost two centuries the authoritative reference work for practitioners in criminal law in Britain and Ireland and other common law jurisdictions. The 38th edition of Archbold, published in 1973, appears to specify just such a duty.[26] The obligation suggested was not that the prosecution should give the defence the unedited statements, but that they should inform the defence that material potentially helpful to them was being excluded. There also appears to be case law to the same effect, dating as far back as 1946.[27] A further Irish authority for the existence of an obligation in 1970 to make helpful material available to the defence is R. L. Sandes's *Criminal Law and Procedure in Eire* (1951), which stated succinctly that the law required the prosecutor 'to call all relevant witnesses at the trial, and should disclose fully all relevant evidence'.[28] Sandes, whose book was described in its foreword by then Chief Justice Conor Maguire as 'an accurate and reliable guide to the criminal law', did not specify if the obligation extended to disclosure in advance of the trial, but that appears to be the implication of the word 'fully' above.

Dermot Walsh, in his authoritative Irish legal handbook *Criminal Procedure* (2002), also addressed the prosecution's duty to disclose material in its possession which could be helpful to the defence. Dealing with exclusions from the Book of Evidence which undermined some aspect of the prosecution case, Walsh suggested that Irish courts saw the obligation to disclose as long-standing, being, as he stated, 'firmly rooted in the individual's constitutional right to fair procedures in a criminal trial'. Relevant material requiring disclosure, he said, was anything that 'tends to undermine the prosecution case, or assists the defence case'.[29] This treatment by Walsh seems to imply that the right of the defence to such disclosure, and the parallel duty of the State to provide it, was no less present in 1970 than in 2002, and included material such as that excluded from Hefferon's statement.

The issue of the obligation on the State in such a situation was considered by McDowell in his 2001 *Report of the Attorney General*. However, his findings on the relevant law in 1970 were inconclusive and appear at best ambiguous. In a section of his report entitled 'Was the editing done in accordance with any guidelines (written or otherwise) then existing?', McDowell stated: 'It does not appear that any guidelines then existed, which have survived, in relation to the preparation of Books of Evidence.'[30] But this observation appeared not to take into account the Archbold reference in the 1973 edition at par. 448, cited above. This dealt with the editing of witness statements – the seemingly applicable circumstances. McDowell only referenced a different section of Archbold, one dealing with disclosure of original statements, which was dealt with separately at par. 443. In the end, his report arrived at no clear conclusion, other than to state that 'the prosecutor, as is still the case, had a duty to be a fair and dispassionate presenter of the evidence, and part of his duty was to ensure that anything relevant that was not led in evidence be brought to the attention of the defence'.[31]

Despite such statements, McDowell did not conclude in his 2001 report that the Attorney General had failed to meet an obligation to disclose relevant material to the defence. In this, he may have been influenced by the fact that the arms trial juries eventually heard the evidence in question from Hefferon – and indeed from Gibbons in regard to his statements – without manifest hindrance. This of course did not address the issue of a duty to disclose *in advance of* the trials – in this specific case, three months in advance. McDowell also said that in Ireland at a later date, in the 1980s, there was 'a general and proper concern' among prosecuting solicitors and barristers 'that the process of editing not conceal from the defence material that might have been helpful or relevant to the defence', whereas the position in 1970, he felt, had been 'much less clear'. Seemingly unable to specify the precise duty or obligation on the State present in 1970, he acknowledged that the practice later – in the mid-1970s – in Irish courts was to notify the defence. He stated without comment that 'the approach adopted by the DPP, who of course took over most prosecutions from the Attorney General in 1975, was to suggest that relevant deleted material be made informally available to the defence'.[32]

Although some of these matters are essentially for lawyers to determine, they remain deeply relevant to any historical review of the conduct of the arms trial prosecution in the period May to September 1970. Since the deletions appear not to have been disclosed, in any form, to the defence in advance of the 1970 arms trials, it seems arguable that the prosecution failed to meet its duty to make such a disclosure. The undoubted effect was that defence counsel were not aware, in advance of the trial, that Hefferon would support Captain Kelly and potentially incriminate the Minister for Defence. He was listed as a prosecution witness, and, accordingly, the defence lawyers had no access to him. Also hidden was the extent to which Gibbons had incriminated himself through what he had revealed on 8 June; Gibbons, unaware of how he was damaging his own credibility by repeating the claims, appeared happy in the witness box to repeat and even amplify what he had said, as did Hefferon.

Throughout the period from June to mid-September the defence side could not marshal the full arguments at their disposal because they were in the dark over significant evidence that the State knew was likely to be given by these two key witnesses. The potential gravity of such conduct is suggested in a later edition of Archbold's *Criminal Pleading* (1995), the 47th edition, where it is stated that a failure to disclose material that should have been disclosed to the defence is, in English law, 'likely to constitute a material irregularity'.[33] Although it refers to a British statute at a later date than 1970, this raises at least the suggestion that there was a material irregularity in the conduct of the State in the arms trials, with all the potential consequences that would follow. These actual or potential infirmities in the conduct of the prosecution became moot once the jury decided to acquit all the accused.

While there is no evidence of direct external political manip- ulation of the prosecution in 1970, the detail of its development, as outlined particularly in the previous chapter, provides ample evidence that political calculations influenced the Attorney General at nearly every turn. The key was the handling of evidence concerning Gibbons – and by the same token, of Hefferon. At no point in the period under review is there evidence that the Attorney General treated Gibbons as even a possible suspect. Conspicuous confirmation of this approach is evident in the editing of Hefferon's and Gibbons's witness statements.

From the end of May, if not much earlier, the accumulated testimony available to the Attorney General pointed to some level of complicity by Gibbons in the gun-running. In the end, the pivotal question that was posed by Garret FitzGerald to the Taoiseach in the Dáil on 14 May – asking whether Gibbons was under investigation or not – is answered resoundingly in the files. He was not, at least not as a possible suspect. Equally, the evidence suggests that the opinion offered by Judge Henchy at the second arms trial – that the Attorney General was justified in bringing criminal charges when he did – was based on faulty information, and, seen in hindsight, comes with diminished authority.

It is now evident that the decision to prefer charges before any statement was taken from Hefferon, and before the Garda investigation had concluded, was highly problematic. It appears to confirm the Attorney General's lack of interest in the most basic of issues: was Captain Kelly's involvement in gun-running, with, or without, the authority of his military superiors? Common sense alone dictated that Captain Kelly's commanding officer was likely to be a central witness in any case involving Kelly; had the investigation been pursued on more normal lines, he would surely have been one of the first to be questioned, instead of one of the last. The decision to issue charges before the statement was eventually taken suggests that the Attorney General's neglect over Hefferon was not *bona fide*. Looking further at the effects of the precipitate decision to bring charges on 27 May, this action has the appearance of a tactical coup by the Attorney General against his own, apparently sceptical, Garda investigators. Later, when important exclusions were made from Hefferon's statement by a senior official in the Attorney General's Office, Declan Quigley, it seems not credible to imagine they were implemented without Colm Condon's full knowledge and authority. His 2001 denial of any role in this is not convincing.

While the controversy that occurred in 2001 was largely over the editing of Hefferon's statement, it appears that two of the other documents considered here – Fleming's 2 June investigation report, and the witness statement of Gibbons on 8 June disclosing his conversation with Captain Kelly – are even more revealing about the arms trial prosecution than the saga over Hefferon's statement. If one excludes, for sake of argument, any possible role for the Attorney General in influencing Fleming's approach, it appears little short of amazing that the Chief Superintendent, in assessing his own investigation, would act as though Hefferon had never implicated Gibbons in the gun-running. It is more likely that in his report, and in the way Gibbons's final statement of 8 June was handled, one should discern the firm hand of the Attorney General in play, setting down the course the prosecution was to take.

In the end, after Fleming's final investigation report had simply ignored the clash of evidence between Hefferon and Gibbons, the prosecution proceeded to court with blindfolds on. They appear to have had no idea whether the minister would be able successfully to rebut Hefferon's charges against him. It became evident in court later that he could not. Gibbons too seems to have been kept in the dark.[34]

On this analysis, the approach adopted by the Attorney General was a courtroom accident waiting to happen. He may well have been relying on other aspects of the prosecution case, as outlined in Chapter 16, to sustain a conviction, but so far as the vulnerability of Gibbons is concerned, Condon can only have assumed that Hefferon would somehow not give the evidence that he had heralded in his statement of 30 May 1970. Even to the author of such a policy, this must have seemed a dangerous gamble, one capable of backfiring spectacularly – as indeed in the end it did.[35]

Clearly, much about this process leading up to the trials remains shrouded. How it was that Hefferon could ever have been presented as a prosecution witness, and his full statement withheld not just from the defence but from the State's own lawyers in court, seems as yet only partially revealed.[36] There may be further implications arising from Fleming's report on his investigation which have not been developed here. It seems arguable, for example, that the nature of his report, circulated directly to the Office of the Chief State Solicitor, indicates that officials in that office were also kept in the dark about the original Hefferon statement. This could be consistent with a failure to brief prosecution counsel McKenna, Walsh and Browne about Hefferon's full statement. Such briefings are a function of the Chief State Solicitor's Office, whose chief source of information is typically the Garda file on the case, and within that the report of the officer leading the investigation. It would seem inconceivable that the Chief State Solicitor, Donough O'Donovan, if he was aware of Hefferon's intended evidence as indicated in his statement on 30 May 1970, would have withheld such key briefing material from prosecution counsel. The possibility, greatly enhanced by the Fleming report, may be that the Chief State Solicitor's Office was also kept in the dark over Hefferon's likely evidence, which would increase even further the importance of the issues here.

16

Arms Trial Issues

Despite any lurking anxieties within the prosecution over the conflicting evidence to be anticipated from their witnesses Gibbons and Hefferon, the State did approach the arms trial proceedings with what appeared to be a strong legal hand. This may seem surprising in the light of uncertainty over how Gibbons's evidence would stand up to cross-examination, and unresolved fears about Hefferon's intentions, but yet the Attorney General had grounds for believing his case was legally formidable. When he issued charges it was evident, as a simple matter of fact, that no import licence had been issued to any of the accused under the 1925 Firearms Act. That in general was likely to render the attempted importation *prima facie* illegal. Given that the arms consignment at the centre of the case appeared to be clearly intended for the use of Northern republicans, and not for the Defence Forces or the Garda Síochána, no other mechanism existed that could legalize Captain James Kelly's plans.

Even if the defence succeeded in proving that Gibbons, as Minister for Defence, had agreed to the importation and unofficially sanctioned it – as Kelly appeared to be claiming – a guilty finding could still be anticipated, because the arms appeared to be clearly not for the use of the Defence Forces. So far as Haughey was concerned, his defence was weakened by the fact that he had suggested to Peter Berry that the arms could go directly to Northern Ireland, in which case there was no question of their use by the Defence Forces. That was broadly how the case must have appeared to the Attorney General, and his confidence in its strength was shown by the quick decision to opt for a retrial after the unexpected collapse of the first trial under Judge Aindrias O'Caoimh.

As Attorney General, Condon had worked hard to get the case to that point. He had protected Gibbons in the Garda investigation and excluded him from all suspicion of involvement in the gun-running. He had also adopted the effective, if somewhat crude, tactic of bringing charges before the increasingly troublesome Garda leading the investigation, Chief Superintendent Fleming, could take statements from either Hefferon or from Haughey, or otherwise finalize his investigation. Condon and his assistant Quigley seemed to have managed any tensions between the gardaí and his Office, and the Attorney General had taken the actions he deemed necessary to ensure that a viable prosecution took place. That prosecution was also, happily, of a kind that Lynch's political circumstances appeared to demand, i.e., one that did not place Gibbons in the dock.

Yet the first trial had only confirmed how, from the State's perspective, Gibbons remained the essential problem. He had already earlier in the summer shown himself to be a headstrong witness, particularly by his startling and unexpected admissions on 8 June, and in the collapsed trial the Attorney General had seen how lawyers for the defence had used Hefferon's evidence in the witness box, given in line with his original statement, to challenge and cast doubt over the former Minister for Defence's truthfulness. Gibbons's inability to provide a credible explanation for his actions remained a combustible issue as the second trial got under way; it continued to haunt the prosecution case, ultimately proving its undoing.

This chapter will attempt to assess the balance of the evidence at the end of the second arms trial, and how the State case came unstuck. Although the difficulties between Gibbons and Hefferon were serious, and, at least by the time of the second trial, were clearly evident to the prosecution barristers, they were not necessarily fatal. Their clash of evidence concerned the minister's alleged foreknowledge and possible authorization of the importation, and while this was in 1970 a dominating *political* question, in law it was only part of the issue. As already stated, even if the importation was deemed to have been authorized by the Minister for Defence, unless it could be established that the arms were 'for the use of the Defence Forces', as the Firearms Act specified, then an illegal act would have been committed. The verdict would be 'guilty'. This major hurdle for the defence was stressed by Judge Henchy several times in the course of the trial.

The manner in which the jury addressed, and finally resolved, the particular issue requiring the imported arms to be 'for the use of the Defence Forces' is a fascinating story; it will be considered here employing a recently uncovered record of an important legal argument at the arms trial on 20 October 1970. A tape-recording of this discussion, plus several other sessions from the second trial, forms part of the Maguire Papers, held privately by Peter Maguire SC, counsel to Charles Haughey in 1970.[1] The tape's discovery is important due to the absence of the official transcript of the arms trials, which has gone missing; with newspapers of the day precluded from reporting legal arguments held in the absence of the jury, the loss of the official transcript has meant the loss of any written record of legal discussion at the trials. The existence of a tape-recording means an exception to the general loss, and the importance of the particular discussion is that it contains pivotal exchanges between judge and legal counsel over the meaning of the phrase 'for the use of the Defence Forces'. No reportage of this legal argument featured in the newspapers; nor was it mentioned in MacIntyre's diary of the trials, *Through the Bridewell Gate*. The outcome of the discussion, other documentation shows, would prove crucial in the eventual jury decision to acquit the four accused.

Apart from this recording, which throws new light on the legal issues the jury were charged to consider, further additional, relevant and unique new material has come to hand which explains even more directly how the jury may have reached their 'not guilty' verdict. This material consists of transcripts of extensive interviews with two jurors, sanctioned by RTÉ in 2001 and conducted in the aftermath of the publication of the State papers for 1970. These unique records emerged in response to comments by Garret FitzGerald TD (Fine Gael), a former Taoiseach, that the arms trial jury had been intimidated, and had brought in a perverse verdict. At the time, in December 2001, jurors expressed a wish to repudiate FitzGerald's charge of intimidation, and RTÉ Television at that time broadcast short quotes from two of them. Their identity was not disclosed. Both jurors interviewed were anxious to deny any intimidation, and to explain how the verdict was based on the evidence before them.[2] The full transcripts of the interviews, otherwise unpublished to date, provide fresh insights into the arms trial outcome, and will be considered below.[3]

The fact that the floor of the Central Criminal Court was a key battleground in the Arms Crisis had important consequences. Politically important material which would have been central to any non-legal, comprehensive investigation of the underlying events was excluded from the trials under rules of evidence. It meant that, for example, no evidence was heard either from, or directly relating to, the Taoiseach Jack Lynch, or indeed his sacked Minister for Agriculture, Neil Blaney. The Taoiseach was not a party to the case, and the failure of defence counsel to call Blaney as a witness for their side, while remarkable in one sense, reflected the defence lawyers' judgement on their clients' best interests. The pursuit of ultimate truth is no part of the agenda in adversarial criminal proceedings.[4] Courtroom decisions in the arms trials on whether or not to reveal facts were inevitably subject to both legal propriety and the arbitrary tactical considerations of defence or prosecution teams. These significant limitations on what was disclosed were offset by the reality of a formal Garda investigation, with key witnesses making statements, giving sworn evidence and being cross-examined under oath.

Without the fact of criminal proceedings, it is likely that Colonel Hefferon's first-hand evidence on several matters, such as the issuing of the 6 February directive, the training of Northerners at Fort Dunree at the end of September 1969, and the urgent transporting of army rifles and ammunition to Dundalk on 2 April 1970, would have been kept from public view under the Official Secrets Act 1963. This prohibits the disclosure of official material touching on the security of the State.[5] Without the trials, much other evidence would have been kept under wraps until the release of the State papers in 2001.

As it was, over four weeks in September and October 1970 the trials offered a dramatic, gladiatorial perspective on the Arms Crisis, catching the imagination of both contemporaries and historians, even if it came from a legal perspective that, of its nature, was not necessarily conducive to revealing the rights and wrongs on either side. In the end, politics came back to the fore; the State went on effectively to ignore the trial verdict, and treated the defendants almost as if they had been deemed guilty. And in the same way that doubts have persisted over whether the criminal trials should ever have happened, so too there have been doubts over the 'not guilty' verdicts. In 2001 Garret FitzGerald, Cosgrave's successor as leader of Fine Gael and later Taoiseach in two coalition governments during the 1980s, told writer Justin O'Brien that there had been a miscarriage of justice:

> It was a totally perverse verdict. They [the jury] were intimidated. The atmosphere in the court was such that the jury were afraid to convict and unwilling to convict, and they weren't going to convict. They totally disregarded the evidence.[6]

FitzGerald's trenchant opinion, delivered more than thirty years after the fact, implied that the defendants were guilty, not innocent. Its publication led to an action for libel which resulted in the payment of compensation to Captain James Kelly.[7] Nonetheless, the fact that this remark came from such

a normally diplomatic source was indicative of the highly
contentious nature of the verdict. Jack Lynch, in New York
for a meeting of the UN General Assembly when the verdict
was given, insisted that, regardless of the acquittals, there *had*
been an attempt to import arms illegally.[8] A similar sporadic
sense of disagreement with the outcome of the arms trials has
persisted ever since. Desmond O'Malley insisted in 2014 that he
had been shocked by the 1970 verdict, and stated: 'There was a
conspiracy to import arms for use by an illegal organization in
Northern Ireland.'[9]

Although strong opinions abound about the arms trials, in the
literature on the period relatively little attention has been given to
the specific legal issues that governed them in 1970. The charges
were based on the terms of Section 17 of the 1925 Firearms Act.
Because the importation of arms had been forestalled and the
consignment had never left Vienna, the Attorney General was
obliged to construct charges in terms of a *conspiracy* to import
illegally, rather than actual gun-running. The charges stemmed
from Section 17 of the Act, sub-section 1, which stated that no
person could import arms or ammunition into the State without
a licence from the Minister for Defence. Since no evidence
existed of the Minister issuing such a licence, the attempted
importation, *prima facie*, appeared illegal. However, sub-
section 8 of Section 17 of the Act was also relevant: it stated that
the rest of Section 17 did not apply if the arms were 'imported
under the authority of the Minister for Defence, for the use of
the Defence Forces'.[10] In other words, no licence was required
so long as the Minister could be shown to have authorized the
importation.[11] The sub-section provided no precise guidance on
how, without a licence, this authorization could be conveyed, but
it was clear that it covered only arms that were 'for the use of the
Defence Forces'.

Captain Kelly's counsel, Tom Finlay, made it clear early on, in
response to a question from Judge Aindrias O'Caoimh in the first
(aborted) trial, that he would be relying on this section:

Judge O'Caoimh: I take it that is the nature of the defence that the whole of this consignment is intended to get into the hands of the Irish army, for use by the Irish army?

Finlay: That is undoubtedly the nature of the defence, that the whole of this consignment of arms with which my client was concerned was to be brought into the control and possession of the defence forces and held there against the contingency of subsequent distribution.[12]

From the start, therefore, the defence accepted the burden of proving not just that the importation had been authorized by the Minister for Defence, Gibbons, but also that the arms, which to all intents and purposes appeared to be destined for the use of Northern nationalists, could be seen under the terms of the Act to be 'for the use of the Defence Forces'. It seemed a high bar.

Judge Henchy made clear to the jury that even the authority of the minister could not make legal something that was banned under the Act; he said that even if certain government ministers had given Captain Kelly and John Kelly reason to believe that what they were doing was acceptable, he had to direct the jury that that was not the law. 'Mere authority to bring in arms, from the minister or any minister, including the Taoiseach, did not legalize the importation.'[13] While this meant that the minister had participated in a crime if he approved an importation that was not 'for the use of the Defence Forces', that situation was outside the scope of the proceedings because the Attorney General had not charged Gibbons, and he was not on trial. On the contrary, he was a principal prosecution witness and one who had never been regarded as a suspect.

The legal argument in the Central Criminal Court on 20 October 1970 occurred following a somewhat startling announcement by Judge Henchy that he was contemplating making a ruling that the arms were *not*, and could not have been, for the use of the Defence Forces. Such a ruling would have removed from the jury any choice in the matter; it would have undercut the defence arguments and left its strategy in shreds.[14] Judge Henchy by that time was fully aware of the defence case, and clearly had not been impressed by it. The resumed trial was already eleven days old and the defence cards were fully on the table, their counsel having already fully ventilated the argument that the arms were intended to be held under Captain Kelly's sole control, pending a government decision to release them to Northern nationalists should circumstances deteriorate north of the border. Colonel Hefferon had given evidence that he had told the Minister for Defence the precise non-military location in Co. Cavan where the arms were to be stored.[15] Hefferon had also testified that Captain Kelly had proposed to him that the arms could be stored in Cathal Brúgha Barracks in Dublin, but that he (Hefferon) had overruled Kelly and said it was better that the arms, given the exceptional nature of the operation, should be held under his personal control, outside of a military barracks.

Despite this presentation of the defence case, Judge Henchy on 20 October said he doubted whether a valid argument had been submitted:

> As at present advised, it does not seem to me, on any version of the evidence, that such agreement as has been shown in evidence to have been given by the Minister, amounted or could amount to an agreement or authority to import arms for the use of the armed forces.[16]

This statement from the judge appeared to shock the defence lawyers. Tom Finlay, counsel for Captain Kelly, rose immediately to protest. Finlay said that, 'with great respect', he did not understand on what basis the judge had said what he had. His side was offering, Finlay said, a complete defence; if the evidence showed that the minister had agreed to the importation of arms which were then going to be held under the control of the army, then it was irrelevant what their ultimate use by the Defence Forces might be:

> Finlay: The jury must consider whether the parties entering into the agreement believed that the Minister was authorizing this importation—
>
> Judge Henchy:— for the use of the Defence Forces?
>
> Finlay:— for the use of the Defence Forces.[17]

Finlay went on to suggest that the judge was being inconsistent in suggesting the minister was not giving authorization:

> Finlay: I don't know whether your Lordship suggests that the bringing in of arms here, to be held under the control of the Defence Forces, to be held by them as surplus arms, and if and when a decision was so made, to be distributed, in contingencies, to persons outside the Defence Forces, is not a use for the Defence Forces, my Lord? But in my submission if that were the point your Lordship was making… it would be at violent variance with the ordinary meaning of the word 'use'…. To say that is something that is not for the use of the Defence Forces, would be, in my submission, straining words entirely.[18]

Finlay's argument here, and throughout the case, was that control of the arms by Captain Kelly, an army intelligence officer, amounted to control by the Defence Forces. The judge responded by saying that the problem was with the phrase 'for the use of the Defence Forces'. Finlay said it was a matter for the jury, properly instructed, to decide what that phrase meant:

> Finlay: If your Lordship were to make a ruling along the lines which your Lordship indicated, in my submission your Lordship

would be falling into error in two ways: firstly, putting an artificial and unprovided restricted meaning on the word 'use' in the Section, and secondly, your Lordship would be usurping the function of the jury.[19]

The judge said he would not at that moment make a ruling; what he had said was that 'as at present advised, my view of the situation was as I stated'. Having invited other counsel to make submissions on the matter, he was told by Niall McCarthy SC (for Haughey) that he also supported Finlay's observations. The arms were being imported to be stored; much material was acquired that was never put to military use, but that didn't mean it was not bought for use by the Defence Forces. It was for the government and the Minister for Defence to determine for what purposes the Defence Forces would be employed, and if they were keeping arms for a given contingency, then that was importation 'for the use of'.

Counsel for the State Eamonn Walsh then stepped in, offering the view that the problem indicated by the judge was not about interpretation, but about whether the evidence offered to date warranted a defence along certain lines. He said there had to be an element of control over the arms:

Arms can't be brought in for the use of the Defence Forces unless they are under the control of the Defence Forces. They have to become Army arms. And not even the Minister can authorise the importation of arms which are not for the use of the Defence Forces. The problem as I apprehend it is a problem of evidence, because the evidence here is to the effect that if it had gone through, a certain consignment of ammunition would have arrived in Dublin docks on a certain date; it would have passed into the custody of a defendant who was, it so happened, a member of the Defence Forces, and a defendant who was not, as it happened, a member of the Defence Forces, and as far as I apprehend it, there will be, so far as the evidence is concerned, grave difficulty for the defendants to point to evidence to support the defence that we are dealing with – an importation of arms that was for the use of the Defence Forces, and which had the sanction of the Minister for Defence.[20]

The State was arguing that control of the arms by Captain Kelly was not the same thing as control by the Defence Forces. It was a substantial part of its case. But the judge concluded the discussion without making a ruling on this matter, nor did he make one at any point thereafter. Finlay and McCarthy had won their point. The judge's hand was stayed, despite his obvious continuing reservations about the arguments of the defence, as shown below, and also despite doubts apparently held among the defence lawyers themselves that this critical aspect of their case could be won.[21]

The stakes in the legal argument on 20 October 1970 had been very high. The judge appeared generally sceptical about the defence case, and the ruling he contemplated making would have been little short of catastrophic for the accused. The exchanges causing him to draw back from such a course would seem to represent a pivotal moment in the second arms trial, and as such are of considerable historical significance.[22] He allowed the matter to go to the jury three days later, as defence counsel requested, without the threatened direction that the arms being imported could not be regarded as being for the use of the Defence Forces.

This important mini-contest within the arms trial still left the defence with the difficulty of persuading the jury that the arms were, or could be described as being, for the army's use, rather than simply for the use of Northern nationalists. It was left as one of two key issues the jury would have to decide. The other one was whether or not the Minister for Defence had authorized the importation, for whatever usage. It seems evident that, for all the conspicuous damage done to the State case by the evidence of Colonel Hefferon and by the weakness of Gibbons's performance as a witness, the prosecution case remained quite powerful at the end of the evidence. This was especially true on the critical question which had so exercised the judge, i.e., for whose use were the arms intended? Eamonn Walsh SC, for the State, was not overstating the case when he told the judge on 20 October that he thought the defence would have 'grave difficulty' in showing that the arms were for the use of the Defence Forces. Henchy had been dissuaded from giving the jury a direction on this, but his doubts over this critical part of the defence case were fully evident in his charge to the jury.

In his closing address for the prosecution, Walsh identified a further, seemingly fundamental, difficulty with the defence argument that the arms were for the use of the Defence Forces. He said the arms were owned by the Northern Defence Committees, not by the Defence Forces. The army had not paid for them; the Defence Committees had. Captain Kelly himself had told the Court that when money was withdrawn by him from the Munster and Leinster Bank, Baggot Street in Dublin to buy the arms, those accounts were controlled by the trustees of the Northern Relief Fund, and had nothing to do with the Defence Forces as such.[23] (Kelly also insisted at the Committee of Public Accounts that, in the end, it was not even the money voted by the Dáil which had bought the arms, but funds that belonged separately to the Northern Defence Committees which had been 'switched' into other accounts to make up the amount expended from the Baggot Street accounts.[24]) Walsh told the jury that it was not credible that, if ownership was claimed in this way, the owners would hand the guns over to the army and then await a government decision on what would be done with them.

Walsh suggested that a key element had been missing from the unsworn address made to the court by John Kelly, one of the four accused; it was something that Walsh said was 'crucial for an acquittal'. This was any statement that John Kelly had acquiesced in the arms coming under the control of the Defence Forces.[25] The Northern Defence Committees wanted guns, and John Kelly had never stated that these would be handed over to the Defence Forces, with an attendant risk, as Walsh put it, that they 'perhaps might never be released'. On this point, Captain Kelly told the second arms trial of the moment when he informed the Defence Committees that, because the imported arms were coming in under the auspices of the Defence Forces, they could not be released until the government gave authority. His counsel James Darcy SC (with Tom Finlay SC) asked him whether the Northerners had agreed to this. Kelly's not entirely convincing answer was: 'They accepted that.'[26]

Walsh noted, in support of his case, that one item being imported which did actually arrive in Dublin, the bullet-proof vests, had been taken away after they arrived on the *City of Dublin* vessel on 19 March 1970, and were not under the control of the army.[27] This point was underlined by Judge Henchy in his charge to the jury: he said that there was no suggestion that the bullet-proof vests had gone under the control of the armed forces. He said Captain Kelly kept them under his control up until the time of his first arrest, on 1 May, but they had since passed from his control. The judge did not state directly that the vests, when they were in Kelly's possession, could not be regarded as being under Defence Forces control, but the implication was that they could not. Henchy appeared to be further implying that had the arms and ammunition arrived in the country, they too would most likely have ended up outside the army's control. He left it to the jury's discretion to determine when, or indeed if, Defence Forces 'control' was in place, but his own scepticism was quite evident.[28]

Henchy also set out, in a way that appeared entirely hostile to the defence case, his view of the purpose behind sub-section 8 of Section 17 of the Firearms Act. His scepticism was implicit rather than explicit, as can be seen from the newspaper account of his words:

> Mr. Justice Henchy said that the purpose of Section 17 of the Firearms Act was to ensure that no firearms or ammunition would come into this State without control. Firearms and

ammunition, like drugs, were dangerous. Each could be a killer, and it was legislative policy that neither dangerous drugs nor arms and ammunition would come into the State without proper checks and proper control. Otherwise, they were likely to cause tragedy. The exception to the section was that the licence was not necessary if the Minister gave an authority that the firearms were being brought in for the use of the Army. The reason for that was that before firearms were put into any armoury they were checked for quality and recorded, and thereafter were kept in safe keeping.[29]

This formulation shows the judge's doubts about the defence argument that the arms were for the use of the Defence Forces. If they were so intended, Henchy implied, they would have been checked into army barracks under the quality and safety controls of the Quartermaster General. It was a very pointed view, for which Judge Henchy gave no reference or authority; but the implication was that arms not checked into official custody – in other words, arms handled as Captain Kelly intended – could not be for the use of the army.[30] At another point in his charge, he made his reservations more explicit when he stated that 'apart from minor exceptions', arms that were for the use of the army were checked into army stores.

While much of this might appear prejudicial to the defence case, crucially Henchy did not tell the jury that it was obliged to accept such views from him. He left jurors free to choose the defence view, in which it was claimed that the arms were still for the army's use, even if they had not been checked into army stores. But the judge appeared to be struggling in his charge to the jury to summarize the defence arguments dispassionately, and without disparaging them. It might be observed that his approach was generally predicated on normal procedures, operating in normal times, whereas the defence were arguing that *ab*normal circumstances existed in Northern Ireland, and, as such, required abnormal responses from the Defence Forces. It was not, in the defence's view, an occasion for regular procedures. It had been with that in mind that Colonel Hefferon agreed with Captain Kelly that in order to avoid a situation where the arms might eventually be traceable to the Irish army, due to serial numbers and official records, it was better that they be sourced and retained outside normal acquisition procedures, i.e., outside Cathal Brúgha Barracks in Dublin.

Kelly's counsel, Tom Finlay SC, made the argument that the army had been directed to prepare for various contingencies, including distributing arms to civilians in Northern Ireland. He claimed: 'It would be a poor army that would have to say to the government that they had not got suitable arms.' Finlay pointed out that Captain Kelly had suggested to his superior officer that the arms might be stored in Cathal Brúgha Barracks, which would have meant the full application of Defence Forces bureaucracy and certification, but Hefferon had decided against that level of control.[31] Henchy told the jury that Captain Kelly's evidence was that the arms were to be held under lock and key in a non-military environment, under his personal control and the control of the Director of Intelligence and the Minister for Defence. He also reminded the jury that Colonel Hefferon had given evidence that he had informed the minister of the precise non-military environment where the arms were to be stored.

A further difficulty confronting the defence argument that the arms were for the use of the Defence Forces arose from the disputed evidence of Peter Berry about his phone conversation with Charles Haughey on 18 April 1970. Haughey knew when making that call that, despite his direction to Revenue officials that the consignment be allowed in without customs inspection, it was in danger of being seized by Special Branch officers. Berry's evidence was that Haughey asked him whether the consignment could be let through if there was a guarantee that it would go directly to Northern Ireland. Berry had told him, no. While Haughey denied Berry's account, Judge Henchy agreed with State counsel Walsh that if Berry's account of this conversation was accepted by the jury, then there could be no question that the arms were for the use of the Defence Forces, because Haughey suggested that they could go straight to the North.[32] The judge allowed that while this conversation was evidence against Haughey, it was not necessarily evidence against the other accused. Tom Finlay in his response simply asked the jury to consider: if the arms were supposed to be going directly to the North, why would Captain Kelly have suggested they be stored in Cathal Brúgha Barracks in Dublin?[33]

It is obvious from this brief account of the evidence facing the jury that the scales were, at best, finely balanced on whether the arms could be seen as 'for the use of the Defence Forces'. The case, in fact, must have seemed on a knife edge. Finlay acknowledged in his closing address what the judge had stressed throughout the trial: that it was possible the defence would succeed in showing that the importation was done with the authority of the Minister for Defence, but still the defendants would stand convicted if the arms were adjudged to be not for the use of the Defence Forces. But Finlay also claimed it was 'as clear as the noonday sun' that the army had been ordered to prepare for all contingencies, one of which was the distribution of arms to civilians in Northern Ireland. Could anyone, he asked, say by any law of common sense that Captain Kelly was not importing arms for the use of the Defence Forces?

Before dealing with the rest of the evidence, in particular whether Jim Gibbons had given his authority to the operation, the response within the jury room to the evidence described above may be considered. The verdict of course was acquittal, but on what basis? A member of the jury at the second arms trial, 'Mr B', was interviewed about the verdict by RTÉ thirty years later in 2001, in the circumstances indicated earlier. Clearly, issues of accuracy of recall arise after such an interval; memory can play tricks, and accordingly caution must be applied in drawing conclusions from such a source. Still, it is manifest from the transcript that 'Mr B' believed himself to have an 'excellent' memory of the arms trial; he also presented as a reasonable man who took the judge's charge very seriously.

The recollection of Mr. B was that, whereas the acquittal of three of the accused – Captain Kelly, John Kelly and Albert Luykx – was swiftly arrived at and required little discussion in the jury room, the acquittal of Haughey took more time. He explained:

> Albert Luykx, Mr Kelly, Captain Kelly, they were the first to be found not guilty by the jury itself. Because we reckoned they were acting on behalf of the Irish government, because we were sure that the army were involved and we were also sure that the Minister for Finance and the Minister for Defence were certainly involved as well. So the three lads were the first to be exonerated. Most of the discussion was to whether Mr Haughey was guilty or not guilty of the importation of the arms without knowledge of the government.... It had to be the arms – even if it were with the knowledge of the government – it still, it had to be for the use of the Irish army. These were the instructions of the judge.... The whole thing revolved around the arms being for the use of the Irish army, and that was the stumbling block really. We weren't sure if, how that could be....[34]

It seems from this transcript, though it is not explicitly stated, that the jury had accepted the evidence of Peter Berry that Haughey *had* referred on the phone on 18 April 1970 to a possible guarantee that the arms might go straight to the North. Haughey denied saying this, but the jury did not believe him. This created serious difficulties for Haughey. The jury had been told that if he said this, it ruled out any possibility of the arms being for the use of the Defence Forces of the Irish State.

In explaining how this issue was resolved in order to reach a 'not guilty' verdict on Haughey, the juror said that during the trial it had emerged that members of the FCA, the part-time local voluntary component of the Defence Forces who had been trained at Fort Dunree, had actual addresses in Derry:

> We came to the conclusion that if there were members of the FCA stationed in Derry, that presumably the arms could have been for the use of the FCA, and their distribution of it was a matter for them to decide. And that's actually how Mr. Haughey got off. The major part of the decision-making was on behalf of Mr Haughey. Yeah, that's the way it worked. We presumed that if they were for use in the North, that the members of the FCA who were stationed there, or living there, the arms would have been for – well, they would have been their responsibility at that stage. So that came under the heading of the judge's instructions as well. And that's how Mr Haughey got off.[35]

The other key issue before the arms trial jury was whether Gibbons as Minister for Defence had authorized the arms importation. This was a major political issue at the time and may have assumed an exaggerated importance in perceptions of the arms trials since; Gibbons's authorization, as shown above, could never have formed more than a *part* of a successful legal defence. Its importance was nonetheless highlighted by the forceful nature of the cross-examination Gibbons endured in the witness box from defence counsel; this forced from him eventually an admission that he had knowledge of the importation plan. He also accepted that he had not acted to stop it.[36] The State countered this, as Judge Henchy later explained to the jury, by arguing that Gibbons had never issued a licence or other formal authorization for the project. In his closing address, State counsel Walsh claimed that Gibbons could have legalized the whole operation 'by writing his name on a piece of paper', but had not. Instead, Walsh argued, the importation had been conducted in an unorthodox, irregular and illicit fashion. If the guns were intended for a doomsday situation, what was the need for such secrecy? Was it claimed the State could have armed the Bogside and the Falls Road and still kept this intervention a secret? 'If this situation ever arose, the need for secrecy would disappear,' Walsh told the jury.

Judge Henchy noted in his charge that when Captain Kelly needed instructions in Vienna on 20 April 1970, he did not turn to his own minister, Gibbons, but instead rang Haughey, who was Minister for Finance. Henchy also reminded the jury that Kelly had referred to Haughey as 'the bossman'.[37] Defence counsel argued in turn that Gibbons was an unreliable witness who, while he denied authorizing the importation, had admitted to having what he called 'vestigial' knowledge of it; they stressed that in his own evidence he accepted that at no point did he make any effort to halt Captain Kelly's activities. In the same fashion, Finlay, Captain Kelly's counsel, pointed out that, by common consent, it was agreed that junior officer Kelly had sought out the minister in early March to tell him of the importation plans; Finlay claimed that this fact 'on its own was enough to acquit Captain Kelly'.[38]

The judge, in an important reference, said it was open to the jury to decide that, if Gibbons did not put his foot down with Captain Kelly and did not say no to his activities in categorical terms, Captain Kelly was entitled to presume he was saying yes.[39] On Haughey's behalf, counsel Peter Maguire put it to the jury that if his client was engaged in a criminal conspiracy to import arms illegally, the last thing he would have done was to phone the Secretary of the Department of Justice, Peter Berry.[40] His colleague, Niall McCarthy SC, claimed the evidence showed that at all times Haughey had acted through official channels, with nothing underhand.

In considering how the jury resolved these matters and reached a decision to acquit all four accused, the interviews with jurors conducted in 2001 provide some further unique assistance to historians. The juror 'Mr B', who even after thirty years said the trial 'is still very real to me', said the initial feeling on the jury when the trial began was that all four accused were likely to be found guilty.[41] He himself felt convinced that 'with all the hype that was going on', they would not have been brought to trial unless they were definitely guilty. However, he recalled the moment when that changed: it was, he said, after James Gibbons got on the witness stand and denied that he had any knowledge of arms coming into the country. He continued:

> Gibbons denied all this, and at a certain point during the trial, Jim Gibbons said that... he was pinned, and said that he was aware of the arms coming in. He had been made aware of it.... You could actually sense the reaction in the jury box, because that was a turning point for the whole thing. A complete denial on the one hand, and then an admission that he was aware of it.... There was another lad on the jury and when we both – when we went in – we were saying, 'that's a revelation', and another few of the jury were in the vicinity and also of the same opinion. That, that was absolutely—I suggested myself that the four lads shouldn't be up on trial, that it was Jim Gibbons should have been up for perjury.[42]

Apart from some further discussion to deal with Haughey's particular situation, referred to above, the juror recalled being able to arrive quickly at a unanimous verdict. Once they had made a key determination that the arms consignment could be deemed to be 'for the use of the Defence Forces', coupled with Gibbons's admitted knowledge, it left the verdict apparently straightforward:

> It didn't take an awful lot of time actually, I would say within an hour – it was a completely unanimous verdict without any browbeating or anything else. It was just—it was discussed completely in a very, very rational way. There was no screaming, ranting, raving—anything like that. It was just a straightforward discussion. And all the points were discussed completely.

As shown in Chapter 14, Judge Henchy had said in his charge to the jury that he believed the prosecution had been properly brought by the Attorney General. He allowed, though, that this was just his opinion, and the jury were free to disregard it. He went on to say that if they decided that the prosecution should never have been brought, then of course they would bring in a verdict of 'not guilty' against each of the accused. This, it appears, was precisely the view arrived at by at least some in the jury room, as the juror quoted above explained:

> We couldn't understand actually why the trial ever took place. Because we were sure that if the Minister for Finance was aware, the Minister for Defence was aware, the top brass in the army were aware and giving Captain Kelly instructions, we couldn't understand why it ever came to trial. They were the initial reactions of the jury when we were sitting down at the final stages.... And we could never understand why Captain Kelly was on the stand at all, why he was ever accused of doing anything illegal? He appeared to have been working for the army under instruction and as such was completely an innocent man.

The second juror interviewed in 2001, 'Mr A', described the trial as 'a joke'. He said: 'The whole thing was a charade.' He believed the government had decided to bring in arms to help Northern nationalists but that Lynch 'got cold feet' and changed his mind 'when Cosgrave blew the whistle'.[43] This juror, unlike his colleague, said his memory of the detail of the trial was 'hazy, to say the least'. But he recalled that in the jury room afterwards, ten of the twelve jurors were quickly of the view that the accused were not guilty, whereas the remaining two were less certain and required some further discussion before joining the majority view in favour of acquittal. Both he and his colleague 'Mr B', speaking separately, were anxious to respond to the claim that there had been juror intimidation.[44] 'Mr A' described Garret FitzGerald's claim that the jury were intimidated as 'ludicrous' and 'absurd'. He said nobody ever intimidated him during the trial and, he said, nobody ever would. He said he was appalled by the suggestion; he had served on other juries, and he took the responsibility seriously. 'Mr B' also described as 'ludicrous' FitzGerald's claim that the jury were afraid to bring in a guilty verdict:

> At no stage, at absolutely no stage prior to the trial or after the trial were we ever contacted or approached by anybody. I certainly wasn't anyway. Nobody on the jury ever voiced intimidation or anything like that. So I am quite convinced they would have been in the same boat as I, that nobody ever tried to interfere with their opinion or verdict or anything like that. Certainly, to my knowledge, nobody was ever touched. No.[45]

What seems clear from the transcript of the interview with 'Mr B' is that he listened carefully to Judge Seamus Henchy's directions, and then strove to produce a judgement in line with the law as it was explained to him. His views of the case seemed to stem from the evidence he heard in court, rather than any prior political views he may have held. The account of 'Mr A' is less coherent, but he also felt the trial should never have happened – 'a charade', he called it. It is simply not clear to what extent this emerged in his case from the evidence. His interview provides some useful corroboration for points made by 'Mr B', and that appears its principal historical value.

Both jurors believed that the prosecution should never have come before them, and this may be the key to the verdict. A view in the jury room that the prosecution had been unwarranted in itself is likely to have led to a feeling that it should not succeed. The judge himself had stated that if any juror felt that way, they should vote to acquit. He had also told them that when Gibbons failed to put his foot down and say 'no' when told of the attempted importation, Captain Kelly – and they as jurors – were entitled to presume he had said 'yes'. Clearly, both jurors interviewed believed Gibbons had known of and approved of the importation.

But perhaps most significant in the interviews is the insight from 'Mr B' into how the jury members reached their most critical finding of fact, i.e., that the arms being imported could be properly seen as intended 'for the use of the Defence Forces'. In reaching this view, the jurors were exercising the discretion that had been left to them by Judge Henchy, after the detailed legal discussion with counsel on 20 October. It was a discretion applied somewhat imaginatively in the case of Charles Haughey, on the basis of the established enlistment of Northerners such as Paddy Doherty in the Fórsa Cosanta Áitiúil. Did that represent the wisdom of Solomon? However one views that, in the end, justice – whether poetic or otherwise – may have been achieved by a process in which the jury's findings of fact ultimately trumped a flawed prosecution, one that the evidence suggests owed more to politics than it did to the law.

17

Conclusions

The 1970 Arms Crisis may have been a landmark of sorts in the history of twentieth-century Ireland, but all was not as it has seemed. Overwhelmingly, the crisis has been seen as stemming from the uncovering by Jack Lynch of a conspiracy within his own government, geared towards ousting him from power, rearming the IRA and breaking partition with the force of arms. The perception has been of a moment when the island of Ireland almost lurched into a sectarian civil war, when democracy and the stability of the Irish State itself were on the line, until the day was saved by Lynch's decisive response to the plotters. It has been a perspective on the 1970 Arms Crisis sketched in tones of black and white, where the good guy, Lynch, defeated the bad guys, Haughey and Blaney, and – under Lynch's decisive leadership – the Irish State chose a path that avoided a dangerous entanglement with the developing Northern Ireland Troubles. As a historical narrative, it has never been fully convincing, and ultimately, it does not withstand proper research and academic scrutiny. It is, in short, a myth, or series of myths. It is a false representation not just of Lynch, but also of Haughey and Blaney, and of the two Irish army officers caught up in the controversy.

The context in which the crisis occurred involved a very particular set of circumstances, a short period of exceptional anxiety inside the Irish government after the August 1969 disturbances in Northern Ireland. It was a time when, in the immediate aftermath of those events, concern in the South for the safety and protection of Northern nationalists mingled dangerously with anti-partitionist rhetoric. While there was a sense that the end of partition might be in sight, this was accompanied by intense short-term fears that the British might lose control, and prove either unwilling or unable to prevent further and much worse sectarian assaults on Northern nationalists. These conflicting instincts existed inside the Irish government and among nationalists generally over the autumn, winter and spring of 1969–70. The fleeting circumstances were unlike anything a Dublin administration had faced since 1922, when Michael Collins, as leader of the Provisional Government, had struggled to respond to pogroms against Catholics in Belfast. The acute anxiety felt in 1969 did not go away, but by the summer of 1970 the British army had established its presence on the streets of the North and a different dynamic was in play. It was within the intervening nine months, from August 1969 to May 1970, that the Arms Crisis was incubated and hatched, a time when, to nationalist eyes, disaster and promise never seemed so close or so intimately bound together.

Establishing the facts on this traumatic period in Irish history has been far from straightforward, and over the years the task has been greatly complicated by double-talk from many of the principal figures involved. John Peck, the British ambassador, was not exaggerating when he said that a feature of the arms trials was 'the intermittent and flexible memories of key witnesses'.[1] The pattern of mendacity Peck hinted at went far beyond the trials, and an exceptional number of dissimulations, untruths and straight lies have littered the narrative of the times. This has created a challenge to which political observers and writers generally have struggled to respond. Aggravating the problem until recently was the absence of official documentation, but that lack of primary source material was substantially remedied by the release in January 2001 of the British and Irish State papers for 1969 and 1970.

This book makes the case, overly delayed though it may be, for a comprehensive reassessment of the place the 1970 Arms

Crisis occupies in twentieth-century Irish history. Little about what Jack Lynch did in 1970, or why he did it, conforms with the conventional understanding. The same is true of Charles Haughey and of Neil Blaney. The case for reviewing the record is based not on any one particular event or 'eureka' moment of discovery, but on a multitude of factors and evidence from a variety of different quarters, some of it new, and almost all of it pointing in one direction. In the face of this multi-pronged assault, the 'Lynch view' of the 1970 Arms Crisis, of Haughey, of Blaney, of the Irish army officer James Kelly and of the celebrated arms trials, dies from a thousand cuts, and from a myriad of provable facts. Some of the facts are major, some less so, but cumulatively they strip the conventional view of its credibility and ultimately create the case for a root-and-branch revision.

The prime need is to acknowledge that Jack Lynch in the spring of 1970 had a covert element to his policy on Northern Ireland. Hidden from view was the provision being made for contingencies, i.e., disaster, within the North, a provision largely but not totally documented after the 6 February 1970 directive was issued to the Defence Forces. The policy envisaged the use of force of various kinds, including army cross-border military incursions and the provision of arms and training in the use of arms to civilians for their own defence. This was a use of force but it was strictly for defensive and humanitarian purposes. Also, the hidden policy's full implementation was contingent on a doomsday situation arising across the border, in which the British authorities might prove unable to protect the lives and property of Northern nationalists. The plans were not inconsistent with Lynch's peaceful approach to the ending of partition, but critically, and for obvious reasons, they could not be disclosed publicly.

The required secrecy left Lynch with a Janus-faced approach to the Northern Irish situation; it led him into systematic deception, including the making of a series of false statements to Dáil Éireann. It necessitated a systematic cover-up of the full contents of the 6 February directive. When in early 1971 the directive's precise terms were sought from the Taoiseach by the chairman of the Committee of Public Accounts inquiry, Patrick Hogan TD (Fine Gael), Lynch withheld the truth; he misrepresented the directive's contents to Hogan while simultaneously refusing to give his Dáil committee access to the original documents. False information was also contained in a Dáil statement from Minister for Defence, Jerry Cronin, in April 1971, about the actions taken in the aftermath of the directive. Other untruthful statements were made to the British and Irish media.

These events underscore a major finding in this book: the general lack of candour shown by both Lynch and Gibbons in the course of the crisis. The core of their pretence was exposed as far back as 1980, when Peter Berry's *Diaries* were published; these corroborated Colonel Michael Hefferon's evidence to the Committee of Public Accounts inquiry, given in 1971, and showed how Lynch and Gibbons hid the truth about their early knowledge of Captain Kelly's offer of money for guns to republicans in Bailieboro in October 1969. The two men engaged in a history of deception and denial over this and other hidden aspects of government policy.

While the sheer extent of Lynch's identifiable deceptions in front of the public and of Dáil Éireann may appear surprising, a thorough deconstruction of all of James Gibbons's various public statements in the period May 1970 to April 1971, including his witness statements to the gardaí in May and June 1970, produces utterly conclusive evidence of evasion, deception and untrustworthiness. Gibbons, whose performance in this period some writers have seen as a 'mystery', about which the truth would never be known, in fact showed himself, in his under-scrutinized April 1971 evidence to the Committee of Public Accounts inquiry, to have been a persistent stranger to the truth. Although his foreknowledge of the arms importation was considerable, throughout 1970 he withheld much of this from the authorities and from the arms trials. He also kept in the dark Colonel P. J. Delaney, Hefferon's successor as Director of Military Intelligence, when he ordered him to investigate Captain Kelly. The evidence is that Delaney was effectively duped by his minister.

Overall, Lynch did much to create the political crisis for which, remarkably, he has been given great credit for resolving. His chosen form of resolution was to make scapegoats of Haughey and Blaney, as well as Captain James Kelly, Belfast republican John Kelly and Belgian expatriate businessman Albert Luykx. Haughey and Blaney, on the evidence, were operating within the broad confines of government policy at the time they were sacked. They have been demonized in the years since as ministers who were supposedly running – in opposition to Lynch – a 'shadow' or 'alternative' government, also termed 'a government within a government'.[2] It appears that, whatever their personal relationship with the Taoiseach, both ministers have been, in this period at least, misrepresented, poorly understood and occasionally maligned. A prime example of such misunderstanding is provided by Blaney's controversial speech in Letterkenny in December 1969; other examples are the exaggerated claims that, in the autumn and winter of 1969–70, Haughey operated with a persistent disregard for Lynch's authority as Taoiseach.

Haughey's own willingness to bend the truth makes it difficult to reach a conclusive finding on his management of the Northern Ireland Relief Fund, but there are many reasons, outlined at length in this book, for questioning whether he was as far out of line as has been claimed. This impression is enhanced by the sluggish manner in which Lynch and Gibbons dealt ultimately with the knowledge that public money had indeed gone to the purchase of arms in early 1970.

The Arms Crisis was precipitated not when the attempted arms importation came to light, but when Lynch made the seemingly snap decision to renounce such activity and to cast Haughey and Blaney from his cabinet. It amounted to a sudden, forced change of policy, which was represented as the unearthing of a plot against him from within his own cabinet; it threw the political world into disarray and generated over-heated fears for the safety of the State, after almost fifty years of institutional stability. With rumours flying and accurate information at a premium, Lynch found himself credited by his supporters with having averted a slide towards a sectarian civil war. Haughey and Blaney, along with Captain Kelly, John Kelly and Albert Luykx, despite being cleared of criminal offences, were demonized.

Ultimately, the sacking of Haughey and Blaney, and their subsequent criminal prosecution, appears to have been a cynical manoeuvre designed primarily to keep Fianna Fáil in power, keep the Opposition parties quiet and, possibly, keep the British government at bay. While Lynch claimed that he sacked his ministers because they did not subscribe fully to the government's Northern policy, the fact of the February directive leaves it unclear what significant disagreements existed – before, that is, Lynch changed his mind and decided that arms could never be made available to beleaguered Northern nationalists.

The factual situation about the gun-running that precipitated the crisis is that it was not initiated by the Irish government or by any of its ministers, not even Blaney; it had its origins north of the border among the Defence Committees. Strictly speaking, it is difficult to describe it as a government scheme at all, though it was known of and supported within the cabinet, and was being given indirect funding through monies disbursed to accounts controlled by Northern Ireland trustees. Above all, it was consistent with a wider – covert – government approach at the time, in which it had been agreed that arms should be made available to Northern nationalists, if required in a future hour of need. The conflicted ownership of the gun-running project, and its *sub rosa* nature, is the key to the haphazard nature of Captain Kelly's planning. It had been conceived by the Northerners to bolster their defence, but the money for it came largely, though not exclusively, from Dublin. The money had been gifted to the Northern account holders, with no apparent strings attached. While the power of the purse gave ministers a big influence, this did not mean that any of them – except possibly for Blaney

– would be prepared to take responsibility, publicly, for the gun-running, if that need ever arose.

The imported guns were to be held in trust under a junior army officer's sole control, until such time as the government decided that the circumstances were right to distribute them. These arrangements appear at best impractical, and could even be categorized as naïve. The planning of the operation was chaotically executed, and with hindsight the plan is easy to see as reckless and calculated to add fuel to the sectarian fires threatening Northern Ireland. However, the same criticism might equally be made of the instructions the Lynch government gave the Defence Forces on 6 February, when Gibbons, as Minister for Defence, envisaged sending the Irish army over the border and distributing guns to Northern republicans. Potentially desperate circumstances were being anticipated, and desperate contingency planning was the result.

The issue that exercised Lynch and his colleagues in the months that followed the events of August 1969 was not whether force should be used to end partition, but whether it could, or should, be used to defend Northern nationalists, if extreme circumstances demanded it. The facts suggest that before May 1970, Lynch's approach on this was closer to Blaney, Haughey and other supposed hardliners within his cabinet than is often supposed. The concern in Dublin over providing defensive cover for nationalists was universal, including in Army GHQ. The military Planning Board reports in September–October 1969 showed how senior officers were driven to recommend some temporary link-up with the State's pledged enemies in the Republican Movement, in what it was hoped could be a common cause.

At the same time, in the autumn of 1969, a parallel courtship was taking place between Fianna Fáil and IRA veterans; their dialogue was never less than awkward, and was ultimately embarrassing to both. It ended badly, with Lynch walking away and seeking to cover his tracks with untruths and evasions. It would remain an issue for writers to ponder thereafter whether this attempted alliance had been – as is strongly argued here – for the provision of defence, or for the generation of war. On the republican side, the evidence is overwhelming that through to at least the middle of 1970, the Provisional IRA, publicly and privately, made their priority the defence of nationalists from pending assault.[3] Their longer-term intentions were more aggressive, but distinctly muted for the time being. There is nothing to suggest the army officers who were in discussions with republicans in autumn 1969, under Colonel Hefferon's supervision, were seeking anything other than reliable allies on the ground who might help them defend nationalist communities.

Hefferon's role as Director of Military Intelligence, and as Kelly's commanding officer, has been seriously neglected in the literature on the Arms Crisis. It is also highly problematic for those who argue for the existence of a conspiracy against Lynch. It was advice from Hefferon that ultimately led to Haughey becoming involved in customs clearance for the arms consignment, and so led indirectly to the phone call between Haughey and Berry on the evening of 18 April 1970. Hefferon emerges in the story as a morally brave and honest soldier, though perhaps prone to an overly secretive way of working that was excessive even for the office he held. He was a central figure in the jigsaw of the Arms Crisis, and his participation in the planning of Captain Kelly's arms importation is difficult to square with any plot to undermine Lynch and subvert the State.

Overall, the evidence is that Haughey and Blaney's supposedly subversive 'plot' was conducted in full view of a number of key public servants such as Hefferon; others in the know included Anthony Fagan, Haughey's civil service assistant, and even Revenue Commissioner Bartholomew Culligan. At the same time, the Army Planning Board reports make it difficult to see Captain Kelly's Bailieboro meeting with Northern Defence Committees as the maverick, subversive operation so frequently claimed. None of these facts suggest a plot to unseat Lynch or to launch a violent campaign against partition.

What the evidence does reveal is the harsh treatment accorded by the State to Captain James Kelly in the affair. He and Hefferon ultimately can be seen as collateral damage in what became a struggle primarily between senior figures in the governing Fianna Fáil party. As Peter Berry rightly observed, the interests of the party trumped everything else in the end, and a junior officer like Kelly was entirely surplus to the concerns of the principals. Attempts have been made by sympathisers to paint him as an Irish Dreyfus, in reference to the celebrated French army officer in the Third Republic, Captain Alfred Dreyfus, who was falsely convicted of treason at the end of the nineteenth century and rehabilitated only after a twelve-year campaign. Parallels can be potent even when they are not one hundred per cent accurate, and Kelly's case, while different in scale and outcome to that of Dreyfus, does offer considerable similarities, especially in regard to his politicized and unwarranted prosecution.

The full restoration of Kelly's reputation would seem an out-standing obligation on the Irish State, a historical anachronism that still awaited rectification half a century after the event. Also awaiting the attention of historians is the dismal record of the Fine Gael and Labour parties throughout the Arms Crisis. It is an open question to what extent the Opposition parties facilitated the gross deceptions that have clouded the historical record – regarding Lynch, regarding Haughey and Blaney, and regarding Captain Kelly. Cosgrave's performance, from his first closeted meeting with Lynch on the evening of 5 May, remains a genuine mystery.

So far as the arms trials are concerned, serious questions arise about the role played by Attorney General Colm Condon SC, and to a lesser extent Garda Chief Superintendent John Fleming. Condon, who sat at cabinet but also carried the responsibility of the role of public prosecutor, appears to have taken a blind-eye approach to the involvement of James Gibbons, then Minister for Defence. In the end, the handling of the evidence surrounding Gibbons left a fatal weakness in the State case. There is nothing to show that he was ever properly investigated, and the exclusion from Hefferon's witness statement in May 1970 of direct evidence of Gibbons's involvement was no isolated event, but part of a revealed pattern in the Attorney General's conduct of the prosecution. Michael McDowell SC's *Report of the Attorney General* in July 2001 erred in concluding that the exclusions from Hefferon's statement were a matter of no great significance.

The facts suggest that a criminal prosecution was never warranted. If there had to be such a prosecution, the suspects had to include both Gibbons, the Minister for Defence, and Hefferon, the army's Director of Military Intelligence. This was because of their proven prior knowledge of the plan, their complicity in Captain Kelly's actions and their high-level status. Such a prosecution, however, would have been politically suicidal and would probably have brought down Lynch's government. Obviously, the Attorney General did not choose to go there.

The head of the Garda Special Branch investigation, Detective Chief Superintendent John Fleming, emerges poorly from the evidence in this book, though to be fair he was clearly struggling with the protective mantle the Attorney General had thrown around Gibbons. In the end, however, Fleming displayed an excessive willingness to comply with the politics that surrounded him. After his colleagues on the investigation, O'Dea and Doocey, had produced, with commendable diligence, a witness statement from Hefferon that laid bare Gibbons's complicity, Fleming's final investigation report discarded the evidence of his own officers and set out a seriously inaccurate version of the facts of the case. In the end, while claims that the arms trials were show trials, in the Stalinist sense, may appear extravagant, there has been no effective rebuttal of Patrick MacEntee SC's opinion that the trials should not have happened as they did, and probably should not have happened at all.[4] Some jurors confessed themselves unable in the end to understand how it was that Captain James Kelly had ever come to trial before them.[5]

On the broader issue of the historical significance of the 1970 Arms Crisis, it seems questionable whether the State itself was under threat in 1970, as so many writers have stated, and far from clear that it stood on the brink of a sectarian civil war.[6] There is in fact little evidence that a crisis existed within the Irish Republic of anything like the dimensions commonly claimed, except in the narrowest political sense, and due largely to the way Lynch chose to handle the situation. This revised understanding of the 1970 Arms Crisis suggests that its importance in twentieth-century Irish history has been overstated. What is manifest is the convulsion it generated in the political life of the Irish Republic, the effects of which lasted for several decades, especially within Fianna Fáil. Equally, it was a moment when the twenty-six-county Irish State drew back from any potential cross-border military involvement – an affirmation, as historian John A. Murphy suggested in 1975, of the Republic's development as a 'homogenous, twenty-six-county, sovereign state'.[7] It might also be described as a significant moment in the emergence of what John M. Regan has called a twenty-six-county 'Southern nationalist ideology'.[8]

A major question mark that remains is the influence of the Arms Crisis on the emergence of the Provisional IRA. Much literary effort has gone into attempts to prove that the actions of Fianna Fáil ministers Haughey and Blaney were a significant factor in the birth of the Provisionals, with claims such as 'the [Irish] State and Northern Ireland were to pay dearly over many years for the mistakes made'.[9] But Tim Pat Coogan's early assessment that the advantage gained by the Provisionals from Blaney and Haughey's actions amounted to just 'a tiny push along the road', still appears appropriate.[10] By way of contrast, Lynch, by his actions at the time, has been widely judged to have done the right thing in keeping the Republic out of the North. A popular verdict to that effect is unlikely to be altered by any evidence here that he did it in different circumstances and for different reasons than he chose to admit. It is also true that, with the exception of Angela Clifford, few writers have had any appetite for querying the wisdom of the course Lynch took.[11] It unquestionably reflected the popular will within his main constituency, the electorate of the twenty-six counties.[12]

But in the light of the bloodshed and death toll of the following twenty-five years, mainly within Northern Ireland, which of the main players, including the Irish government, could state with certainty that, had Lynch done things differently, it might not have produced a better outcome, with fewer lives lost? One view which has been little pursued is whether Lynch, when he chose to disavow so emphatically any possibility that the Irish army could ever intervene to defend Northern nationalists, and allowed John Kelly, the representative of the Northern Defence Committees, to be prosecuted, contributed himself to the growth of the Provisional IRA by leaving a vacuum in the North. His actions, arguably, created a situation where those in nationalist communities who had always looked to Dublin, who distrusted the British forces and felt vulnerable to potential Ulster Volunteer Force assault, were forced to look elsewhere for a means of physical defence. The capacity of the Irish government to influence militant nationalist opinion was reduced almost to nothing after what some chose to see as Jack Lynch's betrayal in 1970.

The emphatic view of Blaney and Boland, among others, was that Lynch's actions did leave the field to the gunmen. In 1990, Blaney said that Lynch had 'helped to create the Provisional IRA' because, after the Arms Crisis, Northern nationalists 'lost their faith in the *bona fide* concern of Dublin and the South'.[13] Boland said the Provisionals were 'called into being by the Irish government's about-turn in May 1970.... This was the achievement of the Taoiseach'.[14] John Kelly, acquitted at the arms trial and later a member of the Provisionals, said in 2014 of the Irish government: 'They created the conditions on the ground for the formation of the Provisional IRA, by their abandonment of Northern nationalism.'[15] Derry man Paddy Doherty, so important in the events of 1970, agreed, saying that if the government 'had taken up the running and accept(ed) responsibility and dealt directly with the British about it, I don't think we would have had thirty years of war'.[16] Captain James Kelly himself wrote in 1976 of the Lynch government's 'inexplicable and disastrous about-face', describing it as 'a foul betrayal' with sharp consequences: 'In the vacuum created by the Dublin desertion, it was inevitable that nationalists should turn to the IRA.... Mr Lynch made certain of the evolvement of a nationalist "people's army".'[17]

More recently, Martin Mansergh, historian and adviser to Haughey on Northern Ireland when he was Taoiseach during the 1980s, has complained that this point has been 'habitually missed' by writers:

> The perceived abandonment of nationalists by the Dublin government after 1970, among more militant and deprived members of the nationalist community, did as much unintentionally to accelerate the development of the IRA as any previous lines of communication.[18]

Finally, historian T. P. O'Neill, biographer of Éamon de Valera, made a noteworthy private comment as the Arms Crisis was developing. In a letter to Minister for External Affairs Patrick Hillery, one which he described himself as 'a friend's reaction to events', O'Neill lamented the words and actions of Jack Lynch:

> Perhaps it was necessary to make the position about arms clear, but why state it in terms which give the impression that the Government would do nothing for those attacked?... The minority in the Six Counties have been given a guarantee by the Taoiseach – a guarantee they never had before. They have been given the guarantee that if they are being murdered by Paisleyite mobs, the Irish Government will stand idly by. The Taoiseach is wise in his rejection of the use of force as a means of ending partition. But is he wise in his washing of hands in regard to protecting the minority? He should not have spelled this out so clearly. The only effect his words will have will be to drive young men into activist groups.[19]

It is of, course, far from clear what different, more nuanced position on the physical protection of Northern nationalists might have been open to the Irish government in the years after 1970. Could there have been found a means of balancing the genuine abhorrence of violence among its own electorate, with a more emphatic determination by the government in Dublin to defend and protect its 'lost tribe' across the border in Northern Ireland? The question posed by O'Neill was whether Lynch ultimately did the right thing in 1970, or whether his blunt approach effectively directed young nationalist men and women in the North into the arms of republican paramilitaries. It remained just another big question meriting consideration by historians, as the 1970 Arms Crisis reached its fiftieth anniversary.

Appendix 1

Prosecution Timeline

20 April (Monday)   First report by Chief Superintendent Fleming on the attempted arms importation, given by Peter Berry to Taoiseach Jack Lynch.

Gibbons asks Delaney to prepare a report on the importation attempt.

21 April   Second Fleming report on attempted importation, given by Berry to Lynch.

22 April

23 April   Statements from Andrew Desmond, Surveyor, Customs and Excise, Dublin Airport; Jack Ryan, Cargo Superintendent, Aer Lingus.

Meeting in Blaney's office – Hefferon, Kelly and Gibbons present.

24 April   Gibbons meets Lynch – delivers Delaney report personally, plus his own oral report on events.

25 April Statement from Seán Carpendale, Inspector, Customs and Excise.

26 April

27 April Statement from Tom Tobin, Inspector, Customs and
(Monday) Excise.

Gibbons tells Kelly to continue contacts; he will be shifted to a quiet job.

28 April Kelly 'arrested', and has leave cancelled. Ordered to cut off contacts; he meets Gibbons to protest, and suspects he is being set up for court-martial.

29 April Kelly places his resignation on Gibbons's desk.

30 April Captain Kelly retires from army.

Conference called by Lynch at his home to 'coordinate' investigation findings; Gibbons in attendance.

1 May Statement from Albert Luykx, Belgian businessman.

Captain Kelly arrested, questioned, released without charge.

2 May

3 May

4 May Lynch demands resignation of Mícheál Ó Móráin,
(Monday) Minister for Justice.

5 May	Cosgrave confronts Lynch with anonymous garda note.
6 May	Haughey and Blaney sacked by Lynch.
7 May	Gibbons promoted within the cabinet.
8 May	Dáil statement by Gibbons; Captain Kelly issues statement to the media in response.
9 May	Tony Fagan, Principal Officer Department of Finance, completes handwritten statement for his superiors.
10 May	
11 May (Monday)	Second statements from Jack Ryan, Aer Lingus, and Andrew Desmond, Customs and Excise.
12 May	Statement from Bartholomew Culligan, Revenue Commissioner.
13 May	Second statements from Bartholomew Culligan, Revenue Commissioner; Tom Tobin, Inspector, Customs and Excise; and Seán Carpendale, Inspector, Customs and Excise.
	Andrew Johnson, Aer Lingus agent in statement from Frankfurt.
	Tony Fagan, Department of Finance, completes second handwritten statement.
14 May	Three formal statements taken from Tony Fagan, Department of Finance.
15 May	

16 May

17 May

18 May   Statements from Murrough Connellan, Assistant
(Monday)   Collector, Customs and Excise; Andrew Desmond,
               Customs and Excise (third statement); Jim Gibbons,
               Minister for Agriculture.

19 May

20 May

21 May   Statement from Peter Berry, Secretary, Department of
               Justice (taken on 21 April).

22 May   Second statement from Jim Gibbons, Minister for
               Agriculture (in Q&A form).

23 May

24 May

25 May   Garda attempt to get a statement from Charles
(Monday)   Haughey on this date is stalled when Haughey asks for
               written questions.

26 May   Statements from Colonel P. J. Delaney, Director of
               Military Intelligence; Tony Fagan, Department of
               Finance (fourth formal statement).

               Warrants issued on 26 May for arrest of
               Captain Kelly, John Kelly, Luykx, Haughey
               and Blaney.

27 May   Statement from Tony Fagan, Department of Finance (fifth formal statement).

Both Kellys and Luykx arrested, charged and released on bail.

Captain James Kelly issues short statement (on being charged).

28 May

29 May   Statement from Diarmaid Ó Ríordáin, Surveyor, Customs and Excise, Dublin Port.

Charles Haughey arrested, charged, released on bail.

30 May   Statement from Colonel Michael Hefferon, former Director of Military Intelligence.

31 May   Second statement from Colonel Hefferon.

1 June (Bank Holiday Monday)

2 June   Statements from Bernard P. Muldoon, Assistant Collector, Customs and Excise, Dublin Port; J. C. Buckley, Customs Officer, Collectors Office, Dublin Port.

Report on the results of garda investigation sent by Chief Superintendent John Fleming to the Office of the Chief State Solicitor.

8 June   Fourth statement from James Gibbons, Minister for
(Monday)   Agriculture (in Q&A form).

10 June   Attempted garda interview in Castlebar with former
                  minister Ó Móráin; Ó Móráin declines to make a
                  statement.

26 June   Sixth formal statement taken from Tony Fagan,
                  Department of Finance.

Appendix 2

Military records concerning the 6 February directive issued by the Minister for Defence James Gibbons, to the Chief of Staff, Lieutenant General Seán MacEoin, in the presence of Colonel Michael Hefferon:

(These documents have been reproduced, by kind permission, from Angela Clifford's *Military Aspects of Ireland's Arms Crisis of 1969–70* (Belfast, 2006). The originals were mainly handwritten and are in the Military Archive. These documents have been transcribed as accurately as possible to replicate the layout of the originals.)

In order, the documents shown below are:

MA, Ops File 3 – Ministerial Directive to Chief of Staff, 6 February
    1970
MA, Ops File 3 – Addendum to Memo of 10/2/70 – Ministerial
    Directive, dated 11 February 1970
MA, SCS 18/1 – Brief for an Ceann Fóirne, 9 June 1970
MA, M.I File 5 – Meeting with An Taoiseach 9 June 1970.

Document a) Ministerial Directive to the
Chief of Staff, 6 February 1970

"TOP SECRET

STRN [Director of Training]   Copy No.
FIVE

RN P & O [Planning & Operations Section]

CCA [Army HQ]

10/2/70

Ministerial Directive

To Chief of Staff

16.30rs Friday

6 Feb. 70

1. <u>Present when conveyed by CF</u> 1700 hrs 6 Feb: AG [Adjutant General], ACS [Assistant Chief of Staff], S Fais [Director of Intelligence], Lt. Col Adams.

2. <u>Directive</u>

   a. "to prepare and train the Army for incursions into Northern Ireland"

   b. Respirators?

   c. Weapons and arms, surplus ?

   d. The exact nature of the directive in regard to b and c was NOT mentioned by CF

   e. The following questions arise out of a.

      (1) the probable purpose of such incursions

      (2) when and in what circumstances

      (3) are the ops to be "large" scale or of a small hit and run nature

      (4) are incursions to be overt or covert

      (5) limitations or stipulations as to the number of pers to be involved

      (6) are the ops to be with or without prejudice to all other tasks such as the security of posts and the protection of vital instls

3. Implications

In view of the possible implications of the directive, it would seem essential that the Minister and the Cabinet would make arrangements to hear the CF on these aspects at 2 e above and on the critical state of the Army to undertake such a mission

4. Suggested planning procedure

a. Meeting   CF and S Fais to get in writing the exact nature of the directive

b. Staff Conference   CF, AG [Adjutant General], ACS [Assistant Chief of Staff] QMG (Quartermaster General] or Deputy, SP&O [Director, Planning and Ops], S Fais [Director of Intelligence], S Im [Director of Transport].

(1) Discussion of mission

(2) Determination of planning sequence

(3) Types of forces to be used, Comd commitments – types of ops

(4) Training

(5) Control of ops – comms

(6) Level to which planning will go

(7) Cover plan

(8) Special Planning staff

c. Command OCs meeting

To attend   Comd ACs [Assistant Commanders?], S Cori [Director of Engineering], Staff as at 4a above

Broad plan / Comd commitments

Cover plan

5. Respirators, Surplus arms and amn
   Distr a Q problem
   a. How many
   b. Where to be held
   c. How to be packed
   d. To whom to be delivered
   e. Stand by transport
   f. Officer i/c.

                                                        J.A"

                                              [NA MDA.]

"TOP SECRET

S Im   Copy No 5

RN P & O

CCA

11/2/70

Addendum to Memo of 10/2/70

Ministerial directive

To CF

<u>Present</u> CF, S/P&I, Lt Col Adams

1. At a meeting held on 11/2/70/ CF recapitulated on Ministers directive as follows.

  a. "At a meeting of the Government held this morning (Friday 6 Feb 70) I was instructed to direct you to prepare the Army for incursions into Northern Ireland."

  b. "The Taoiseach and other Ministers have met delegations from the North. At these meetings urgent demands were made for respirators, weapons and ammunition the provision of which the Government agreed. Accordingly truck loads of these items will be put at readiness so that they may be available in a matter of hours.["]

  c. Minister asked what were the natures of critical deficiencies to which CF answered

           Manpower

           AFVs [Armoured Fighting Vehicles]

           TPT [Transport]

  d. The Minister directed that the FCA should be required to take on more security tasks than at present in order to free PDF [Permanent Defence Forces] pers for training and ops.

  e. The Minister instructed CF to hold himself in readiness to discuss estimates with Mr Haughey as soon as the latter was out of hospital.

J.A."

[NA MDA.]

"TOP SECRET   SCS 18/1
BR CEANN FÓIRNE,
CCA.
5 JUNE 1970.

BRIEF FOR CEANN FÓIRNE

1. DEFENCE POLICY

   a. The lack of a clear-cut Governmental Directive on the form which Defence Policy should take, has created a considerable degree of uncertainty and frustration within the Defence Forces. No long-term procurement policy in regard to personnel or equipment can be drawn up in such a climate.

   b. Critical deficiencies in personnel strength and in equipment, allied to the present very high incidence of duties, have created a situation in which training for combat is not possible. In these circumstances combat efficiency is very low.

   c. Following a directive from the then Taoiseach in June 1962, various major studies were initiated by the General Staff. These were

Ireland in a Major War	1962
Defence Policy Memorandum	1963
Defence Review Board Report	1965
Defence Policy memorandum	1967

   These documents were very comprehensive; they examined every facet of the Defence Forces, suggested roles and responsibilities and set out the requirements of the Defence Forces to implement these.

   d. None of the papers above have been submitted to the Government.

   e. The events since August 1969, have only served to confirm the lack of combat effectivity [sic]: when no one unit could from its own resources provide an effective force, and when it became necessary to form ad-hoc groups hastily drawn together and made up from personnel from administrative,

technical and training staffs to provide sufficient numbers
to protect and support the refugee centres and field hospitals

f. Early examination of the military submissions by the
Government is essential and urgent, coupled with a clear-
cut directive as to the mission of the Defence Forces, the
designation of their roles and responsibilities, and a clear
statement as to the means in manpower and equipment
which will be made available to them.

g. A brief appraisal of the capabilities of the Defence Forces
is referred to in Paragraph 2 of this paper and is set out in
Appendix I attached [not included here]."

"2. Situation in Northern Ireland

a. In August 1969 following on civil strife in Northern
Ireland, the Defence Forces deployed three hastily-formed
infantry groups along the border, to support and protect
Field Hospitals and Refugee Centres.

b. Following a directive from the Minister for Defence, the
General Staff had an "Estimate of the Situation" prepared
which assessed the situation in Northern Ireland and the
capabilities of the Defence Forces to provide more positive
assistance should the strife in Northern Ireland continue
at the level of mid August 1969 or even deteriorate. The
assessment indicated a very low standard of combat
effectivity [sic], and a critical situation in regard to personnel
deficiencies and shortage of essential equipment, which
precluded action.

c. In November '69 the Defence Forces took over from
the gardaí the commitment of protecting certain vital
installations threatened by Ulster Volunteer Force activity.
The Defence Forces still retain this responsibility in
addition to their other commitments. This has forced
a reduction in the strength of units deployed near the
border. In spite of these reductions the incidence of duties,

particularly 24 hour-out-of-bed duty, is very high and
places a considerable strain on morale.

d. At 1630 hours on Friday 6 Feb 1970, the Minister for
Defence informed the Chief of Staff and the then Director
of Intelligence that the Government at a Cabinet Meeting
on that date had instructed the Minister to order the Chief
of Staff to prepare and train the Army for incursions into
Northern Ireland if and when such a course became
necessary, and to have respirators and arms and ammunition
made ready in the event that it would be necessary for the
minority to protect themselves. The Minister explained
that the Taoiseach and other Ministers had met delegations
from the North. At these meetings urgent demands were
made for respirators, weapons and ammunition, the
provision of which the Government agreed as and when
necessary. Accordingly the Chief of Staff was instructed to
put truck loads of these items at readiness so that they could
be available in a matter of hours if required. The Minister
asked the Chief of Staff the nature of the most critical
deficiencies of the Defence Forces, to which the Chief of Staff
replied

> Manpower
> Armoured fighting vehicles
> Transport

The Minister instructed the Chief of Staff to hold himself
in readiness to discuss estimates with Mr Haughey on his
release from hospital.

e. A military study of the directive was undertaken and the
Chief of Staff sought a meeting with the Minister on 13 Feb
1970 to seek clarification as follows..."

"(1) The Military assume that incursions would only be mounted in circumstances where there would be a complete break-down of law and order in N. Ireland and where the Security Forces were unable or unwilling to protect the Minority

The Minister confirmed that such a situation was what was envisaged

(2) The Military assume that the sole object of incursions would be the protection of the lives and property of the majority

The Minister confirmed that such an arrangement was envisaged

(3) The military requested information regarding the Government's intention to make diplomatic representations before incursions

The Minister did not consider that such representations would be made

(4) The Chief of Staff queried if the Government intended in the circumstances of incursions,
(a) to declare a state of emergency
(b) to introduce the National Security Bill
(c) to introduce a form of compulsory military service

The Minister thought that the Government would declare a state of emergency

(5) In view of the absolute necessity to ensure secrecy in contingency planning, the Chief of Staff enquired how much information had been given to the Northern delegations of the Government's intensions

The Minister indicated that the Northern delegations had not been informed of the directive to the Defence Forces

(6) In view of the critical shortage of armoured cars, can the Panhards be withdrawn from Cyprus

The Government does not approve of their withdrawal

(7) In view of critical shortages of AFV, will the Government approve a Purchase mission to the United States

A Council of Defence meeting would be necessary to determine priorities

(8) In view of the nature of the directive can the financial restrictions on the employment of FCA be eased to provide for greater FCA participation and the consequent release of PDF personnel for urgently needed training?

This would have to be examined in detail

(9) Can the overall limitation on the permitted strength of the PDF be lifted in view of the directive?

Estimates provide for 7500 but Minister for Finance is likely to sanction an increase

(10) Can the present strength   Approved
on border posts be reduced in
view of the heavy commitments
on vital installations and
the need to release men for
training?

(11) Has the Secretary of the   Yes
Department been informed of
the nature of the directive?

(12) With regard to the arms,   The Minister has no
ammunition and respirators,   idea but agreed that
(a) How many are to be made   stockpiles were to be
available?   held in Dublin and
(b) To whom and in what   Athlone
circumstances are they to be
handed over?

"f. On 18 Feb 1970, the following items were assembled in
Dublin and Athlone

Each	500	Rifles No 4
	200	Gustav MGs [machine guns]
	3000	Respirators
	80,000	rounds 303 amn
	99,000	rounds 9 mm. amn.

"g. On 2 April 1970 Minister rang Chief of Staff from NAAS.
He indicated that he had received information from
Mr Blaney that attacks on the minority were planned
and the British security forces would be withdrawn and
accordingly would not afford protection for the minority.
The Minister felt that material stored in Dublin should be
moved forward.

h. On the night of 2 April 1970, the following items were stored in DUNDALK military barracks. 500 rifles, 80,000 rounds ammunition and 3000 respirators.

i. Military intelligence subsequently ascertained that the information given to the Minister regarding reported attacks on the Minority and the withdrawal of British security forces were without foundation.

j. On 4 Apr 350 rifles were returned to stores in Dublin because of storage problems in Dundalk.

k. Meanwhile the Chief of Staff had formed a small selected planning Board to prepare contingency plans to implement the Government's directive.

Following intelligence reports, of the possibility of a raid by a subversive organisation on Dundalk military barracks, the balance of 150 rifles and 80,000 rounds of ammunition stored in Dundalk were returned to stores in Dublin on Fri 1 May 1970."

Meeting with an Taoiseach   RN P.O.
9 June 1970   CCA
16 June

Present
An Taoiseach
Aire Cosanta [Minister for Defence]
Ceann Fóirne
Runai Roinn Cosanta [Secretary, Department of Defence]

1. An Taoiseach indicated his pleasure at the meeting with an Ceann Fóirne and expressed his regret that pressing business had prevented his having a meeting sooner.

Defence Policy

2. An Ceann Fóirne referred to the lack of clear-cut Government policy on defence and indicated the urgency of this matter apart altogether from the situation in the North of Ireland. At this stage however he was not prepared to go into detail. He felt that he should fully brief the new Minister as a first step on the question of defence policy generally.

3. In the various studies made of the defence situation, an Ceann Fóirne emphasised that Northern Ireland was examined in the following contexts
   a. as an area which could provide the Western Bloc with a secure land base from which hostile operations could be mounted against the State
   b. as an area from which assistance could be expected in the event of an Eastern Bloc invasion of the State.

4. In view of the reiteration of Government policy from time to time regarding the aim of reunification of the national territory by peaceful means, no military studies had been undertaken nor had plans been prepared even on a contingency basis for military action in Northern Ireland prior to August 1969.

Northern Ireland

5. The Taoiseach recounted the events of last August in which the following military deployment took place, and enquired if the Chief of Staff was satisfied with and clear on the tasks set. The Chief of Staff replied that he was
   a. Field Hospitals were set up in Rockhill, Fort Dunree, Dundalk, Castleblaney and Cavan.
   b. Refugee centres were set up in Gormanstown, Finner Camp and Kildare.
   c. Casualty collection points were set-up forward of the field hospitals and mobile patrols operated between the casualty collection posts and the field hospitals and refugee centres.
   d. About 1000 troops were deployed in Dundalk, Gormanstown, Castleblaney, Cavan, Mullingar, Longford, Finner Camp, Rockhill and Fort Dunree to protect and support the field hospitals, the refugee centres and the casualty collection posts.

6. The Taoiseach enquired if the field hospitals were open still. An Ceann Fóirne replied that the equipment and beds were in location but that the personnel had been withdrawn. They could however be reactivated at very short notice.

7. In further reply to the Taoiseach, an Ceann Fóirne indicated that an overall reduction in the strength of troops in border posts had been effected and he outlined the present approximate strength in each.

8. Direction of 6 Feb 1970
   a. In reference to the direction of 6 Feb 70, which was made known to an Ceann Fóirne by the Minister of Defence (Mr James Gibbons) and which required the Army to be trained and prepared to make incursions into Northern Ireland,

the Chief of Staff had assumed that these incursions would be made in circumstances in which there would be a complete break-down in law and order in which the lives of the minority would be in grave danger and in which the Security Forces in Northern Ireland would be unable or unwilling to protect the minority.

b. The Taoiseach confirmed that the circumstances envisaged by the Government were those assumed by the Chief of Staff.

c. Regarding the use of the term "incursion" the Chief of Staff explained that this term had been used in conveying the Government directive and that it conveyed to him that cross border activity was not intended as an invasion but rather as a short temporary stay to carry out a mercy mission and return.

d. Further to the discussion at c above the Chief of Staff indicated that a military study had been compiled including an incursion to Newry. This Northern town, which although considered to be close to the border is considered as the extreme limit of incursion capability at present strength and status of supply. The study indicated that some 800 troops would be necessary for such an operation, that the stay might well have to be limited to 24 hours at most, and that even then considerable casualties could be anticipated.

9. The Taoiseach re-affirmed that it was the policy of the Government that force would NOT [emphasis in original] be used as a means to re-integrate the national territory. He recounted the various means used by the Minister for External Affairs to bring the matter before the United Nations Organisation. While Dr. Hillery had advocated the presence of a United Nations Peace Keeping Force which would include Irish troops, the Government had not been very hopeful that such a course would be acceptable to the British Government.

10. The Taoiseach himself had given considerable thought to the possibility that Irish troops could work in conjunction with British troops in the event that a situation would arise in the future in which the British troops would be unable to defend the minority. In reply to a question by the Chief of Staff the Taoiseach indicated that should incursions into the North be required, they would not be preceded by political or diplomatic representations.

11 Capabilities of the Defence Forces
   a. The Chief of Staff referred to the very limited capabilities of the Defence Forces in view of critical deficiencies in manpower and equipment and he informed the Taoiseach of the military proposals to incorporate the FCA into a "First Step" organisation which would provide some 15,000 personnel, which in the military view was the minimum force necessary if incursions were to be undertaken.
   b. The Taoiseach was aware of meetings which took place between the General Staff and Mr Gibbons and Mr Haughey. He was also aware that further meetings had been planned. He was more familiar with the situation with regard to the deficiencies in equipment than he was with the state of deficiencies in personnel. He was of course aware that the standard of training was low. He stated that he would arrange to have the new Minister for Finance meet the Minister for Defence and the Chief of Staff on the question of personnel and equipment at an early date.

SECRET"

[NA MI 5 p2–8.]

Appendix 3

Exchanges on the 6 February directive between Garret FitzGerald TD and Colonel Michael Hefferon, at the Committee of Public Accounts inquiry, 17 February 1971, paragraphs 8142–56 (edited):

FitzGerald: On the directive, could you tell us precisely what your view of it is, because I think you referred to it on two occasions (in previous evidence)....

Hefferon: Yes, I have.

FitzGerald: Volume 7, page 313, 4,164, and the other reference is... 4,360 (quoting):

—*You felt that he was working under ministerial direction, did you? In reference to Captain Kelly?*

—*I felt, certainly after the 6th of February, that the possibility might arise, that this directive was a very plain and very responsible statement of policy by the government, as I understood it, conveyed to the Chief of Staff at the time, that the army would make preparations for incursions into Northern Ireland and I told the Minister for Defence and put him in the picture about it at this time and I certainly did not feel at that time that I should do anything to stop him, to stop Captain Kelly from—*

Then you were interrupted at that point.

In other words it could have been part of government policy to allow this activity?

—*It could have been government policy to prepare for the contingency which indeed in the climate of the time seemed to be going that way....*

FitzGerald: Would you like to state... in what way you felt in replying to these two questions that it was relevant to the matter being discussed?... You quoted from it in court?

Hefferon: Yes.

FitzGerald: Yes. I think what you said in court was that the directive was subject to a government decision to implement it and you agreed that no decision had been made?

Hefferon: Yes.

FitzGerald: 8152. You may not be able to comment, but that would suggest to me that it has no relevance to what we are discussing, although you did bring it in on two occasions?

Hefferon: Yes, but I think if you read the directive you will see that it has relevance.

FitzGerald: 8153. Even though you told the court that the directive was subject to a government decision to implement it and that no such decision had been made?

Hefferon: Yes, even so.

FitzGerald: 8154. Could you suggest how a directive whose implementation had not been decided could be relevant to action taken?

Hefferon: Well, as a directive, naturally, it was of such a nature that it would only be implemented in the case of some grave situation developing on the border. Plans had to be made to cater for this.

FitzGerald: 8155. Do you include, under plans, action involving the purchase of arms, because I would call that implementation rather than planning?

Hefferon: You mean, did the directive give direct authority for the importation of arms?

FitzGerald: 8156. Yes?

Hefferon: No, it didn't.

Endnotes

Introduction (pages 1–16)

[1] Diarmaid Ferriter, *The Transformation of Ireland, 1900–2000* (Dublin, 2004), p. 622.

[2] T. P. O'Mahony, *Jack Lynch – A Biography* (Dublin, 1991), pp. 10–14.

[3] Speech by Cosgrave's front-bench colleague, Richie Ryan TD (Fine Gael), *Dáil Debates*, 7 May 1970, col. 668, in which he revealed that Gibbons's name was on Cosgrave's list; see also James Kelly, *The Thimble Riggers* (Dublin, 1999), p. 62, in which Kelly reported a confirmation of this two years later by Garret FitzGerald, Cosgrave's successor as Fine Gael leader.

[4] Kelly, *The Thimble Riggers*, p. 63; Kelly here reproduced a document received by him also from an anonymous source in late 1970 and signed simply 'a friend', which purported to be a copy of the original note Cosgrave had received. It bore similar phraseology to that used by Cosgrave when reporting to the Dáil. The document, whose authenticity has never been challenged, listed both Gibbons and Hefferon as being involved in the gun-running.

[5] Speech by Liam Cosgrave (Fine Gael), *Dáil Debates*, 7 May 1970, col. 644–45.

[6] NAUK FCO 33/1207, Sir John Peck, British Ambassador to Ireland, report to Foreign and Commonwealth Office, 'Aftermath of the Arms Trial', 16 December 1970.

[7] Peter Berry, *Diaries*, *Magill* current affairs magazine, June 1980, p. 67, entry for 14 May 1970.

[8] Justin O'Brien, *The Arms Trial* (Dublin, 2000).

[9] Angela Clifford, *The Arms Conspiracy Trial Ireland 1970: The Prosecution of Charles Haughey, Captain Kelly and Others* (Belfast, 2009).

[10] Stephen Collins, *The Power Game: Fianna Fáil Since Lemass* (Dublin, 2000, 2nd ed., 2001); Bruce Arnold, *Jack Lynch: Hero in Crisis* (Dublin, 2001); Dermot Keogh, *Jack Lynch: A Biography* (Cork, 2008).

[11] Arnold, *Jack Lynch: Hero*, p. 132.

[12] Keogh, *Lynch*, p. 286.
[13] Collins, *The Power Game*, p. 61.
[14] Clifford, *The Arms Conspiracy Trial*, p. 7.

Chapter 1: Aftermath of August 1969 (pages 17–33)

[1] Ronan Fanning, 'Playing it Cool: The Response of the British and Irish Governments to the Crisis in Northern Ireland, 1968–69', *Irish Studies in International Affairs*, Vol. 12 (2001), p. 85.

[2] T. P. Coogan, *The IRA* (London 1971, rev. ed., 1995), p. 369.

[3] NA 2000/5/12, Lynch TV address, 13 August 1969, also reprinted in O'Brien, *The Arms Trial*, pp. 42–43.

[4] James Callaghan, *A House Divided* (London, 1973), p. 39: 'we had to consider the possibility that within the next 24 hours we might face both civil war in the North and an invasion from the South'.

[5] J. J. Lee, *Ireland 1912–1985: Politics and Society* (Cambridge, 1989), pp. 429–30.

[6] See Michael Kennedy, *Division and Consensus – The Politics of Cross Border Relations in Ireland, 1925–1969* (Dublin, 2000), pp. 336–37, for an account of the successive cabinet initiatives of 13 August.

[7] NA 2000/5/12, Lynch TV address, 13 August 1969.

[8] Jack Lynch speech, *Dáil Debates*, 22 October 1969, col. 1406.

[9] Neil Blaney, 'Lawyers, Guns and Money', interview in *Hot Press* magazine, 14 June 1990.

[10] Kevin Boland, *We Won't Stand (Idly) By* (Dublin, 1972), p. 50.

[11] *Evening Press*, 14 August 1969, quoted by P. O'Donnell TD (FG), *Dáil Debates*, 22 October 1969, col. 1470. See also Kennedy, *Division and Consensus*, p. 342.

[12] NA 2000/5/12, Government Information Bureau statement, 14 August 1969.

[13] Padraig Faulkner, *As I Saw It: Reviewing Over 30 Years of Fianna Fáil and Irish Politics* (Dublin, 2005), p. 90; see also Arnold, *Lynch: Hero in Crisis* (Dublin, 2001), p. 106.

[14] MA S P70, Deployment to the Border, OO 8/69, 14 August 1969.

[15] MA S 650, Supply Requirements, Memo from the Quartermaster General to the Secretary, Department of Defence, 19 August 1969.

[16] NA 2000/5/12, memorandum on Northern Ireland policy from Hugh McCann, Secretary, Department of External Affairs, 19 November 1969.

[17] NAUK FCO 33/1200, Gilchrist report, 'Republic of Ireland: Annual Review for 1969', 23 January 1970.

[18] Angela Clifford, *Military Aspects of Ireland's Arms Crisis of 1969–70* (Belfast, 2006), p. 22; Clifford is unique in the literature on the Arms Crisis in her detailed analysis of the military records.

[19] Ibid., p. 33.

[20] Donnacha Ó Beacháin, *Destiny of the Soldiers: Fianna Fáil, Irish Republicanism and the IRA, 1926–1973* (Dublin, 2010), p. 290.

[21] Blaney interview, 'Lawyers, Guns and Money'.

[22] Dick Walsh, *The Party: Inside Fianna Fáil* (Dublin, 1986), p. 99, also cited by Kennedy, *Division and Consensus*, p. 342.

[23] Kennedy, *Division and Consensus*, p. 342; this view that the government decided at this time that a further deterioration in the situation could require Irish troops to be sent over the border was shared by Noel Whelan, *Fianna Fáil – A Biography of the Party* (Dublin, 2011), p. 159.

[24] It was a policy that later received formal expression from the government, through the 6 February 1970 directive to the Defence Forces – see Chapter 5, pp. 101–11.

[25] Mary Daly, *Sixties Ireland: Reshaping the Economy, State and Society 1959–1973* (Cambridge, 2016), p. 343.

[26] NAUK FCO 33/1200, Gilchrist to Foreign and Commonwealth Office, 'Republic of Ireland: Annual Review for 1969', 23 January 1970.

[27] Blaney interview, 'Lawyers, Guns and Money'.

[28] Lynch speech, *Dáil Debates*, 23 October 1969, col. 1587.

[29] NA 2001/6/513, minutes of Hillery's meeting in London with George Thomson, 20 February 1970.

[30] John Walsh, *Patrick Hillery: The Official Biography* (Dublin, 2008), p. 191.

[31] Gibbons's cross-examination by Niall McCarthy SC (for Haughey) at the first arms trial, *Irish Times*, 26 September 1970.

[32] NA Tsch 2/2/29, minutes of cabinet meetings, August 1969. There has been persistent misreporting of the brief and functions of this sub-committee; it was set up to maintain 'permanent liaison with opinion in the Six Counties'.

[33] See Daly, *Sixties Ireland*, p. 351, where she attributes the Arms Crisis in large part to 'Lynch's lack of control over his cabinet, and at least a tacit willingness to turn a blind eye to defiant Ministers'.

[34] Arnold, *Lynch: Hero*, p. 160: 'by the end of 1970 Lynch... surveyed, as Hercules might, the desolation left after his own victories'.

[35] Martin Mansergh, *The Legacy of History* (Cork, 2003), p. 397.

[36] See Chapter 3, pp. 68–73, and Chapter 9, pp. 161–2.

[37] Kennedy, *Division and Consensus*, p. 331.

[38] NA 2000/6/658, Hillery meeting at Foreign and Commonwealth Office London with Lord Chalfont and Lord Stoneham, 15 August 1969.

[39] See Fanning, 'Playing it Cool', pp. 57–85.

[40] In this regard, see NAUK FCO 33/758, Sir Edward Peck (Foreign and Commonwealth Office) to Gilchrist, UK Irish Ambassador, 5 September 1969; FCO 33/759, Gilchrist to Foreign and Commonwealth Office,

25 October 1969; and FCO 33/1205, Peck to Foreign and Commonwealth Office, 15 May 1970.

41 See for example a speaking note prepared in the Foreign and Commonwealth Office in London for the Foreign Secretary on 7 May 1970, considering whether London could make some helpful gesture to assist Lynch in his cabinet crisis: this could be done only subject to 'the over-riding consideration that Chichester Clark's position must not be weakened'.

42 NAUK FCO 33/759, Gilchrist to Foreign and Commonwealth Office, 23 October 1970.

43 NAUK FCO 33/759, Gilchrist Report to Foreign and Commonwealth Office, 'Lynch's Dilemma', 3 October 1969.

44 NAUK FCO 33/1200, Gilchrist's Annual Review for 1969, 23 January 1970.

45 NAUK FCO 33/759, Gilchrist's report to the Foreign and Commonwealth Office, 3 October 1969.

Chapter 2: Captain Kelly: Maverick Officer? (pages 34–51)

1 Eunan O'Halpin, 'A Greek Authoritarian Phase? The Irish Army and the Irish Crisis, 1969/70', *Irish Political Studies*, Vol. 23, No. 4 (December 2008), p. 477. See also Arnold, *Lynch: Hero*, p. 111; Keogh, *Lynch*, p. 233.

2 Tom MacIntyre, *Through the Bridewell Gate: A Diary of the Dublin Arms Trial* (London, 1971), p. 143.

3 United Nations Truce Supervision Organisation in Palestine (UNTSOP) report by Lieutenant General Odd Bull, Chief of Staff, August 1965, reproduced in James Kelly, *Orders for the Captain?* (Dublin, 1971), p. 246.

4 MacIntyre, *Through the Bridewell Gate*, p. 18.

5 See Chapter 16, pp. 317, 320–1.

6 Hefferon's evidence to Justin Keating TD (Labour), at the Committee of Public Accounts inquiry, par. 8448, 18 February 1971.

7 Kelly, *Orders*, p. 8.

8 Kelly, *Orders*, p. 10.

9 NA Tsch2/2/29, cabinet minutes for 16 August 1969.

10 Ibid., p. 11.

11 Boland, *We Won't Stand (Idly) By*, p. 74; also Boland, *Up Dev* (Rathcoole, 1977), p. 71; Haughey's evidence to Niall McCarthy SC (for Haughey) at the second arms trial, 19 October 1970 (trial transcript for that particular day held in Hefferon Papers in Military Archive); see also interview by the author with Captain Kelly, April 2001, transcript p. 9 (in the author's possession). Gibbons denied knowing anything of Kelly before early 1970.

[12] Haughey's evidence to McCarthy SC at the second arms trial, *Irish Times*, 20 October 1970.

[13] Kelly, *The Thimble Riggers*, p. 18.

[14] Hefferon gave a detailed account at the Committee of Public Accounts inquiry of how Kelly was acting with his full authority at Bailieboro, noting that he and Kelly went to Haughey's home in Kinsealy for discussions before the meeting. Kelly made it clear both at the arms trials and at the Committee of Public Accounts inquiry that he kept Blaney fully informed, meeting him regularly during the autumn of 1969.

[15] Arnold, *Lynch: Hero*, p. 119.

[16] Kelly, *The Thimble Riggers*, p. 20.

[17] MA SCS 29, containing Interim Report of the Planning Board on Northern Ireland Operations, 27 Mean Fómhair, 1969, plus Recommendations of Planning Board, 13/10/69.

[18] MA SCS 29, Interim Report, p. 5, and Recommendations of Planning Board.

[19] MA SCS 29, Interim Report, pars. 18–19.

[20] MA SCS 29, Recommendations, p. 3.

[21] Clifford, *Military Aspects*, p. 45.

[22] MA, Hefferon Papers, typed notes, undated and unsigned, but probably put together in preparation for his appearance at the Committee of Public Accounts hearings in 1971.

[23] Hefferon commented on the reports in typed unsigned notes contained in the Hefferon Papers, MA.

[24] NA 3–58367, Minutes of the Council of Defence, 13 October 1969, cited in Angela Clifford, *Military Aspects*, pp. 57–59. The Council, according to Clifford, was set up under Section 11 of the 1954 Defence Act, and its purpose was 'to aid and counsel' the minister. Clifford felt its meetings 'must have been a rare occurrence', because the files included a note setting out the Council's legal status. A copy of these minutes is in the author's possession; precise Military Archive reference is not currently confirmed. The Recommendations of Planning Board states the reports were prepared 'to meet the needs of the General Staff for the Council of Defence meeting to be held at 1500 hours on 15/10/69'.

[25] See, in particular, MA SCS 29, Military Preparedness, 27/2/1970, prepared by the Chief of Staff for the Minister for Defence in February 1970, and heavily stressing the army's lack of preparation.

[26] Captain Kelly's cross-examination by Seamus McKenna SC (for the State) at the second arms trial, 15 October 1970, reported in *Irish Times*, 16 October 1970, also in Clifford, *The Arms Conspiracy Trial*, pp. 298–99.

[27] Kelly, *The Thimble Riggers*, pp. 18–19; this contains a photocopy of his

short report to Colonel Hefferon, dated 6 October 1969 and referring to the 'acquisition of arms for defensive purposes'.

[28] Peter Taylor, *States of Terror* (London, 1993), p. 221.

[29] Ibid.

[30] See interview with an unnamed representative of Provisional Army Council (identified as MacStiofáin by R. W. White in his 2006 biography, *Ruairí Ó Brádaigh: The Life and Politics of an Irish Revolutionary* (Bloomington, Indiana, 2006), in *This Week* magazine, August 1970.

[31] Patrick Bishop and Eamonn Mallie, *The Provisional IRA* (London, 1987), pp. 94–95.

[32] According to White's biography, *Ó Brádaigh*, p. 151, five of the seven-man Provisional Army Council set up in December 1969, including its Chief of Staff, were from south of the border, with only Joe Cahill and Leo Martin representing the North.

[33] Seán MacStiofáin, *Memoirs of a Revolutionary* (Salisbury, 1975), p. 140.

[34] O'Brien, *The Arms Trial*, p. 94.

[35] James Downey, *In My Own Time: Inside Irish Politics and Society* (Dublin, 2009), p. 124; Martin Dillon in *The Dirty War* (London, 1990), p. 24, said of the Provisionals' plans for the guns: 'There is little doubt that they would have endured no interference on the part of Captain Kelly'; Vincent Browne felt Captain Kelly 'maintained a naïve impression of all this', 'The Arms Crisis, 1970', *Magill* magazine, May 1980, p. 46.

[36] Hefferon's evidence to McKenna SC (for the State) at the second arms trial, 13–14 October 1970, reported in *Irish Times*, 14–15 October 1970; see also the sparkling account in Tom MacIntyre's *Through the Bridewell Gate*, pp. 119–23.

[37] Captain Kelly's evidence at the Committee of Public Accounts inquiry, 2 February 1971, par. 4579.

[38] See Seán Cronin, *Irish Nationalism: A History of its Roots and Ideology* (Dublin, 1980), p. 194: 'In times of tension in Northern Ireland, Belfast is the focus of Catholic fears.'

[39] Paddy Doherty, *Paddy Bogside* (Cork, 2001), p. 225; Doherty describes how Billy Kelly made an emotional demand directly to Jack Lynch in February 1970, as outlined in Chapter 9, p. 171.

[40] Chief Superintendent John Fleming, head of the Special Branch, evidence to the Committee of Public Accounts inquiry, 9 February 1971, par. 5662, *et seq.*

[41] See in particular Blaney's interview with *Hot Press* magazine, June 1990, and with English reporter Peter Taylor in *States of Terror*, pp. 239, 242; see also Captain Kelly's testimony at the two arms trials in September–October 1970 and at the Committee of Public Accounts inquiry in 1971, where he made clear throughout that he was in close and constant touch with Neil Blaney in the autumn of 1969.

[42] *Fianna Fáil and the IRA*, Official IRA pamphlet, published anonymously in the early 1970s, p. 19.

[43] O'Brien, *The Arms Trial*, pp. 142, 254.

[44] Assistant Garda Commissioner Pat Malone's evidence to Justin Keating TD (Labour) at the closed-door Committee of Public Accounts hearings, 30 March 1971.

[45] Hefferon's evidence at the Committee of Public Accounts inquiry, 17 February 1971, par. 8005.

[46] NA 2000/36/3, Memorandum for Government, 14 July 1969, p. 2.

[47] Peter Berry *Diaries*, entry for 2 July 1969.

[48] NA 2000/36/3, Memorandum for Government, 14 July 1969, p. 2.

[49] O'Brien, *The Arms Trial*, p. 238, fn. 30, noted Berry's advice on splitting the IRA, but curiously treated it only in a short footnote. Unusually, Berry, although later scandalized by reports of dealings between army officers and government ministers with the IRA, made no apparent connection between the policy he had himself advocated and that being employed shortly afterwards by Military Intelligence.

Chapter 3: Haughey–Blaney: Where's the Plot? (pages 52–73)

[1] Blaney and Haughey had signalled their leadership ambitions clearly in 1966 when Lemass stood down: see John Horgan, *Seán Lemass: The Enigmatic Patriot* (Dublin, 1997), pp. 332–39.

[2] Kennedy, *Division and Consensus*, p. 331.

[3] NAUK FCO 33/1205, Peck to Foreign and Commonwealth Office, 6 May 1970.

[4] NA 2001/6/514, Department of External Affairs file of newspapers coverage, including a copy of the *Financial Times* of 7 May 1970.

[5] Desmond O'Malley, *Conduct Unbecoming* (Dublin, 2014), pp. 67, 68.

[6] Lee, *Politics and Society*, p. 458.

[7] 'Fianna Fáil Plots Takeover of Civil Rights', *United Irishman*, November 1969, p. 2.

[8] In this regard, see Arnold, *Lynch: Hero*, p. 21; Michael Mills, *Hurler on the Ditch: Inside Politics and Society* (Dublin, 2005), p. 81; and Downey, *In My Own Time*, p. 124.

[9] FitzGerald to Hefferon, at the Committee of Public Accounts inquiry, 3 March 1971, par. 9758.

[10] *The Party*, pp. 102–03.

[11] Eunan O'Halpin, 'Greek Authoritarian Phase? p. 477. O'Halpin described the Arms Crisis as 'a conspiracy led by two ambitious Ministers', p. 475.

[12] This phrase was used by Patrick Hillery to his biographer John Walsh in *Hillery*, p. 214; Dermot Keogh saw Blaney leading what he called

a 'shadow, parallel government', *Lynch*, p. 232; Stephen Collins said Haughey was 'running what looked like an alternative Government from his home' in autumn 1969, *The Power Game*, p. 64.

[13] O'Brien worked as a television producer in Belfast and Dublin, Collins as a Dublin political correspondent, and Arnold as a political columnist, also in Dublin. Keogh worked as a sub-editor in Irish national newspapers before eventually becoming an eminent Professor of Irish History at University College Cork.

[14] Arnold, *Lynch: Hero,* p. 159.

[15] The books in question are Dwyer's *Charlie – The Political Biography of C. J. Haughey* (Dublin, 1987) and also *Lynch–Nice Fellow: A Biography of Jack Lynch* (Cork, 2001); John Walsh's *Hillery*; and Patrick Maume's profiles of Haughey and of Blaney in *Dictionary of Irish Biography* (Cambridge, 2009).

[16] Diarmaid Ferriter, *Ambiguous Republic – Ireland in the 1970s* (London, 2012), p. 144; Vincent Browne, 'Arms Trial Re-appraisal', *Magill* magazine, July 1980, pp. 23–25.

[17] Clifford, *The Arms Conspiracy Trial*, p. 10.

[18] Conor Lenihan, *Haughey, Prince of Power* (Dublin, 2015), p. 78.

[19] Ibid., p. 72.

[20] Ó Beacháin, *Destiny of the Soldiers*, p. 294.

[21] NA 2001/8/7, Peter Berry's Notes for the Taoiseach, 8 June 1970, par. xiii.

[22] Stephen Kelly, *A Failed Political Entity Charles Haughey and the Northern Ireland Question, 1945–1992*, (Dublin, 2016), p. 61.

[23] See John Bowman, *De Valera and the Ulster Question 1917–1973* (Oxford, 1982), pp. 103–04 for a consideration of de Valera's speeches in North America in 1927 and 1930; Bowman said de Valera, while bellicose on Northern Ireland, distinguished between a moral justification for force – 'an argument he approved' – and a rejection of force on the grounds that it would be counter-productive. In New York on 22 March 1930, de Valera stated that British troops were still in the North 'because at the present time we are not able to put them out'. In an interview with the *News Chronicle* on 17 February 1932 (reported by Bowman on p. 112), de Valera used the same phrase employed by Haughey in 1968, that the use of force was 'out of the question'.

[24] UCDA Whitaker Papers, p. 175/25.

[25] See in regard to Fianna Fáil policy at this time on the use of force in the North, Fanning, 'Playing it Cool', p. 70. Fanning cites the minutes of a meeting of the Fianna Fáil Parliamentary Party on 15 January 1957, which Patrick Hillery viewed as having laid down the parameters of party policy on the use of force, still applicable in 1969. The minutes said the party view was that 'the employment of force at any time in the foreseeable future would be undesirable and likely to be futile'.

[26] UCDA P 176/280, Fianna Fáil Papers, letter of C. J. Haughey to Thomas

Mullins, 15 January 1955, also reported in Stephen Kelly, *Fianna Fáil, Partition and Northern Ireland 1926–1971* (Dublin, 2013), pp. 167–76.

[27] Doherty, *Paddy Bogside*, p. 222.

[28] These thoughts are contained in an undated article by Haughey, 'Call for UN Intervention in the North', apparently prepared for *This Week* magazine sometime in 1970/71, and included in *The Spirit of the Nation – The Speeches and Statements of Charles J. Haughey, 1957–1986*, ed. Martin Mansergh (Cork and Dublin, 1986), pp. 146–47.

[29] Blaney interview, 'Lawyers, Guns and Money'.

[30] Dwyer, *Nice Fellow*, p. 178. For differing accounts of how the Lynch cabinet divided on 13 August, see Arnold, *Lynch: Hero*, p. 92; Collins, *The Power Game*, p. 48; Boland, *Up Dev*, p. 42; and Walsh, *Hillery*, p. 191.

[31] Lynch TV address to the nation, 13 August 1969, reproduced in O'Brien, *The Arms Trial*, pp. 42–43.

[32] Walsh, *Hillery*, p. 204.

[33] Dwyer, *Haughey's: 40 Years of Controversy* (Cork, 2005), p. 48.

[34] Downey, *In My Own Time*, p. 117.

[35] Kelly, *Fianna Fáil and Partition*, p. 302.

[36] Lynch claimed that 'arms imported for defensive purposes could easily, in the tense situation that exists in the North, be used for offensive purposes…', reported in *Irish Times*, 2 June 1970, and quoted in Keogh, *Lynch*, p. 265.

[37] Conor Cruise O'Brien, *States of Ireland* (London, 1972), p. 200.

[38] Arnold, *Lynch: Hero*, p. 119; Eunan O'Halpin, *Defending Ireland: The Irish State and its Enemies since 1922* (Oxford, 1999), felt that by October 1969 the justification for guns 'had long gone', as public order had been restored, pp. 309–10.

[39] NA 2001/6/513, A Note for the Taoiseach, a two-page Department of External Affairs addendum to memorandum on Policy in Relation to Northern Ireland.

[40] NA 2001/6/513, Meeting between Minister for External Affairs and the Chancellor of the Duchy of Lancaster at Foreign and Commonwealth Office, 20 February 1970.

[41] NA 2001/6/513, memo from Seán Ronan, assistant Secretary, Department of External Affairs, of his meeting with Ivan Cooper MP, 6 March 1970.

[42] Hillery Papers, UCDA P 205/36, minutes of meeting at Foreign and Commonwealth Office in London, 23 March 1970.

[43] Hillery Papers, UCDA P 205/36, confidential internal memo from Gallagher, dated 20 April 1970.

[44] Hillery Papers, UCDA P 205/36, memo from Ambassador O'Sullivan to Department of External Affairs, 20 April 1970.

[45] Hillery Papers, UCDA P 205/36, Minutes of meeting at the Foreign and Commonwealth Office in London between Ambassador O'Sullivan

and Home Office and Foreign Office officials Burroughs, Peck, Langdon and White, 27 April 1970.

[46] Ronan Fanning, *Independent Ireland* (Dublin, 1983), p. 209.

[47] Ibid., p. 33.

[48] P. M. Sachs, in *The Donegal Mafia: An Irish Political Machine* (New Haven and London, 1976), challenged the conventional view of Blaney as 'blunt-spoken' when he described his speeches as 'masterpieces of ambiguity', p. 201.

[49] NA 2000/6/662, speech by Neil Blaney at the Golden Grill restaurant, Letterkenny, 8 December 1969.

[50] Boland, *We Won't Stand (Idly) By*, p. 61; Boland was in attendance in Letterkenny on the night Blaney delivered his speech, and felt it was intended 'to flush the Taoiseach into the open'.

[51] Collins, *The Power Game*, p. 68.

[52] NA 2000/6/662, statement from Government Information Bureau, 9 December 1969.

[53] Blaney speech, *Dáil Debates*, 8 May 1970, col. 865.

[54] Neil Blaney, 'My Past – My Future', interview with Liam MacGabhann, *This Week*, August 1970.

[55] Blaney speech, *Dáil Debates*, 4 November 1970, col. 668.

[56] Boland, *Up Dev*, p. 31. Further analysis of Blaney's Letterkenny speech is contained in Chapter 9, pp. 157–159.

[57] Taylor, *States of Terror*, p. 214.

[58] Ó Beacháin, *Destiny of the Soldiers*, p. 287, cited James Downey's observation, *In My Own Time*, p. 36, that rather than having any military purpose, calls for the army to cross the border were intended to 'force' a UN intervention.

[59] Bruce Arnold, *Haughey – His Life and Unlucky Deeds* (London, 1993), pp. 94–98.

[60] Arnold, *Lynch: Hero*, pp. 142–3.

[61] Thomas Hennessey, *Northern Ireland: The Origins of the Troubles* (Dublin, 2005), p. 343.

[62] Ó Beacháin, *Destiny of the Soldiers*, p. 298.

[63] Kelly, *Fianna Fáil and Partition*, p. 300.

Chapter 4: Haughey: Treacherous Schemer? (pages 74–94)

[1] Arnold, *Haughey*, p. 78.

[2] Kennedy, *Division and Consensus*, p. 331.

[3] Justin O'Brien, *The Modern Prince: Charles J. Haughey and the Quest for Power* (Dublin, 2002), p. 22.

[4] Kelly, *A Failed Political Entity*, p. 21.

[5] NAUK FCO 33/759, Gilchrist telegram to Foreign Office, 4 October 1969.

[6] NAUK FCO 33/758, Gilchrist's account (taken from O'Donovan personally) of what Lynch had said on 29 August was relayed to the Foreign and Commonwealth Office in London, 1 September 1969.

[7] O'Brien, *The Arms Trial*, pp. 73–74; Collins, *The Power Game*, p. 64. A more realistic view of the Gilchrist meeting was taken by Haughey's policy adviser Martin Mansergh in a February 2000 address to the UCC Historical Society, reprinted in Mansergh, *The Legacy of History*, p. 401.

[8] Dwyer, *Nice Fellow*, p. 204.

[9] Evidence of Seamus Brady at the Committee of Public Accounts inquiry, 16 February 1971, par. 7624.

[10] Evidence of Captain Kelly to the Committee of Public Accounts inquiry, 3 February 1971, par. 4754.

[11] *Final Report of the Committee of Public Accounts Inquiry*, July 1972, par. 77.

[12] NA 2001/61/1, Berry Explanatory Note, Part I, par. IX, p. 3.

[13] NA 2001/8/7, Berry letter to Lynch, Notes for the Taoiseach, dated 8 June 1970.

[14] NA 2001/61/1, copy of Berry's witness statement, with handwritten annotation.

[15] NA 2001/61/1, Berry's memo for the advice of the arms trial prosecution, Explanatory Note, in which Ryan was replaced in the deal by Goulding, and the date moved back to 19 August.

[16] NA 2001/61/1, Berry Explanatory Note, Part I, par. IX, p. 3.

[17] Seamus Brady, *Arms and the Men* (Dublin, 1971), p. 37.

[18] *Fianna Fáil and the IRA*, Official IRA pamphlet, p. 19.

[19] Ibid. p. 24. Padraig 'Jock' Haughey was a quantity surveyor who ended up as a taxi driver, and according to his friend John Kelly, one of the arms trial defendants, 'he never leaned on his brother; he made his own way in life'. Jock Haughey featured at this time in several Special Branch reports reaching Berry; discussions with IRA members brought him to Garda attention, and he clearly was quite active in seeking to raise funds for Northern republicans. John Kelly described how Jock Haughey delivered two boxes of weapons, comprising some twenty to fifty short arms, to Cathal Goulding personally in the autumn of 1969. John Kelly's interview with Liam Clarke, dated August 2005, has been posted online on the website *From the Blanket*, January 2008.

[20] NA 2001/61/1, Berry Explanatory Note, Part II, par. 4, p. 2; elsewhere Henry Patterson, in *Ireland's Violent Frontier* (London, 2013), p. 21, claimed incorrectly that Haughey admitted meeting Goulding.

[21] Berry, *Diaries*, entry for 19 August 1969, p. 51.

[22] Chief Superintendent John Fleming's evidence to the Committee of

Public Accounts inquiry, 9 February 1971, par. 5662; see also O'Halpin, *Defending Ireland*, p. 310.

[23] *Fianna Fáil and the IRA*, Official IRA pamphlet, p. 24.

[24] NA 2001/8/7, Berry memorandum to the Taoiseach, Notes for the Taoiseach, 8 June 1970.

[25] Terms of the cabinet decision were cited in the *Final Report of the Committee of Public Accounts Inquiry*, Part III, par. 20.

[26] British Ambassador Peck advised his colleagues in the Foreign and Commonwealth Office in London in December 1970 that the inquiry was likely to be a re-run of the arms trials – NAUK FCO 33/1207, 17 December 1970.

[27] *Final Report of the Committee of Public Accounts Inquiry*, July 1972.

[28] See Captain Kelly's evidence at the Committee of Public Accounts inquiry, 2 February 1971, par. 4470, and 3 February 1971, par. 5239; also Colonel Hefferon's evidence, 18 February 1971, par. 8480.

[29] NA 2003/4/546, file containing copy of the Supreme Court judgement in the case taken by Padraig 'Jock' Haughey against the State, March 1971.

[30] See Keogh's appraisal of the work of the Committee, *Lynch*, p. 279.

[31] As an example, Stephen Kelly, in his 2016 book on Haughey, *A Failed Political Entity*, p. 63, referred to how Haughey was responsible for ensuring that the £100,000 was 'used for its intended purpose', the purpose being taken as self-evident.

[32] Early in the Committee of Public Accounts inquiry, on 26 January 1971, the chairman, Patrick 'Surgeon' Hogan TD (FG), said that it had 'apparently' been the interpretation of the Dáil that money was voted 'for relief purposes and relief purposes only', but he failed to explain what evidence he was relying on; see Committee of Public Accounts inquiry proceedings, 26 January 1971, par. 3302. For further unqualified references to 'the intentions of the Dáil' or the 'purposes envisaged' by the Dáil or government, see 14 January 1971, par. 547; 26 January 1971, par. 3308; and 10 February 1971, pars. 6663, 7015 and 7206.

[33] The first reference to money 'misappropriated' in the *Final Report* came only in paragraph seventy-nine of a total of ninety paragraphs.

[34] *Final Report of the Committee of Public Accounts Inquiry*, 1972, par. 23, part 3.

[35] The term 'relief of distress' did not feature in the government statement allocating money to the Northerners on 16 August; it can be traced to a letter signed two months later by the three account holders, Messrs F,G and H, as they were known, to the Agent, Bank of Ireland Clones, Co., on 17 October 1969, instructing him to open an account to be designated 'The Belfast Committee for the Relief of Distressed'[sic] – NA 2003/26/1; see also submission of the Department of Finance, 9 December 1970, par. 12, p. 3, Appendix 9 of *Final Report of the Committee Inquiry*.

[36] *Final Report*, par. 20, part 3.
[37] Charles Murray's evidence at Committee of Public Accounts inquiry, 7 January 1971, par. 67.
[38] John Kelly's unsworn statement at the second arms trial, *Irish Times*, 15 October 1970.
[39] NA 2000/6/658, file note from Hugh McCann, Secretary, Department of External Affairs; also present with Devlin and Kennedy in Dublin was Paddy O'Hanlon MP.
[40] NA 2000/6/658, memo from Seán Ronan, 18 August 1969, Visit of N. Ireland MPs to Department.
[41] Devlin's plea at the GPO in August 1969, 'We want guns!', was reported in 'Resistance', published as part of *United Irishman*, 18 November 1969.
[42] Paddy Devlin, *Straight Left: An Autobiography* (Dublin, 1993), p. 109.
[43] Even Captain Kelly, one person who did admit such a connection, argued that the money used for guns from the Baggot Street bank account had been replaced through what he called a 'switching' device, by other funds in the possession of the Defence Committees – see Kelly's evidence to the chairman of the Committee of Public Accounts inquiry, 26 January 1971, pars. 3258–60. In this, Kelly was echoing an argument first advanced to Charles Murray by the three Northern account holders themselves on 28 November 1970 – Murray memorandum of 6 January 1971, NA 2003/26/1.
[44] Kelly, *The Thimble Riggers*, p. 12.
[45] See Browne's foreword in Kelly, *A Failed Political Entity*, p. xviii.
[46] Dwyer, *Charlie*, p. 76; Browne, 'Misconduct of the Arms Trial', *Magill*, July 1980, p. 23.
[47] See Michael Heney, 'Colonel Michael Hefferon and the 1970 Arms Crisis' (M.A. thesis, University College Dublin, 2014), pp. 57–58, for more on this.
[48] Haughey's evidence at the Committee of Public Accounts inquiry, 24 February 1971, par. 9095.
[49] Captain Kelly's cross-examination at the second arms trial by Seamus McKenna SC (for the State), *Irish Times*, 17 October 1970.
[50] Kelly, *The Thimble Riggers*, p. 258.
[51] Haughey's evidence to the Committee of Public Accounts chairman Patrick Hogan TD (FG), 2 March 1971, pars. 8970–73.
[52] Haughey's evidence to Justin Keating TD (Labour), Committee of Public Accounts inquiry, 2 March 1971, pars. 9020–22.
[53] Murray's evidence to the Committee of Public Accounts inquiry, 7 January 1971, par. 67.
[54] MacStiofáin, *Memoirs of a Revolutionary*, p. 141.
[55] Taylor, *States of Terror*, p. 234.
[56] Arnold, *Haughey*, p. 80.
[57] Browne, 'Misconduct of the Arms Trial', p. 23.

Chapter 5: Lynch's Hidden Policy (pages 95–111)

[1] Evidence of Colonel Hefferon at first arms trial, *Irish Times*, 29–30 September 1970.

[2] See, for example, Keogh, *Lynch*, pp. 206–09.

[3] Gibbons's evidence to Tom Finlay SC (for Captain Kelly) at the second arms trial, 9 October 1970.

[4] Hefferon's evidence to McKenna SC (for the State) at the first arms trial, 29 September 1970.

[5] Gibbons's statement, *Dáil Debates*, 8 May 1970, col. 841.

[6] Gibbons's cross-examination by Finlay SC (for Captain Kelly) at the second arms trial, 9 October 1970.

[7] Hefferon's evidence to Niall McCarthy SC (for Haughey) at the first arms trial, 29 September 1970.

[8] Kelly, *The Thimble Riggers*, pp. 15–16.

[9] Report reproduced in Kelly, *The Thimble Riggers*, p. 19.

[10] MA 3 58367, Meeting of Council of Defence, 13 October 1969, also reproduced in Clifford, *Military Aspects,* pp. 56–58.

[11] Ó Beacháin, *Destiny of the Soldiers*, p. 291, with further explanatory note on p. 486. See also Chapter 2 pp. 41–45 for the Planning Board recommendations, which specifically advised that FCA training courses be established.

[12] See Doherty, *Paddy Bogside*, pp. 224–6.

[13] Author's interview with Billy Kelly in December 2001, transcript pp. 8–9.

[14] Kelly, *The Thimble Riggers*, p. 16.

[15] Ibid., pp. 16–18.

[16] Kennedy, *Division and Consensus*, p. 353.

[17] NA 2001/6/513: this file contains a document from the Department of the Taoiseach referring to forthcoming plans to hold a long-awaited discussion on a memorandum from the Minister for External Affairs on Northern Ireland policy, on 6 February 1970.

[18] MA, Hefferon Papers.

[19] Hefferon made brief notes shortly afterwards on what Gibbons said; these are contained in his diaries, part of the Hefferon Papers in the Military Archive in Dublin.

[20] A comment attributed to Lieutenant Colonel Joe Adams, GHQ staff, recorded in the Hefferon Papers.

[21] MA Ops File 3, Copy No. 1, Ministerial Directive to An Ceann Fóirne [Chief of Staff], 6 February 1970, dated 10 February 1970; reprinted in Appendix 2.

[22] MA, Ops File 3, Addendum to Memo of 10/2/70, Ministerial Directive to CF [*Ceann Fóirne, i.e., Chief of Staff*], 11 February 1970; reprinted in Appendix 2.

[23] MA, SCS 18/1, Brief for the Ceann Fóirne, 9 June 1970, par. E 12; reprinted in Appendix 2.

[24] MA, Brief for the Ceann Fóirne, 9 June 1970; this document shows the direct connection between the 6 February directive and the rifles sent north by Gibbons on 2 April 1970. See Appendix 2.

[25] The claim was first made by O'Brien in *The Arms Trial*, p. 116, without citing any source or giving further details.

[26] See cross-examination of Gibbons by Finlay SC (for Captain Kelly) in the transcript of the first arms trial, 25 September 1970, contained as part of the Maguire Papers; Blaney himself said later that his suggestion to Gibbons on 2 April was that the rifles be moved specifically to Dundalk, which had an army barracks close to the border – ref. NAUK/FCO/1596, Peck to FCO, 19 April 1971, reporting a speech by Blaney to a Fianna Fáil dinner in Arklow, Co. Wicklow, on 16 April 1971.

[27] Mills, *Hurler*, p. 60. The claim was repeated by Keogh, *Lynch*, p. 239, also without any official reference to support the claim; see also Downey, *In My Own Time*, p. 119.

[28] NA S/67/01, document in the Lynch Papers, released to *Irish Times*, 23 April 2001.

[29] See, in particular, Arnold, *Lynch: Hero*; John Walsh's authorized biography, *Hillery*; the memoirs of Padraig Faulkner, *As I Saw It*; and Desmond O'Malley, *Conduct Unbecoming*.

[30] MA, File MI 5/3, in which the issue was succinctly set out by Colonel P. J. Delaney in his memorandum Ministerial Directive (undated, but probably written between the two arms trials).

[31] Ó Beacháin, *Destiny of the Soldiers*, p. 301.

[32] See Keogh, *Lynch*, p. 237, where it was stated: 'clearly the directive covered a hypothetical situation'; see also Garret FitzGerald's suggestion at the Committee of Public Accounts inquiry, in questioning Hefferon, that no action resulted, 17 February 1971, pars. 8142–56.

[33] Both documents are reproduced in Appendix 2.

[34] Meeting with Taoiseach on 9–6–70, cited by Clifford, *Military Aspects*, p. 112. A copy is in the author's possession.

[35] MA, SCS 18/1, Brief for the Ceann Fóirne, also cited by Clifford, *Military Aspects*, pp. 108–10.

[36] Memo from Minister for Defence Jerry Cronin to Lynch, 1 July 1970, cited by Clifford, *Military Aspects*, p. 113.

[37] Cited in Clifford, *Military Aspects*, p. 112.

[38] Lynch's speech, *Dáil Debates*, 9 May 1970, col. 1342.

[39] MA, SCS 18/1, Brief for the Ceann Fóirne.

[40] Clifford, *The Arms Conspiracy Trial*, p. 10; Kelly, *Orders for the Captain?*, p. 212.

[41] See Ó Beacháin, *Destiny of the Soldiers*, p. 301, for a particularly clear perspective on the 6 February directive.

[42] Lynch stated that he sacked Haughey and Blaney 'because I am satisfied that they do not subscribe fully to government policy in relation to the present situation in the Six Counties', *Irish Times*, 6 May 1970, cited in O'Brien, *The Arms Trial*, p. 124.

Chapter 6: Directive Cover-up (pages 112–22)

[1] O'Malley, *Conduct Unbecoming*, pp. 52, 58.

[2] Notes of interview with Patrick Hillery on 28 November 2001, in the author's possession.

[3] Faulkner, *As I Saw It*, pp. 90, 94.

[4] Boland, *Up Dev*, p. 44.

[5] Haughey entered hospital on 6 February 1970, and seemed uncertain at the second arms trial as to when he had first heard of the directive.

[6] It is noteworthy that the only record of any related decisions at the 6 February government meeting is the 'pink slip' in the official records indicating a decision 'informally' to cancel the sale of surplus rifles. It may have been the same 'informal' meeting of selected ministers, plus Lynch, which signed off on the directive to the Defence Forces.

[7] Hefferon's exchanges with Garret FitzGerald at the Committee of Public Accounts inquiry are reproduced in part in Appendix 3; for a full consideration of how the directive affected Hefferon's view of Kelly, see Heney, 'Hefferon and the Arms Crisis', pp. 38–44.

[8] MacIntyre, *Through the Bridewell Gate*, pp. 68–69; McKenna SC (for the State) reported to the judge on 29 September that a quite detailed search overnight had failed to unearth the directive.

[9] Evidence of Colonel Hefferon to the first arms trial, *Irish Times*, 30 September 1970.

[10] MA, File MI 5/3, handwritten unsigned memo, describing how Colonel P. J. Delaney consulted the Chief of Staff, Lieutenant General MacEoin, before complying with a request from the recently appointed Minister for Defence, Jerry Cronin, to make the files available to former Minister for Defence Gibbons.

[11] Boland, *Up Dev*, p. 86.

[12] Kelly, *The Thimble Riggers*, p. 161; Kelly stated that Boland's source was Patrick Murphy, later Secretary of the Department of Defence.

[13] Contrast the statement of Niall McCarthy SC (for Haughey) on 29 September 1970 in the first arms trial, with his attitude on 12 October in the second trial, when State counsel offered to produce the directive. McCarthy had said in the first trial that the directive should be produced, as it

was the best evidence; when offered it in the second, he said he was not interested in its contents and effectively declined the offer.

14 See Clifford, *The Arms Conspiracy Trial*, pp. 240–43.

15 MA, File MI 5/3.

16 Blaney's speech was reported only locally at the time, but was quoted in British Ambassador John Peck's message to the Foreign and Commonwealth Office in London on 19 April 1971, NAUK FCO 33/1596.

17 Cronin, *Dáil Debates*, in reply to a question from Gerry L'Estrange TD (FG), 28 April 1971, col. 678.

18 NAUK FCO 33/1206, memo from P. T. C. Evans, official in the British Embassy in Dublin, writing in the ambassador's absence to K. W. W. White, Foreign and Commonwealth Office in London, 19 May 1970.

19 Letter to the Committee of Public Accounts from Chief of Staff MacEoin, read to the committee by Justin Keating TD (Labour), 10 February 1971, par. 6477.

20 Hefferon to Finlay SC (for Captain Kelly) at the second arms trial, *Irish Times*, 14 October 1970.

21 See Hefferon's reply to Fine Gael TD Garret FitzGerald at the Committee of Public Accounts inquiry, 17 February 1971, par. 8152.

22 Hefferon's evidence to the Committee of Public Accounts inquiry, 2 February 1971, pars. 4360–61.

23 MacEoin simply revealed the letter sent to him by his minister, Jerry Cronin, instructing him on the precise language he was to use to the Committee of Public Accounts, i.e., 'You will inform the committee that... the directive gave no authority whatever, direct or indirect... to purchase, procure or acquire arms' in a private session of the Committee of Public Accounts, 2 February 1971.

24 For a fuller account of this, see Heney, 'Hefferon and the Arms Crisis', pp. 70–71.

25 NA 2002/8/431, memorandum personally signed and handwritten by Jack Lynch, describing his conversation that day with Patrick Hogan TD (FG), dated 2 February 1971.

26 See Appendix 3 for a transcript of Hefferon's exchanges with FitzGerald at the Committee of Public Accounts inquiry, 17 February 1971, pars. 8142–56.

27 Interview for RTÉ Television with Justin Keating, conducted November 2001, full transcript in the author's possession. Several short extracts were included in *Secret Orders*, an RTÉ television programme transmitted in December 2001.

Chapter 7: Berry's Warning (pages 123–32)

[1] Uncorrected official (partial) transcript of the second arms trial, Gibbons's cross-examination by Finlay SC (for Captain Kelly), 9 October 1970, in Maguire Papers.

[2] Hefferon's cross-examination by Finlay SC (for Captain Kelly) at the second arms trial, *Irish Times*, 14 October 1970.

[3] Captain Kelly's cross-examination by Seamus McKenna SC (for the State) at the second arms trial, *Irish Times*, 17 October 1970.

[4] Hefferon's evidence at the Committee of Public Accounts inquiry, 17 February 1971, par. 7891.

[5] Ibid., par. 7895; see also further replies from Hefferon, pars. 8593, 8596.

[6] Gibbons's evidence at the Committee of Public Accounts inquiry, 21 February 1971, pars. 11150, 11168.

[7] See Heney, 'Hefferon and the Arms Crisis', pp. 28–29, for more on the fraught relationship between Hefferon and Berry.

[8] Berry, *Diaries*, p. 54; Captain Kelly, as noted above, had already given evidence to the second arms trial suggesting something similar.

[9] Lynch speech, *Dáil Debates*, 25 November 1980, col. 1196.

[10] Berry, *Diaries*, p. 54; while Berry had clear concerns about Captain Kelly's activities at the time and was reporting an apparently serious act of sedition, an identifiable 'plot to import arms' existed only as an aspiration in October 1969, and did not take shape until months later.

[11] Dwyer, *Charlie*, p. 80.

[12] Ibid., p. 80; also *Nice Fellow*, p. 200; Ó Beacháin, *Destiny of the Soldiers*, p. 293; Downey, *In My Own Time*, p. 120; and O'Brien, *The Arms Trial*, p. 74.

[13] Keogh, *Lynch*, p. 219.

[14] Arnold, *Lynch: Hero*, p. 118.

[15] Collins, *The Power Game*, p. 66.

[16] Lynch's speech, *Dáil Debates*, 25 November 1980, col. 1196.

[17] Collins, *The Power Game*, p. 66.

Chapter 8: Gibbons's Deceits (pages 133–154)

[1] *Irish Press*, 26 October 1970.

[2] Hefferon's statement of evidence, and its editing by the prosecution, are examined fully in Chapters 14 and 15 below, pp. 272–3, 283–7.

[3] Arnold, *Lynch: Hero*, pp. 126–27, 149.

[4] Keogh, *Lynch*, p. 244.

[5] Collins, *The Power Game*, p. 78.

[6] Gibbons's cross-examination by Seamus Sorahan BL (for John Kelly), first arms trial, 25 September 1970. See also an exchange at the Committee of Public Accounts inquiry with Garret FitzGerald TD, 21 April 1971, par. 11219.

[7] Gibbons's evidence at the Committee of Public Accounts inquiry, 21 April 1971, pars. 11200–19.

[8] Gibbons's cross-examination by Finlay SC (for Captain Kelly) at the second arms trial, *Irish Times*, 10 October 1970.

[9] Maguire's address to the jury at the second arms trial, 16 October 1970, transcribed by the author from original tape-recording of proceedings, held in the Maguire Papers.

[10] Gibbons's evidence to Eamonn Walsh SC (for the State) at the first arms trial, *Irish Times*, 25 September 1970.

[11] See, for example, Dwyer, *Nice Fellow*, p. 254, and Downey, *In My Own Time*, p. 121.

[12] See Boland's *We Won't Stand (Idly) By*, p. 73, wherein Gibbons is stated to have told Blaney on 29 April 1970 that he expected Lynch was going to sack him as well as Haughey and Blaney.

[13] NA 2001/61/1, Gibbons's first Garda witness statement, to Chief Superintendent Pat Malone, 18 May 1970.

[14] NA 2001/61/1, Hefferon's second Garda statement, to Detective Inspector Ned O'Dea, 31 May 1970.

[15] Hefferon's cross-examination by McKenna SC (for the State) at the second arms trial, *Irish Times*, 14–15 October 1970; see also the more subjective, but sharply observed account of these courtroom exchanges in MacIntyre, *Through the Bridewell Gate*, pp. 119–22. Hefferon did not identify in court the precise quotation, but had told the first arms trial that the location in question was a monastery in Co. Cavan; Clifford said she was informed that the quotation came from Chaucer's *The Canterbury Tales*, in relation to 'The Abbot's Tale' (*The Arms Conspiracy Trial*, p. 268).

[16] Gibbons's evidence at the Committee of Public Accounts inquiry, 21 April 1971, par. 10928.

[17] MacIntyre in his account of Gibbons's cross-examination by counsel for Captain Kelly, Tom Finlay SC, at the first arms trial, describes the witness as 'marked for life' by the experience, a man whose breath 'will never quite free itself from the rancid air of this court-room', MacIntyre, *Through the Bridewell Gate*, p. 53.

[18] Eamonn Walsh SC (for the State), closing submission to the jury at the second arms trial, *Irish Times*, 23 October 1970.

[19] Gibbons's evidence to the Committee of Public Accounts inquiry, 21 April 1971, pars. 11134, 11198, 11265 and 11447.

[20] Fleming's two reports, dated 19 and 20 April 1970, are reproduced in full in Clifford's *Arms Conspiracy Trial*, pp. 598–601.

21 The oversight reflects a curious lack of scrutiny of the extended hearings and voluminous documentation of the Committee of Public Accounts inquiry, which are rarely cited as references in the historiography of the Arms Crisis.

22 NA 2001/61/1, Gibbons's witness statement on 8 June 1970. The question put to him probably arose from a witness statement taken weeks earlier from Tony Fagan, Haughey's personal assistant in the Department of Finance, in which Fagan had alluded to such a conversation on that date between Haughey and Gibbons.

23 Haughey had proposed for Kelly the job of pig-smuggling prevention officer on the border.

24 Gibbons's evidence to Finlay SC (for Captain Kelly) at the first arms trial, *Irish Times*, 29 September 1970.

25 Lynch's closing speech, *Dáil Debates*, 9 May 1970, col. 1336.

26 Gibbons's promotion from Minister for Defence to Minister for Agriculture and Fisheries was not effective until after 9 May 1970.

27 Lynch at Question Time, *Dáil Debates*, 14 May 1971, col. 1596.

28 Lynch's closing speech, *Dáil Debates*, 14 May 1970, col. 1757.

29 Gibbons's evidence at the Committee of Public Accounts inquiry to Garret FitzGerald TD (Fine Gael), 21 April 1971, par. 11140; also his reply to Justin Keating TD (Labour), 21 April, par. 11371.

30 Official (partial) transcript of the first arms trial (uncorrected), 24 September 1970, held in Maguire Papers. This exchange was not reported in *Irish Times* of 25 September 1970.

31 Gibbons's evidence to Walsh SC (for the State) at the second arms trial, *Irish Times*, 10 October 1970.

32 Gibbons's letter to the Committee of Public Accounts inquiry, 19 January 1971, outlined in the Committee of Public Accounts evidence, 21 April 1971, par. 10799.

33 Gibbons's evidence at the Committee of Public Accounts inquiry, 21 April 1971, par. 10805.

34 Ibid., par. 11380.

35 NA 2001/61/1, Gibbons's statement to Chief Superintendent John Fleming, 22 May 1970; although it is not clear from the record if this was a written or an oral interrogation, the questions were probably written.

36 Gibbons's evidence to the Committee of Public Accounts inquiry, 22 April 1971, par. 11417.

37 Gibbons's evidence-in-chief to Walsh SC (for the State) at the second arms trial, *Irish Times*, 10 October 1970; Gibbons on this occasion said Captain Kelly had told him on 1 May 1970 of the source of the money used to buy arms. He did not specify any further, and defence counsel chose not to pursue the issue.

38 NA 2001/61/1, statements of evidence from Anthony Fagan, Department of Finance, May–June 1970.

[39] Berry, *Diaries*, p. 68, June 1980, entry for 21 May 1970.

[40] Gibbons's evidence to Justin Keating TD (Labour) at the Committee of Public Accounts inquiry, 21 April 1971, par. 11376.

[41] Lynch may have been uneasy about his reliance on his former defence minister and privately let off steam to British Ambassador Sir John Peck about Gibbons's largely inept performance in the witness box at the arms trials, ref. NAUK FCO 33/1207; this was contained in Peck's report to London, detailing a conversation with Lynch in October 1970.

[42] Final Report of the Committee of Public Accounts, July 1971, p. 57, par. 70. It is unclear whether this was intended as a criticism of Lynch personally, or of those advising him.

[43] NA 2001/6/551, memorandum from Department of An Taoiseach, to Lynch, detailing a report in that evening's newspaper, 7 May 1970, linking money which went through the Irish Red Cross with the gun-running attempt for which Haughey and Blaney had been sacked. Lynch was informed that a statement was being issued by the organization denying the *Evening Herald*'s claims.

[44] NA 2001/61/1, memorandum containing a transcript of the conversation between Berry and Murray, 20 May 1970.

[45] NA 2001/61/1, letter from Berry to Murray, 21 May 1970.

[46] Berry *Diaries*, *Magill* magazine, June 1980, p. 68, entry for 20 May 1970.

[47] NA S/67/01, Lynch's personal 1980 memo of his conversation with Browne.

[48] NAUK/PREM/19/283/1, memorandum from Hayden to Carrington, on the occasion of Charles Haughey's accession to the office of Taoiseach in 1980.

Chapter 9: Blaney Reassessed (pages 155–75)

[1] MacIntyre, *Through the Bridewell Gate*, p. 12.

[2] Kennedy, *Division and Consensus*, p. 331.

[3] Blaney's Letterkenny speech is quoted in Chapter 3, pp. 68–71 the directive in Chapter 5, pp. 101–111.

[4] Clifford argued that the directive showed that Blaney at Letterkenny had been 'spelling out in public what the cabinet agreed in private: to send the army into the North in the event of large-scale attacks on Catholic communities', Clifford, *The Arms Conspiracy Trial*, p. 567.

[5] NA 2000/6/62, speech by Neil Blaney, December 1969, including Lynch's response, 9 December 1969.

[6] Boland, *We Won't Stand (Idly) By*, p.61.

[7] NAUK FCO 33/1206, Peck's Diplomatic Report to Foreign Minister Michael Stewart, 28 May 1970.

[8] NAUK FCO 33/1201, Gilchrist telegram to Foreign and Commonwealth Office in London, 20 January 1970.

[9] Cited by Stephen Kelly, *Failed Political Entity,* p. 58, quoting from NAUK CJ 3/22, telegram from Gilchrist to the Foreign and Commonwealth Office, 14 August 1969.

[10] Daly, *Sixties Ireland,* p. 351.

[11] Downey, *In My Own Time,* p. 114.

[12] See, in particular, Blaney's interview with *Hot Press* magazine, June 1990, and with English reporter Peter Taylor in *States of Terror,* pp. 239, 242. See also Captain Kelly's testimony at the two arms trials September–October 1970 and at the Committee of Public Accounts inquiry in 1971, where he made clear throughout that he was in constant touch with Neil Blaney in the autumn of 1969.

[13] Fleming's evidence at the Committee of Public Accounts inquiry, 9 February 1971, par. 5662, *et seq.*

[14] NA JUS 2000/36/3, Memorandum for Government, 14 July 1969.

[15] Hefferon's unchallenged evidence at the Committee of Public Accounts inquiry, 17 February 1971, par. 8005.

[16] O'Brien, *The Arms Trial,* p. 94.

[17] From *On the Blanket* website, interview with John Kelly by Liam Clarke, conducted August 2005.

[18] Ó Beacháin, *Destiny of the Soldiers,* quoting John Kelly interview, pp. 294–95.

[19] *This Week,* August 1970. Further evidence of Ó Brádaigh's contempt for Blaney and Fianna Fáil was provided by him in a conversation in July 1970 with Conor Cruise O'Brien, reported in *States of Ireland,* p. 229.

[20] O'Brien, *The Arms Trial,* p. 108.

[21] See Blaney interview, 'Lawyers, Guns and Money'.

[22] Taylor, *States of Terror,* p. 242.

[23] O'Brien, *The Arms Trial,* p. 116.

[24] Ciarán de Baróid, *Ballymurphy and the Irish War* (Belfast, 1989, rev. ed. 1990, 2000), p. 6.

[25] Ibid., p. 6; also, Gerry Adams, *Before the Dawn: An Autobiography* (Dingle, Co. Kerry, 1996), p. 146.

[26] MA, Brief for the Ceann Fóirne [Chief of Staff], 9 June 1970; this document shows the direct connection between the 6 February directive and the rifles sent north by Gibbons on 2 April 1970 – see Appendix 2.

[27] *This Week,* current affairs magazine, August 1970, interview with Ruairí Ó Brádaigh and 'an official spokesman for the Provisional Army Council' (identified by R. W. White as MacStiofáin).

[28] John Kelly, in a 2007 Liam Clarke interview, posted in *On the Blanket* website.

[29] *Fianna Fáil and the IRA,* anonymous Official IRA pamphlet, p. 27.

[30] Bishop and Mallie, *The Provisional IRA,* pp. 95, 100.

[31] MacStiofáin, *Memoirs of a Revolutionary,* pp. 139–40. See Adams memoir,

Before the Dawn, p. 127; Brendan Anderson, *Joe Cahill: A Life in the IRA* (Dublin, 2002), p. 163; Billy Kelly, in an unpublished 2001 RTÉ interview with the author; and White, *Ó Brádaigh*, p. 368.

[32] See O'Brien, *The Arms Trial*, pp. x, xvi, 96; Arnold, *Lynch: Hero*, p. 119; Collins, *The Power Game*, pp. 62, 68.

[33] Richard English, *Armed Struggle: The History of the IRA* (London, 2003), p. 119.

[34] Hennessey, *Origins of the Troubles*, p. 392.

[35] Coogan, *The IRA*, p. 368.

[36] *Freedom Struggle*, a pamphlet by P. O'Neill, representing the Provisional IRA (1973), pp. 10–11. This document listed five reasons for the split, of which the first was the abandonment of abstentionism; there was no mention of the role of Irish government ministers.

[37] MacStiofáin, *Memoirs of a Revolutionary*, pp. 139–40.

[38] See 'Blaney was Right, Says McAteer', *Irish Press*, 11 December 1969.

[39] NA 2000/6/660, Eamon Gallagher memo to Seán Ronan, assistant Secretary, Department of External Affairs, after a visit by him to Derry, and describing Paddy Doherty as 'possibly being groomed as successor to Eddie McAteer' and 'the real leader of the Derry Citizens Defence Association', 20 September 1969.

[40] Interview with Doherty by the author, conducted in the first week of December 2001, transcript is in the author's possession.

[41] Doherty, *Paddy Bogside*, p. 226.

[42] Kelly, *The Thimble Riggers*, p. 69.

[43] Henry Patterson, *Ireland Since 1939: The Persistence of Conflict* (Oxford, 2002), p. 178.

[44] NA 2001/6/513, includes 'pink slip' dated 6 February 1970, indicating the government had 'informally agreed' that the sale of surplus weapons, 'for which tenders were recently invited, should not now take place'.

[45] Lynch speech in Cork, 24 April 1971, cited by Colonel Hefferon in a presentation to the Committee of Public Accounts inquiry, 30 November 1971.

[46] Paddy Doherty interview with the author, December 2001, transcript p. 11.

[46a] Billy Kelly interview with the author December 2001, transcript pp. 4, 6.

[47] *Paddy Bogside* is described on its title page as having been 'edited' by Peter Hegarty, a journalist and author.

[48] A detailed account of how Doherty was contacted by Blaney, through his wife in the Bogside, in early April 1970 about an urgent return to Ireland is contained in the interview between the author and Doherty conducted in December 2001 (transcript in the author's possession). The message from Blaney to Doherty was that material was being sent north and he had to return to take responsibility for it.

Chapter 10: Climactic Weekend (pages 176–196)

[1] NA 2001/61/1, Fagan's handwritten statement (13 May 1970) and witness statement to gardaí (14 May 1970), where Fagan quoted Haughey as telling him 'I know about it', and Fagan added, 'I think he said that Blaney had been on.'

[2] NA 2003/4/536, Berry's witness statement in the arms trial Book of Evidence.

[3] Kelly, *The Thimble Riggers*, p. 38.

[4] Haughey's evidence in cross-examination by Eamonn Walsh SC (for the State) at the second arms trial, *Irish Times*, 20 October 1970.

[5] Fagan's evidence-in-chief at the first arms trial, *Irish Times*, 24 September 1970.

[6] Haughey's evidence-in-chief to Niall McCarthy SC (for Haughey) at the second arms trial, *Irish Times*, 20 October 1970.

[7] Gibbons himself referred in his court evidence to the information he got on Friday, 17 April 1970 as being 'of such urgency' that there should be 'no delay', and thus a reason why he believed his conversation with Haughey took place on Friday evening, not on Monday, 20 April: see his evidence-in-chief at the first arms trial, *Irish Times*, 25 September 1970.

[8] See Eamonn Walsh SC (for the State), closing submission to the jury at the second arms trial, *Irish Times*, 23 October 1970.

[9] See partial transcript of the first arms trial, Ó Móráin to Peter Maguire SC (for Haughey), 28 September 1970, held in the private papers of Peter Maguire. This reference appears to have been incorrectly reported in the national newspapers the following day. Ó Móráin's words in the transcript were 'In the days immediately before 18 April, there were different conflicting reports... certainly at one of these stages I thought this was an official importation.' The *Irish Times* report erroneously quoted him as follows: 'certainly at one of these stages I thought this was a case of one official implicating another'. The immediately subsequent passages in both the transcript and the newspaper report suggest that the transcript version is the accurate one.

[10] NA 2001/61/1, undated, single page, Explanatory Statement from Andrew Ward, Deputy Secretary, Department of Justice.

[11] Clifford, *The Arms Conspiracy Trial*, p. 29; see also Ó Móráin's evidence to Peter Maguire SC (for Haughey) at the first arms trial, *Irish Times*, 29 September 1970.

[12] A withering forensic analysis of the Haughey/Berry phone conversation is contained in Angela Clifford's *The Arms Conspiracy Trial*, pp. 29–30; Clifford was exceptionally cynical, more than any other writer, of Berry's motivation and behaviour.

[13] Jurors appear not to have accepted Haughey's denial that he suggested the

arms could go direct to the North, judging by an interview with juror 'Mr B' conducted in particular circumstances for RTÉ in 2001, the transcript of which is in the author's possession, and which is discussed in detail in Chapter 16.

[14] NA 2001/61/1, Berry memorandum to the AG, Explanatory Note, part 1, par. viii, advising on data he felt might assist the prosecution.

[15] Berry, *Diaries*, entry for 18 April 1970, p. 61. Haughey denied he would ever have described a ministerial colleague as 'the man from Mayo' to a 'very punctilious' civil servant like Berry, in his evidence-in-chief at second arms trial, 19 October 1970.

[16] Clifford, *The Arms Conspiracy Trial*, p. 47.

[17] Maguire's address to the jury at the second arms trial, 16 October 1970, transcribed from the original tape of the proceedings by the author; the tape is held as part of the Maguire Papers; also reported in *Irish Times*, 17 October 1970.

[18] Clifford, *The Arms Conspiracy Trial*, p. 45.

[19] NA 2001/61/1, Explanatory Note, Part II, par. 9.

[20] See Chapter 4 above, pp. 79–82.

[21] See Chapter 2 above, pp. 41–45.

[22] Hefferon's evidence to Finlay SC (for Captain Kelly), at the first arms trial, *Irish Times*, 29 September 1970.

[23] NA 2001/61/1, handwritten statement of Tony Fagan, dated 13 April 1970.

[24] Berry *Diaries*, entry for 4 October 1969, p. 52.

[25] Judge Seamus Henchy's charge to the jury at the second arms trial, *Irish Times*, 24 October 1970.

[26] Gibbons had been forced repeatedly to deny Colonel Hefferon's evidence that he and the minister had on a number of occasions discussed Captain Kelly's arms-buying trips to the Continent; Haughey equally denied Peter Berry's evidence on the content of their phone conversation on 18 April 1970.

[27] Fagan's cross-examination by Peter Maguire SC (for Haughey) at the second arms trial, *Irish Times*, 8 October 1970.

[28] Eamonn Walsh SC (for the State), closing address to the jury at the second arms trial, *Irish Times*, 23 October 1970.

[29] Walsh's closing address at the second arms trial, *Irish Times*, 23 October 1970.

[30] Fagan was equally emphatic and unequivocal in regard to the timing of the events of Monday, 20 October when questioned by Garret FitzGerald TD (Fine Gael) at the Committee of Public Accounts inquiry the following year – see exchanges at par. 3022 on 26 January 1971.

[31] NA 2001/61/1, Fagan's Notes on Northern Ireland Aid Relief Fund, With Particular Reference to the Army Intelligence Service, dated 9 May and 13 May 1970.

[32] Fagan's questioning by Justin Keating TD (Labour) at the Committee of Public Accounts inquiry, 27 January 1971, pars. 3950–3963.

[33] Fagan's formal witness statement, taken by Detective Inspector O'Dea on 14 May 1970, described Haughey as having said to him: 'He said he had been speaking to Gibbons, Minister for Defence, and they agree that the whole thing has got to be called off' (NA 2001/61/1). The same version appeared in the Book of Evidence.

[34] Haughey's stance during the arms trial, and subsequently, was almost always highly controlled; he appears throughout to have been balancing the requirement of defending his own position with avoiding inflicting extra or unnecessary damage on his party in government.

[35] Haughey in cross-examination by Eamonn Walsh SC (for the State) at the second arms trial, reported in *Irish Times*, 20 October 1970.

[36] In fairness to Judge Henchy, counsel for Charles Haughey, Niall McCarthy SC, did not choose to argue, as he could have, that Fagan's evidence pointed to an earlier undisclosed conversation.

Chapter 11: Hanging Fire (pages 197–215)

[1] Frank Dunlop, *Yes Taoiseach: Irish Politics from Behind Closed Doors* (Dublin, 2004), p. 15.

[2] NA 2001/61/1, Gibbons's first Garda witness statement, 18 May 1970.

[3] For an extensive consideration of Delaney's accusations against Hefferon, see Heney, 'Hefferon and the Arms Crisis', pp. 73–79.

[4] Hefferon's evidence at the Committee of Public Accounts inquiry, to Ben Briscoe TD (FF), 2 February 1971, par. 4306.

[5] MA, MI File 5/3, Memorandum, 7 May 1970.

[6] NA 2001/61/1, Gibbons's witness statement on 8 June 1970.

[7] MA, MI File 5/3, Verbal Briefing, Wednesday, 22 April 1970, appendix B.

[8] NA 2001/61/1, Gibbons's first witness statement to gardaí, 18 May 1970.

[9] NA 2001/6/552, draft answer to Dáil Question to the Taoiseach for answer, 12 November 1970, noting the date of their first discussion of the gun-running – 24 April – was 'determined by Taoiseach and Minister for Agriculture and Fisheries [*Gibbons*] in consultation'.

[10] One writer who has been alert to the hollowness of Delaney's report was Vincent Browne, who described it as 'mere window-dressing' – see 'The Arms Crisis 1970', p. 54.

[11] Lynch's detailed account of his actions at this time was given in his closing speech at the marathon debate on 8–9 May 1970, *Dáil Debates*, col. 1329–1331.

[12] NA 2003/4/533, report of Chief Superintendent Fleming, 20 April 1970, to Assistant Garda Commissioner; John Squire, a director of Aer Turas, told Fleming that Albert Luykx, one of those involved in the attempt

to import the arms the previous weekend, had told him he had been invited to assist in the importation by Neil Blaney.

[13] Justin Keating TD (Labour) speech, *Dáil Debates*, col. 918, 8 May 1970.

[14] Berry, *Diaries*, p. 63, entry for 30 April 1970.

[15] Report of Boland's RTÉ radio interview, *Irish Press*, 13 November 1970.

[16] Boland, *We Won't Stand (Idly) By*, p. 73.

[17] Walsh, *Hillery*, pp. 218–25.

[18] Arnold, *Lynch: Hero*, p. 129.

[19] Blaney's interview with *Hot Press* magazine, 'Lawyers, Guns and Money'.

[20] NA 2001/6/552, includes a report of Lynch's Dáil statement on 14 May 1970; see also Lynch's response to a question from Barry Desmond TD (Labour), *Dáil Debates*, col. 1426, 17 November 1970.

[21] Arnold, *Lynch: Hero*, p. 56.

[22] Collins, *The Power Game*, p. 79.

[23] Kelly, *A Failed Political Entity*, p. 73.

[24] Browne, 'The Arms Crisis, 1970', p. 56.

[25] Lynch speech, *Dáil Debates*, col. 1198, 25 November 1980.

[26] O'Mahony, *Jack Lynch: A Biography* (Dublin, 1991), p. 174; also Mills, *Hurler*, p. 51. Lynch earlier had denied to Vincent Browne, on 6 May 1980, that Ó Móráin ever told him of 'a conspiracy to import arms' – ref. NA/Tsch 2001/8/11.

[27] Boland, *Up Dev*, p. 46.

[28] Ó Móráin's evidence to James Darcy SC (for Captain Kelly), contained in a partial official transcript (uncorrected) of the first arms trial, 28 September 1970, in Maguire Papers.

[29] See Berry, *Diaries*, entry for 13 April 1970, p. 59.

[30] NA 2001/61/1, Berry's Explanatory Notes for Counsel, Part II.

[31] Berry, *Diaries*, p. 61, entry for 18 April 1970.

[32] Berry may well have mentioned this matter when he spoke to Lynch on 13 April.

[33] Berry, *Diaries*, p. 62, entry for 21 April 1970.

[34] Ibid., pp. 62–63, entries for 20, 23 April 1970.

[35] Lynch's closing speech in the marathon debate on the nomination of replacement ministers to the government, *Dáil Debates*, col. 1331, 9 May 1970.

[36] Berry, *Diaries*, p. 63, entry for 30 April 1970.

[37] Lynch's closing speech, *Dáil Debates*, col. 1331, 9 May 1970.

[38] Berry, *Diaries*, p. 63, entry for 30 April 1970.

[39] Browne, 'The Arms Crisis, 1970', p. 55.

[40] 'Gibbons Expected to be Sacked', Emily O'Reilly, *Sunday Business Post*, 6 May 2001, reporting the contents of an interview given by Neil Blaney to a Kilkenny schoolteacher in 1982.

[41] Justin O'Brien commented that the extrication of Gibbons from

involvement in the gun-running became Lynch's 'key imperative', *The Modern Prince*, p. 42.

42 Kelly, *The Thimble Riggers*, pp. 42–56.

43 Kelly, *The Thimble Riggers*, p. 55; see also the evidence of Captain Kelly at the Committee of Public Accounts inquiry, 9 February 1971, par. 6287.

44 Chief Superintendent John Fleming's evidence at the Committee of Public Accounts inquiry, 9 February 1971, par. 5640.

45 The claim was first made by T. P. Coogan in *The Troubles* (1995), p. 101, and given further credence by Clifford, *The Arms Conspiracy Trial*, p. 69.

46 NAUK FCO 33/1205, Ms McGhashann, British Embassy official, to Foreign and Commonwealth Office, 6 May 1970.

47 NAUK FCO 33/1205, 'Speaking Note' from Foreign and Commonwealth Office officials (unsigned) regarding a British cabinet meeting, 7 May 1970.

48 NAUK FCO 33/1206, Peck's Diplomatic Report, sent to the Foreign Secretary Michael Stewart, 28 May 1970.

49 NAUK FCO 33/1205, Foreign Secretary Stewart's memorandum to the Dublin Embassy, Priority Guidance, 12 May 1970.

50 Collins, *The Power Game*, p. 80; the theory that the Cosgrave tip-off resulted from Special Branch impatience with Lynch's prevarication is consistent with the thrust of Peter Berry's account in the *Diaries*.

Chapter 12: Hefferon's Defiance (pages 216–235)

1 Peggy Hefferon in RTÉ interview with the author, December 2001.

2 MacIntyre, *Through the Bridewell Gate*, p. 56.

3 Interview with the author, December 2001.

4 RTÉ interview with his son Colm Hefferon, conducted by the author in December 2001, the transcript of which is in the author's possession.

5 M.A., Hefferon Papers, typed unsigned notes prepared by Hefferon in relation to a forthcoming appearance at the Committee of Public Accounts inquiry.

6 See, for example, Justin O'Brien's *The Arms Trial*, with its references to 'Military Intelligence... cooking up schemes for arming insurgents' (p. 117), and 'acting under orders from government Ministers openly hostile to their party leader' (preface, p. xi). Dermot Keogh saw Hefferon as a 'victim of the ruthlessness' of Haughey and Blaney (*Lynch*, p. 244).

7 NA 2003/4/534, Hefferon's witness statement, 30 May 1970; see Chapters 14 and 15 for a full consideration, pp. 272–3, and 283–7.

[8] Had the arms trials ended in a guilty verdict, it appears Hefferon would have been at risk of prosecution.

[9] Collins, *The Power Game*, p. 64.

[10] Arnold, *Lynch: Hero*, p. 109.

[11] Hefferon's evidence to the Committee of Public Accounts inquiry, 2 February 1971, par. 4356.

[12] See the Hillery Papers, P 205/36, UCDA – in particular, memos from senior Irish diplomat Eamon Gallagher and Ireland's ambassador to the UK, Donal O'Sullivan, on 20 April, 27 April and 6 May 1970.

[13] Arnold, *Lynch: Hero*, p. 119.

[14] M.A., Hefferon Papers, typed memo of five stapled pages, undated and unsigned, but probably written by Hefferon in 1971 as an *aide-mémoire* for his evidence at the Committee of Public Accounts inquiry hearings.

[15] Hefferon's evidence to Justin Keating TD (Labour) at the Committee of Public Accounts inquiry, 18 February 1971, pars. 8377–78.

[16] M.A., Hefferon Papers; in unsigned typed pages, Hefferon recorded the events of 6 February.

[17] Hefferon's evidence to Seamus McKenna SC (for the State) at the first arms trial, *Irish Times*, 30 September 1970.

[18] NA 2003/4/534, Hefferon's statement of evidence to gardaí, 30 May 1970.

[19] Hefferon to Finlay SC (for Captain Kelly) at the second arms trial, *Irish Times*, 14 October 1970; see also Hefferon's evidence to the Committee of Public Accounts inquiry, 2 February 1971, pars. 4360–61; see Chapter 5 for a fuller account of this.

[20] As shown in Chapter 6, pp. 119–20.

[21] 'We Can't Wait for Árd Fheis', Ó Móráin interview, *Sunday Press*, 25 October 1970.

[22] See Chapter 11, pp. 200–02.

[23] M.A., Brief for the Prosecution, dated 1 October 1970, Critique for CS of Evidence given at Parliamentary Inquiry, dated 5 October 1970, and Ministerial Directive 6 February (undated), in Military Intelligence Files, Nos 2 & 5.

[24] O'Malley's speech, *Dáil Debates*, 6 July 2001, Vol. 540, cols. 1054–59.

[25] O'Halpin, 'Greek Authoritarian Phase?', p. 476.

[26] Keogh, *Lynch*, p. 244.

[27] Ibid., p. 239.

[28] Henry Patterson, *Ireland Since 1939: The Persistence of Conflict* (Dublin, 2002), p. 175.

[29] Mills, *Hurler*, p. 88.

[30] Clifford, *The Arms Conspiracy Trial*, pp. 80–81.

[31] Hefferon's submission to the Committee of Public Accounts, regarding the evidence given by Gibbons, 30 November 1971.

[32] In conversation with the author in 2014, Hefferon's son Colm remembered his father telling him that MacEoin was not happy that Hefferon had not told him of the arms importation scheme.

[33] Hefferon's evidence to Tom Finlay SC (for Captain Kelly) at the first arms trial, *Irish Times*, 29 September 1970.

[34] M.A., Critique for the CS [Chief of Staff] of Evidence Given at Parliamentary Inquiry, MI File No 2, par. 17, dated 5 October 1970.

[35] Hefferon's evidence to Finlay SC (for Captain Kelly) at the first arms trial, *Irish Times*, 29 September 1970.

[36] MA, Brief for Ceann Fóirne, 9 June 1970, pars. f and g.

[37] Hefferon to McKenna, SC (for the State) at the second arms trial, *Irish Times*, 15 October 1970.

[38] Gibbons's evidence to Finlay SC (for Captain Kelly) in the first arms trial, *Irish Times*, 26 September 1970.

[39] Hefferon's evidence at the Committee of Public Accounts inquiry, 30 November 1971.

[40] Ibid., 17 February 1971, pars. 7949–8018.

[41] Ibid., 3 March 1971, par. 9672.

[42] NA 2003/4/534, Hefferon's witness statement, dated 30 May 1970.

[43] Hefferon's evidence at the Committee of Public Accounts, 27 January 1971, par. 4177.

[44] Arnold, *Lynch: Hero*, p. 111; O'Brien, *The Arms Trial*, p. 86; Keogh, *Lynch*, p. 244.

[45] Kelly, *The Thimble Riggers*, p. 263.

[46] Intelligence memo quoted by O'Brien, *The Arms Trial*, p. 58.

[47] Arnold, *Lynch: Hero*, p. 115.

[48] Frank Fitzpatrick's letter to the late Sheila Kelly, widow of Captain Kelly, copy in the author's possession, dated 5 August 2005; see also Clifford, *The Arms Conspiracy Trial*, pp. 79–80.

[49] Clifford, *The Arms Conspiracy Trial*, pp. 195–207.

[50] Colm Hefferon (son), in an interview for RTÉ *Prime Time* 'Evidence of the Colonel', tx. 10 April 2001; see also Michael Mills's verdict on Hefferon: 'a most honourable man whose name was damaged by this affair', *Hurler*, p. 58.

[51] Colm Hefferon's interview with the author, June 2014.

[52] Gibbons's speech, *Dáil Debates*, col. 1488, 9 November 1971.

Chapter 13: Honest Jack? (pages 236–254)

[1] T. K. Whitaker, *Irish Times*, 21 October 1999, quoted by Ronan Fanning in 'Jack Lynch', *Dictionary of Irish Biography* Cambridge University Press, 2009.

2 Boland, *Up Dev*, pp. 72–73.

3 M.A., MI File 5/3, in which the issue was succinctly set out by Colonel P. J. Delaney in his memorandum Ministerial Directive (undated, but probably written between the two arms trials).

4 Clifford reflected a general distrust of Berry when describing him, as part of her analysis of his writings, as 'a tricky mandarin' – *The Arms Conspiracy Trial*, p. 35.

5 See Keogh, *Lynch*, pp. 240–57.

6 Berry, *Diaries*, p. 61, entry for 18 April 1970; Lynch denied in November 1980 ever receiving this information, by which time Berry had died.

7 Ibid., p. 67, entry for 14 May 1970.

8 Ibid., p. 54, entry for 17 October 1969.

9 Ibid., p. 66, entry for 7 May 1970.

10 *Dáil Debates*, 9 May 1970, col. 1342; 4 November 1970, col. 711.

11 NAUK FCO 33/1206, memorandum of P. T. C. Evans.

12 *Irish Press*, 11 November 1970.

13 NA 2002/8/431, personal memo by Jack Lynch.

14 *Dáil Debates*, 25 November 1980, col. 1196.

15 Ibid., 7 May 1970, cols. 641/718; 9 May, col. 1338; 14 May, col. 1752.

16 Ibid., 7 May, col. 716; 9 May, cols. 1338/39; 14 May, col. 1750/53.

17 Ibid., 7 May, col. 642.

18 Ibid., 9 May 1970, col. 1336; 14 May, cols. 1596/1757.

19 Ibid., 7 May, col. 720; 9 May, cols. 1335/1339/1346; 14 May, col. 1753; 4 November 1970, col. 715.

20 NA 2003/4/536, statement of Delaney in the arms trial Book of Evidence.

21 NA 2001/61/1, handwritten statement by Tony Fagan, in two parts, dated 9 May and 13 May 1970.

22 NA 2001/61/1, see Gibbons's various witness statements on 18, 22 and 28 May 1970, as well as 8 June 1970; see also his extensive evidence at both arms trials and at the Committee of Public Accounts inquiry in April 1971.

23 Lynch's speeches in *Dáil Debates*, col. 717, 7 May 1970, and col. 1356, 9 May 1970.

24 Ó Beacháin, *Destiny of the Soldiers*, p. 300.

25 Lee, *Politics and Society*, p. 459.

26 Arnold, *Lynch: Hero*, p. 126.

27 Boland, *Up Dev*, p. 72, where Boland wrote, in apparent awe, 'how could I or any other member of the Government dream for one moment that the Head of Government could possibly be so devious in dealing with his colleagues?'

28 Walsh, *Hillery*, p. 215.

29 Ibid., p. 231.

30 Dick Walsh, *The Party*, p. 109.

[31] Ibid., p. 121.

[32] Mills, *Hurler*, p. 82.

[33] Downey, *In My Own Time*, p. 127; Downey approvingly quoted journalist John Healy on how Lynch had set a cunning 'tiger trap', using Gibbons as the 'donkey'.

[34] Cited by Stephen Kelly, *Failed Political Entity*, p. 58, quoting from NAUK CJ 3/22, telegram from Gilchrist to the Foreign and Commonwealth Office, 14 August 1969.

[35] Peck appears here to accept the term 'honest Jack' at face value, despite its origination as a term of derision. Both these observations by Peck are contained in his nine-page report to Alec Douglas-Home, Foreign Secretary, entitled 'Aftermath of the Arms Trials', NAUK FCO/1207, 16 December 1970. The same report concluded with the comment above about Lynch being more devious than he appeared.

[36] Dunlop, *Yes Taoiseach*; Dunlop, apart from working directly with Lynch, was from Co. Kilkenny, part of Gibbons's Dáil constituency; while visiting his parents over weekends in the mid-1970s, he and Gibbons shared nights drinking and discussing party affairs.

[37] Ibid., p. 8.

[38] Ibid., p. 16.

[39] Ibid., p. 34.

[40] Ibid., p. 15.

[41] Ibid., p. 42.

[42] The files contain nothing to suggest that Whitaker was aware of the 6 February 1970 directive.

[43] NAUK FCO 33/1200, Gilchrist's Annual Review for 1969, 23 January 1970.

Chapter 14: The Arms Trial Prosecution (1) (pages 255–281)

[1] MacIntyre, *Through the Bridewell Gate*, p. 117.

[2] Peter Maguire SC's address to the jury (for Haughey) in the second arms trial, *Irish Times*, 17 October 1970.

[3] Seamus Sorahan BL's address to the jury (for John Kelly) in the second arms trial, *Irish Times*, 22 October 1970.

[4] Ernest Wood SC's address to the jury (for Luykx) in the second arms trial, *Irish Times*, 22 October 1970.

[5] Niall McCarthy SC's address to the jury (for Haughey) in the second arms trial, *Irish Times*, 21 October 1970.

[6] 'We Can't Wait for Árd-Fheis', Ó Móráin interview in *Sunday Press*, 25 October 1970.

[7] Dermot Keogh, *Twentieth-Century Ireland: Nation and State* (Dublin, 1994), p. 312.

[8] Judge Henchy's charge to jury in second arms trial, *Irish Times*, 24 October 1970.

[9] For example, see *Report of the Attorney General*, par. 2, p. 42, July 2001.

[10] The editing of Hefferon's witness statement taken on 30 May 1970 will be considered below and in the following chapter.

[11] Lynch's closing speech, *Dáil Debates*, col. 1339, 9 May 1970.

[12] FitzGerald's speech, *Dáil Debates*, col. 1694, 14 May 1970.

[13] Lynch's speech, *Dáil Debates*, col. 1750, 14 May 1970.

[14] Response by Lynch to Opposition queries, *Dáil Debates*, col. 1595, 14 May 1970.

[15] The role of Director of Public Prosecutions was created in 1974, established by the Prosecution of Offences Act 1974.

[16] Lynch's closing speech, *Dáil Debates*, col. 708, 4 November 1970.

[17] Ibid., col. 713, 4 November 1970.

[18] Reported in O'Mahony, *Jack Lynch – A Biography* (Dublin, 1991), p. 170.

[19] A subsequent holder of the Office of the DPP, James Hamilton, observed that Condon 'behaved with unquestioned propriety and impartiality' in the arms trials. He was speaking at a seminar on 'Accountability in the Public Sector', 14 November 2008; a copy of his remarks is in the author's possession.

[20] Ronan Fanning, 'Political Trial Showed Arms Trial Was Over', *Sunday Independent*, 29 April 2001.

[21] Covering letter to the Minister for Justice, John O'Donoghue TD, accompanying McDowell's *Report of the Attorney General*, p. 2; see also Ferriter, *Transformation of Ireland*, p. 689: 'It is likely the definitive story of the arms trial will never be told satisfactorily, at least not until all the documentation is released.'

[22] See in particular NA 2001/61/1.

[23] This apparently innocent bureaucratic error was described by Attorney General Rory Brady SC in a letter to his predecessor in that Office, Michael McDowell, on the occasion of the discovery and transfer of the mislaid files to the National Archives, 4 December 2002, copy in the author's possession.

[24] NA 2003/4/537, Fleming report to Chief State Solicitor, headed 'Conspiracy to Import Arms and Ammunition into the State: Five Prisoners Charged', 2 June 1970.

[25] The detailed timeline for the prosecution is contained in Appendix 1.

[26] See, in particular, NA 2001/61/1 and NA 2003/4/533.

[27] NA 2003/4/533, Fleming's reports to Assistant Garda Commissioner John Lincoln, 19–20 April 1970, 'Re: Illegal Importation of Arms and Ammunition at Dublin Airport'.

[28] Berry, *Diaries*, entry for 23 April 1970, p. 63. This matter was discussed in Chapter 11, p. 212.

[29] One final statement was taken from Tony Fagan on 26 June 1970, on the management of the Northern Ireland Relief Fund.

[30] It had been clear since 1970 that charges were issued before a statement was taken from Colonel Hefferon, but the significance of this somehow escaped attention.The prosecution timeline highlights the anomalous treatment accorded Hefferon, and how late, relative to other witnesses, the taking of his statement was.

[31] NA 2003/4/533, note of Hefferon's interview by gardaí, 28 May 1970.

[32] Ibid.

[33] Ibid., entry for February 1970, p. 58.

[34] Ibid., entry for 18 April 1970, p. 61, Chief Superintendent John Fleming's evidence to the Committee of Public Accounts inquiry, 9 February 1971, par. 5795; also Heney, 'Hefferon and the Arms Crisis', pp. 21–29.

[35] Berry, Diaries, p. 72, entry for 15 September 1970.

[36] NA 2001/61/1, Fagan's statement – Notes on Relief Fund, 9 May 1970.

[37] NA 2003/4/523, memo of Diarmaid O'Donovan, Chief State Solicitor, to Attorney General, 22 May 1970.

[38] See Chapter 15, pp. 282–87.

[39] NA 2001/61/1, Gibbons's statement to Chief Superintendent Pat Malone, 18 May 1970.

[40] NA 2001/61/1, Gibbons's fourth statement to gardaí, 8 June 1970.

[41] NA 2003/4/525, Fleming's memo to the Attorney General regarding the questioning of Haughey, 25 May 1970.

[42] Fleming's cross-examination by Niall McCarthy SC (for Haughey) at the second arms trial, Irish Times, 13 October 1970.

[43] 1925 Firearms Act, Section 17 (8); clause 8 specified that the Minister for Defence had authority to import weapons without licence, but only if they were for the use of the Defence Forces.

[44] NA 2001/61/1, Hefferon's statement to gardaí, 30 May 1970; See Heney, 'Hefferon and Arms Crisis', pp. 49–54, for a full account.

[45] Hefferon's evidence in court, supported by that of Captain Kelly, was that the issue of the resignation had been effectively set aside by Gibbons before 16 February and was not being pursued by Kelly thereafter – Hefferon's evidence to Finlay SC (for Captain Kelly) at the first arms trial, Irish Times, 29 September 1970.

[46] The file in which it rests in the National Archives, NA 2003/4/537, consists mainly of copies of witness statements being edited for the Book of Evidence. This suggests a possible double misfiling as it was among the files missed in 2001 but later discovered in 2002 by staff of the then Attorney General, Rory Brady, who explained that this material had been 'mis-filed in a Northern Ireland file', within the basement area of the Registry section of the Attorney General's Office. Having been released belatedly in January 2003,

the copy of Fleming's report was further removed from the public gaze by being included in file NA 2003/4/537, an unusual location for a copy of such a central Garda document. These factors may at least partly explain why this document has been missed hitherto by researchers. Another factor is that, to appreciate its full significance, it has to be read in conjunction with Hefferon's original unedited statement.

47 NA 2001/61/1, statement of Diarmaid Ó'Ríordáin, Customs and Excise surveyor, Dublin Port, 29 May 1970, describing in detail the activities of the two Kellys on 25 October 1969.

48 Fleming's evidence at the Committee of Public Accounts inquiry, 3 November 1971, par. 12080.

49 Berry, *Diaries*, entry for 1 May 1970, p. 65.

50 Kelly, *The Thimble Riggers*, p. 55.

51 Fleming's evidence at the Committee of Public Accounts inquiry, 3 November 1971, par. 11937.

52 NA 2001/61/1, Gibbons's fourth statement – Answers to Questions from gardaí, 8 June 1970.

53 Gibbons told Tom Finlay SC (for Captain Kelly) at the second arms trial, that he never expressed any disapproval to Captain Kelly of what he had said he was engaged in *vis-à-vis* the arms importation, *Irish Times*, 10 October 1970.

54 Transcript of interview with 'Mr B', member of jury at second arms trial, pp. 2–3, conducted for RTÉ in May 2001; transcript in the author's possession.

55 NA 2001/61/1, witness statement of Bartholomew Culligan, Revenue Commissioner, to gardaí, 13 May 1970.

56 NA 2001/61/1, witness statement of Tom Tobin, Customs and Excise inspector, to gardaí, 27 April 1970.

57 NA 2001/61/1, Ó Ríordáin witness statement, 29 May 1970.

58 Gibbons's speech, *Dáil Debates*, col. 840, 8 May 1970.

Chapter 15: The Arms Trial Prosecution (2) (pages 282–300)

1 Criminal Procedure Act 1967, section 6, par. (d).

2 Although the reports claimed to be pursuing issues raised by the RTÉ television programme 'Evidence of the Colonel', the transcript of the programme shows that the question of a conspiracy to obstruct justice was not a charge made in the programme.

3 NA 2001/61/1, Hefferon's statement to gardaí, 30 May 1970, p. 3. Compare with NA 2003/4/536, Hefferon's statement as in the Book of Evidence.

4 NA 2001/61/1, Hefferon's statement to gardaí, 30 May 1970, p. 4.

[5] Ibid.

[6] Ibid.

[7] Ibid.

[8] Ibid., p. 7.

[9] For those who have argued that the editing was proper, see Collins, *The Power Game*, p. 92; Arnold, *Lynch: Hero*, p. 149; O'Brien, *The Modern Prince*, p. 33. For those who felt the editing was problematic, see Clifford, *The Arms Conspiracy Trial*, p. 80; Dwyer, *Nice Fellow*, pp. 232–33; Ó Beacháin, *Destiny of the Soldiers*, pp. 304–05.

[10] Statement issued by Desmond O'Malley TD, 9 May 2001, p. 12, reported in *Irish Times*, 10 May 2001.

[11] *Report of the Attorney General*, passim, July 2001.

[12] See, for reference, the United Kingdom *Attorney General's Guidelines on Disclosure*, pars. 8–12, on the Crown Prosecution website. Matters deemed to require disclosure by the prosecution in English law include material capable of undermining the prosecution case, or of assisting the defence case.

[13] NA 2003/4/534, Hefferon's statement of 30 May, with Quigley's handwritten notation directing the sections to be edited. The handwriting is similar to other examples of Quigley's script found in the files, and was confirmed to McDowell by officials in the Attorney General's Office as 'the distinctive handwriting' of Declan Quigley; see also McDowell letter to Heney, 24 December 2002, in the author's possession.

[14] Condon's denials were made directly to the author, by telephone, in April 2001, and reported in the RTÉ TV documentary 'Evidence of the Colonel', tx. 10/04/2001, transcript p. 15. Significantly, Condon never resiled from this position.

[15] NA 2003/4/520.

[16] Transcript of 'Evidence of the Colonel', p. 11.

[17] MacIntyre, *Through the Bridewell Gate*, p. 60.

[18] McKenna's letter to Heney, 5 April 2001, copy in the author's possession; McKenna had already indicated informally to the author that the material was new to him, and that the deleted matter was 'important'.

[19] Although the sudden end to the first trial was unhelpful to the defence case, it appears to have been inadvertent, a function of a historically querulous relationship between senior counsel Ernest Wood and Judge O'Caoimh.

[20] Gibbons, having volunteered this information on 8 June, then seeing it edited out of the Book of Evidence, volunteered it again in his evidence-in-chief at the first arms trial, and even added to it – see Gibbons's direct evidence to Walsh SC (for the State) at the first arms trial, *Irish Times*, 25 September 1970.

[21] This information comes from a confidential legal source, present at the

District Court hearing on 2 July 1970. Liam Hamilton later became Chief Justice.

22 Patrick MacEntee SC, from transcript of 'Evidence of the Colonel', pp. 15–16.

23 *Report of the Attorney General*, pars. 4–5, p. 42.

24 'Evidence of the Colonel' transcript, p. 15 (copy in the author's possession).

25 John O'Donoghue, *The Arms Trial – Changes Made to Colonel Hefferon's Statement: Report by the Minister for Justice, Equality and Law Reform* (July 2001), par. 19.

26 J. H. Archbold, *Criminal Pleading – Evidence and Practice*, eds. T. R. W. Butler and S. Mitchell (38th ed., London, 1973), par. 448, pp. 206–07. This stated that the law at the time governing the editing of statements in a situation where 'prejudicial and inadmissible matter' was being excluded: 'The prosecutor or his legal representative, as the case may be, must exercise a discretion to notify the defence in a suitable manner of any matter arising from the preparation of a statement, e.g. where it is material, of the existence and contents of the original statements or the exclusion of some matter. The duty is the same as that which may arise where original statements materially differ from depositions of evidence given orally.'

27 Archbold, *Criminal Pleading – Evidence and Practice*, general ed. P. J. Richardson (47th ed., London, 1995), p. 544, detailed the case law on the duty of the prosecution to disclose unused material to the defence. It was first formulated in *R. v. Bryant and Dickson* (1946), and extended in *Dallison v. Caffrey* (1965). In the latter, Lords Denning and Diplock agreed that material helpful to the defence must be made known to the defence, although they differed on whether or not the obligation required that the witness's actual original statement be made available. In addition, Celia Hampton's English legal textbook *Criminal Procedure and Evidence* (London, 1973), pp. 109–10, under the heading 'Prosecution to make material evidence available to Accused', states: 'Where the prosecution has discovered evidence which tends to show that the accused is innocent or which is otherwise helpful to the accused, and therefore does not intend to call it, the prosecutor, his counsel or solicitor, must make it available to the defence. It is not certain whether the duty extends to furnishing the accused with a copy of a witness's statement.'

28 R. L. Sandes, *Criminal Law and Procedure in Eire* (London, 1951), p. 123.

29 Dermot Walsh, *Criminal Procedure* (Dublin, 2002), p. 717.

30 *Report of the Attorney General*, par. 1, p. 22.

31 Ibid., par. 3, p. 24. The approach adopted by the DPP, who took over most prosecutions from the Attorney General in 1975, was to suggest

that relevant deleted material be made informally available to the defence.

[32] Ibid., par. 1, p. 24.

[33] Archbold, *Criminal Pleading – Evidence and Practice*, 47th ed., par. 4-281, p. 551.

[34] Gibbons's first apparent attempt to rebut Hefferon's evidence as given at the first trial is to be found in handwritten notes he prepared for the prosecution between the first and second trials, cited in Clifford, *The Arms Conspiracy Trial*, pp. 594–97.

[35] For further consideration of the issues here, see Heney, 'Hefferon and the Arms Crisis', pp. 62–63.

[36] Seamus McKenna's statement, contained in a letter to RTÉ, was broadcast on the RTÉ *Prime Time* programme 'Evidence of the Colonel'.

Chapter 16: Arms Trial Issues (pages 301–323)

[1] The tape-recording of the arms trials was ordered initially by Judge O'Caoimh (and later Judge Henchy) as a backup, unique at the time, for the stenographers, 'so that possible disputes as to what is said can be satisfactorily resolved' (NA 2001/55/4). Tapes of the proceedings were described as missing in July 2001 by then Attorney General Michael McDowell SC; however, it has emerged that three tapes from the recording of the second arms trial have survived, fortuitously held in the possession of Peter Maguire SC, having been received by him, it seems from his solicitor, at the end of the trials.

[2] RTÉ television documentary, *Secret Orders*, tx. December 2001.

[3] These interviews took place when a juror approached the author, then an RTÉ television producer, in May 2001 to voice unhappiness at the FitzGerald allegations about juror intimidation, claiming that the verdict had been perverse and against the evidence. While the law prohibits jurors from speaking publicly about cases, and prohibits news media from seeking or reporting such opinions, RTÉ made a decision at the time to report comments recorded with two members of the 1970 jury. This decision to broadcast, it is understood, was based on the historical nature of the matters involved and, in the particular context of FitzGerald's charges, the importance of vindicating the integrity of the jury verdict. The interview tapes have recently been transcribed, and copies of the transcripts, as well as the original, sound-only recordings, are in the author's possession. Further copies of the transcripts are retained in the RTÉ Archive, under conditions of restricted access.

[4] See Kevin Rafter, *Neil Blaney: Soldier of Destiny* (Dublin, 1993), p. 75: Blaney was in court and expecting to be called as a defence witness,

but may have been judged too unpredictable by defence lawyers. In addition, with a joint strategy apparently in place among the defence teams, Blaney's evidence, while it would help Captain Kelly, could have been harmful to the case being run by Charles Haughey that he knew nothing of a specific plan to bring in arms.

5 Official Secrets Act 1963, Section 4, sub-section 1.

6 Interview with O'Brien, cited in *The Arms Trial*, p. 220.

7 'Former Army Officer Awarded £70,000 Over Arms Trial Libel', *Irish Independent*, 16 May 2003.

8 'Missing £100,000 Fund Probed by gardaí', *Irish Independent*, 25 October 1970.

9 O'Malley, *Conduct Unbecoming*, p. 77.

10 Firearms Act 1925, Section 17, sub-section 8.

11 Clifford suggests that when Judge Henchy stated that being part of a conspiracy could be conveyed simply by a nod of the head, that meant that the authorization of the minister could be similarly conveyed: *The Arms Conspiracy Trial*, p. 437, footnote 4.

12 Exchange between Finlay and Judge O'Caoimh at the first arms trial, during the cross-examination of James Gibbons, *Irish Times*, 26 September 1970.

13 Judge Henchy's charge to the jury at the second arms trial, *Irish Times*, 24 October 1970.

14 MacIntyre, in *Through the Bridewell Gate*, p. 105, records briefly a statement by Judge Henchy, in the absence of the jury on 12 October 1970, that he would make a ruling later in the trial on 'whether the state of the evidence would permit the jury to hold that the importation was for the use of the Defence Forces'.

15 Hefferon in cross-examination by McKenna SC (for the State) at the second arms trial, *Irish Times*, 15 October 1970.

16 Transcribed note by the author from the recording of the legal discussion between Judge Henchy, defence counsel Finlay and McCarthy, and State counsel Walsh, 20 October 1970; the recording is part of the Maguire Papers.

14 Transcript of tape-recorded discussion at the second arms trial, 20 October 1970.

18 Ibid.

19 Ibid.

20 Ibid.

21 Browne, 'Misconduct of the Arms Trial', p. 18.

22 The tape-recording of the legal argument, although in Maguire's possession since 1970, was largely untouched until the barrister, in 2016, gave the author permission to peruse his papers in relation to the arms trials.

²³ Captain Kelly in cross-examination by McKenna SC (for the State) at the second arms trial, *Irish Times*, 16 October 1970.

²⁴ Captain Kelly's evidence to the Committee of Public Accounts inquiry, 26 January 1971, pars. 3258–3260 and par. 3297. It was a position that had initially been set out by the Northern account holders as early as November 1970, but all documents relating to the bank accounts were destroyed once a criminal prosecution was begun in Dublin, so the claim was incapable of validation (NA 2003/26/1).

²⁵ John Kelly, as reported in *Irish Times*, 15 October 1970, declined to give sworn evidence to the court; he claimed that he was concerned about the risk, if he was subject to cross-examination, of endangering people living in the North. The judge then permitted him to deliver an unsworn statement of his position.

²⁶ Captain Kelly's evidence-in-chief at the second arms trial, *Irish Times*, 16 October 1970.

²⁷ Eamonn Walsh SC (for the State), final address to the jury at the second arms trial, *Irish Times*, 23 October 1970.

²⁸ It is noteworthy that Colonel Hefferon, in his very honest evidence to the Committee of Public Accounts in 1971, also made a clear distinction between control by Captain Kelly and control by the Defence Forces. Hefferon stated that, in his view, Captain Kelly could not be taken to be representing the army. See questioning of Hefferon by Ben Briscoe TD (Fianna Fáil) at the Committee of Public Accounts inquiry, 2 February 1971, pars. 4317–4322.

²⁹ Report of Judge Henchy's charge to the second arms trial jury, *Irish Times*, 24 October 1970.

³⁰ Clifford believed that Judge Henchy reviewed these matters in a way that was biased towards the prosecution – see *The Arms Conspiracy Trial*, pp. 455, 457.

³¹ Closing address to the jury by Finlay SC (for Captain Kelly) at the second arms trial, *Irish Times*, 22 October 1970.

³² Judge Henchy's charge to the jury at the second arms trial, *Irish Times*, 24 October 1970.

³³ Tom Finlay SC's final address to the jury at second arms trial, *Irish Times*, 22 October 1970.

³⁴ Interview with jury member 'Mr B', conducted in December 2001 for RTÉ programme *Secret Orders*.

³⁵ This proposition finds support in Paddy Doherty's account of the events of 2 April 1970, when rifles were rushed north to Dundalk and Captain Kelly was initially recalled from Germany to assist in distributing the rifles north of the border. Doherty, who had joined the FCA in autumn 1969 (*Paddy Bogside*, pp. 190–91) and led a group of Derry men being given military training at Fort Dunree in Co. Donegal, was summoned personally by Neil Blaney from the

West Indies, where he was working in construction, so that he could receive the rifles in Derry: 'I was on standby to accept weapons in Derry on behalf of the Irish government,' he said in an interview with the author in December 2001.

36 Gibbons's concession that he had 'vestigial' knowledge of the arms importation in advance was given while under cross-examination by Seamus Sorahan BL (for John Kelly) at the second arms trial, *Irish Times*, 9 October 1970.

37 Judge Henchy's charge to the jury at the second arms trial, *Irish Times*, 24 October 1970.

38 Finlay SC's final address (for Captain Kelly) to the jury at the second arms trial, *Irish Times*, 22 October 1970.

39 Judge Henchy's charge to the jury at the second arms trial, *Irish Times*, 24 October 1970.

40 Interim summary of the defence case given to the jury by Peter Maguire SC (for Haughey) at the second arms trial, *Irish Times*, 17 October 1970.

41 Although the identity of the two jurors was withheld in the RTÉ programme in 2001, documentation made available to the producer/ reporter at the time – the current author – authenticated each person's participation as jurors at the trial.

42 Transcript of interview with 'Mr B', juror at the second arms trial, recorded December 2001 for RTÉ.

43 Transcript of interview with 'Mr A', juror at the second arms trial, recorded December 2001 for RTÉ.

44 This claim was aired by Garret FitzGerald, as cited above in this chapter, in O'Brien's book *The Arms Trial*, and may have been based on information he got from Tánaiste Erskine Childers: Childers's views were reported to London by British ambassador Sir John Peck in Summary: The Arms Conspiracy Trial, NAUK FCO 33/1207, dated 10 November 1970, in which Peck stated that Childers told him that 'to his certain knowledge' an associate of Neil Blaney, Gerry Jones, had tracked down and got in touch with each of the arms trial jurors.

45 Transcript of interview with arms trial juror 'Mr B', December 2001.

Chapter 17: Conclusions (pages 324–337)

1 NAUK FCO 33/1209, Peck to the Foreign and Commonwealth Office, 27 October 1970.
2 These terms were employed by Collins (*The Power Game*, p. 64), O'Brien (*The Arms Trial*, p. 63) and Keogh (*Lynch*, p. 232), as well as being attributed to Patrick Hillery in Walsh's biography, *Hillery*, p. 214.
3 See *Freedom Struggle*, the Provisional IRA pamphlet published in 1973, p. 11; see also MacStiofáin, *Memoirs of a Revolutionary*, p. 146.

[4] Allegations that the arms trials were 'show trials' were made on the cover of Clifford's *The Arms Conspiracy Trial*, while claims that the Lynch government had 'fabricated' the case against the accused were made by Captain Kelly on the cover of *The Thimble Riggers*. Patrick MacEntee SC's opinion on the arms trials was broadcast in 'Evidence of the Colonel' on RTÉ Television on 10 April 2001 and is contained in the transcript of that programme.

[5] Transcript of interview with juror 'Mr B', December 2001.

[6] Among the many writers on similar lines, O'Brien saw Haughey and Blaney as plotting 'a boardroom take-over' (*The Arms Trial*, p. 63); Dick Walsh (*The Party*, p. 236) saw 'a real prospect of civil war on the island of Ireland' if the alleged plot had succeeded; Fanning described the Arms Crisis as 'the most dangerous threat to democracy in independent Ireland since the civil war' (*Dictionary of Irish Biography*, 'Jack Lynch'); Desmond O'Malley saw in the events of 1970 'a threat of unparalleled gravity to the Irish State' (*Conduct Unbecoming*, p. 50).

[7] John A. Murphy, *Ireland in the Twentieth Century* (Dublin, 1975), p. 171.

[8] John M. Regan, 'Southern Irish Nationalism as a Historical Problem', *The Historical Journal*, Vol. 50, No. 1 (2007), pp. 197–223.

[9] O'Halpin, *Defending Ireland*, p. 311.

[10] Coogan, *The IRA*, p. 368. See Chapter 9 pp. 168–69, above for a fuller consideration of this question.

[11] Clifford, *The Arms Conspiracy Trial*, p. 10; she argued that had Lynch not 'reneged' on his policy in 1970, the changes that came later with the Good Friday Agreement in 1998 might have come about 'in a more measured way', and without the intervening Provisional IRA campaign.

[12] An early poll conducted by news magazine *This Week* in June 1970 showed substantial support for Lynch's actions at that stage.

[13] Blaney's interview with *Hot Press* magazine, 'Lawyers, Guns and Money'.

[14] Boland, *We Won't Stand (Idly) By*, p. 84.

[15] John Kelly, *The Detail* website, interview by Steven McCaffery, 3 February 2014.

[16] From Doherty's extended interview in 2001 with the author.

[17] James Kelly, *The Genesis of Revolution* (Dublin, 1976), p. 17.

[18] Martin Mansergh, in a review of Stephen Kelly's book *A Failed Political Entity*, *History Ireland*, January–February 2017, p. 58.

[19] UCDA, P 205/36, Hillery Papers, letter of T. P. O'Neill to Minister for External Affairs P. J. Hillery, 11 May 1970.

Primary Sources

National Archives of Ireland:

Cabinet Minutes, August–September 1969
Department of Justice Files, 1969–70
Department of the Taoiseach Files, 1969–70
Department of Defence Files, 1969–70
Department of External Affairs Files, 1969–70
Attorney General's Office Files, 1969–70

United Kingdom National Archives, Kew, London:

United Kingdom Foreign and Commonwealth Office Files,
1969–70

Official Reports:

Report of the Attorney General on Questions Concerning the Prosecution of the Arms Trial in 1970, July 2001.
The Arms Trial: Changes Made to Colonel Hefferon's Statement, Report by the Minister for Justice, Equality and Law Reform, July 2001.
Final Report of the Committee of Public Accounts Inquiry into the Expenditure of Grant-in-Aid for Northern Ireland Relief, including proceedings, correspondence and appendices, July 1972.

Collections:

University College, Dublin Archives (UCDA):
Fianna Fáil Papers
P. J. Hillery Papers
T.K. Whitaker Papers

Military Archives, Dublin:
Hefferon Papers

Privately Held:
Maguire Papers

Interviews by the Author:

Colm Condon SC
Paddy Doherty
Justin Keating TD
James Kelly
John Kelly
Jurors at second arms trial, 'Mr. A', and 'Mr. B'

Newspapers and Periodicals:

The Irish Times, reports on first and second arms trials, September–
    October 1970
The Sunday Press, October–November 1970
The Irish Press, May/October 1970
The Irish Independent, May/October 1970
The Voice of the North, October–November 1969
The United Irishman, September–November 1969
This Week, current affairs magazine, August–October 1969
Magill, current affairs magazine, May–July 1980

Secondary Sources

Television Programmes:

'Evidence of the Colonel', RTÉ TV, transmitted 10 April 2001
'Secret Orders', RTÉ TV, transmitted December 2001

Bibliography

Adams, Gerry, *Before the Dawn: An Autobiography* (Dingle, Co. Kerry, 1996).

Anderson, Brendan, *Joe Cahill: A Life in the IRA* (Dublin, 2002).

Archbold, J. F., *Criminal Pleading: Evidence and Practice, 38th edition*, eds. T. R. F. Butler and S. G. Mitchel (London, 1973).

—*Criminal Pleading, 47th edition*, ed. P. J. Richardson (London, 1995).

Arnold, Bruce, *Haughey – His Life and Unlucky Deeds* (London, 1993).

—*Jack Lynch: Hero in Crisis* (Dublin, 2001).

Bell, J. Bowyer, *The Secret Army: A History of the IRA 1916–70* (London, 1970).

—*The Irish Troubles* (Dublin, 1993).

Berry, Peter, *The Berry Papers* (otherwise Berry *Diaries*), *Magill* current affairs magazine (ed. Vincent Browne), June 1980.

Bew, Paul, *The Politics of Enmity: Ireland 1789–2006* (Oxford, 2007).

Bishop, Patrick and Eamonn Mallie, *The Provisional IRA* (London, 1987).

Boland, Kevin, *We Won't Stand (Idly) By* (Dublin, 1972)

—*Up Dev* (Rathcoole, 1977).

Bowman, John, *De Valera and the Ulster Question 1917–1973* (Oxford, 1982).

Brady, Seamus, *Arms and the Men* (Dublin, 1971).

Browne, Vincent, 'The Arms Crisis 1970' (and various articles), *Magill* current affairs magazine, May and July 1980.

Callaghan, James, *A House Divided: The Dilemma of Northern Ireland* (London, 1973).

Clifford, Angela, *Military Aspects of Ireland's Arms Crisis 1969–70* (Belfast, 2006).

—*The Arms Conspiracy Trial, Ireland 1970: The Prosecution of Charles Haughey, Captain Kelly and Others* (Belfast, 2009).

Collins, Stephen, *The Power Game: Ireland under Fianna Fáil* (Dublin, 2000).

Coogan, Tim Pat, *The IRA* (London, 1971).

—*The Troubles* (London, 1995).

Cronin, Seán, *Irish Nationalism: A History of Its Roots and Ideology* (Dublin, 1980).

Daly, Mary, *Sixties Ireland: Reshaping the Economy, State and Society 1959–1973* (Cambridge, 2016).

de Baróid, Ciarán, *Ballymurphy and the Irish War* (Belfast, 1989; rev. ed. 1990, 2000).

Devlin, Paddy, *Straight Left: An Autobiography* (Dublin, 1993).

Dillon, Martin, *The Dirty War* (London, 1990).

Doherty, Paddy, *Paddy Bogside* (Cork, 2001).

Downey, James, *Lenihan – His Life and Loyalties* (Dublin, 1998).

—*In My Own Time: Inside Irish Politics and Society* (Dublin, 2009).

Dunlop, Frank, *Yes Taoiseach: Irish Politics from Behind Closed Doors* (Dublin, 2004).

Dwyer, T. Ryle, *Charlie – The Political Biography of C. J. Haughey* (Dublin, 1987).

—*Haughey's 30 years of Controversy* (Cork, 1992).

—*Short Fellow* (Dublin, 1995).

—*Fallen Idol - Haughey's Controversial Career* (Cork, 1998).

—*Lynch - Nice Fellow: A Biography of Jack Lynch* (Cork, 2001).

—*Haughey's 40 Years of Controversy* (Cork, 2005).

English, Richard, *Armed Struggle: The History of the IRA* (London, 2003).

Fanning, Ronan, *Independent Ireland* (Dublin, 1983).

—'Jack Lynch', *Dictionary of Irish Biography* (Cambridge, 2009).

—'Playing it Cool: The Response of the British and Irish

Governments to the Crisis in Northern Ireland, 1968–69', *Irish Studies in International Affairs*, Vol. 12 (2001).

Faulkner, Padraig, *As I Saw It: Reviewing Over 30 Years of Fianna Fáil and Irish Politics* (Dublin, 2005).

Ferriter, Diarmaid, *The Transformation of Ireland 1900–2000* (Dublin, 2004).

—*Ambiguous Republic: Ireland in the 1970s* (London, 2012).

Hampton, Celia, *Criminal Procedure and Evidence* (London, 1973).

Hanly, Brian and Scott Millar, *The Lost Revolution: The Story of the Official IRA & The Workers Party* (Dublin, 2009).

Haughey, Charles, *The Spirit of the Nation – The Speeches and Statements of Charles J. Haughey, 1975–1978*, ed. Martin Mansergh (Cork and Dublin, 1986).

Heney, Michael, 'Colonel Michael Hefferon and the 1970 Arms Crisis' (M.A. thesis, University College, Dublin, 2014).

Hennessey, Thomas, *A History of Northern Ireland, 1920–1996* (Dublin, 1997).

—*Northern Ireland: The Origins of the Troubles* (Dublin, 2005).

Horgan, John, *Seán Lemass: The Enigmatic Patriot* (Dublin, 1997).

Keating, Justin, *Nothing is Written in Stone*, eds. Barbara Hussey and Anna Kealy (Dublin, 2017).

Kelly, James, *Orders for the Captain?* (Dublin, 1971).

—*The Genesis of Revolution* (Dublin, 1976).

—*The Thimble Riggers* (Dublin, 1999).

Kelly, Stephen, *Fianna Fáil, Partition and Northern Ireland 1926–1971* (Dublin, 2013).

—*A Failed Political Entity: Charles Haughey and the Northern Ireland Question, 1945–1992* (Dublin, 2016).

Kennedy, Michael, *Division and Consensus – The Politics of Cross-Border Relations in Ireland, 1925–1969* (Dublin, 2000).

Keogh, Dermot, *Jack Lynch: A Biography* (Cork, 2008)

—*Twentieth-Century Ireland: Nation and State* (Dublin, 1994).

Lee, J.J., *Ireland 1912–1985: Politics and Society* (Cambridge, 1989).

Lenihan, Conor, *Haughey, Prince of Power* (Dublin, 2015).

MacIntyre, Tom, *Through the Bridewell Gate: A Diary of the Dublin Arms Trial* (London, 1971).

MacStiofáin, Seán, *Memoirs of a Revolutionary* (Salisbury, 1975).

Mansergh, Martin, *The Legacy of History* (Cork, 2003).

—'The Big Book', review of Stephen Kelly's *Failed Political Entity*, in *History Ireland*, January–February 2017, p. 58.

Maume, Patrick, 'James Gibbons', *Dictionary of Irish Biography* (Cambridge, 2009).

—'James Kelly' (*DIB*, 2009).

—'Charles Haughey' (*DIB*, 2009).

—'Neil Blaney' (*DIB*, 2009).

McDermott, Jim, *Northern Divisions: The Old IRA and the Belfast Pogroms, 1920–1922* (Belfast, 2001).

Mills, Michael, *Hurler on the Ditch, Memoir of a Journalist who became Ireland's First Ombudsman* (Dublin, 2005).

Moloney, Ed, *A Secret History of the IRA* (London and New York, 2002).

Murphy, John A., *Ireland in the Twentieth-Century* (Dublin, 1975).

Ó Beacháin, Donnacha, *Destiny of the Soldiers: Fianna Fáil, Irish Republicanism and the IRA, 1926–73* (Dublin, 2010).

O'Brien, Conor Cruise, *States of Ireland* (London, 1972).

O'Brien, Justin, *The Arms Trial* (Dublin, 2000).

—*The Modern Prince: Charles J. Haughey and the Quest for Power* (Dublin, 2002).

O'Donnell, Catherine, *Fianna Fáil, Irish Republicanism and the Northern Ireland Troubles, 1968–2005* (Dublin and Portland, Oregon, 2007).

O'Halpin, Eunan, 'A Greek Authoritarian Phase? The Irish army and the Irish Crisis 1969–70' *Irish Political Studies*, Vol. 23, No. 4 (December 2008), pp. 475–90.

—*Defending Ireland: The Irish State and its Enemies Since 1922* (Oxford, 1999)

O'Mahony, T. P., *Jack Lynch: A Biography* (Cork, 1991).

O'Malley, Desmond, *Conduct Unbecoming* (Dublin, 2014).

O'Neill, P., *Freedom Struggle* (Dublin, 1973).

Patterson, Henry, *The Politics of Illusion: A Political History of the IRA* (Oxford, 1997).

—*Ireland Since 1939: The Persistence of Conflict* (Dublin, 2006).

Rafter, Kevin, *Neil Blaney: Soldier of Destiny* (Dublin, 1993).

Sachs, P. M., *The Donegal Mafia: An Irish Political Machine* (New Haven and London, 1976).

Sandes, R. L., *Criminal Law and Procedure in Eire* (London, 1951).

Staunton, Enda, *The Nationalists of Northern Ireland, 1918–73* (Dublin, 2001).

Taylor, Peter, *States of Terror* (London, 1993).

—*Provos: The IRA and Sinn Fein* (London, 1997).

Walsh, Dermot, *Criminal Procedure* (Dublin, 2002).

Walsh, Dick, *The Party: Inside Fianna Fáil* (Dublin, 1986).

Walsh, John, *Patrick Hillery: The Official Biography of the Party* (Dublin, 2008).

Whelan, Noel, *Fianna Fáil: A Biography of the Party* (Dublin, 2011).

White, R. W., *Ruairí Ó Brádaigh: The Life and Politics of an Irish Revolutionary* (Bloomington, Indiana, 2006)

Whyte, J. H., 'The North Erupts: Ireland Enters Europe, 1968–72', *A New History of Ireland Vol. VII, Ireland 1921–84*, ed. J. R. Hill (Oxford, 2003).

Image credits

1. Copyright Larry Doherty, c/o Victor Patterson.

2. Copyright Lensmen & Associates, Irish Photo Archive.

3. Copyright Lensmen & Associates, Irish Photo Archive.

4. Copyright Lensmen & Associates, Irish Photo Archive.

5. Copyright Lensmen & Associates, Irish Photo Archive.

6. Copyright, Lensmen & Associates, Irish Photo Archive.

7. Photograph: Tommy Collins, *The Irish Times*.

8. Photograph: Jimmy McCormack, *The Irish Times*.

9. Photograph: Dermot O'Shea, *The Irish Times*.

10. Photograph: Tommy Collins, *The Irish Times*.

11. Photograph: Jimmy McCormack, *The Irish Times*.

12. Photograph: Dermot Barry, *The Irish Times*.

Acknowledgements

This book has been fashioned after a journalistic career over almost forty-three years that was book-ended by the Arms Crisis: I reported on it in 1970 while a junior reporter with *The Irish Times*, and it featured in recurring reports I made during the 1970s, 1980s, and 1990s and in 2001 for RTÉ radio and television. For all my continuing acquaintance with the mysteries of the arms saga, the ultimate responsibility for this book rests back in time with the late John Lee, my inspiring history teacher at the King's Hospital Bluecoat School in Dublin; it was his early influence that thrust me, in the mid-1960s, into the arms of the late Theo Moody, distinguished professor of history at Trinity College, Dublin, whose rigour and insistence on precise and comprehensive referencing left its own mark on a young student of history. Later Douglas Gageby, Donal Foley and Michael Viney were among the many sources of inspiration as my journalistic career got under way at *The Irish Times*. There followed thirty-eight entirely exhilarating years with RTÉ radio and television, in the company of great journalists and broadcasters such as Olivia O'Leary, Kevin Healy, Kevin O'Kelly, Seán Duignan, Gerry Barry, Shane Kenny, Mike Burns, and later Brendan O'Brien, Forbes McFall, Joe Mulholland, Miriam O'Callaghan and Noel Curran, among many others.

In the latter part of my professional career, I produced and presented in 2001 two significant television documentaries on the subject of the Arms Crisis, based on the State Papers released to the National Archives that year, under the thirty-year rule. Gary Agnew, then head of current affairs television, gave me time and space to tell an important story, and Andrea Martin, at the time one of RTÉ's legal advisers, offered shrewd advice. The assistance of the late Captain Jim Kelly, and his late widow, Sheila, was of particular help in 2001; more recently, their eldest daughter Suzanne has been a source of consistently sensible advice. Colonel Michael Hefferon's son, Colm, has been helpful and supportive throughout. The unresolved issues raised by the Arms Crisis had been a target for my retirement years after 2010, driven in large measure by dissatisfaction at the historiography of the 1969–70 period, and the sense that an untold story lay resting in the files. The impression lingered in my senses that loyal Irish army officers had been mistreated and abused in the political cauldron that existed in 1970. I was lucky enough then to come under the supervision of a consummate historian, Professor Diarmaid Ferriter, my academic supervisor at UCD, whose guidance and encouragement were invaluable in the course of the doctoral research that underlies this book. I am significantly indebted to Peter Maguire SC who gave me permission to peruse his invaluable papers from 1970. David O'Donoghue and Aisling Maguire are also owed thanks for their invaluable help in the later stages of research.

Throughout four years of full-time inquiry, punctuated by the periodic and thrilling discovery of fresh documents and other previously unnoticed material, the staff of the National Archives in Dublin, and of the Military Archives in Cathal Brúgha Barracks were consistently helpful; likewise, the staff at the United Kingdom Archives at Kew in London. I have also found the public library service in Dublin to be of constant and courteous assistance. Tony Phillips, my brother-in-law, provided invaluable assistance in the preparation of the manuscript, as did my good friend Denis Coghlan, who read and commented on portions of the text. Special mention for Mary Menton, a consistent source of moral support, and encouragement, and in particular, for Willie and Jennifer Maxwell, who provided technical, editorial and moral support without which this endeavour would have even greater blemishes than those currently in evidence. Jonathan Williams has been a rock of solid advice and assistance, and I am also grateful to Neil Belton for his belief in the project, and his willingness to take it on. In the end, of course, the failings and infirmities which remain, in what has undeniably been a labour of love, are entirely my own responsibility.

Michael Heney, September 2019.

About the author

Dr Michael Heney is an award-winning former journalist and producer with RTÉ Television, having previously worked with *The Irish Times* and with RTÉ Radio. His achievements include two Jacobs Television awards, Cross Broadcaster of the Year, and Liam Hourican European Journalist of the Year. His television exposés on the criminal convictions of the Tallaght Two led to the verdicts in that case being overturned in the Irish Court of Criminal Appeal. Since retiring from journalism in 2010, Michael has conducted six years of full-time academic investigation into the 1970 Arms Crisis, for which he was awarded a Ph.D by University College Dublin in 2018. He lives in Dublin.

Index